W9-BSU-154

Better Homes and Gardens®

BIGGEST BOOK OF ITALIAN RECIPES

Meredith® Books
Des Moines, Iowa

BIGGEST BOOK OF ITALIAN RECIPES

Editor: Jessica Saari
Project Editor and Indexer: Spectrum Communication Services, Inc.
Writer: Annie Krumhardt
Contributing Designer: Joyce DeWitt
Cover Designer: Daniel Pelavin
Copy Chief: Terri Fredrickson
Publishing Operations Manager: Karen Schirm
Senior Editor, Asset and Information Manager: Phillip Morgan
Edit and Design Production Coordinator: Mary Lee Gavin
Editorial Assistant: Cheryl Eckert
Book Production Managers: Pam Kvitne, Marjorie J. Schenkelberg, Rick von Holdt, and Mark Weaver
Contributing Copy Editor: Carolyn Stern
Contributing Proofreaders: Nicole Clausing, Amy LaMar, and Donna Segal
Test Kitchen Director: Lynn Blanchard
Test Kitchen Product Supervisor: Juliana Hale
Test Kitchen Home Economists: Elizabeth Burt, R.D.; Marilyn Cornelius; Juliana Hale; Maryellyn Krantz;
    Laura Marzen, R.D.; Jill Moberly; Dianna Nolin; Colleen Weeden; Lori Wilson; Charles Worthington

Meredith® Books
Executive Director, Editorial: Gregory H. Kayko
Executive Director, Design: Matt Strelecki
Managing Editor: Amy Tincher-Durik
Senior Editor/Group Manager: Jan Miller
Marketing Product Manager: Gina Rickert

Publisher and Editor in Chief: James D. Blume
Editorial Director: Linda Raglan Cunningham
Executive Director, Marketing: Steve Malone
Executive Director, New Business Development: Todd M. Davis
Executive Director, Sales: Ken Zagor
Director, Operations: George A. Susral
Director, Production: Douglas M. Johnston
Director, Marketing: Amy Nichols
Business Director: Jim Leonard

Vice President and General Manager: Douglas J. Guendel

Better Homes and Gardens® Magazine
Editor in Chief: Karol DeWulf Nickell
Deputy Editor, Food and Entertaining: Nancy Hopkins

Meredith Publishing Group
President: Jack Griffin
Executive Vice President: Bob Mate

Meredith Corporation
Chairman and Chief Executive Officer: William T. Kerr
President and Chief Operating Officer: Stephen M. Lacy

In Memoriam: E. T. Meredith III (1933-2003)

Copyright © 2006 by Meredith Corporation, Des Moines, Iowa. First Edition.
All rights reserved. Printed in China.
Library of Congress Control Number: 2006921303
ISBN-13: 978-0-696-23051-6
ISBN-10: 0-696-23051-8

All of us at Meredith® Books are dedicated to providing you with the information and ideas you need to create delicious foods. We welcome your comments and suggestions. Write to us at: Meredith Books, Cookbook Editorial Department, 1716 Locust St., Des Moines, IA 50309-3023.

Our Better Homes and Gardens® Test Kitchen seal on the back cover of this book assures you that every recipe in *Biggest Book of Italian Recipes* has been tested in the Better Homes and Gardens® Test Kitchen. This means that each recipe is practical and reliable, and meets our high standards of taste appeal. We guarantee your satisfaction with this book for as long as you own it.

TABLE OF CONTENTS

INTRODUCTION

Fabulous Italian Cooking!

Not only do Italians have a rich and varied cuisine in their own country, but as they have settled around the globe they have influenced the way people eat everywhere. That's why pizza, lasagna, and fettuccine Alfredo are universal favorites.

The *Biggest Book of Italian Recipes* explores the many facets of Italian cooking. With more than 350 recipes, this comprehensive collection brings you the best of Italian-style cuisine. Whether you're looking for traditional recipes, such as pesto and tiramisu, or you're up for novel twists on old-world tastes, such as Italian-style enchiladas and Tuscan mac and cheese, these dishes will tempt you.

Start with the classics chapter. It shows you how to prepare a variety of Italian standards, from Linguine in White Clam Sauce and Sicilian Meat Roll to Zuppa Inglese and Biscotti d'Anici. Then move on and discover lively appetizers to take to that get-together next week, or comforting main dishes to try out on the family. You'll also find incredible pizza and sandwiches for an easy supper on the weekend, soups and salads for when you want a light meal, and spectacular desserts for that special dinner party. Two bonus chapters will help you fit great Italian meals into your busy schedule. When time is short, try one of the 25-minute entrées. Or when you have a few moments to plan ahead, opt for an appealing Italian specialty adapted for the slow cooker. And if you have questions, check the basics section and the tips throughout the book for the help you need.

If you love flavorful food, any time is the right time to cook Italian. So don't hesitate. Start using the *Biggest Book of Italian Recipes* and enjoy a great meal soon.

ITALIAN BASICS

PREP YOUR PANTRY— ITALIAN-STYLE!

A well-stocked pantry is an integral part of an Italian cook's kitchen. Pair fresh meats and vegetables with items you keep on hand, and delicious Italian meals will come together in a snap. Here are the Italian ingredients you'll probably use most often.

Amaretti cookies: These versatile amaretto-flavored cookies make it easy to prepare a quick and elegant dessert. They also pair well with after-dinner espresso.

Anchovies: Not just a pizza topper, canned anchovies also can be used to add robust flavor to salad dressings and sauces. Store them on your cupboard shelf for up to a year.

Beans: Dried and canned beans are useful in soups and stews, adding protein and heartiness. Popular Italian choices include: Cannellini beans (white kidney beans), fava beans, and garbanzo beans (chickpeas). You can keep dried beans in an airtight container for up to a year.

Bread crumbs: Dried bread crumbs often are included in dishes titled "alla parmigiana," as well as in meatballs and in meat loaves. They are available both plain and with Italian seasonings. In an airtight container, they have a shelf life of six months.

Canned tomato products: Canned whole tomatoes, diced tomatoes, crushed tomatoes, tomato puree, and tomato paste have an infinite number of uses in Italian cuisine. Take your choice of domestic or imported brands.

Capers: Sun-dried and pickled in brine or packed in salt, these small berries add a pungent flavor to a variety of Mediterranean dishes. After opening, they should be refrigerated.

Cheeses: Cheese is an essential part of Italian fare. For a listing of the most commonly used Italian cheeses, see "Cheese, Please!" on page 6. Firm, semi-firm, and semi-soft cheeses, such as Parmesan, pecorino, or fontina, should be wrapped in plastic and refrigerated. They will last for several weeks. Fresh cheeses, such as ricotta or fresh mozzarella, should be stored in the refrigerator and kept for no more than two weeks.

PASTA PAIRING

Italian pastas come in all shapes and sizes. It can be a bit confusing to know which pasta pairs best with which sauce. Use this list of popular pasta shapes, descriptions, and uses to achieve optimal results for all your pasta creations.

• **Angel hair:** Long, very narrow strands of pasta, angel hair works best with thin, light sauces.

• **Bucatini:** Long, narrow, hollow strands of pasta, bucatini is ideal for smooth sauces.

• **Bucatoni:** Like long strands of elbow macaroni, the wide, hollow tubes are great for thick sauces.

• **Campanelle:** Shaped like small cones or flowers with ruffled edges, campanelle is ideal for pasta salads and chunky suces.

• **Elbow macaroni:** Short, hollow, bent tubes, elbow macaroni is best for thick, cheesy sauces, as in American macaroni and cheese, and works well in pasta salads.

• **Farfalle:** Also called "bow-tie" pasta because of its shape, farfalle is great for pasta salads and baked dishes.

• **Fettuccine:** Wide, long, and flat, fettuccine works well for slightly chunky, robust sauces.

• **Fusilli:** Short and twisted to resemble a screw, fusilli is great for pasta salads and smooth to slightly chunky sauces.

• **Linguine:** Long, flat, and narrow, linguine is best paired with pesto and other fresh herb sauces.

• **Manicotti:** Large tubes with smooth or ridged surfaces, manicotti are ideally stuffed with cheese, covered with sauce, and baked.

• **Orecchiette:** Disk-shaped, small pasta, orecchiette is great for thick, hearty soups.

• **Orzo:** Small and rice-shaped, orzo is perfect for soups.

• **Penne:** Tubular, short, ridged, and cut diagonally, penne holds chunky sauces well.

• **Rigatoni:** Wide, short tubes with ridges, rigatoni can hold the chunkiest full-flavored sauces.

• **Rotini:** Short, spiral-shaped pasta, rotini is perfect for slightly chunky sauces.

• **Shells:** Shaped like conch shells, large ones are great for stuffing, and medium and small ones work well for pasta salads or chunky sauces.

• **Spaghetti:** Long, round strands, spaghetti pairs well with smooth or slightly chunky sauces and seafood mixtures.

• **Ziti:** Narrow, short or long tubes with ridges, ziti is great with chunky sauces and works ideally in baked dishes.

Garlic: A trademark of many Italian dishes, garlic is available fresh, bottled, minced, and dried, and in powder and juice forms. Bottled garlic is sold both crushed and minced. Store fresh garlic in a cool, dark place for up to three months.

Herbs and spices: All types of herbs and spices, both fresh and dried, are used in Italian cooking. The ones called for most often include: basil, bay leaves, crushed red pepper, fennel seeds, marjoram, oregano, parsley, rosemary, sage, and thyme. Italian seasoning is a handy mix of ingredients, including oregano, basil, ground red pepper, rosemary, and, sometimes, garlic powder. Fresh herbs will last several days in the refrigerator. Dried herbs and spices can be kept in airtight containers for up to six months.

Olives: Both green and ripe olives make snappy additions to many Italian dishes. They also are welcomed items on any antipasto tray. Olives can be brine-, salt-, or dry-cured. Some of the most common varieties called for in Italian dishes include: sicilian, gaeta, cerignola, kalamata, and ligurian.

Olive oil: Olive oil is the cooking and salad oil of choice in Italy. To learn more about the common types, see "Olive Oil 101" on page 7.

Nuts: Pine nuts, almonds, hazelnuts, and pistachio nuts often are used in Italian cooking. They will last for up to a year in the freezer.

Pancetta: This Italian bacon is cured with salt and spices rather than smoked. Keep it in the refrigerator for up to three weeks. Or freeze it for up to six months.

Pasta: Stock several sizes and shapes of pasta for a variety of recipes. Rely on "Pasta Pairing" on page 5 to help you decide which pastas work best for the dishes you typically prepare.

Peppers: Canned and often pickled, peppers are a hallmark of Italian cooking and make great additions to antipasto trays. The kinds to keep in your pantry include: chile peppers, cherry peppers, and pepperoncini peppers. Bottled or canned roasted red peppers have an intense sweet, smoky flavor. They save you the time and effort of roasting fresh sweet peppers.

Prosciutto: Italy's famous ham, prosciutto is salt cured and air dried. Wrapped around various fruits or breadsticks, it makes a great start to any meal.

Rice: Arborio and long-grain rice are good to keep on hand. Arborio rice is used to make risotto, a classic Italian dish. Rice can be stored almost indefinitely in a cool, dry place in an airtight container.

Tuna: Canned tuna is a great convenience product. For a more authentic flavor, opt for Italian tuna, or tonno, packed in olive oil.

Vinegars: Keep balsamic, red wine, and white wine vinegars in your pantry for salad dressings, marinades, and sauces.

Wine: Wine plays a big part in Italian cooking and dining. It enhances and melds flavors in sauces, soups, and stews. Pinot Grigio *(a white)* and Chianti *(a red)* are two popular Italian choices. Both are great used in cooking and for drinking during the meal.

CHEESE, PLEASE!

Italian cheeses are as diverse as each region of Italy. But which cheese works best for which use? Rely on this list of popular Italian cheeses to guide you in your culinary adventures.

• **Asiago:** A hard, slightly sharp cow's milk cheese, Asiago is perfect for grating on pasta or salads.

• **Fontina:** A dense, smooth, slightly elastic cheese with a mild, nutty flavor, fontina makes a great dessert cheese.

• **Gorgonzola:** In both creamy and crumbly versions, this blue-veined cheese is great paired with fruit, sprinkled on salads, or mixed into risotto.

• **Grana padano:** Hard, slightly sharp, and somewhat sweet, it is great for grating over pasta and salads.

• **Mascarpone:** With a buttery flavor, and light, creamy texture, mascarpone is ideal for desserts like tiramisu or cheesecake.

• **Mozzarella:** Fresh mozzarella is soft and has a mild flavor. Use it on pizza or team it with basil and tomatoes. Pasteurized mozzarella has a slightly nutty flavor and is great in baked dishes.

• **Parmigiano-Reggiano:** A hard cheese, with a sharp, nutty flavor, this cheese is commonly called Parmesan cheese by most Americans. It is perfect for grating over salads and pasta, as well as mixing with olive oil for bread dipping.

• **Pecorino Romano:** A hard, sharp-flavored cheese, Romano cheese is good for grating over pasta.

• **Provolone:** A semi-firm to hard cheese with a mellow or sharp flavor, depending on how long it is allowed to age, provolone is terrific for sandwiches and pizza.

• **Ricotta:** Creamy, thick, and mild, ricotta is great in baked dishes, such as lasagna, as well as in desserts, such as cheesecake.

• **Scamorza:** Smooth, rubbery, and stringy, Scamorza is often smoked and used in a variety of pasta dishes.

OLIVE OIL 101

All olive oils are not created equal. Depending on how the olives are pressed, olive oils have several different flavors and uses. Here are the most common retail grades:

• **Extra-virgin olive oil:** Highly fragrant and flavorful, it is best used for drizzling on pasta and salads, in dressings, or for bread dipping.

• **Virgin olive oil:** Slightly fruity, this grade lacks the same depth of flavor as extra-virgin olive oil. Use it on pasta and salad as you would use an extra-virgin version.

• **Refined olive oil:** Made from lower-quality virgin olive oil, it is chemically treated to remove flavor flaws. Use it for frying and in salad dressings and marinades.

• **Olive oil or pure olive oil:** A low-cost blend of virgin and refined olive oil, it has a very mild flavor. Use it as an all-purpose cooking oil and in salad dressing and marinades.

KNOW THE REGIONS OF ITALY

Delights of Italian cuisine vary distinctly from region to region. The food culture from each is based heavily upon local vegetables, herbs, seafood, and wildlife. For this reason, Italian cuisine differs depending on the area of Italy from which it originated. Here is a quick rundown of the culinary specialties of each Italian region. Let one inspire your next dinner party or combine dishes from several regions for an eclectic Italian meal.

NORTHERN ITALY

Valle d'Aosta
• Polenta
• Risotto
• Fontina cheese

Piedmont
• Mushrooms
  (including white truffles)
• Pasta stuffed with various fillings
• Cheese fondue

Liguria
• Pesto
• Pine nuts
• Anchovies

Lombardy
• Butter and cream
  (instead of olive oil)
• Osso buco *(veal shank in tomato sauce over rice)*
• Polenta

Veneto
• Risotto
• Clams, mussels, and shrimp
• Beans

Trentino-Alto Adige
• Rye bread
• Strudel
• Sauerkraut

Friuli-Venezia Giulia
• Espresso
• Ginger, anise, nutmeg, and cinnamon
• Horseradish

Emilia-Romana
• Bolognese meat sauce
• Soffrito *(celery, peppers, garlic, onions, and herbs sautéed in olive oil)*
• Parmesan cheese

CENTRAL ITALY

Tuscany
• Fava and cannellini beans
• Porcini mushrooms
• Spinach

Umbria
• Lentils
• Pecorino cheese
• Sausages and salami

Marche
• Sole, mollusks, and sardines
• White wine sauces
• Blackberries, peaches, and apricots

Lazio
• Artichokes
• Fresh and cured pork
• Pecorino Romano cheese

Abruzzo
• Garlic and hot red peppers
• Lamb
• Gnocchi

Molise
• Chile peppers
• Lamb
• Shaped pastas

SOUTHERN ITALY

Campania
• Pizza
• Tomatoes, eggplant, and zucchini
• Mozzarella, mascarpone, and ricotta cheese

Puglia
• Oysters and squid
• Brushcetta
• Orecchiette

Basilicata
• Chile peppers
• Vegetable and bean soups
• Pork and lamb

Calabria
• Spicy and sweet peppers
• Pancetta
• Citrus fruits and figs

THE ISLANDS

Sicily
• Swordfish and tuna
• Olives and capers
• Caponata *(a dish with olives, tomatoes, anchovies, and eggplant)*

Sardinia
• Lobster, squid, and sardines
• Wild mushrooms
• Spit-roasted meats

HELPFUL HINTS
SIMPLE SHORTCUTS

Take note of these convenience products that work well in Italian dishes. They can help cut your time in the kitchen.

- Refrigerated polenta
- Refrigerated pasta
- Frozen ravioli
- Prepared pasta sauces
- Dried Italian seasoning
- Bottled Italian salad dressing
- Prepared pesto
- Bottled roasted red peppers

SAVVY SUBSTITUTIONS

For the best results, we recommend that you use the specified ingredients in each recipe. However, when you don't have an ingredient on hand, use this list of simple substitutions for quick solutions to dinner dilemmas.

Arborio rice (1 cup) = 1 cup short-grain rice or 1 cup brown rice

Balsamic vinegar (1 tablespoon) = 1 tablespoon cider or red wine vinegar plus 1/2 teaspoon sugar

Bread crumbs (fine dry, 1/4 cup) = 3/4 cup soft bread crumbs, 1/4 cup cracker crumbs, or 1/4 cup cornflake crumbs

Broth (beef or chicken, 1 cup) = 1 teaspoon or 1 cube instant beef or chicken bouillon plus 1 cup hot water

Fresh herbs (snipped, 1 tablespoon) = 1/2 to 1 teaspoon dried herb, crushed

Garlic (1 clove) = 1/2 teaspoon bottled minced garlic or 1/8 teaspoon garlic powder

Half and half or light cream (1 cup) = 1 tablespoon melted butter or margarine plus enough whole milk to equal 1 cup

Onion (chopped, 1/2 cup) = 2 tablespoons dried minced onion or 1/2 teaspoon onion powder

Red wine (1 cup) = 1 cup beef or chicken broth in savory recipes; cranberry juice in desserts

Tomato juice (1 cup) = 1/2 cup tomato sauce plus 1/2 cup water

Tomato sauce (2 cups) = 3/4 cup tomato paste plus 1 cup water

White wine (1 cup) = 1 cup chicken broth in savory recipes; apple juice or white grape juice in desserts

TOOLS OF THE TRADE

The right tools in the kitchen can make all the difference in great cooking. Take inventory of your kitchen supplies to make sure you have the essential utensils. Here is a list of supplies that simplify cooking and make it more fun.

Aluminum foil
Baking pans and dishes
Brown bags for ripening fruits
Casseroles
Colander and/or sieve
Cutting boards
   (plastic and wooden)
Dutch oven
   (or a pan equivalent in size)
Electric mixer
Electric slow cooker
Food processor
Grater and/or shredder
Hot pads
Kitchen shears
Knives
   (chef's, paring, and serrated)
Ladle
Measuring cups *(liquid and dry)*
Measuring spoons
Mixing bowls
Pastry blender
Pastry brush
Pie plate
Pizza cutter
Pizza pan
Rolling pin
Rotary beater
Rubber scrapers
Saucepans
Skillets
Slotted spoon
Spatulas
Thermometers
   (instant read and meat)
Vegetable peeler
Waxed paper
Wire cooling racks
Wooden spoons for mixing
Zester for citrus fruits

APPETIZERS

1

This recipe is surprisingly simple to prepare. In only 20 minutes, you'll have a hot and tasty appetizer for last-minute guests.

HOT ARTICHOKE DIP

START TO FINISH:
20 minutes

MAKES:
3 cups dip

2   14-ounce cans artichoke hearts, drained and coarsely chopped

1   10¾-ounce can condensed cream of chicken or cream of mushroom soup

1   teaspoon dried Italian seasoning, crushed

¼   cup grated Parmesan cheese

2   green onions, sliced

¼   teaspoon crushed red pepper

Red sweet pepper wedges and/or crackers

1 In a medium saucepan combine artichoke hearts, cream of chicken soup, and Italian seasoning. Cook and stir over medium heat until heated through. Remove from heat.

2 Stir in Parmesan cheese, green onions, and crushed red pepper. Serve warm or at room temperature with sweet pepper wedges and/or crackers.

Per ¼ cup dip: 54 cal., 2 g total fat (1 g sat. fat), 3 mg chol., 430 mg sodium, 6 g carbo., 2 g fiber, 2 g pro.

Artichoke lovers, take note: You'll be amazed at how well the tangy flavor of dried tomatoes meshes with artichoke hearts in this vibrant dip.

TOMATO & ARTICHOKE DIP

½ cup oil-packed dried tomatoes

2 9-ounce packages frozen artichoke hearts, thawed and chopped

8 ounces provolone or fontina cheese, shredded (2 cups)

½ cup dairy sour cream

¼ cup mayonnaise or salad dressing

3 cloves garlic, minced

¼ teaspoon crushed red pepper

2 tablespoons finely shredded Parmesan or Asiago cheese

48 toasted baguette-style French bread slices or crackers

1 Preheat oven to 350°F. Drain dried tomatoes on paper towels to remove excess oil; snip dried tomatoes. In a large bowl combine snipped tomatoes, artichoke hearts, provolone cheese, sour cream, mayonnaise, garlic, and crushed red pepper. Transfer mixture to a 9-inch pie plate or 10-inch quiche dish. Sprinkle with Parmesan cheese.

2 Bake about 25 minutes or until mixture is heated through. Serve warm with bread or crackers.

Per serving: 144 cal., 7 g total fat (3 g sat. fat), 9 mg chol., 277 mg sodium, 16 g carbo., 2 g fiber, 6 g pro.

PREP:
20 minutes

BAKE:
25 minutes

OVEN:
350°F

MAKES:
24 servings

Layers of pesto and cheese create an outstanding presentation. Short on time? Use purchased pesto.

PESTO-HAZELNUT CHEESE PÂTÉ

PREP:
30 minutes

CHILL:
8 to 24 hours

MAKES:
16 servings

8	ounces soft goat cheese (chèvre)
2	3-ounce packages cream cheese, softened
1	cup fresh basil leaves
½	cup fresh spinach leaves
¼	cup freshly grated Parmesan cheese
2	tablespoons fresh flat-leaf parsley
2	tablespoons pine nuts
1	clove garlic, quartered
3	tablespoons olive oil
¼	cup finely chopped hazelnuts (filberts) or pecans, toasted
	Toasted French bread slices, crackers, and/or sliced pears

1 Line two 4½×2½×1½-inch loaf pans with plastic wrap, leaving enough excess plastic wrap to cover finished pâté.

2 In a food processor combine goat cheese and cream cheese. Cover and process with several on-off turns until smooth, stopping the machine several times and scraping the side. Remove cheese mixture from food processor; set aside. Wash food processor bowl.

3 For basil-spinach pesto, in the food processor combine basil, spinach, Parmesan cheese, parsley, pine nuts, and garlic. Cover and process with several on-off turns until paste forms, stopping machine several times and scraping the side. With machine running slowly, gradually add olive oil, processing until almost smooth.

4 Spread about ⅓ cup of the goat cheese mixture onto the bottom of one of the prepared pans. Sprinkle with 1 tablespoon of the hazelnuts. Carefully spread half of the basil-spinach pesto (about ¼ cup) over nuts. Sprinkle basil-spinach pesto with another 1 tablespoon of the hazelnuts. Spread with another ⅓ cup of the cream cheese mixture. Repeat layering remaining ingredients in the second prepared pan. Cover with plastic wrap and chill for 8 to 24 hours.

5 To serve, fold back plastic wrap; invert onto a small serving platter. Remove and discard plastic wrap. Serve pâté with bread slices, crackers, and/or pears.

Per serving pâté: 124 cal., 12 g total fat (5 g sat. fat), 19 mg chol., 104 mg sodium, 1 g carbo., 0 g fiber, 5 g pro.

When shopping for tomatillos, look for firm skin and dry, tight-fitting husks. Serve this caponata with toasted Italian bread slices.

TOMATILLO CAPONATA

3	tablespoons olive oil
2	tablespoons pine nuts or chopped almonds
1	large onion, chopped
1	pound tomatillos, husks removed and coarsely chopped, or 1 pound green tomatoes, seeded and coarsely chopped (3 to 3½ cups)
2	tablespoons red wine vinegar
2	tablespoons drained capers
2	tablespoons tomato paste
4	olive oil-packed anchovies, drained and mashed
½	teaspoon black pepper
¼	teaspoon salt

PREP:
45 minutes

COOL:
1 hour

MAKES:
about 2 cups

1 In a large skillet heat olive oil over medium heat. Add nuts; cook and stir for 2 to 3 minutes or until lightly golden brown. Remove with a slotted spoon to paper towels to drain. Set aside.

2 Add onion to skillet. Cook and stir for 3 to 4 minutes or just until tender. Add chopped tomatillos or green tomatoes; cook for 4 minutes more, stirring occasionally.

3 Stir in red wine vinegar, capers, tomato paste, anchovies, pepper, and salt. Bring to boiling; reduce heat. Simmer, uncovered, for 5 to 10 minutes or until thickened, stirring occasionally. Remove from heat. Transfer to a serving bowl; cover and cool for 1 hour.

4 To serve, top with the nuts.

Per 2-tablespoon serving: 44 cal., 4 g total fat (0 g sat. fat), 1 mg chol., 107 mg sodium, 3 g carbo., 0 g fiber, 1 g pro.

These appetizers make entertaining easy. Four ingredients and a slow cooker—that's all you need.

COCKTAIL MEATBALLS

PREP:
10 minutes

COOK:
Low 4 hours, High 2 hours

MAKES:
16 servings

1 16-ounce package frozen cooked meatballs (32), thawed
½ cup bottled roasted red and/or yellow sweet peppers, cut into 1-inch pieces
⅛ teaspoon crushed red pepper
½ of a 26-ounce jar onion-garlic pasta sauce (1½ cups)

1 In a 1½- to 2-quart slow cooker combine meatballs and roasted peppers. Sprinkle with crushed red pepper. Pour pasta sauce over mixture in slow cooker.

2 Cover and cook on low-heat setting for 4 to 5 hours or on high-heat setting for 2 to 2½ hours. If no heat setting is available, cook for 4 to 5 hours. Skim fat from sauce, if necessary. Stir gently before serving. Serve immediately or keep warm, covered, on low-heat setting for up to 2 hours.

Per serving: 109 cal., 8 g total fat (3 g sat. fat), 10 mg chol., 321 mg sodium, 6 g carbo., 1 g fiber, 4 g pro.

NOTE: For 32 servings, prepare as directed, except use a 3½- or 4-quart slow cooker and use two 16-ounce packages meatballs (64 total); 1 cup bottled roasted red or yellow sweet peppers, cut into 1-inch pieces; ¼ teaspoon crushed red pepper; and one 26-ounce jar onion-garlic pasta sauce.

Italian sausage and dry Italian salad dressing mix add pizzazz to these zippy meatballs.

ZIPPY MINI MEATBALLS

1	slightly beaten egg
⅓	cup fine dry bread crumbs
1	0.7-ounce envelope Italian salad dressing mix
½	teaspoon crushed red pepper
2	cloves garlic, minced
1	pound lean ground beef
8	ounces bulk Italian sausage
¼	cup canned crushed pineapple, well drained
¼	cup canned diced green chile peppers, well drained
¼	cup shredded mozzarella cheese (1 ounce)
½	cup bottled Italian salad dressing
½	cup pineapple or plum preserves
½	cup bottled chili sauce

1 Preheat oven to 350°F. For meatballs, in a large bowl combine egg, bread crumbs, dry salad dressing mix, crushed red pepper, and garlic. Add ground beef, Italian sausage, pineapple, chile peppers, and mozzarella cheese; mix well. Shape into 48 meatballs.

2 In a 15×10×1-inch baking pan arrange meatballs in a single layer. Bake for 20 minutes. Drain well. Transfer meatballs to a 3½- or 4-quart slow cooker.

3 For sauce, in a medium bowl combine bottled salad dressing, pineapple preserves, and chili sauce. Pour over meatballs in slow cooker. Cover and cook on low-heat setting for 3 to 4 hours or on high-heat setting for 1½ to 2 hours.

4 Stir gently before serving. Serve meatballs with toothpicks.

Per meatball: 62 cal., 4 g total fat (1 g sat. fat), 14 mg chol., 165 mg sodium, 4 g carbo., 0 g fiber, 3 g pro.

PREP:
30 minutes

BAKE:
20 minutes

COOK:
Low 3 hours, High 1½ hours

OVEN:
350°F

MAKES:
48 meatballs

Eyecatching and fun to eat, these kabobs make great party food.

ANTIPASTO KABOBS

START TO FINISH:
25 minutes

MAKES:
12 kabobs

6 ounces sliced salami

6 ounces mozzarella or provolone cheese, cubed

1½ cups cantaloupe and/or honeydew melon balls

1 cup purchased large pitted herbed green olives*
   and/or large pitted ripe olives

¾ cup cherry tomatoes

1 On six 6-inch bamboo skewers, alternately thread salami slices, cheese cubes, and melon balls, folding salami slices if desired. On six additional 6-inch skewers, thread salami slices, cheese cubes, olives, and cherry tomatoes, folding salami slices if desired. Place on a serving plate. Serve immediately or cover and chill for up to 2 hours before serving.

Per kabob: 117 cal., 10 g total fat (4 g sat. fat), 24 mg chol., 620 mg sodium, 2 g carbo., 0 g fiber, 6 g pro.

*NOTE: Herbed green olives can be found in Italian markets. However, if you want to make your own, here's how. In a small bowl combine 1 cup large pitted green olives, pimento-stuffed olives, and/or pitted ripe olives; 1½ teaspoons olive oil; 1 clove garlic, minced; ½ teaspoon dried Italian seasoning, crushed; and ⅛ teaspoon crushed red pepper. Stir until olives are evenly coated. Cover and chill for at least 2 hours.

Loaded with great Italian flavors, these treats-on-a-stick can be made up to 24 hours in advance.

PEPPER, OLIVE & CHEESE SKEWERS

4   to 6 very thin slices prosciutto or smoked ham,
cut into ½-inch-wide strips

8   ounces provolone or Asiago cheese, cut into ¾-inch cubes

1   16-ounce jar whole cherry peppers, drained

1   12-ounce jar pepperoncini salad peppers, drained

20   to 24 pitted ripe olives, drained

2   tablespoons olive oil

2   tablespoons balsamic vinegar

1 Wrap a prosciutto strip around each provolone cheese cube; set aside. On 6-inch wooden skewers, alternately thread wrapped provolone cheese, cherry peppers, pepperoncini peppers, and olives. Place on a large serving platter. Serve immediately or cover and chill for up to 24 hours.

2 In a small bowl whisk together olive oil and balsamic vinegar. Serve with skewers.

Per skewer: 67 cal., 5 g total fat (2 g sat. fat), 9 mg chol., 472 mg sodium, 2 g carbo., 0 g fiber, 3 g pro.

START TO FINISH:
40 minutes

MAKES:
20 to 24 skewers

Great dipped in pizza sauce, these scrumptious appetizers bring out the veggie lover in just about anyone.

CRUMB-COATED VEGGIE DUNKERS

PREP:
25 minutes

BAKE:
20 minutes

OVEN:
400°F

MAKES:
6 servings

Nonstick cooking spray

⅔ cup seasoned fine dry bread crumbs

2 tablespoons grated Parmesan cheese

⅛ teaspoon salt

2 slightly beaten egg whites

1 tablespoon milk

4 cups cauliflower florets and/or broccoli florets

2 tablespoons butter or margarine, melted

1 15-ounce can pizza sauce

1 Preheat oven to 400°F. Lightly coat a 15×10×1-inch baking pan with nonstick cooking spray; set aside. In a large resealable plastic bag combine bread crumbs, Parmesan cheese, and salt. In another large resealable plastic bag combine egg whites and milk.

2 Add vegetables to the plastic bag with the egg white mixture. Close bag and shake to coat well. Add vegetables to plastic bag with crumb mixture. Close bag and shake to coat well. Place coated vegetables on the prepared baking pan. Drizzle melted butter over vegetables.

3 Bake about 20 minutes or until golden brown, stirring twice. Meanwhile, in a small saucepan heat pizza sauce over medium heat. Serve vegetables with warm pizza sauce.

Per serving: 144 cal., 6 g total fat (3 g sat. fat), 13 mg chol., 543 mg sodium, 18 g carbo., 3 g fiber, 7 g pro.

Crostini means "little toasts" in Italian. Top these with a mouthwatering pesto and bean topping or a tangy tomato and olive mixture.

CROSTINI APPETIZERS

1   8-ounce loaf baguette-style French bread
2   tablespoons olive oil
     Freshly ground black pepper
1   recipe Basil Pesto and White Beans or 1 recipe
     Fresh Tomato and Olives
     Finely shredded Parmesan or Asiago cheese (optional)

1 Preheat oven to 425°F. For crostini, bias-cut bread into ½-inch-thick slices. Lightly brush one side of each bread slice with olive oil. Lightly sprinkle oiled side with pepper. Arrange in a single layer on an ungreased baking sheet. Bake for 4 minutes. Turn slices over and bake for 3 to 4 minutes more or until crisp and light brown.

2 To serve the Basil Pesto and White Beans, spread pesto topping on the oiled side of each toast; top each with a small amount of bean mixture. To serve the Fresh Tomato and Olives, top oiled side of each toast with tomato mixture. If desired, sprinkle with cheese.

BASIL PESTO AND WHITE BEANS: In a small bowl combine 1 cup purchased basil pesto; 1 hard cooked egg, finely chopped; and 1 teaspoon lemon juice or red wine vinegar. In another small bowl combine half of a 19-ounce can cannellini beans (white kidney beans) or half of a 15-ounce can Great Northern beans, rinsed and drained; 1 tablespoon thinly sliced green onion or chopped shallot; 1 tablespoon olive oil; and ⅛ teaspoon crushed red pepper.

Per serving with Basil Pesto and White Beans: 371 cal., 27 g total fat (1 g sat. fat), 31 mg chol., 468 mg sodium, 25 g carbo., 3 g fiber, 9 g pro.

FRESH TOMATO AND OLIVES: In a small bowl combine 1 cup seeded and finely chopped tomatoes, 1 cup coarsely chopped assorted pitted black olives (such as gaeta, sicilian, or kalamata), ⅓ cup finely chopped red onion, 2 tablespoons snipped fresh cilantro or parsley, 2 tablespoons balsamic vinegar or red wine vinegar, and 2 cloves garlic, minced.

Per serving with Fresh Tomatoes and Olives: 140 cal., 6 g total fat (1 g sat. fat), 0 mg chol., 322 mg sodium, 19 g carbo., 2 g fiber, 3 g pro.

MAKE-AHEAD DIRECTIONS: Cool toast; place in an airtight container and store at room temperature for up to 24 hours. For the Basil Pesto and White Beans, transfer the pesto and bean toppings into two separate plastic containers with tight-fitting lids. For the Fresh Tomato and Olives, transfer topping into a plastic container with a tight-fitting lid. Chill toppings for up to 24 hours.

PREP:
25 minutes

BAKE:
4 minutes + 3 minutes

OVEN:
425°F

MAKES:
8 to 10 servings

Bruschetta comes from the Italian word, "bruscare," which means to roast over coals. This recipe uses a broiler instead of hot coals.

FRESH TOMATO-BASIL BRUSCHETTA

PREP:
20 minutes

BROIL:
2 minutes

MAKES:
16 servings

16 ½-inch-thick slices baguette-style French bread

3 ounces part-skim mozzarella cheese, thinly sliced

1 cup seeded and chopped fresh red, orange, and/or yellow tomatoes

2 tablespoons small fresh basil leaves or snipped fresh basil

1 Preheat broiler. Arrange bread slices on the unheated rack of broiler pan. Broil 3 to 4 inches from heat about 2 minutes or until toasted, turning once.

2 Top toasted bread slices with mozzarella cheese. If desired, broil about 1 minute to melt cheese.

3 In a small bowl combine tomatoes and basil. Top bread slices with tomato mixture.

Per serving: 54 cal., 1 g total fat (1 g sat. fat), 3 mg chol., 120 mg sodium, 8 g carbo., 1 g fiber, 3 g pro.

Marsala or Madeira complements the figs. If you don't have either of these wines on hand and would rather not buy a bottle of wine just for 2 tablespoons, use the white grape juice option.

MASCARPONE-FIG BRUSCHETTA

¼   cup olive oil

3   cloves garlic, minced

1   10- to 12-ounce loaf baguette-style French bread, cut into ½-inch-thick slices

1   8-ounce carton mascarpone or 8 ounces soft goat cheese (chèvre)

4   ounces thinly sliced prosciutto, torn into bite-size pieces (about 1 cup)

20   to 24 small or 15 medium fresh figs, sliced (about 1 pound)*

2   tablespoons Marsala, Madeira, or white grape juice

PREP:
20 minutes

BAKE:
5 minutes

OVEN:
425°F

MAKES:
24 servings

1 Preheat oven to 425"F. In a small bowl combine olive oil and garlic; lightly brush both sides of each bread slice with the oil mixture. Arrange bread slices on a baking sheet. Bake about 5 minutes or until crisp and lightly browned, turning once.

2 To assemble, spread each slice of toast with a scant tablespoon of the mascarpone cheese; top with some of the prosciutto and two or three fig slices. Brush fig slices with wine. Serve at room temperature or return slices to baking sheet and bake in the 425°F oven about 3 minutes or until heated through.

Per serving: 119 cal., 7 g total fat (3 g sat. fat), 15 mg chol., 205 mg sodium, 10 g carbo., 1 g fiber, 4 g pro.

*NOTE: When fresh figs aren't available, plump 4 to 5 ounces of dried figs to use instead. To plump the figs, in a small saucepan combine the figs and ¼ cup Marsala or Madeira; heat just until boiling. Remove from the heat; cover and chill for 1 to 8 hours before using.

These bite-size treats are party pleasers. For make-ahead convenience, toast the bread and store it in an airtight container up to 24 hours in advance.

SHRIMP-TOMATO BRUSCHETTA

PREP:
30 minutes

BAKE:
5 minutes

OVEN:
425°F

MAKES:
24 appetizers

¼ cup olive oil

1 teaspoon snipped fresh oregano

1 clove garlic, minced

   Dash cayenne pepper

24 ½-inch-thick baguette-style French bread slices (about 8 ounces)

5 or 6 plum tomatoes, thinly sliced

12 ounces peeled, deveined, and cooked medium shrimp

   Fresh oregano sprigs (optional)

1 Preheat oven to 425°F. In a small bowl combine olive oil, snipped oregano, garlic, and cayenne pepper; lightly brush both sides of each bread slice with some of the oil mixture. Arrange bread slices on a baking sheet. Bake about 5 minutes or until crisp and lightly browned, turning once.

2 To assemble, top each slice of toast with some tomato slices and one or two shrimp. If desired, garnish with oregano sprigs.

Per appetizer: 63 cal., 3 g total fat (0 g sat. fat), 28 mg chol., 90 mg sodium, 6 g carbo., 1 g fiber, 4 g pro.

The robust flavors of marinated artichokes, olives, and herbs create an out-of-this-world combination.

ARTICHOKE & OLIVE PIZZA WEDGES

1	12-inch Italian bread shell (such as Boboli brand)
1	6-ounce jar marinated artichoke hearts, drained
1¼	cups shredded mozzarella cheese (5 ounces)
1	cup sliced fresh mushrooms
⅓	cup pitted black olives (such as gaeta, sicilian, or kalamata), drained and sliced
2	tablespoons sliced pimiento, drained
1	to 2 tablespoons snipped fresh basil
2	teaspoons snipped fresh thyme
⅓	cup shredded Parmesan cheese

PREP:
20 minutes

BAKE:
8 minutes

OVEN:
450°F

MAKES:
16 servings

1 Preheat oven to 450°F. Place bread shell on a baking sheet or pizza pan; set aside. If necessary, cut up any large artichoke heart pieces.

2 Sprinkle 1 cup of the mozzarella cheese over bread shell. Top with artichoke pieces, mushrooms, olives, pimiento, basil, and thyme. Sprinkle with remaining ¼ cup mozzarella cheese and the Parmesan cheese.

3 Bake for 8 to 10 minutes or until cheese is melted. Cut into wedges and serve warm.

Per serving: 113 cal., 5 g total fat (2 g sat. fat), 9 mg chol., 277 mg sodium, 12 g carbo., 1 g fiber, 6 g pro.

All-time favorites, pizza and grilling, combine forces in this fast-fixing appetizer.
Purchased bread shells cut preparation time.

CANADIAN BACON PIZZA

PREP:
20 minutes

GRILL:
5 minutes

MAKES:
8 servings

1	6-ounce jar marinated artichoke hearts, quartered
2	6-inch Italian bread shells (such as Boboli brand)
1	cup shredded fontina or mozzarella cheese (4 ounces)
6	slices Canadian-style bacon, cut into strips (about 5 ounces)
3	plum tomatoes, sliced
¼	cup crumbled feta cheese (1 ounce)
2	green onions, thinly sliced
1	tablespoon snipped fresh oregano or basil

1 Drain artichoke hearts, reserving marinade. Brush bread shells with some of the reserved marinade (discard any remaining marinade). Sprinkle half of the fontina cheese over bread shells. In a large bowl toss together artichoke hearts, Canadian-style bacon, tomatoes, feta cheese, green onions, and oregano; divide among shells. Sprinkle with remaining fontina cheese.

2 Transfer bread shells to a pizza grill pan or a large double-thick piece of heavy foil. On a grill that has a cover, place the pan or foil on the rack of the grill directly over medium heat. Cover and grill for 5 to 8 minutes or until cheese is melted and pizza is heated through.

Per serving: 192 cal., 10 g total fat (4 g sat. fat), 30 mg chol., 626 mg sodium, 16 g carbo., 1 g fiber, 12 g pro.

Turn bakery focaccia into an Italian masterpiece with the addition of sweet, juicy pears and robust Gorgonzola. This recipe couldn't be easier—or more impressive!

GORGONZOLA & PEAR FOCACCIA

1   12-inch Italian flatbread (focaccia) or one 12-inch Italian bread shell (such as Boboli brand)

1   medium pear, cored, halved, and very thinly sliced

1   small red onion, cut into thin wedges

1   tablespoon olive oil

1   cup crumbled Gorgonzola cheese (4 ounces)

¼   cup chopped walnuts, toasted

1 Preheat oven to 425°F. Place bread shell on an ungreased baking sheet or pizza pan. Arrange pear slices and onion slices on top. Drizzle with olive oil. Sprinkle with Gorgonzola cheese.

2 Bake for 10 minutes. Sprinkle with toasted walnuts. To serve, cut into wedges.

Per serving: 175 cal., 8 g total fat (2 g sat. fat), 10 mg chol., 364 mg sodium, 19 g carbo., 1 g fiber, 7 g pro.

START TO FINISH:
25 minutes

OVEN:
425°F

MAKES:
12 to 16 servings

Salsiccia, which is Italian for "sausage," is the star ingredient in this bread. Frozen dough makes this recipe a snap.

SALSICCIA BREAD

PREP:
25 minutes

RISE:
30 minutes

BAKE:
25 minutes

COOL:
30 minutes

OVEN:
350°F

MAKES:
6 to 8 servings

8   ounces bulk Italian sausage

½   cup chopped peeled potato

2   cloves garlic, minced

½   of a 10-ounce package frozen chopped spinach, thawed and well drained

1   8-ounce can pizza sauce

2   tablespoons drained snipped oil-packed dried tomatoes

1   16-ounce loaf frozen bread dough, thawed

1   teaspoon olive oil

1 For filling, in a large skillet cook sausage, potato, and garlic until sausage is brown and potato is tender. Drain off fat. Stir in spinach, ⅓ cup of the pizza sauce, and the dried tomatoes. Set aside.

2 On a lightly floured surface, roll dough to a 12×9-inch rectangle, stopping occasionally to let dough relax a few minutes for easier rolling. Spread sausage mixture evenly over dough, leaving a 1-inch border on all sides. Starting from a short side, roll up dough into a spiral. Moisten edge and ends; pinch seams to seal. Transfer to a lightly greased baking sheet. Cover and let rise in a warm place until nearly double (30 to 45 minutes).

3 Preheat oven to 350°F. Lightly brush loaf with olive oil. Bake for 25 to 30 minutes or until loaf is golden brown. Transfer to a wire rack; cool for 30 minutes before cutting. Serve with remaining pizza sauce for dipping. (Store leftovers, wrapped in foil, in refrigerator for up to 2 days. To reheat, bake wrapped loaf in a 350°F oven for 15 to 20 minutes or until heated through.)

Per serving: 373 cal., 16 g total fat (4 g sat. fat), 29 mg chol., 830 mg sodium, 42 g carbo., 2 g fiber, 12 g pro.

You'll be amazed at the abundance of flavor in these one-ingredient morsels.

PARMESAN CHEESE CRISPS

6 ounces Parmesan cheese

1 Preheat oven to 400°F. Coarsely shred cheese. Line a baking sheet with a silicone baking mat (Silpat), parchment paper, or nonstick foil. Place about 1 tablespoon cheese on prepared baking sheet; pat into a 2-inch circle. Repeat with remaining cheese, allowing 2 inches between circles. Bake for 7 to 8 minutes or until bubbly and lightly golden brown. Let stand on baking sheet for 1 to 2 minutes or until firm enough to remove. Transfer to wire rack; let cool.

Per crisp: 29 cal., 2 g total fat (1 g sat. fat), 5 mg chol., 120 mg sodium, 0 g carbo., 0 g fiber, 3 g pro.

MAKE-AHEAD DIRECTIONS: Prepare as directed. Store in an airtight container for up to 24 hours or freeze for up to 1 month.

PREP:
20 minutes

BAKE:
7 minutes

STAND:
1 minute

OVEN:
400°F

MAKES:
24 crisps

These appetizers package all the flavor of a delicious cheese pizza into bite-size puffs.

ITALIAN PEPPERONI-CHEESE PUFFS

PREP:
30 minutes

BAKE:
15 minutes per batch

OVEN:
450°F

MAKES:
about 40 puffs

1¼ cups water

⅓ cup shortening

1½ cups all-purpose flour

4 eggs

¾ cup finely chopped pepperoni (3 ounces)

¾ cup finely shredded pecorino Romano cheese or Parmesan cheese (3 ounces)

2 tablespoons snipped fresh flat-leaf parsley

⅛ teaspoon garlic powder

⅛ teaspoon black pepper

Purchased pizza sauce, warmed (optional)

1 Preheat oven to 450°F. Lightly grease two large baking sheets; set aside. In a large saucepan combine the water and shortening. Bring to boiling. Add flour all at once, stirring vigorously. Cook and stir until mixture forms a ball. Remove from heat. Cool for 10 minutes. Add eggs, one at a time, beating well with a wooden spoon after each addition. Stir in pepperoni, cheese, parsley, garlic powder, and pepper.

2 Drop dough by rounded teaspoons into small mounds 2 inches apart on prepared baking sheets. Position the two baking sheets on separate oven racks. Bake for 15 to 17 minutes or until firm and golden brown, switching oven racks halfway through baking. Transfer to a wire rack. Repeat, as needed, for remaining dough. Serve warm. If desired, serve with pizza sauce.

Per puff: 57 cal., 4 g total fat (1 g sat. fat), 25 mg chol., 81 mg sodium, 4 g carbo., 0 g fiber, 2 g pro.

MAKE-AHEAD DIRECTIONS: Bake puffs as directed; let cool. Place in sealed freezer containers. Freeze for up to 3 months. To serve, preheat oven to 350°F. Arrange frozen puffs on a large baking sheet. Bake about 10 minutes or until heated through.

Toasted ravioli were made famous by one of the restaurants on The Hill, an Italian neighborhood in St. Louis. The original recipe used made-from-scratch ravioli. For extra convenience this version uses frozen ravioli.

TOASTED RAVIOLI

¼ cup finely chopped onion

1 clove garlic, minced

1 tablespoon olive oil or butter

2 pounds tomatoes, peeled, seeded, and cut up

2 tablespoons snipped fresh basil or 1 teaspoon dried basil, crushed

½ teaspoon salt

⅛ teaspoon black pepper

2 tablespoons tomato paste

1 egg

2 tablespoons milk

1 16- to 20-ounce package frozen meat-filled ravioli, thawed

⅔ to 1 cup seasoned fine dry bread crumbs

Cooking oil or shortening for deep-fat frying

Grated Parmesan cheese (optional)

1 For sauce, in a medium saucepan cook onion and garlic in hot oil or butter until onion is tender. Stir in tomatoes, dried basil (if using), salt, and pepper. Cover; cook over medium heat about 10 minutes or until tomatoes are soft, stirring occasionally.

2 Stir in tomato paste. Bring to boiling; reduce heat. Simmer, uncovered, about 20 minutes or until mixture reaches desired consistency, stirring occasionally. Stir in fresh basil, if using. Cover sauce; keep warm.

3 Meanwhile, preheat oven to 300°F. In a small bowl beat together egg and milk. Dip each ravioli in egg mixture, then dip in bread crumbs to coat.

4 Pour 2 inches of oil into a heavy 3-quart saucepan; heat to 350°F. Fry ravioli, a few at a time, in hot oil about 2 minutes or until golden brown, turning once. Drain on paper towels. Keep warm in the 300°F oven while frying the remaining ravioli.

5 If desired, sprinkle ravioli with Parmesan cheese. Serve with warm sauce for dipping.

Per two ravioli: 222 cal., 13 g total fat (1 g sat. fat), 47 mg chol., 429 mg sodium, 19 g carbo., 1 g fiber, 8 g pro.

PREP:
35 minutes

COOK:
2 minutes per batch

OVEN:
300°F

MAKES:
24 to 28 ravioli

These cheese-stuffed tomatoes are a surefire hit for an outdoor party or gathering.

STUFFED CAPRESE

START TO FINISH:
25 minutes

MAKES:
4 servings

4	small tomatoes (3 to 4 ounces each)
¼	teaspoon sea salt or salt
⅛	teaspoon freshly ground black pepper
3	tablespoons olive oil
3	tablespoons white wine vinegar or vinegar
½	teaspoon sugar
3	ounces fresh mozzarella or fresh buffalo mozzarella, drained and cut into small chunks (about ½ cup)
¼	cup slivered red onion
¼	cup snipped fresh basil
	Sea salt or salt
	Freshly ground black pepper

1 Cut a ¼-inch-thick slice from the stem end of each tomato. Using a spoon, carefully scoop out and discard tomato core, seeds, and pulp, leaving up to a ½-inch-thick shell. Sprinkle tomato shells with the ¼ teaspoon salt and the ⅛ teaspoon pepper. Stand tomato shells on a plate; set aside.

2 For dressing, in a screw-top jar combine olive oil, vinegar, and sugar. Cover and shake well. Set aside 1½ tablespoons of the dressing. Spoon remaining dressing into tomato shells.

3 In a medium bowl combine mozzarella, red onion, basil, and reserved dressing; toss to mix. Spoon cheese mixture into tomato shells. Serve immediately or cover and chill for up to 2 hours. Sprinkle with additional salt and pepper before serving.

Per serving: 177 cal., 15 g total fat (4 g sat. fat), 16 mg chol., 187 mg sodium, 6 g carbo., 1 g fiber, 5 g pro.

Generally available year-round, plum or roma tomatoes are a natural pairing with tangy goat cheese and zesty pesto.

ROASTED PLUM TOMATOES WITH CHÈVRE & PESTO

10   plum tomatoes, halved lengthwise (1½ to 2 pounds)

¼   teaspoon dried thyme, crushed

     Salt

     Black pepper

⅓   cup purchased pesto

⅓   cup soft goat cheese (chèvre)

2   tablespoons snipped fresh parsley or basil

1 Preheat oven to 400°F. Sprinkle cut sides of tomato halves with thyme, salt, and pepper. Place tomatoes, cut sides up, in a greased shallow baking pan. Bake about 5 minutes or until heated and beginning to soften.

2 Spoon a scant teaspoon of the pesto onto each tomato half. Top each with a scant teaspoon of the goat cheese. Bake about 2 minutes more or until cheese is softened. Sprinkle tomatoes lightly with parsley.

Per appetizer: 50 cal., 4 g total fat (1 g sat. fat), 3 mg chol., 68 mg sodium, 2 g carbo., 0 g fiber, 2 g pro.

PREP:
10 minutes

BAKE:
5 minutes + 2 minutes

OVEN:
400°F

MAKES:
20 appetizers

Aged Asiago is an Italian hard cheese with a rich and sweet to robust flavor, depending on the variety. Although often grated and used in cooking, as in this savory filling, Asiago also is delicious for nibbling by itself.

SAUSAGE & ASIAGO-STUFFED MUSHROOMS

PREP:
35 minutes

BAKE:
5 minutes + 8 minutes

OVEN:
425°F

MAKES:
24 stuffed mushrooms

24 fresh mushrooms (1½ to 2 inches in diameter)

4 ounces bulk sweet Italian sausage

2 tablespoons finely chopped onion

1 clove garlic, minced

¼ cup seasoned fine dry bread crumbs

¼ cup finely shredded Asiago cheese (1 ounce)

¼ cup finely chopped bottled roasted red sweet peppers, well drained

2 tablespoons snipped fresh basil

⅛ teaspoon black pepper

1 to 2 tablespoons olive oil

1 Preheat oven to 425°F. Clean mushrooms with a damp paper towel. Remove stems; reserve caps. Chop enough stems to make ⅔ cup (discard remaining stems). Place mushrooms, stem sides down, in a 15×10×1-inch baking pan. Bake for 5 minutes.

2 Meanwhile, for stuffing, in a medium skillet cook the ⅔ cup chopped mushroom stems, the sausage, onion, and garlic until sausage is brown. Drain sausage mixture in a colander; return to skillet. Stir in bread crumbs, cheese, roasted red peppers, basil, and black pepper.

3 Carefully turn mushrooms stem sides up. Brush edges of mushrooms with olive oil. Spoon about 1 tablespoon of the stuffing into each mushroom cap. Bake for 8 to 10 minutes more or until heated through. Serve immediately.

Per stuffed mushroom: 35 cal., 2 g total fat (1 g sat. fat), 4 mg chol., 79 mg sodium, 2 g carbo., 0 g fiber, 2 g pro.

Your guests will marvel at these appetizers. Provolone and prosciutto provide an elegant touch.

PROSCIUTTO-TOPPED EGGPLANT SLICES

1	1-pound eggplant
1	tablespoon kosher salt or salt
2	beaten eggs
1	tablespoon water
¾	cup seasoned fine dry bread crumbs
2	tablespoons grated Parmesan cheese
3	tablespoons cooking oil
¾	to 1 cup purchased pasta sauce
3	ounces provolone cheese, shredded
2	ounces very thinly sliced prosciutto, cut into short, thin strips
¼	cup walnuts, toasted and finely chopped

START TO FINISH:
45 minutes

OVEN:
425°F

MAKES:
about 36 appetizers

❶ With a vegetable peeler, remove 1-inch-wide strips lengthwise down the eggplant at equal intervals. Cut eggplant crosswise into ½-inch-thick slices. Place slices on a double layer of paper towels. Sprinkle eggplant with the salt, turning to lightly coat both sides. Let stand for 15 to 30 minutes or until liquid is visible on the surfaces. Rinse salt and liquid off eggplant rounds; pat dry with paper towels. Halve or quarter large eggplant slices.

❷ Preheat oven to 425°F. In a shallow dish combine eggs and the water. In another shallow dish combine bread crumbs and Parmesan cheese. Dip eggplant slices in egg mixture, then in bread crumb mixture to coat both sides.

❸ In a large skillet heat 2 tablespoons of the oil over medium-high heat. Add half of the eggplant slices; cook about 4 minutes or until golden brown, turning once. Transfer to baking sheet(s). Add remaining 1 tablespoon oil to skillet; repeat with remaining eggplant slices.

❹ Top each eggplant slice with about 1 teaspoon of the pasta sauce. In a small bowl combine cheese, prosciutto, and walnuts; place a small mound on top of each eggplant slice. Bake for 3 to 4 minutes or until cheese melts.

Per appetizer: 43 cal., 3 g total fat (1 g sat. fat), 15 mg chol., 220 mg sodium, 3 g carbo., 1 g fiber, 2 g pro.

A true melding of Eastern and Western cuisine, these treats are easy and fun to make.

ITALIAN-STYLE WONTONS

PREP:
35 minutes

COOK:
1 minute per batch

OVEN:
300°F

MAKES:
24 wontons

½ cup finely shredded mozzarella cheese (2 ounces)

¼ cup snipped fresh basil

¼ cup chopped walnuts

3 tablespoons oil-packed dried tomatoes, drained and finely chopped

2 tablespoons finely chopped pitted ripe olives

1 green onion, thinly sliced

24 wonton wrappers

Cooking oil or shortening for deep-fat frying

¾ cup purchased marinara sauce (optional)

1 Preheat oven to 300°F. For filling, in a small bowl stir together mozzarella cheese, basil, walnuts, dried tomatoes, ripe olives, and green onion.

2 For each wonton, place one wonton wrapper on a flat surface with one corner toward you. Spoon a rounded teaspoon of the filling just below the center of the wonton wrapper. Fold the bottom point over the filling and tuck it under the filling. Roll the wonton wrapper once to cover filling, leaving about 1 inch unrolled at the top of the wrapper. Moisten the right corner with water. Grasp right and left corners and bring them toward you below the filling. Overlap the left corner over the right corner. Press firmly to seal.

3 Pour 2 inches of oil into a heavy saucepan or deep-fat fryer; heat to 365°F. Fry wontons, a few at a time, for 1 to 2½ minutes or until golden brown. Drain on paper towels. Keep warm in oven while frying the remaining wontons. If desired, serve with heated marinara sauce for dipping.

Per wonton: 55 cal., 4 g total fat (1 g sat. fat), 2 mg chol., 41 mg sodium, 4 g carbo., 0 g fiber, 1 g pro.

Prosciutto is an Italian ham that has been seasoned, salt cured, and air dried. It marries perfectly with the mild flavor of fresh mozzarella.

PROSCIUTTO-WRAPPED MOZZARELLA

4   1¾-ounce or two 4-ounce balls fresh mozzarella cheese

8   thin slices prosciutto (about 5½ ounces)

1   tablespoon olive oil

1   cup bottled spaghetti sauce, warmed

Snipped fresh basil

Snipped fresh tarragon

1 Cut the 1¾-ounce mozzarella balls in half or cut the 4-ounce balls into quarters. Wrap a slice of prosciutto around each mozzarella piece. In a large skillet heat olive oil over medium-high heat. Place wrapped mozzarella in skillet; cook for 1 to 2 minutes or until prosciutto is lightly browned and mozzarella softens, turning frequently.

2 Spoon 2 tablespoons of the warmed spaghetti sauce onto the center of each of eight small warmed plates; sprinkle with basil and tarragon. Set a hot wrapped mozzarella piece in the sauce on each plate. Serve immediately.

Per serving: 138 cal., 9 g total fat (4 g sat. fat), 31 mg chol., 747 mg sodium, 4 g carbo., 1 g fiber, 10 g pro.

START TO FINISH:
15 minutes

MAKES:
8 servings

This convenient, make-ahead appetizer makes a cool, refreshing treat on a hot day. Try it at your next summer get-together.

ITALIAN-STYLE MARINATED SHRIMP & ARTICHOKES

PREP:
20 minutes

CHILL:
2 to 4 hours

MAKES:
10 to 12 servings

1	9-ounce package frozen artichoke hearts
1	12-ounce package frozen peeled and deveined medium shrimp
½	cup bottled roasted red sweet peppers, drained and cut into bite-size strips
⅓	cup white wine vinegar
¼	cup olive oil
1	tablespoon thinly sliced green onion
2	cloves garlic, minced
1	teaspoon dried Italian seasoning, crushed
1	teaspoon finely shredded lemon peel
½	teaspoon dry mustard
¼	teaspoon salt
⅛	teaspoon black pepper

1 In a large saucepan cook artichoke hearts according to package directions, adding shrimp for the last 2 to 3 minutes of cooking or until shrimp are opaque and artichokes are tender. Drain well. When cool enough to handle, halve any large artichoke pieces. In a medium nonmetal bowl combine artichokes, shrimp, and roasted red pepper strips.

2 In a screw-top jar combine white wine vinegar, olive oil, green onion, garlic, Italian seasoning, lemon peel, dry mustard, salt, and black pepper. Cover and shake well. Pour over artichoke mixture; toss gently to coat. Cover and chill for 2 to 4 hours, stirring occasionally.

3 To serve, drain mixture; transfer to a shallow serving bowl or platter. Serve with a slotted spoon or toothpicks.

Per serving: 77 cal., 3 g total fat (0 g sat. fat), 52 mg chol., 97 mg sodium, 3 g carbo., 2 g fiber, 8 g pro.

Use olive oil infused with herbs or roasted garlic for extra flavor in these crowd-pleasing morsels.

MARINATED MOZZARELLA WITH BASIL

¼   cup fresh basil leaves

¼   cup olive oil

2   tablespoons balsamic vinegar

1   teaspoon coarsely ground black pepper

1   teaspoon finely shredded lemon peel

¼   teaspoon salt

1   pound fresh mozzarella cheese

     Tomato slices (optional)

     Baguette slices or crackers

PREP:
25 minutes

STAND:
30 minutes

MAKES:
15 servings

1 Set aside several whole basil leaves for garnish. Using a sharp knife, chop remaining basil. In a medium bowl combine chopped basil, olive oil, balsamic vinegar, pepper, lemon peel, and salt. Cut mozzarella into 1-inch cubes; toss cheese cubes gently with herb and oil mixture until cheese is well coated. Cover and let stand for 30 minutes before serving.

2 Transfer cheese mixture to a serving dish; garnish with reserved basil leaves and, if desired, tomato slices. Serve with baguette slices or crackers.

Per serving: 121 cal., 10 g total fat (5 g sat. fat), 21 mg chol., 130 mg sodium, 1 g carbo., 0 g fiber, 5 g pro.

MAKE-AHEAD DIRECTIONS: Prepare as directed in step 1. Cover and chill for up to 5 days. Let stand at room temperature for 30 minutes before serving.

Antipasto means "before the meal" in Italian. A snap to make, this colorful appetizer is a superb party starter.

ANTIPASTO-STYLE RELISH TRAY

START TO FINISH:
30 minutes

MAKES:
12 servings

1   recipe Salami Rolls

1   recipe Italian Cheese Bites

1   7-ounce jar roasted red and/or yellow sweet peppers, drained and cut into strips

2   6-ounce jars marinated artichoke hearts, drained

8   ounces black olives
    (such as gaeta, sicilian, or kalamata)
    or herbed green olives, drained and pitted
    (see note, page 16)

    Capers, drained

    Thinly sliced ciabatta or Italian bread (optional)

1 Arrange Salami Rolls, Italian Cheese Bites, roasted red peppers, artichoke hearts, and olives on serving platter(s). Sprinkle artichokes with capers. If desired, serve with thinly sliced ciabatta or Italian bread.

SALAMI ROLLS: Using ¼ cup purchased black olive paste, spread some of the olive paste on each of 24 thin slices garlic salami (about 4 ounces). Place a strip of purchased roasted red pepper along one edge of each salami slice; roll up. Cut in half crosswise.

ITALIAN CHEESE BITES: Cut 4 ounces thinly sliced prosciutto into narrow strips. Cut 1½ pounds Taleggio, Asiago, and/or aged provolone cheese into bite-size pieces. Wrap a prosciutto strip around each cheese piece, securing with wooden picks if necessary.

Per serving: 426 cal., 37 g total fat (17 g sat. fat), 69 mg chol., 1,406 mg sodium, 6 g carbo., 1 g fiber, 19 g pro.

SOUPS & SALADS

2

Because veal cooks quickly, this meal-in-a-bowl can be on the table faster than most stews.

VEAL STEW WITH POLENTA

START TO FINISH:
40 minutes

MAKES:
4 main-dish servings

1	pound boneless veal round steak or lean boneless pork
2	tablespoons olive oil
1	medium onion, cut into thin wedges
1	medium green or red sweet pepper, seeded and coarsely chopped
2	cloves garlic, minced
1	14½-ounce can diced tomatoes, undrained
¼	cup dry red wine
1	teaspoon instant chicken bouillon granules
1	teaspoon dried Italian seasoning, crushed
½	teaspoon salt
2¾	cups water
¼	teaspoon salt
¾	cup quick-cooking polenta mix
2	cups torn fresh spinach

1 Trim fat from veal or pork. Cut meat into ½-inch pieces. In a large saucepan heat 1 tablespoon of the olive oil over medium heat. Cook meat, half at a time, in hot oil until brown, stirring occasionally. Remove meat and drain; set aside. Add remaining 1 tablespoon olive oil to the same pan. Add onion, sweet pepper, and garlic; cook for 5 to 8 minutes or just until vegetables are tender, stirring occasionally. Add drained meat, undrained tomatoes, wine, bouillon granules, Italian seasoning, and the ½ teaspoon salt. Bring to boiling; reduce heat. Cover and simmer for 10 minutes.

2 Meanwhile, in a 2-quart saucepan heat the water and the ¼ teaspoon salt to boiling. Stir in polenta mix. Cook, stirring frequently, for 5 minutes.

3 Stir spinach into veal mixture. To serve, divide polenta among four shallow soup bowls. Top with veal mixture.

Per serving: 370 cal., 11 g total fat (2 g sat. fat), 91 mg chol., 1,180 mg sodium, 33 g carbo., 4 g fiber, 30 g pro.

Lamb shanks, which are generally tough cuts of meat, are simmered until they transform into fork-tender morsels in this rich, flavorful soup.

LAMB & ORZO SOUP

2½	pounds lamb shanks
4	cups water
4	cups chicken broth or vegetable broth
2	bay leaves
1	tablespoon snipped fresh oregano or 1 teaspoon dried oregano, crushed
1½	teaspoons snipped fresh marjoram or ½ teaspoon dried marjoram, crushed
¼	teaspoon black pepper
2	medium carrots, cut into short thin strips (1 cup)
2	stalks celery, sliced
¾	cup dried orzo pasta
3	cups torn fresh spinach or half of a 10-ounce package frozen chopped spinach, thawed and well drained
	Finely shredded Parmesan cheese (optional)

1 In a large Dutch oven combine lamb shanks, the water, broth, bay leaves, oregano, marjoram, and pepper. Bring to boiling; reduce heat. Cover and simmer for 1¼ to 1½ hours or until meat is tender.

2 Remove lamb shanks from Dutch oven. When cool enough to handle, cut meat off bones; coarsely chop meat. Discard bones. Strain broth through a large sieve or colander lined with two layers of 100%-cotton cheesecloth; discard bay leaves and herbs. Skim off fat; return broth to Dutch oven.

3 Stir chopped meat, carrots, celery, and uncooked pasta into broth in Dutch oven. Return to boiling; reduce heat. Cover and simmer about 15 minutes or until vegetables and pasta are tender. Stir in spinach. Cook for 1 to 2 minutes more or just until fresh spinach wilts or frozen spinach is heated through. If desired, serve with Parmesan cheese.

Per serving: 345 cal., 14 g total fat (5 g sat. fat), 99 mg chol., 769 mg sodium, 20 g carbo., 2 g fiber, 33 g pro.

PREP:
25 minutes

COOK:
1¼ hours + 15 minutes

MAKES:
6 main-dish servings

Keep the ingredients for this recipe on hand and you can whip up a hearty Italian soup for your family in no time.

MEATBALL SOUP WITH TINY PASTA

PREP:
10 minutes

COOK:
10 minutes

MAKES:
4 main-dish servings

1	14½-ounce can diced tomatoes with onion and garlic, undrained
1	14-ounce can beef broth
1½	cups water
½	teaspoon dried Italian seasoning, crushed
½	of a 16-ounce package frozen cooked Italian-style meatballs
1	cup loose-pack frozen Italian-blend vegetables (zucchini, carrots, cauliflower, lima beans, and Italian beans) or desired frozen mixed vegetables
½	cup small dried pasta (such as tripolini, farfallini, ditalini, stellini, or orzo)
2	tablespoons finely shredded or grated Parmesan cheese

1 In a large saucepan stir together undrained tomatoes, beef broth, the water, and Italian seasoning; bring to boiling.

2 Add meatballs, frozen vegetables, and uncooked pasta. Return to boiling; reduce heat. Cover and simmer about 10 minutes or until pasta and vegetables are tender. Sprinkle individual servings with Parmesan cheese.

Per serving: 280 cal., 14 g total fat (6 g sat. fat), 38 mg chol., 1,335 mg sodium, 23 g carbo., 4 g fiber, 15 g pro.

This soup is packed with zesty Italian flavors. To add some spiciness, use hot Italian sausage.

SAUSAGE SOUP

PREP:
30 minutes

COOK:
1 hour + 30 minutes

MAKES:
8 main-dish servings

1   pound bulk Italian sausage

1   large onion, chopped

1   medium carrot, chopped

1   stalk celery, chopped

8   cups chicken broth

1   14½-ounce can diced tomatoes, undrained

1   8-ounce can tomato sauce

1   clove garlic, minced

1   teaspoon dried oregano, crushed

½   teaspoon dried rosemary, crushed

½   teaspoon dried basil, crushed

¼   teaspoon dried thyme, crushed

¼   teaspoon fennel seeds, crushed

1   bay leaf

½   cup dried orzo pasta or finely broken capellini pasta

Finely shredded Parmesan cheese (optional)

1 In a 4-quart Dutch oven cook sausage, onion, carrot, and celery over medium heat until sausage is brown. Drain well.

2 Add chicken broth, undrained diced tomatoes, tomato sauce, garlic, oregano, rosemary, basil, thyme, fennel seeds, and bay leaf to mixture in Dutch oven. Bring to boiling; reduce heat. Cover and simmer for 1 hour. Add uncooked pasta. Return to boiling; reduce heat. Cook, uncovered, for 30 minutes more. Discard bay leaf. If desired, serve with shredded Parmesan cheese.

Per serving: 285 cal., 18 g total fat (6 g sat. fat), 46 mg chol., 1,600 mg sodium, 17 g carbo., 1 g fiber, 11 g pro.

Kale adds a hint of cabbage flavor to this soup. For an alternative to kale, use fresh spinach.

WHITE BEAN SOUP WITH SAUSAGE & KALE

START TO FINISH:
30 minutes

MAKES:
5 main-dish servings

12 ounces uncooked mild Italian sausage links, cut into ½-inch-thick slices

¼ cup water

1 tablespoon cooking oil

1 medium onion, chopped

2 cloves garlic, minced

2 15-ounce cans cannellini beans (white kidney beans), rinsed and drained

2 14-ounce cans chicken broth

1 14½-ounce can diced tomatoes with basil, oregano, and garlic, undrained

4 cups coarsely chopped kale or fresh spinach

Black pepper

1 In a large skillet combine sliced sausage and the water. Bring to boiling; reduce heat. Cover and simmer about 10 minutes or until sausage is no longer pink. Uncover and cook about 5 minutes more or until sausage is browned, stirring frequently. Remove sausage with a slotted spoon; set aside.

2 Meanwhile, in a large saucepan heat oil over medium heat. Add onion and garlic; cook about 5 minutes or until onion is tender. Stir in beans, chicken broth, and undrained tomatoes. Bring to boiling; reduce heat. Cover and simmer for 5 minutes.

3 Stir in cooked sausage and kale or spinach. Simmer, uncovered, about 3 minutes more or until kale or spinach is tender. Season to taste with pepper.

Per serving: 394 cal., 19 g total fat (7 g sat. fat), 48 mg chol., 1,720 mg sodium, 38 g carbo., 9 g fiber, 23 g pro.

A mellow combination of cabbage, onion, and navy beans is pepped up with Italian sausage and tomatoes.

SAUSAGE~NAVY BEAN STEW

2⅓	cups dry navy beans
6	cups water
1	pound uncooked Italian sausage links, cut into ½-inch-thick slices
1	large onion, chopped
1	clove garlic, minced
3½	cups beef broth
¾	cup water
1	teaspoon dried oregano, crushed
2	bay leaves
3	cups chopped cabbage
1	14½-ounce can diced tomatoes, undrained
	Salt
	Black pepper

PREP:
30 minutes

STAND:
1 hour

COOK:
1 hour + 15 minutes

MAKES:
8 main-dish servings

1 Rinse beans. In a 4-quart Dutch oven combine beans and the 6 cups water. Bring to boiling; reduce heat. Simmer for 2 minutes. Remove from heat. Cover and let stand for 1 hour. (Or in Dutch oven combine beans and the 6 cups water. Cover and let soak in a cool place for 6 to 8 hours or overnight.) Drain and rinse beans; set aside.

2 In the same Dutch oven cook sausage, onion, and garlic over medium-high heat until meat is brown and onion is tender. Drain off fat. Stir in beans, beef broth, the ¾ cup water, the oregano, and bay leaves. Bring to boiling; reduce heat. Cover and simmer for 1 to 1½ hours or until beans are tender, stirring occasionally.

3 Stir in cabbage and undrained tomatoes. Return to boiling; reduce heat. Cover and simmer about 15 minutes more or until cabbage is tender. Discard bay leaves. Skim off fat. Season to taste with salt and pepper.

Per serving: 391 cal., 14 g total fat (6 g sat. fat), 38 mg chol., 840 mg sodium, 41 g carbo., 15 g fiber, 22 g pro.

Broccoli rabe, a leafy green with stalks and broccolilike buds that is popular in Italy, has a pungent, somewhat bitter flavor. If it is not available, substitute Swiss chard.

TUSCAN RAVIOLI STEW

START TO FINISH:
35 minutes

MAKES:
4 main-dish servings

1	tablespoon olive oil
1	large leek, thinly sliced (about ½ cup)
3	cloves garlic, minced
1	14½-ounce can stewed tomatoes, undrained
1	14-ounce can beef broth
¾	cup water
¼	teaspoon crushed red pepper (optional)
5	cups coarsely chopped broccoli rabe or Swiss chard (about 6 ounces)
1	9-ounce package refrigerated chicken-filled or cheese-filled ravioli
1	tablespoon snipped fresh rosemary or 1 teaspoon dried rosemary, crushed
	Fresh rosemary sprigs (optional)
¼	cup finely shredded Asiago cheese (1 ounce)

1 In a large saucepan heat olive oil over medium heat. Add leek and garlic; cook about 3 minutes or until tender, stirring occasionally. Stir in undrained tomatoes, beef broth, the water, and, if desired, crushed red pepper; bring to boiling.

2 Stir in broccoli rabe, ravioli, and rosemary. Return to boiling; reduce heat. Cover and simmer for 7 to 8 minutes or until broccoli rabe and ravioli are tender. Ladle into shallow bowls. If desired, garnish with rosemary sprigs. Top individual servings with Asiago cheese.

Per serving: 332 cal., 15 g total fat (4 g sat. fat), 68 mg chol., 890 mg sodium, 36 g carbo., 2 g fiber, 14 g pro.

A delicious slice of Parmesan-and-pesto toast tops each bowl of this easy-to-make chicken soup.

PARMESAN-PESTO CHICKEN SOUP

2   14-ounce cans chicken broth

1   teaspoon dried Italian seasoning, crushed

2   cloves garlic, minced

12 ounces skinless, boneless chicken breast halves, cut into bite-size pieces

¾   cup small shell macaroni

2   ½-inch-thick slices Italian bread, halved crosswise

2   tablespoons purchased basil pesto

¼   cup finely shredded Parmesan cheese (1 ounce)

¾   cup loose-pack frozen peas

¼   cup thinly sliced green onions

START TO FINISH:
35 minutes

MAKES:
4 main-dish servings

1 In a medium saucepan combine chicken broth, Italian seasoning, and garlic; bring to boiling.

2 Add chicken and uncooked macaroni to broth. Return mixture to boiling; reduce heat. Simmer, uncovered, for 8 to 9 minutes or until pasta is tender and chicken is no longer pink, stirring occasionally.

3 Meanwhile, preheat broiler. Spread one side of each halved bread slice with pesto. Sprinkle with Parmesan cheese. Place bread on broiler rack. Broil 3 to 4 inches from heat about 2 minutes or just until cheese begins to melt.

4 Add peas and green onions to broth mixture; cook for 2 minutes more. Top individual servings with the cheesy toasted bread.

Per serving: 330 cal., 9 g total fat (1 g sat. fat), 56 mg chol., 1,103 mg sodium, 31 g carbo., 2 g fiber, 29 g pro.

Cioppino, a delightful fish and tomato stew, is credited to San Francisco's Italian immigrants. For added interest, use two different kinds of fish for the recipe.

SHORTCUT CIOPPINO

START TO FINISH:
35 minutes

MAKES:
8 main-dish servings

2 pounds fresh or frozen skinless cod, salmon, and/or sea scallops

2 medium fennel bulbs (about 2 pounds)

3 tablespoons olive oil

4 cloves garlic, minced

3 large tomatoes, coarsely chopped

1 14-ounce can chicken broth

1 teaspoon dried oregano, crushed

½ teaspoon anise seeds, crushed (optional)

Salt

Freshly ground black pepper

⅓ cup shredded fresh basil leaves (optional)

1 Thaw fish and/or scallops, if frozen. Rinse fish and/or scallops; pat dry with paper towels. If using fish, cut into 2-inch pieces. Set fish and/or scallops aside.

2 Remove green leafy tops from fennel; snip enough of the tops to make 2 tablespoons. Set aside. Cut off and discard upper stalks of fennel. Remove wilted outer layers and cut off a thin slice from the fennel bases. Thinly slice fennel bulbs, removing cores (if desired).

3 In a 4- to 6-quart Dutch oven heat olive oil over medium heat. Add fennel slices; cook about 10 minutes or until fennel is tender, stirring occasionally. Add garlic; cook and stir for 1 minute. Add tomatoes, chicken broth, oregano, and, if desired, anise seeds. Bring to boiling.

4 Add fish and/or scallops to fennel mixture. Return to boiling; reduce heat. Simmer, uncovered, for 6 to 8 minutes or until fish flakes easily when tested with a fork or scallops are opaque. Season to taste with salt and pepper. Stir in the reserved fennel tops. If desired, stir in the fresh basil. Serve immediately.

Per serving: 163 cal., 6 g total fat (1 g sat. fat), 49 mg chol., 335 mg sodium, 5 g carbo., 2 g fiber, 21 g pro.

Because much of Italy is surrounded by sea, it's easy to understand why fish is popular in Italian soups. If your family loves seafood, this rosemary-flavored soup is sure to be a winner.

ITALIAN FISH & VEGETABLE SOUP

12	ounces fresh or frozen sea bass, haddock, or cod fillets
2	14-ounce cans chicken broth
1	14½-ounce can diced tomatoes, undrained
1½	cups packaged shredded cabbage with carrot (coleslaw mix)
1	small zucchini, chopped (about 1 cup)
1	stalk celery, chopped
1	small onion, chopped
¼	cup dry white wine or water
2	teaspoons snipped fresh rosemary
2	bay leaves
2	cloves garlic, minced

1 Thaw fish, if frozen. Rinse fish; pat dry with paper towels. Cut into 1-inch pieces; set aside.

2 In a large saucepan combine chicken broth, undrained tomatoes, coleslaw mix, zucchini, celery, onion, wine, rosemary, bay leaves, and garlic. Bring to boiling; reduce heat. Cover and simmer about 10 minutes or until vegetables are crisp-tender.

3 Add fish. Return to boiling; reduce heat. Simmer, uncovered, about 5 minutes more or just until fish flakes easily when tested with a fork. Discard bay leaves.

Per serving: 100 cal., 1 g total fat (0 g sat. fat), 25 mg chol., 692 mg sodium, 7 g carbo., 1 g fiber, 12 g pro.

START TO FINISH:
35 minutes

MAKES:
6 main-dish servings

A mixture of mild, white fish fillets and succulent shrimp serves as the seafood in this fish soup. Use white wine instead of chicken broth for a more robust flavor.

FISH SOUP

START TO FINISH:
30 minutes

MAKES:
4 main-dish servings

8 ounces fresh or frozen skinless cod or sea bass fillets

6 ounces fresh or frozen peeled and deveined shrimp

⅓ cup chopped onion

2 stalks celery, sliced

1 clove garlic, minced

2 teaspoons olive oil

1 cup chicken broth

¼ cup dry white wine or chicken broth

1 14½-ounce can diced tomatoes, undrained

1 8-ounce can tomato sauce

1 teaspoon dried oregano, crushed

¼ teaspoon salt

⅛ teaspoon black pepper

1 tablespoon snipped fresh parsley

1 recipe Crostini

1 Thaw fish and shrimp, if frozen. Rinse fish and shrimp; pat dry with paper towels. Cut fish into 1½-inch pieces. Cut shrimp in half lengthwise. Cover and chill fish and shrimp until needed.

2 In large saucepan cook onion, celery, and garlic in hot olive oil until tender. Carefully stir in chicken broth and wine. Bring to boiling; reduce heat. Simmer, uncovered, for 5 minutes. Stir in undrained tomatoes, tomato sauce, oregano, salt, and pepper. Return to boiling; reduce heat. Cover and simmer for 5 minutes.

3 Gently stir in fish and shrimp. Return just to boiling; reduce heat to low. Cover and simmer for 3 to 5 minutes or until fish flakes easily when tested with a fork and shrimp are opaque. Stir in parsley.

4 To serve, ladle into soup bowls and top with Crostini.

CROSTINI: Preheat oven to 425°F. Lightly brush both sides of four ½-inch-thick slices of baguette-style French bread with 1 tablespoon olive oil. Place slices on an ungreased baking sheet. Bake for 5 to 7 minutes or until crisp and lightly browned, turning once.

Per serving: 274 cal., 8 g total fat (1 g sat. fat), 90 mg chol., 1,072 mg sodium, 24 g carbo., 2 g fiber, 22 g pro.

Thanks to refrigerated tortellini and seasoned tomatoes, this recipe can be made in just 20 minutes.

TORTELLINI & TOMATO SOUP

1   9-ounce package refrigerated cheese tortellini

1   14-ounce can chicken broth

1   14½-ounce can diced tomatoes with basil, garlic, and oregano, undrained

1   cup water

2   tablespoons tomato paste

1   small zucchini, finely chopped (1 cup)

1   tablespoon snipped fresh sage or 1 teaspoon dried sage, crushed

¼   cup shredded Asiago or Parmesan cheese (1 ounce)

1 Cook tortellini according to package directions; drain.

2 Meanwhile, in a large saucepan combine chicken broth, undrained diced tomatoes, the water, and tomato paste. Bring to boiling. Stir in zucchini, sage, and drained tortellini; heat through. Top individual servings with Asiago cheese.

Per serving: 287 cal., 8 g total fat (3 g sat. fat), 39 mg chol., 1,246 mg sodium, 41 g carbo., 1 g fiber, 14 g pro.

START TO FINISH:
20 minutes

MAKES:
4 main-dish servings

This recipe calls for green soybeans, which are picked when they're fully grown but not fully mature. They are often referred to by their Japanese name, edamame.

THREE-BEAN ITALIAN-STYLE CHILI

PREP:
25 minutes

COOK:
20 minutes + 5 minutes

MAKES:
6 main-dish servings

2	tablespoons olive oil
1	medium red onion, chopped
1	clove garlic, minced
1	15-ounce can tomato sauce
1	15-ounce can black beans, rinsed and drained
1	15-ounce can Great Northern beans, rinsed and drained
1	14½-ounce can diced tomatoes, undrained
1	cup loose-pack frozen green soybeans (edamame)
1	4-ounce can diced green chile peppers
½	cup water
1	tablespoon balsamic vinegar
⅓	cup sliced pitted ripe olives
2	tablespoons snipped fresh cilantro
	Hot cooked rice, pasta, or couscous
	Shredded mozzarella cheese (optional)

1 In a large saucepan heat olive oil over medium heat. Add red onion and garlic; cook about 5 minutes or until tender. Add tomato sauce, black beans, Great Northern beans, undrained diced tomatoes, soybeans, chile peppers, the water, and balsamic vinegar. Bring to boiling; reduce heat. Cover and simmer for 20 minutes, stirring occasionally.

2 Stir in olives and cilantro. Simmer, covered, for 5 minutes more. Ladle into soup bowls over rice, pasta, or couscous. If desired, top with mozzarella cheese.

Per serving: 436 cal., 12 g total fat (3 g sat. fat), 11 mg chol., 828 mg sodium, 62 g carbo., 10 g fiber, 23 g pro.

Lentils are a good source of protein and several vitamins and minerals. Combine them with a medley of vegetables and you have a healthful and satisfying meal.

LENTIL-CABBAGE SOUP

3	medium carrots, sliced
2	stalks celery, sliced
1	medium onion, chopped
1	tablespoon olive oil
5¾	cups water
1	14-ounce can vegetable broth
½	of a medium head cabbage, cored and cut into 1-inch pieces (about 5 cups)
1½	cups dry brown or yellow lentils, rinsed and drained
1	15-ounce can tomato puree
2	teaspoons sugar
1	teaspoon salt
1	teaspoon dried oregano, crushed
¼	teaspoon black pepper

1 In a 4-quart Dutch oven cook carrots, celery, and onion in hot olive oil about 5 minutes or until crisp-tender. Stir in the water, vegetable broth, cabbage, lentils, tomato puree, sugar, salt, oregano, and pepper. Bring to boiling; reduce heat. Cover and simmer about 45 minutes or until lentils are very soft.

Per serving: 193 cal., 3 g total fat (0 g sat. fat), 0 mg chol., 631 mg sodium, 33 g carbo., 15 g fiber, 13 g pro.

PREP:
20 minutes

COOK:
45 minutes

MAKES:
8 main-dish servings

For a special presentation, serve this flavorful stew in eggplant bowls. Simply halve two medium eggplants lengthwise. Carefully hollow out the eggplants, leaving 1/4- to 1/2-inch-thick shells. Use some of the pulp in the soup.

CHUNKY RATATOUILLE STEW

START TO FINISH:
35 minutes

MAKES:
4 side-dish servings

1	large onion, chopped
1/2	cup chopped green sweet pepper
1	tablespoon olive oil
2	cups peeled and chopped eggplant (1/2 of a small eggplant)
1	14-ounce can beef broth
1	cup frozen cut green beans
1/2	cup water
2	tablespoons dry red wine
1	14 1/2-ounce can diced tomatoes with roasted garlic, undrained
1	4 1/2-ounce jar (drained weight) whole mushrooms, drained
1	tablespoon snipped fresh basil or 1/2 teaspoon dried basil, crushed
1/2	cup shredded provolone cheese (2 ounces)

1 In a Dutch oven cook onion and sweet pepper in hot olive oil until tender. Stir in eggplant, beef broth, green beans, the water, and wine. Bring to boiling; reduce heat. Cover and simmer for 8 to 10 minutes or until vegetables are tender.

2 Stir in undrained diced tomatoes, drained mushrooms, and basil; heat through. Sprinkle individual servings with provolone cheese.

Per serving: 179 cal., 8 g total fat (3 g sat. fat), 10 mg chol., 1,045 mg sodium, 20 g carbo., 4 g fiber, 7 g pro.

Quick-cooking sugar snap peas, spinach, and refrigerated tortellini make this recipe a snap to prepare.

SPINACH & TORTELLINI SOUP

3 medium onions, finely chopped

5 cloves garlic, minced

1 teaspoon dried Italian seasoning, crushed

1 tablespoon olive oil

2 14-ounce cans chicken broth

2 cups water

1 9-ounce package refrigerated cheese-filled tortellini

2 cups fresh sugar snap peas, trimmed and halved crosswise

2 cups shredded fresh spinach

2 teaspoons lemon juice

2 tablespoons finely shredded Parmesan cheese

1 In a 4-quart Dutch oven cook onions, garlic, and Italian seasoning in hot olive oil about 5 minutes or until onion is tender. Add chicken broth and the water. Bring to boiling. Add tortellini. Return to boiling; reduce heat. Simmer, uncovered, for 4 minutes.

2 Stir sugar snap peas, spinach, and lemon juice into mixture in Dutch oven. Return to boiling; reduce heat. Simmer, uncovered, for 2 minutes more. Sprinkle individual servings with Parmesan cheese.

Per serving: 333 cal., 9 g total fat (2 g sat. fat), 34 mg chol., 1,098 mg sodium, 47 g carbo., 4 g fiber, 15 g pro.

START TO FINISH:
35 minutes

MAKES:
4 main-dish servings

To clean leeks, slice them, then soak them in a large bowl of cold water. Any sand and dirt trapped in the layers will fall to the bottom of the bowl. Use a slotted spoon to lift the leeks out of the water.

BREAD SOUP WITH LEEKS

START TO FINISH:
35 minutes

MAKES:
8 to 12 side-dish servings

1	tablespoon olive oil
4	leeks, halved lengthwise and cut into ¼-inch-thick slices (1⅓ cups)
8	ounces crusty country bread, cut into bite-size pieces (6 cups)
4	cups chopped tomatoes
½	to 1 teaspoon crushed red pepper
3	14-ounce cans beef broth
2	tablespoons snipped fresh basil
⅓	cup shredded Parmesan cheese
	Small fresh basil leaves (optional)

1 In a 5- to 6-quart Dutch oven heat olive oil over medium heat. Add leeks; cook about 5 minutes or until tender. Turn heat to medium-low. Add bread, tomatoes, and crushed red pepper. Cook for 5 minutes, stirring frequently.

2 Add beef broth. Cook over medium heat until heated through. Stir in snipped basil just before serving. Top individual servings with Parmesan cheese and, if desired, basil leaves.

Per serving: 147 cal., 7 g total fat (3 g sat. fat), 11 mg chol., 724 mg sodium, 14 g carbo., 1 g fiber, 9 g pro.

This quick recipe calls for flank steak or beef top round steak. If you use flank steak, be sure to slice it across the grain of the fibers to ensure the meat is as tender as possible.

HOT ITALIAN BEEF SALAD

12	ounces beef flank steak or beef top round steak, cut 1 inch thick
2	teaspoons olive oil or cooking oil
1	medium red or green sweet pepper, seeded and cut into bite-size strips
½	cup bottled clear Italian salad dressing
6	cups torn mixed salad greens
¼	cup finely shredded Parmesan cheese (1 ounce)
	Coarsely ground black pepper

START TO FINISH:
20 minutes

MAKES:
4 main-dish servings

1 Trim fat from steak. Thinly slice steak across the grain into bite-size strips.*

2 In a large nonstick skillet heat oil over medium-high heat. Add steak and sweet pepper strips. Cook and stir for 3 to 5 minutes or until steak is desired doneness and sweet pepper is crisp-tender; drain. Add salad dressing to skillet. Cook and stir until heated through.

3 Divide salad greens among four dinner plates. Top with the beef mixture. Sprinkle with Parmesan and black pepper. Serve immediately.

Per serving: 279 cal., 18 g total fat (5 g sat. fat), 38 mg chol., 625 mg sodium, 8 g carbo., 2 g fiber, 22 g pro.

*NOTE: Partially freeze the beef for easier slicing.

Slices of juicy Italian-flavored pork crown a mixture of fennel, sweet pepper, romaine, and radicchio. The hot pork causes the greens to wilt slightly, creating a pleasing texture variation.

FENNEL-PORK SALAD

PREP:
20 minutes

ROAST:
25 minutes

STAND:
15 minutes

OVEN:
425°F

MAKES:
4 main-dish servings

1 ¾- to 1-pound pork tenderloin

Salt

Black pepper

⅔ cup bottled clear Italian salad dressing

8 cups mixed Italian salad greens
(romaine and radicchio)

½ cup very thinly sliced fennel bulb

½ cup thinly sliced yellow sweet pepper

1 ounce Parmesan cheese

❶ Preheat oven to 425°F. Place meat on a rack in a shallow roasting pan. Sprinkle with salt and pepper. Insert an oven-going meat thermometer into thickest portion of tenderloin. Brush meat with 2 tablespoons of the salad dressing. Roast for 25 to 35 minutes or until thermometer registers 155°F. Cover with foil; let stand for 15 minutes before slicing. Temperature of the meat after standing should be 160°F.

❷ Meanwhile, arrange salad greens on four dinner plates. Top with fennel and sweet pepper. Use a vegetable peeler to shave thin pieces of Parmesan cheese on top of salads. Thinly slice meat; arrange slices on salads. Serve with remaining salad dressing.

Per serving: 266 cal., 16 g total fat (4 g sat. fat), 60 mg chol., 968 mg sodium, 9 g carbo., 2 g fiber, 22 g pro.

Reminiscent of the famous Italian wedding soup, this warm pasta salad combines hearty meatballs, spinach, and orzo pasta.

ITALIAN WEDDING SALAD

6 ounces dried orzo pasta

1 16-ounce package frozen cooked meatballs (32), thawed

½ cup bottled clear Italian salad dressing

1 6-ounce jar marinated artichoke hearts, drained and chopped

1 6-ounce package purchased baby spinach

¼ cup chopped walnuts, toasted

Salt

Black pepper

Finely shredded Parmesan or Romano cheese (optional)

1 Cook pasta according to package directions. Drain well.

2 Meanwhile, in a 4-quart Dutch oven combine meatballs and salad dressing; cook over medium heat until meatballs are heated through, stirring occasionally. Stir in drained pasta, artichoke hearts, spinach, and walnuts. Heat and stir just until spinach is wilted. Season to taste with salt and pepper. If desired, sprinkle with Parmesan cheese.

Per serving: 730 cal., 52 g total fat (15 g sat. fat), 40 mg chol., 1,383 mg sodium, 48 g carbo., 8 g fiber, 23 g pro.

START TO FINISH:
25 minutes

MAKES:
4 main-dish servings

Sometimes called Italian cress, arugula has a slightly bitter and peppery flavor. It's very perishable, so use it within two days of purchasing.

SAUSAGE & ARUGULA SALAD

PREP:
15 minutes

GRILL:
20 minutes

MAKES:
4 main-dish servings

1 pound uncooked Italian sausage links

6 cups arugula

1 15½-ounce can cannellini beans (white kidney beans), rinsed and drained

1 cup bottled roasted red sweet peppers, drained and coarsely chopped

1 tablespoon drained capers

¼ cup bottled balsamic vinaigrette

⅓ cup finely shredded Parmesan cheese

1 Using a fork, prick each sausage link several times. Test for medium heat above drip pan. Place sausage on grill rack over drip pan. Cover and grill about 20 minutes or until juices run clear (170°F).

2 Divide arugula among four dinner plates. Cut sausage links into ½-inch-thick slices; arrange sausage over arugula. Top with beans, sweet peppers, and capers. Drizzle with vinaigrette. Sprinkle with Parmesan cheese.

Per serving: 477 cal., 32 g total fat (12 g sat. fat), 81 mg chol., 1,146 mg sodium, 20 g carbo., 6 g fiber, 26 g pro.

Bulgur consists of wheat kernels that have been steamed, dried, and crushed. When cooked, it has a pleasantly tender and chewy texture.

BEANS WITH PESTO

1	14-ounce can chicken broth or vegetable broth
¾	cup bulgur
1	medium red sweet pepper, chopped
⅓	cup purchased basil pesto
¼	cup thinly sliced green onions
2	tablespoons balsamic vinegar
2	cups cooked or canned red kidney beans, pinto beans, Christmas lima beans, and/or other white beans*
	Black pepper
8	cups torn mixed salad greens

PREP:
15 minutes

COOK:
15 minutes

CHILL:
4 hours to 3 days

MAKES:
4 main-dish servings

1 In a large saucepan combine broth and bulgur. Bring to boiling; reduce heat. Cover and simmer about 15 minutes or until bulgur is tender. Remove from heat. Stir in sweet pepper, pesto, green onions, and balsamic vinegar. Stir in beans. Season with black pepper. Transfer to an airtight storage container. Cover and chill for 4 hours to 3 days.

2 Divide salad greens among four dinner plates. Spoon bean mixture over salad greens.

Per serving: 389 cal., 15 g total fat (0 g sat. fat), 4 mg chol., 570 mg sodium, 52 g carbo., 13 g fiber, 15 g pro.

*NOTE: To cook dry beans, rinse ¾ cup dry beans. In a large saucepan combine rinsed beans and 5 cups water. Bring to boiling; reduce heat. Simmer, uncovered, for 2 minutes. Remove from heat. Cover and let stand for 1 hour. Drain; rinse beans and return to saucepan. Add 5 cups fresh water. Bring to boiling; reduce heat. Cover and simmer for 1¼ to 1½ hours or until beans are tender; drain.

Prosciutto gives this pasta salad an authentic Italian flair. Also referred to as Parma ham, look for it at Italian specialty food stores.

PROSCIUTTO & RADIATORE SALAD

START TO FINISH:
25 minutes

MAKES:
6 side-dish servings

2   cups dried radiatore pasta

1   small yellow summer squash or zucchini, quartered lengthwise and sliced

½   cup loose-pack frozen peas

2   medium tomatoes, coarsely chopped

2   ounces prosciutto or cooked ham, chopped (about ⅓ cup)

¼   cup snipped fresh basil

⅓   cup bottled balsamic vinaigrette

1 Cook pasta according to package directions; add yellow summer squash and peas to pasta for the last minute of cooking. Drain. Rinse with cold water; drain again.

2 In a large bowl combine pasta-vegetable mixture, tomatoes, prosciutto, and basil. Pour vinaigrette over pasta mixture; toss lightly to coat.

Per serving: 183 cal., 5 g total fat (1 g sat. fat), 7 mg chol., 426 mg sodium, 26 g carbo., 2 g fiber, 7 g pro.

Take this out-of-the-ordinary pasta salad to your next potluck or picnic. Packed full of vibrant Italian flavors, including marinated artichoke hearts and white wine vinegar, it's sure to have everyone coming back for seconds.

SALAMI-PASTA SALAD

4	ounces dried spaghetti or vermicelli
1	6-ounce jar marinated artichoke hearts
1	small zucchini, halved lengthwise and sliced
1	carrot, sliced
1	cup shredded mozzarella cheese (4 ounces)
2	ounces sliced salami, cut into strips
2	tablespoons grated Parmesan cheese
2	tablespoons white wine vinegar
1½	teaspoons snipped fresh basil or ½ teaspoon dried basil, crushed
1	teaspoon snipped fresh oregano or ¼ teaspoon dried oregano, crushed
¾	teaspoon dry mustard
1	clove garlic, minced

1 Break pasta strands in half. Cook pasta according to package directions; drain. Rinse with cold water; drain again. Set aside.

2 Drain artichoke hearts, reserving marinade; coarsely chop artichoke hearts. In a large bowl combine cooked pasta, the artichokes, zucchini, carrot, mozzarella cheese, salami, and Parmesan cheese.

3 In a screw-top jar combine reserved artichoke marinade, the vinegar, basil, oregano, mustard, and garlic. Cover and shake well. Pour dressing over pasta mixture; toss to coat evenly.

4 Cover and chill for 4 to 24 hours.

Per serving: 148 cal., 7 g total fat (3 g sat. fat), 15 mg chol., 318 mg sodium, 15 g carbo., 1 g fiber, 8 g pro.

PREP:
25 minutes

CHILL:
4 to 24 hours

MAKES:
8 to 10 side-dish servings

Anchovy dressing gives the salad a robust, salty flavor. If you're not crazy about the intense flavor, soak the anchovies in water for 30 minutes, then pat them dry. This will decrease the saltiness significantly.

SICILIAN ESCAROLE SALAD

START TO FINISH:
25 minutes

MAKES:
12 to 16 side-dish servings

6   cups torn escarole

6   cups torn leaf lettuce

1   English cucumber or cucumber, quartered lengthwise and cut into ½-inch pieces

1   cup pitted ripe olives or oil-cured black olives, chopped

1   cup thinly sliced red onion or Vidalia onion

3   cups desired Salad Stir-Ins

1   recipe Anchovy Dressing

1 In a very large salad bowl combine escarole, lettuce, cucumber, olives, and onion. Add desired Salad Stir-Ins. Pour Anchovy Dressing over salad; toss to coat well.

SALAD STIR·INS: Take your choice of chopped bottled roasted red sweet peppers, drained and rinsed canned cannellini beans (white kidney beans), drained and flaked canned Italian tuna (packed in olive oil), Parmesan croutons, tomato slices, snipped fresh basil, snipped fresh oregano, chopped salami, chopped mortadella, cubed Asiago cheese, and/or shredded provolone cheese.

ANCHOVY DRESSING: In a screw-top jar combine ⅓ cup olive oil; 2 tablespoons white wine vinegar; one 2-ounce can anchovy fillets, drained and chopped; 3 cloves garlic, minced; ½ teaspoon dried basil, crushed; ½ teaspoon dried oregano, crushed; ¼ teaspoon salt; ¼ teaspoon crushed red pepper; and ⅛ teaspoon black pepper. Cover and shake well.

Per serving: 178 cal., 14 g total fat (4 g sat. fat), 20 mg chol., 608 mg sodium, 6 g carbo., 2 g fiber, 8 g pro.

This is a perfect recipe to try when summer's bounty of fresh tomatoes arrives. An intensely flavored balsamic reduction provides just the right complement to sweet, juicy tomatoes.

TOMATO SALAD WITH PICKLED RED ONIONS

1   cup balsamic vinegar

4   to 6 assorted heirloom tomatoes or other tomatoes, sliced

Salt

Black pepper

½   cup olive oil

1   recipe Pickled Red Onions

1   cup shredded ricotta salata cheese or mozzarella cheese (4 ounces)

1   cup loosely packed small basil leaves

1 In a small saucepan bring balsamic vinegar to boiling. Reduce heat to medium. Simmer, uncovered, about 20 minutes or until reduced to ⅓ cup. Let cool.

2 Arrange tomato slices on four salad plates. Sprinkle with salt and pepper. Drizzle with olive oil. Drizzle the reduced balsamic vinegar over tomatoes. Sprinkle tomatoes with Pickled Red Onions and shredded ricotta salata cheese. Top with basil leaves. Serve immediately.

PICKLED RED ONIONS: In a medium saucepan cook 1 cup thin wedges red onion in lightly salted boiling water for 45 seconds; drain. In a medium bowl combine the red onion; 1 cup cold water; 1 cup rice vinegar; 2 cloves garlic, halved; and 2 teaspoons cumin seeds. Cover and chill for 3 to 24 hours. Drain before using.

Per serving: 487 cal., 34 g total fat (4 g sat. fat), 25 mg chol., 656 mg sodium, 31 g carbo., 4 g fiber, 8 g pro.

PREP:
20 minutes

COOK:
20 minutes

CHILL:
3 to 24 hours (onions)

MAKES:
4 side-dish servings

The lively flavors of garden fresh vegetables are accentuated by a tangy lemon dressing. For optimum flavor and color, cook the delicate baby vegetables only until crisp-tender.

LEMON-MARINATED BABY VEGETABLES

PREP:
20 minutes

CHILL:
2 to 24 hours

MAKES:
8 side-dish servings

2	pounds tiny whole fresh vegetables (such as carrots, zucchini, and/or yellow summer squash)*
8	ounces fresh sugar snap peas
12	cherry tomatoes
½	teaspoon finely shredded lemon peel
2	tablespoons lemon juice
2	tablespoons water
1	tablespoon olive oil
1	tablespoon snipped fresh basil or oregano
1	teaspoon Dijon-style mustard
1	clove garlic, minced
½	teaspoon salt

1 In a covered large saucepan cook the 2 pounds tiny vegetables in a small amount of lightly salted boiling water for 3 minutes. Add sugar snap peas. Cook, covered, about 2 minutes more or until vegetables are crisp-tender; drain. Rinse with cold water; drain again. Transfer to a large bowl. Add cherry tomatoes.

2 Meanwhile, for dressing, in a screw-top jar combine lemon peel, lemon juice, the water, olive oil, basil or oregano, mustard, garlic, and salt. Cover and shake well to combine.

3 Pour dressing over vegetables; toss gently to coat. Cover and chill for 2 to 24 hours.

Per serving: 65 cal., 2 g total fat (0 g sat. fat), 0 mg chol., 193 mg sodium, 10 g carbo., 3 g fiber, 2 g pro.

*NOTE: If baby vegetables are not available, use packaged peeled baby carrots, and cut zucchini and/or yellow summer squash into thin bite-size strips.

Baked polenta croutons give this salad a delightful variation of texture. Bottled roasted red peppers and pitted olives are quick add-ins that make it memorable.

TOSSED SALAD WITH GARLIC-POLENTA CROUTONS

½	of a 16-ounce tube refrigerated cooked polenta or 8 ounces leftover polenta
1	tablespoon olive oil
½	teaspoon garlic-pepper seasoning
6	cups torn romaine or mixed salad greens
½	cup bottled roasted red sweet peppers, drained and cut up
½	cup chopped tomato
⅓	cup sliced pitted ripe olives or pitted kalamata olives, halved
2	tablespoons grated Parmesan cheese
¼	cup bottled Italian salad dressing

PREP:
15 minutes

BAKE:
15 minutes

OVEN:
425°F

MAKES:
6 side-dish servings

1 Preheat oven to 425°F. Grease a 15×10×1-inch baking pan; set aside. For croutons, cut polenta into ¾-inch cubes. In a small bowl combine cubed polenta, olive oil, and garlic-pepper seasoning; toss to coat. Spread polenta cubes in prepared baking pan. Bake for 15 to 20 minutes or until golden brown, turning once halfway through baking.

2 Meanwhile, in a large bowl toss together romaine, roasted sweet peppers, tomato, and olives. Divide salad mixture among six salad plates. Top individual salads with warm polenta croutons and sprinkle with Parmesan cheese. Serve with Italian salad dressing.

Per serving: 113 cal., 7 g total fat (1 g sat. fat), 1 mg chol., 404 mg sodium, 12 g carbo., 3 g fiber, 3 g pro.

Bread salad—called panzanella in Italy—provides a great use for day-old bread.

BREAD SALAD

START TO FINISH:
20 minutes

MAKES:
6 side-dish servings

¼	cup olive oil
3	tablespoons red wine vinegar
3	tablespoons snipped fresh oregano
½	teaspoon sugar
¼	teaspoon salt
¼	teaspoon black pepper
4	ounces whole wheat sourdough or other country-style bread, cut into 1½-inch cubes
½	of a 10-ounce package Italian-style torn mixed salad greens (about 5 cups)
1	medium tomato, cut into thin wedges
¼	cup halved yellow cherry tomatoes or yellow sweet pepper cut into ½-inch pieces
½	cup pitted ripe olives

1 For dressing, in a screw-top jar combine olive oil, wine vinegar, oregano, sugar, salt, and black pepper. Cover and shake well.

2 In a large salad bowl combine bread cubes, mixed greens, tomato wedges, cherry tomatoes or sweet pepper, and olives. Pour dressing over; toss gently to coat. Serve immediately.

Per serving: 151 cal., 11 g total fat (1 g sat. fat), 0 mg chol., 238 mg sodium, 13 g carbo., 1 g fiber, 2 g pro.

Insalata mista means "mixed salad" in Italian. Create a mixture of your own using the best selections from your grocery. Or buy mesclun, a blend of young, small salad greens.

INSALATA MISTA

START TO FINISH:
25 minutes

MAKES:
4 side-dish servings

4   cups torn mixed salad greens
     (such as radicchio, spinach, arugula, and/or chicory)

1   cup yellow and/or red cherry tomatoes, halved

¼   cup snipped fresh oregano or basil

½   cup pitted black olives

1   recipe Balsamic Vinaigrette

3   ounces thinly sliced fresh mozzarella cheese

1 In a large serving bowl toss together mixed greens, cherry tomatoes, oregano or basil, and olives. Drizzle Balsamic Vinaigrette over salad; toss to coat. Top with mozzarella cheese.

BALSAMIC VINAIGRETTE: In a screw-top jar combine 2 tablespoons olive oil or salad oil, 2 tablespoons balsamic vinegar, 2 teaspoons snipped fresh oregano or basil, ⅛ teaspoon salt, and ⅛ teaspoon black pepper. Cover and shake well to combine. Serve immediately or cover and store in the refrigerator for up to 2 weeks. Shake before serving. Makes about ¼ cup.

Per serving: 166 cal., 13 g total fat (4 g sat. fat), 15 mg chol., 298 mg sodium, 7 g carbo., 1 g fiber, 5 g pro.

So simple and so delicious, this salad is ready to go on the table in 10 minutes.

FRESH MOZZARELLA SALAD

START TO FINISH:
10 minutes

MAKES:
8 side-dish servings

4 medium tomatoes or 6 plum tomatoes

4 ounces fresh mozzarella

2 tablespoons bottled balsamic vinaigrette

½ cup loosely packed fresh basil leaves, thinly sliced

Salt

Freshly cracked black pepper

1 Cut tomatoes into ½-inch-thick slices. Cut mozzarella into ¼-inch-thick slices. Arrange tomato and cheese slices on a platter. Drizzle with vinaigrette. Sprinkle basil on top. Sprinkle with salt and pepper.

Per serving: 64 cal., 4 g total fat (2 g sat. fat), 11 mg chol., 174 mg sodium, 4 g carbo., 1 g fiber, 3 g pro.

This is a great dish for a summer potluck. Make it a day ahead, and it's ready to go when you are.

FENNEL-OLIVE SALAD

1	medium fennel bulb (about 1 pound)
⅓	cup sliced pitted green olives
2	tablespoons olive oil
1	tablespoon white wine vinegar
1	tablespoon snipped fresh oregano or 1 teaspoon dried oregano, crushed
1	clove garlic, minced
⅛	teaspoon salt
⅛	teaspoon crushed red pepper

1 Cut off and discard upper stalks of fennel. Remove wilted outer layer of fennel stalks and cut off a thin slice from base. Cut fennel bulb in half lengthwise; cut crosswise into very thin slices, removing core (if desired). In a medium bowl combine fennel slices and olives.

2 For dressing, in a screw-top jar combine olive oil, white wine vinegar, oregano, garlic, salt, and crushed red pepper. Cover and shake well. Pour dressing over fennel mixture; toss to coat. Cover and chill for 1 to 24 hours.

Per serving: 81 cal., 7 g total fat (1 g sat. fat), 0 mg chol., 306 mg sodium, 5 g carbo., 2 g fiber, 1 g pro.

PREP:
25 minutes

CHILL:
1 to 24 hours

MAKES:
5 side-dish servings

Peppery arugula and licorice-like fennel team up with a tangy pear dressing for an outstanding flavor combination. Walnuts provide a pleasing crunch.

ARUGULA-FENNEL SALAD WITH PEAR VINAIGRETTE

START TO FINISH:
25 minutes

MAKES:
4 side-dish servings

⅔   cup pear nectar

3   tablespoons seasoned rice vinegar

1   tablespoon olive oil

½   teaspoon coarsely ground black pepper

1   fennel bulb

2   cups arugula leaves

2   cups romaine leaves

2   small pears, cored and thinly sliced

½   of a small red onion, thinly sliced
     and separated into rings

¼   cup broken walnuts, toasted

1   ounce Parmesan cheese

1 For vinaigrette, in a small bowl whisk together pear nectar, rice vinegar, olive oil, and pepper. Set aside.

2 Cut off and discard upper stalks of fennel. Remove wilted outer layer of fennel stalks and cut off a thin slice from base. Cut the fennel bulb in half lengthwise; cut crosswise into thin slices, removing core (if desired).

3 In a medium bowl toss together sliced fennel, arugula, and romaine. Pour about half of the vinaigrette over fennel mixture; toss to coat. Arrange the fennel mixture on four salad plates. Top with pears, red onion, and walnuts.

4 Use a vegetable peeler to thinly shave Parmesan cheese. Top salads with shaved cheese. Drizzle with remaining vinaigrette.

Per serving: 217 cal., 11 g total fat (2 g sat. fat), 6 mg chol., 282 mg sodium, 28 g carbo., 5 g fiber, 6 g pro.

SIDE DISHES

3

Marinated artichoke hearts are key in this recipe. They provide a distinct and unique vegetable and also the dressing for the dish.

ITALIAN-STYLE VEGETABLES

PREP:
15 minutes

CHILL:
4 to 24 hours

MAKES:
5 or 6 servings

1   10-ounce package frozen lima beans

1   8-ounce package frozen sugar snap peas or one
    9-ounce package frozen Italian green beans

1   6-ounce jar marinated artichoke hearts, undrained

1   tablespoon snipped fresh dill

⅛   teaspoon crushed red pepper

    Romaine leaves

1   green onion, thinly sliced (optional)

    Fresh dill sprigs (optional)

1 In a medium saucepan cook lima beans and sugar snap peas in a small amount of boiling water for 5 to 8 minutes or until crisp-tender; drain. Rinse with cold water; drain again.

2 In a medium bowl combine lima bean mixture, undrained artichoke hearts, snipped dill, and crushed red pepper. Cover and chill for 4 to 24 hours.

3 To serve, line salad plates with romaine. Spoon lima bean mixture over romaine. If desired, sprinkle with sliced green onion and garnish with fresh dill sprigs.

Per serving: 131 cal., 2 g total fat (0 g sat. fat), 0 mg chol., 141 mg sodium, 22 g carbo., 5 g fiber, 6 g pro.

Roasting the vegetables concentrates their flavor, making this dish tastier than ever. If you're a fan of cannellini beans (white kidney beans), substitute them for the garbanzo beans.

ROASTED VEGETABLES PARMIGIANA

2   medium zucchini, cut into 1-inch chunks

1   medium yellow summer squash, cut into 1-inch chunks

1   medium red or green sweet pepper, cut into 1-inch pieces

8   ounces fresh mushrooms (stems removed, if desired)

2   tablespoons olive oil

½   teaspoon dried rosemary, crushed

¼   teaspoon salt

¼   teaspoon cracked black pepper

1   15-ounce can garbanzo beans (chickpeas), rinsed and drained

1   14½-ounce can Italian-style stewed tomatoes, undrained

⅓   cup shredded mozzarella cheese

⅓   cup finely shredded Parmesan cheese

PREP:
15 minutes

ROAST:
12 minutes + 5 minutes

OVEN:
450°F

MAKES:
6 servings

1 Preheat oven to 450°F. In a large roasting pan combine zucchini, summer squash, sweet pepper, and mushrooms. Drizzle the vegetable mixture with olive oil; sprinkle with rosemary, salt, and pepper. Toss lightly to coat.

2 Roast for 12 minutes. Remove from oven. Gently stir in garbanzo beans and undrained tomatoes. Roast about 5 minutes more or just until vegetables are tender. Transfer vegetable mixture to a serving dish; sprinkle with mozzarella cheese and Parmesan cheese.

Per serving: 223 cal., 10 g total fat (3 g sat. fat), 9 mg chol., 558 mg sodium, 26 g carbo., 6 g fiber, 10 g pro.

Italian flavors such as garlic and olive oil combine with zucchini and mint for a tasty side dish.

ZUCCHINI ALLA ROMANA

START TO FINISH:
20 minutes

MAKES:
6 servings

1   tablespoon olive oil

2   cloves garlic, minced

4   small zucchini, sliced (4 cups)

1   teaspoon dried mint or dried basil, crushed,
    or 1 tablespoon snipped fresh mint or basil

¼   teaspoon salt
    Dash black pepper

2   tablespoons finely shredded Romano
    or Parmesan cheese

1 In a large skillet heat olive oil over medium heat. Add garlic; cook for 30 seconds.

2 Add zucchini, dried mint or basil (if using), salt, and pepper to oil in skillet. Cook, uncovered, over medium heat about 5 minutes or until zucchini is crisp-tender, stirring occasionally.

3 To serve, sprinkle with Romano cheese and fresh mint or basil (if using).

Per serving: 40 cal., 3 g total fat (1 g sat. fat), 2 mg chol., 125 mg sodium, 3 g carbo., 1 g fiber, 2 g pro.

Reduced balsamic vinegar is the dressing for a melange of roasted fresh vegetables. The medley is a great complement to any quick-cooking entrée such as steak, pork chops, or salmon.

ROASTED VEGETABLES WITH BALSAMIC VINEGAR

8   ounces fresh green beans, ends trimmed

1   small red onion, cut into thin wedges

1   clove garlic, minced

1   tablespoon olive oil

     Dash salt

     Dash black pepper

2   medium yellow summer squash, halved lengthwise
     and cut into ¼-inch-thick slices

⅓   cup balsamic vinegar

1 Preheat oven to 450°F. In a shallow roasting pan combine green beans, red onion, and garlic. Drizzle with olive oil; sprinkle with salt and pepper. Toss mixture until beans are evenly coated. Spread into a single layer on bottom of roasting pan.

2 Roast for 8 minutes. Stir in summer squash. Roast for 5 to 7 minutes more or until vegetables are tender and slightly browned.

3 Meanwhile, in a small saucepan bring balsamic vinegar to boiling over medium-high heat; reduce heat. Boil gently about 5 minutes or until vinegar is reduced by half (vinegar will thicken slightly).

4 Drizzle the vinegar over roasted vegetables; toss until vegetables are evenly coated.

Per serving: 92 cal., 4 g total fat (0 g sat. fat), 0 mg chol., 44 mg sodium, 14 g carbo., 3 g fiber, 2 g pro.

START TO FINISH:
25 minutes

OVEN:
450°F

MAKES:
4 to 6 servings

Robust ingredients—including fennel, capers, and olives—fill these stuffed sweet peppers. They go great alongside grilled chicken or fish.

TUSCAN STUFFED PEPPERS

PREP:
40 minutes

BROIL:
12 minutes

COOL:
15 minutes

BAKE:
20 minutes

OVEN:
375°F

MAKES:
6 servings

6   red and/or yellow sweet peppers (about 8 ounces each)

1   large eggplant (about 1½ pounds)

1   to 2 teaspoons salt

1   medium fennel bulb, chopped (about 1 cup)

3   tablespoons olive oil

8   cloves garlic, minced

⅓   cup drained capers, rinsed

8   to 10 canned anchovies, drained and finely chopped (optional)

¾   cup olives (black or green), pitted and quartered

½   cup snipped fresh flat-leaf parsley

¼   cup snipped fresh sage

2   tablespoons freshly grated Parmesan cheese

1 Preheat broiler. Slice the stem end off each pepper and carefully remove the core and seeds. Place peppers on foil-lined baking sheet. Broil about 4 inches from the heat for 12 to 15 minutes or until charred, turning to brown all sides. Place in a closed container or wrap in foil and cool for 15 minutes; carefully peel off the skin. Set aside.

2 Meanwhile, for filling, cut eggplant into ½-inch-thick slices. Lightly sprinkle both sides of each eggplant slice with salt. Let stand for 30 minutes to drain. Wipe excess salt off eggplant slices; cut eggplant into ½-inch cubes.

3 Preheat oven to 375°F. In a large skillet cook fennel in hot olive oil for 4 minutes. Add eggplant and garlic to skillet; cook for 8 minutes more. Stir in capers and, if desired, anchovies. Remove skillet from heat.

4 Stir olives, parsley, and sage into the eggplant mixture. Divide filling among sweet peppers. Place filled peppers in a single layer in a large baking dish. Sprinkle filled peppers with grated Parmesan cheese. Bake for 20 to 25 minutes or until heated through and slightly browned.

Per serving: 170 cal., 10 g total fat (2 g sat. fat), 6 mg chol., 1,001 mg sodium, 18 g carbo., 10 g fiber, 5 g pro.

Frozen hash browns make this recipe a snap to prepare. Serve this hearty side dish for breakfast, brunch, or even dinner.

HERBED POTATOES

1	tablespoon butter
3	green onions, sliced
½	teaspoon dried Italian seasoning, crushed
4½	cups loose-pack frozen hash brown potatoes
¼	teaspoon salt
⅓	cup grated Parmesan cheese
1	tablespoon snipped fresh flat-leaf parsley

1 In a large nonstick skillet melt butter over medium heat. Add green onions and Italian seasoning; cook about 2 minutes or until green onions are tender. Stir in frozen potatoes and salt.

2 Cook about 15 minutes or until potatoes are tender and lightly browned, stirring twice. Stir in Parmesan cheese and parsley.

Per serving: 257 cal., 7 g total fat (4 g sat. fat), 13 mg chol., 354 mg sodium, 44 g carbo., 4 g fiber, 8 g pro.

PREP:
10 minutes

COOK:
15 minutes

MAKES:
4 servings

Tomatoes, crusty bread, and dill combine in this tasty side dish that shouts "summer!"

TOMATO BREAD PUDDING

PREP:
25 minutes

BAKE:
15 minutes

OVEN:
350°F

MAKES:
4 to 6 servings

4	ounces French bread, Italian bread, or Italian country-style bread, torn into 1-inch chunks
2	tablespoons olive oil
2	cloves garlic, minced
2	pounds tomatoes, cored, seeded, and coarsely chopped (about 4 cups)
3	tablespoons snipped fresh dill or 1 teaspoon dried dill, crushed
¼	teaspoon black pepper
¼	cup chicken broth
	Finely shredded Parmesan cheese (optional)
	Fresh dill sprigs (optional)

1 Preheat oven to 350°F. Place bread pieces in a large shallow baking pan. Bake about 15 minutes or until golden brown, stirring once.

2 In a large skillet heat olive oil over medium heat. Add garlic; cook for 30 seconds. Add tomatoes, snipped or dried dill, and pepper. Cook for 2 minutes, stirring occasionally. Add chicken broth; bring to boiling. Remove from heat.

3 To serve, place toasted bread pieces in a serving bowl. Pour tomato mixture over bread; toss gently to mix. Top with Parmesan cheese. If desired, garnish with dill sprigs. Serve immediately.

Per serving: 189 cal., 8 g total fat (1 g sat. fat), 0 mg chol., 232 mg sodium, 26 g carbo., 3 g fiber, 5 g pro.

Italian ingredients have become so much a part of American cuisine that they are frequently used with ingredients from other cuisines. Here tomatoes, basil, garlic, and Asiago cheese combine with tofu for an extraordinary side dish.

ASIAGO-TOPPED TOFU & TOMATOES

1	16-ounce package extra-firm tub-style tofu (fresh bean curd), drained and cut into ½-inch cubes
1	cup halved cherry tomatoes or 1 cup coarsely chopped plum tomatoes (3 medium)
⅓	cup olive oil
⅓	cup white wine vinegar
2	tablespoons snipped fresh basil or oregano or 2 teaspoons dried basil or oregano, crushed
2	cloves garlic, minced
¼	teaspoon salt
⅛	teaspoon black pepper
1	tablespoon olive oil
¼	cup finely shredded Asiago or Parmesan cheese (1 ounce)
	Snipped fresh basil or oregano (optional)

1 Place tofu and tomatoes in a resealable plastic bag set in a deep bowl. In a screw-top jar combine the ⅓ cup olive oil, the white wine vinegar, the 2 tablespoons snipped basil or the dried basil, the garlic, salt, and pepper. Cover and shake well; pour over tofu and tomatoes. Seal bag; gently turn to coat tofu and tomatoes. Marinate in the refrigerator for 30 to 60 minutes, gently turning bag once or twice. Gently drain tofu and tomatoes; discard marinade.

2 In a large skillet heat the 1 tablespoon olive oil over medium heat. Add tofu and tomatoes; cook and stir for 3 to 5 minutes or until heated through, gently stirring occasionally. Using a slotted spoon, transfer to a serving dish. Sprinkle with Asiago cheese. Let stand about 1 minute or until cheese is slightly melted. If desired, sprinkle with additional snipped basil.

Per serving: 176 cal., 15 g total fat (3 g sat. fat), 4 mg chol., 114 mg sodium, 3 g carbo., 1 g fiber, 7 g pro.

PREP:
20 minutes

MARINATE:
30 to 60 minutes

STAND:
1 minute

MAKES:
8 servings

Plum tomatoes, sometimes called roma tomatoes, work very well for this recipe. Roasting the tomatoes gives them a robust, sweet flavor that's perfect for pesto.

ROASTED TOMATO PESTO

PREP:
25 minutes

STAND:
30 minutes

ROAST:
20 minutes

COOL:
20 minutes

OVEN:
450°F

MAKES:
4 cups

16 to 20 plum tomatoes, halved lengthwise and seeded (3 pounds)

1 teaspoon salt

2 small onions, cut into thin wedges

4 cloves garlic, peeled and quartered

6 tablespoons olive oil

2 tablespoons balsamic vinegar

¼ teaspoon black pepper

1 Preheat oven to 450°F. Place tomatoes, cut sides up, in a shallow roasting pan. Sprinkle with salt. Let stand for 30 minutes.

2 Add onions and garlic to roasting pan. Drizzle with 4 tablespoons of the olive oil, gently tossing to coat. Roast about 20 minutes or until tomatoes are tender, stirring occasionally. Cool in pan on wire rack for 20 minutes.

3 Place half of the tomato mixture in a large food processor bowl. Add 1 tablespoon of the olive oil, 1 tablespoon of the balsamic vinegar, and ⅛ teaspoon of the pepper. Cover and process with 4 or 5 on/off turns until coarsely chopped and mixture just begins to form a paste. Transfer to a large bowl; repeat with remaining ingredients. (Or place one-fourth of the tomato mixture in a blender container. Add 1½ teaspoons of the olive oil, 1½ teaspoons of the balsamic vinegar, and a dash of the pepper. Cover and blend with 4 or 5 on/off turns until coarsely chopped and mixture just begins to form a paste. Transfer to a bowl; repeat with remaining ingredients in three more batches.)

4 To serve, divide pesto into four 1-cup portions. Place three portions into 3 airtight freezer containers. Freeze up to 3 months. Use remaining pesto tossed with hot cooked pasta, as a sandwich spread, or as a topper for soups.

Per tablespoon: 68 cal., 5 g total fat (1 g sat. fat), 0 mg chol., 153 mg sodium, 5 g carbo., 1 g fiber, 1 g pro.

Arborio rice makes this authentic risotto extra creamy and delicious. While it cooks, this high-starch rice transforms the broth into a luscious sauce.

SPINACH RISOTTO WITH ACORN SQUASH

1	1½- to 2-pound acorn or butternut squash, halved lengthwise and seeded
1	tablespoon olive oil
2	medium red onions, chopped
4	cloves garlic, minced
1	cup Arborio rice or short grain rice
3	cups vegetable broth or chicken broth
3	cups packed chopped fresh spinach
2	tablespoons shredded Parmesan cheese

START TO FINISH:
30 minutes

MAKES:
4 servings

1 Cut each squash half crosswise into 1-inch-thick slices. In a covered large saucepan cook squash in a small amount of boiling water for 10 to 15 minutes or until tender. Drain and keep warm.

2 Meanwhile, in another large saucepan heat olive oil over medium heat. Add red onions and garlic; cook about 4 minutes or until onions are tender. Add uncooked rice; cook and stir for 1 minute more.

3 In a medium saucepan bring broth to boiling; reduce heat to keep broth simmering. Carefully add 1 cup of the broth to the rice mixture, stirring constantly. Continue to cook and stir over medium heat until the liquid is absorbed. Add another 1 cup of the broth to the rice mixture, stirring constantly. Continue to cook and stir until liquid is absorbed. Add another ½ cup broth, stirring constantly until liquid is absorbed. (This should take about 18 to 20 minutes total.)

4 Stir in remaining ½ cup broth. Cook and stir until rice is slightly firm (al dente) and creamy. Stir in spinach and Parmesan cheese. Serve risotto with squash slices.

Per serving: 296 cal., 6 g total fat (1 g sat. fat), 2 mg chol., 778 mg sodium, 60 g carbo., 5 g fiber, 8 g pro.

Simple, yet flavorful, ingredients come together in this sophisticated side for a company-special meal.

TANGY LEMON & TOMATO RISOTTO

START TO FINISH:
30 minutes

MAKES:
6 servings

1   tablespoon olive oil

2   medium shallots, finely chopped

1   cup Arborio rice or medium grain rice

3   cups chicken broth

1   cup cherry tomatoes, quartered

1   teaspoon finely shredded lemon peel

2   tablespoons lemon juice

     Lemon peel strips (optional)

1 In a large saucepan heat olive oil over medium heat. Add shallots; cook until tender. Add the uncooked rice. Cook and stir about 5 minutes more or until rice is golden brown.

2 Meanwhile, in a medium saucepan bring chicken broth to boiling; reduce heat to keep broth simmering. Carefully add 1 cup of the broth to the rice mixture, stirring constantly. Continue to cook and stir over medium heat until liquid is absorbed. Add another 1 cup of the broth to the rice mixture, stirring constantly. Continue to cook and stir until the liquid is absorbed. Add remaining broth, $\frac{1}{2}$ cup at a time, stirring constantly until the broth has been absorbed and the rice is slightly firm (al dente) and creamy. (This should take 18 to 20 minutes total.)

3 Stir in tomatoes, shredded lemon peel, and lemon juice. Serve immediately. If desired, garnish with lemon peel strips.

Per serving: 116 cal., 3 g total fat (0 g sat. fat), 1 mg chol., 483 mg sodium, 21 g carbo., 0 g fiber, 3 g pro.

Using refrigerated cooked polenta makes this recipe quick and easy. All you have to do is slice and fry it for an ideal complement to the delicious tomato sauce.

POLENTA WITH FRESH TOMATO SAUCE

4   teaspoons olive oil

1   clove garlic, minced

6   plum tomatoes, coarsely chopped (about 2 cups)

¼   cup sliced pitted ripe olives

2   teaspoons snipped fresh rosemary

    Salt

    Black pepper

1   16-ounce tube refrigerated cooked polenta

½   cup shredded smoked Gouda or Swiss cheese (2 ounces)

    Fresh rosemary sprigs (optional)

START TO FINISH:
25 minutes

MAKES:
4 servings

1 For sauce, in a medium saucepan heat 2 teaspoons of the olive oil and the garlic over medium heat. Add tomatoes; cook for 2 minutes. Stir in olives and the snipped rosemary. Bring to boiling; reduce heat. Simmer, uncovered, for 8 minutes, stirring occasionally. Season to taste with salt and pepper.

2 Meanwhile, cut polenta crosswise into 8 slices. In a large nonstick skillet or on a griddle, heat the remaining 2 teaspoons olive oil over medium heat. Add polenta; cook about 6 minutes or until golden brown, turning once. Remove from heat and sprinkle with cheese. Serve sauce on the polenta. If desired, garnish with rosemary sprigs.

Per serving: 226 cal., 10 g total fat (3 g sat. fat), 16 mg chol., 608 mg sodium, 27 g carbo., 5 g fiber, 8 g pro.

Use Italian tuna packed in olive oil for knockout flavor.

ITALIAN GRITS

START TO FINISH:
30 minutes

MAKES:
8 servings

3½	cups water
¼	teaspoon salt
1	cup quick-cooking grits*
½	cup grated Parmesan cheese
2	tablespoons olive oil
1	medium yellow sweet pepper, cut into bite-size strips
3	anchovy fillets, finely chopped
2	cloves garlic, minced
2	tablespoons lemon juice
1	tablespoon capers, drained
2	teaspoons snipped fresh oregano
⅛	teaspoon black pepper
1	6-ounce can tuna, drained and flaked

1 In a large saucepan heat the water and salt to boiling. Gradually stir in grits. Reduce heat to medium-low. Simmer, uncovered, for 5 minutes, stirring frequently. Remove from heat. Stir in Parmesan cheese. Cover and keep warm over very low heat.

2 Meanwhile, in a large skillet heat olive oil over medium heat. Add sweet pepper; cook and stir until pepper is crisp-tender. Stir in anchovy fillets, garlic, lemon juice, capers, oregano, and black pepper; cook and stir for 1 minute. Fold in tuna; cook 1 minute more, gently tossing occasionally.

3 Spoon grits into serving dish; top with tuna mixture.

Per serving: 157 cal., 6 g total fat (1 g sat. fat), 15 mg chol., 333 mg sodium, 17 g carbo., 1 g fiber, 9 g pro.

*NOTE: If you prefer, you can use steel-cut (coarse) grits. In a medium saucepan combine 4½ cups water and ¼ teaspoon salt; heat to boiling. Gradually stir in 1⅓ cups steel-cut grits. Reduce heat to medium. Simmer, uncovered, for 20 to 30 minutes, stirring frequently. Use a long-handled wooden spoon to stir because mixture may spatter. Continue as directed.

Tomatoes and cream are an outstanding combination. Tomatoes add tanginess and character to the sauce, while cream rounds it out, making it rich and decadent.

TOMATO-VODKA CREAM SAUCE WITH FETTUCCINE

1	tablespoon olive oil
1	cup chopped onion
2	cloves garlic, minced
2	14½-ounce cans or one 28-ounce can Italian-style stewed tomatoes, undrained, cut up
1	6-ounce can tomato paste
1½	teaspoons dried oregano, crushed
½	teaspoon salt
¼	teaspoon freshly ground black pepper
½	cup whipping cream
2	tablespoons vodka (optional)
¼	cup snipped fresh flat-leaf parsley
8	ounces dried fettuccine, spaghetti, linguine, capellini, or other long pasta, cooked according to package directions and drained
	Finely shredded Parmigiano-Reggiano, Romano, or Parmesan cheese (optional)
	Fresh basil sprigs (optional)

START TO FINISH:
35 minutes

MAKES:
8 servings

1 In a medium saucepan heat olive oil over medium heat. Add onion and garlic; cook until onion is tender. Stir in undrained tomatoes, tomato paste, oregano, salt, and black pepper. Bring to boiling; reduce heat. Simmer, uncovered, about 10 minutes or until desired consistency, stirring occasionally.

2 Slowly add the whipping cream and, if desired, vodka, stirring constantly. Cook and stir for 3 minutes more. Remove from heat. Stir in parsley.

3 Serve sauce over hot cooked pasta. If desired, sprinkle with Parmigiano-Reggiano cheese and garnish with basil sprigs.

Per serving: 143 cal., 8 g total fat (4 g sat. fat), 21 mg chol., 385 mg sodium, 14 g carbo., 2 g fiber, 3 g pro.

Try using pitted kalamata olives in this recipe. Their intense flavor adds just the right punch to the robust sauce.

PUTTANESCA SAUCE WITH PASTA

PREP:
25 minutes

COOK:
15 minutes

MAKES:
4 servings

1	medium onion, chopped
2	cloves garlic, minced
1	tablespoon olive oil
1	14½-ounce can diced tomatoes, undrained
1	4-ounce can (drained weight) sliced mushrooms, drained
¼	cup dry red wine or chicken broth
2	tablespoons tomato paste
⅛	teaspoon crushed red pepper
12	small pitted ripe olives, sliced
3	canned anchovy fillets, cut into ½-inch pieces (optional)
3	tablespoons snipped fresh flat-leaf parsley
8	ounces dried pasta, cooked according to package directions and drained
	Fresh flat-leaf parsley sprigs (optional)

1 In a large skillet cook onion and garlic in hot olive oil until tender. Add undrained diced tomatoes, mushrooms, wine, tomato paste, and crushed red pepper. Bring to boiling; reduce heat. Simmer, uncovered, for 15 to 20 minutes or until sauce is desired consistency.

2 Stir in olives, anchovies (if desired), and snipped parsley; heat through. Serve over hot pasta. If desired, garnish with parsley sprigs.

Per serving: 317 cal., 6 g total fat (1 g sat. fat), 0 mg chol., 413 mg sodium, 54 g carbo., 4 g fiber, 9 g pro.

A splash of vermouth melds the flavors together, and spiral-shaped fusilli captures the colorful vegetable mixture wonderfully.

FUSILLI PRIMAVERA

8	ounces dried fusilli, fettuccine, linguine, or other long pasta noodles
16	fresh asparagus spears (about 12 ounces)
1	tablespoon cooking oil
4	cloves garlic, very thinly sliced
½	teaspoon crushed red pepper
2	medium carrots, very thinly bias-sliced
1	leek, thinly sliced
6	plum tomatoes, seeded and chopped (about 2¼ cups)
¼	cup extra-dry vermouth, dry white wine, or vegetable broth
¼	teaspoon salt
2	tablespoons butter
¼	cup shredded fresh basil
½	cup coarsely chopped cashews or sliced almonds, toasted
1	ounce smoked Gouda or provolone cheese, thinly shaved

START TO FINISH:
30 minutes

MAKES:
4 to 6 servings

1 In a Dutch oven cook pasta according to package directions. Drain well. Return pasta to hot pan; cover and keep warm.

2 Trim asparagus. Remove tips; set tips aside. Bias-slice asparagus stalks into 1½-inch-long pieces; set stalks aside.

3 In a 12-inch nonstick skillet heat oil over medium-high heat. Add garlic and crushed red pepper; cook and stir for 15 seconds. Add carrots and leek; cook and stir for 2 minutes. Add tomatoes; cook and stir for 1 minute more. Add asparagus stalks, vermouth, and salt. Cook, uncovered, for 2 to 3 minutes or until asparagus is crisp-tender. Add asparagus tips. Cook, uncovered, for 1 minute more. Add butter, stirring until melted.

4 Add asparagus mixture and basil to pasta; toss gently to coat. Transfer to a warm serving dish. Sprinkle with nuts and shaved cheese.

Per serving: 476 cal., 20 g total fat (7 g sat. fat), 21 mg chol., 331 mg sodium, 59 g carbo., 5 g fiber, 14 g pro.

Gorgonzola, Italy's great blue cheese, is named for the northern Italian town in which it originated. Available in both creamy and crumbly varieties, either version works delightfully in this recipe.

GORGONZOLA-CREAM-SAUCED PASTA

START TO FINISH:
15 minutes

MAKES:
6 servings

12	ounces dried fettuccine
½	cup chicken broth
½	cup whipping cream
¼	cup unsalted butter, cut up
4	ounces Gorgonzola cheese, at room temperature
¼	teaspoon salt
¼	teaspoon black pepper
⅛	teaspoon freshly grated nutmeg
1	recipe Walnut and Bread Crumb Topping

1 Cook pasta according to package directions. Drain. Return pasta to hot pan; cover and keep warm.

2 Meanwhile, for sauce, in a large saucepan combine chicken broth, whipping cream, and butter. Bring to boiling over medium heat, stirring occasionally. Simmer, uncovered, about 3 minutes or until slightly thickened. Whisk in Gorgonzola cheese until melted and sauce is smooth. Whisk in salt, pepper, and nutmeg.

3 Spoon sauce over hot cooked pasta. Sprinkle with Walnut and Bread Crumb Topping. Serve immediately.

WALNUT AND BREAD CRUMB TOPPING: Preheat oven to 350°F. In a small bowl toss together ¼ cup soft bread crumbs, 3 tablespoons chopped walnuts, 1 tablespoon snipped fresh parsley, and 1 tablespoon olive oil. Spread in an 8×8×2-inch baking pan. Bake for 6 to 8 minutes or until golden brown.

Per serving: 469 cal., 27 g total fat (14 g sat. fat), 63 mg chol., 465 mg sodium, 45 g carbo., 2 g fiber, 13 g pro.

ARTICHOKE-GORGONZOLA CREAM SAUCE: Prepare pasta as directed in step 1. Prepare sauce as directed in step 2. Stir in one 14-ounce can artichoke hearts, well drained and chopped. Heat through. Continue as directed in step 3.

Per serving: 487 cal., 27 g total fat (14 g sat. fat), 63 mg chol., 675 mg sodium, 48 g carbo., 4 g fiber, 13 g pro.

In Italy, pecorino refers to any cheese made with sheep's milk. Most are aged, resulting in a hard cheese with a granular texture and sharp flavor. It's a key ingredient in this recipe.

FUSILLI WITH GARLIC PESTO & AGED PECORINO

15	cloves garlic
⅓	cup fresh basil leaves
¾	cup olive oil
⅓	cup pine nuts, toasted
4	teaspoons finely shredded pecorino Romano cheese
¾	teaspoon salt
⅛	teaspoon freshly ground black pepper
1	tablespoon olive oil
1	pound dried fusilli, gemelli, or tagliatelle pasta
¼	cup freshly grated pecorino Romano cheese
1	cup small basil leaves

START TO FINISH:
35 minutes

MAKES:
8 servings

1 In a 4-quart Dutch oven bring a large amount of salted water to boiling. Add garlic; cook for 8 minutes. Remove garlic with a slotted spoon and immerse in a bowl of ice water. Add the ⅓ cup basil leaves to the boiling water and cook for 5 seconds; remove with a slotted spoon and drain well on paper towels. Peel garlic when cool enough to handle. Do not discard water (it is used for cooking pasta).

2 For pesto, in a blender or food processor combine the garlic, blanched basil, and the ¾ cup olive oil; cover and blend or process just until combined. Add 2 tablespoons of the pine nuts, the 4 teaspoons cheese, the salt, and pepper. Cover and blend or process until nearly smooth.

3 Meanwhile, add the 1 tablespoon olive oil to the boiling water in which the garlic and basil were cooked. Add pasta and cook according to package directions or until pasta is tender but still slightly firm. Drain well. Return to hot Dutch oven. Add pesto; toss well. Transfer to a serving bowl. Sprinkle with the ¼ cup cheese and the remaining pine nuts. Top with the 1 cup basil leaves.

Per serving: 463 cal., 27 g total fat (4 g sat. fat), 3 mg chol., 261 mg sodium, 46 g carbo., 2 g fiber, 10 g pro.

Orecchiette means "little ears" in Italian. The disk-shaped pasta holds the chunky sauce perfectly.

ORECCHIETTE WITH PANCETTA & BROCCOLI RABE

START TO FINISH:
35 minutes

MAKES:
6 servings

4   ounces pancetta, coarsely chopped

6   ounces dried orecchiette pasta or medium shell pasta

2   teaspoons olive oil

4   cloves garlic, minced

¼   teaspoon crushed red pepper

3   cups cut-up broccoli rabe or broccoli

⅓   cup chicken broth

¼   cup ripe olives or 2 tablespoons drained capers

¼   cup finely shredded Parmesan cheese (1 ounce)

1 In a large skillet cook pancetta over medium heat about 10 minutes or until browned and crisp. Drain on paper towels, reserving 1 tablespoon drippings in skillet. Set aside.

2 In a large saucepan cook pasta according to package directions. Drain well. Return to hot pan. Toss with olive oil; cover and keep warm.

3 In the same skillet heat the reserved drippings over medium heat. Add garlic and crushed red pepper; cook and stir for 30 seconds. Add broccoli rabe or broccoli and chicken broth. Bring to boiling; reduce heat. Cover and simmer about 3 minutes or until tender. Stir in pancetta and olives or capers; heat through.

4 Add broccoli rabe mixture to pasta in saucepan. Add half of the Parmesan cheese; toss to combine. Transfer to a serving dish. Sprinkle with remaining Parmesan cheese.

Per serving: 211 cal., 9 g total fat (3 g sat. fat), 11 mg chol., 244 mg sodium, 25 g carbo., 2 g fiber, 8 g pro.

This is a great recipe to try if using capers in cooking is new to you. The pungent, salty flavor is showcased wonderfully in this dish.

PASTA WITH GARLIC-CAPER-HERB OIL

8   ounces dried campanelle pasta or bow tie pasta

3   tablespoons olive oil

3   cloves garlic, minced

3   tablespoons snipped fresh chives

3   tablespoons drained capers

⅛   teaspoon black pepper

½   cup chopped walnuts, toasted

2   tablespoons Champagne vinegar, red wine vinegar, or white wine vinegar

8   canned anchovy fillets, drained and chopped (1 tablespoon)

¼   cup finely shredded Parmesan cheese (1 ounce)

START TO FINISH:
25 minutes

MAKES:
6 servings

❶ In a large saucepan cook pasta according to package directions. Drain, reserving some of the pasta cooking water. Return pasta to hot pan; cover and keep warm.

❷ Meanwhile, in a small saucepan combine olive oil, garlic, chives, capers, and pepper. Cook over medium-low heat for 5 minutes.

❸ Add oil mixture to pasta along with walnuts, vinegar, and anchovies. Toss to coat. Add 1 to 2 tablespoons of the reserved pasta cooking water; toss to coat. Transfer to a serving bowl. Sprinkle with Parmesan cheese.

Per serving: 296 cal., 15 g total fat (2 g sat. fat), 7 mg chol., 382 mg sodium, 31 g carbo., 2 g fiber, 9 g pro.

A staple in Italy, this bread goes well with just about any Italian dish.

ITALIAN BREAD

PREP:
10 minutes

BAKE:
per bread machine directions

MAKES:
a 1½-pound loaf (16 slices)

¾   cup milk

1   egg

3   tablespoons water

1   tablespoon butter or margarine

3   cups bread flour

1   teaspoon salt

1¼   teaspoons active dry yeast
     or bread machine yeast

1 Add all the ingredients to a bread machine according to the manufacturer's directions. Select the basic white bread cycle. Remove hot bread from machine as soon as it is done. Cool on a wire rack.

Per slice: 110 cal., 2 g total fat (1 g sat. fat), 16 mg chol., 160 mg sodium, 19 g carbo., 1 g fiber, 4 g pro.

ITALIAN CHEESE BREAD: Prepare as directed, except add ¾ cup shredded Romano cheese with the bread flour.

Per slice: 127 cal., 3 g total fat (1 g sat. fat), 19 mg chol., 218 mg sodium, 19 g carbo., 1 g fiber, 5 g pro.

ITALIAN WHOLE WHEAT-SAGE BREAD: Prepare as directed, except decrease bread flour to 2 cups and add 1 cup whole wheat flour and 1 tablespoon snipped fresh sage or 1 teaspoon dried sage, crushed, with the flour. Select whole wheat cycle, if available.

Per slice: 105 cal., 2 g total fat (1 g sat. fat), 16 mg chol., 160 mg sodium, 19 g carbo., 1 g fiber, 4 g pro.

For a great start to a meal, invite guests to dip slices of this rosemary-and-garlic-scented bread into a dish of olive oil sprinkled with finely shredded Parmesan cheese.

ITALIAN COUNTRY LOAVES

1	package active dry yeast
2	cups all-purpose flour
⅔	cup milk
1	teaspoon sugar
⅓	cup olive oil
1	tablespoon snipped fresh rosemary
2	cloves garlic, minced
7½	to 8 cups all-purpose flour
	Cornmeal

PREP:
40 minutes

STAND:
4 hours to 4 days

RISE:
2 hours + 30 minutes

BAKE:
40 minutes

OVEN:
400°F

MAKES:
2 loaves (24 servings)

1 Stir together 1 cup warm water (105°F to 115°F) and the yeast. Let stand about 3 minutes or until mixture looks creamy. Stir in the 2 cups flour, ¼ cup at a time; stir in milk and sugar. Cover and let stand in a warm place for 4 to 24 hours or in the refrigerator for up to 4 days.

2 Add 1¾ cups warm water (105°F to 115°F), the oil, rosemary, garlic, and 2 teaspoons salt to yeast mixture; beat with an electric mixer on low speed until combined. Beat in as much of the 7½ to 8 cups flour as you can with mixer, adding 1 cup at a time. Using a wooden spoon, stir in as much of the remaining flour as you can. Turn out dough onto a lightly floured surface. Knead in enough of the remaining flour to make a moderately stiff dough that is smooth and elastic (6 to 8 minutes total). Shape into a ball. Place dough in a greased bowl; turn once to grease surface. Cover; let rise in warm place until double (about 2 hours).

3 Grease a large baking sheet; sprinkle with cornmeal. Punch down dough. Turn out onto a lightly floured surface. Divide in half. Cover; let rest for 10 minutes. Shape each half into a round 7 inches in diameter. Place on the prepared baking sheet. Cover; let rise until nearly double (about 30 minutes).

4 Preheat oven to 400°F. Adjust two oven racks so one is in the lowest position and the other is in the middle of the oven. Place a broiler pan on bottom rack while oven preheats. When pan is hot, pour about 1 cup hot water into pan. Rub loaves lightly with flour. Cut a crisscross design in each loaf, about ¼ inch deep. Place bread on the middle rack.*

5 Bake for 40 to 50 minutes or until loaves sound hollow when tapped. If necessary to prevent overbrowning, cover with foil for last 10 minutes of baking. (Water in pan will evaporate after about 10 minutes of baking time; remove dry pan from oven.) Transfer loaves to wire racks to cool.

Per serving: 200 cal., 4 g total fat (1 g sat. fat), 1 mg chol., 198 mg sodium, 36 g carbo., 1 g fiber, 5 g pro.

> ***TEST KITCHEN TIP:** If you only have room to bake one loaf at a time, place one loaf, covered, in the refrigerator. Remove it from the refrigerator 15 minutes before baking. Repeat heating broiler pan and adding water before baking second loaf.

This bread is wonderful for sopping up every last bit of a soup or stew. Look for cracked wheat at the supermarket or at health food stores.

PEASANT LOAF

PREP:
25 minutes

RISE:
45 minutes + 30 minutes

BAKE:
25 minutes

OVEN:
375°F

MAKES:
1 loaf (16 servings)

1 cup water

¼ cup cracked wheat

¾ cup milk

1 tablespoon olive oil

¾ teaspoon salt

3½ to 4 cups all-purpose flour

¼ cup finely shredded Parmesan cheese (1 ounce)

1 package active dry yeast

1 egg

Cracked wheat

1 In a small saucepan bring the water to boiling; remove from heat. Stir in the ¼ cup cracked wheat. Let stand for 3 minutes; drain well. Add milk, olive oil, and salt to drained cracked wheat; let stand until cooled to lukewarm (120°F to 130°F).

2 In a large mixing bowl stir together 1½ cups of the flour, the Parmesan cheese, and yeast. Add warm milk mixture and egg. Beat with an electric mixer on low to medium speed for 30 seconds, scraping bowl constantly. Beat on high speed for 3 minutes. Using a wooden spoon, stir in as much of the remaining flour as you can.

3 Turn out dough onto a lightly floured surface. Knead in enough of the remaining flour to make a moderately stiff dough that is smooth and elastic (6 to 8 minutes total). Shape dough into a ball. Place in a lightly greased bowl, turning once to grease surface. Cover; let rise in a warm place until double (45 to 60 minutes).

4 Punch down dough. Turn out dough onto a lightly floured surface. Cover and let rest for 10 minutes. Grease a baking sheet.

5 Shape dough into a round 6 inches in diameter. Place on prepared baking sheet. Cover and let rise in a warm place until nearly double (30 to 40 minutes).

6 Preheat oven to 375°F. Using a sharp knife, cut 2 or 3 slashes on top of loaf in each direction to make a diamond pattern. Brush with water; sprinkle with additional cracked wheat.

7 Bake for 25 to 30 minutes or until loaf sounds hollow when lightly tapped.

Per serving: 130 cal., 2 g total fat (1 g sat. fat), 16 mg chol., 140 mg sodium, 23 g carbo., 1 g fiber, 5 g pro.

SOUPS & SALADS

LAMB & ORZO SOUP
page 41

MEATBALL SOUP WITH TINY PASTA
page 42

SOUPS & SALADS

TUSCAN RAVIOLI STEW
page 46

SOUPS & SALADS

CHUNKY RATATOUILLE STEW
page 54

SOUPS & SALADS

**LEMON-
MARINATED
BABY
VEGETABLES**

page 66

**BREAD
SALAD**

page 68

SOUPS & SALADS

INSALATA MISTA

page 69

ARUGULA-FENNEL SALAD WITH PEAR VINAIGRETTE

page 72

SIDE DISHES

**ROASTED
VEGETABLES
WITH
BALSAMIC
VINEGAR**
page 77

SIDE DISHES

TUSCAN STUFFED PEPPERS
page 78

SIDE DISHES

**POLENTA
WITH
FRESH
TOMATO
SAUCE**

page 85

**PESTO-
GARLIC
BREAD**

page 114

MEATS

**INDIVIDUAL
SICILIAN
MEAT
LOAVES**
page 123

MEATS

BAKED
PENNE
WITH
MEAT
SAUCE

page 130

MEATS

PORK MEDAILLONS WITH FENNEL & PANCETTA

page 140

TOMATO-PEPPER SAUCE WITH SAUSAGES

page 146

POULTRY & FISH

**ROASTED
TARRAGON
CHICKEN**

page 170

**CHICKEN
WITH
CHUNKY
VEGETABLE
SAUCE**
page 175

POULTRY & FISH

**POLLO
SALTIMBOCCA
CON PESTO**

page 180

**LINGUINE
WITH
FENNEL &
SHRIMP**

page 198

MEATLESS PASTA
MAIN DISHES

PIZZA & SANDWICHES

PIZZA MARGHERITA

page 242

A perfect bread for the holidays, these fruit-filled loaves will delight family and friends. If you have a small group, serve one loaf now and freeze the other for later.

FRUITED ITALIAN BREAD

6¼   to 6¾ cups all-purpose flour

⅔   cup golden raisins and/or dark raisins

1   cup coarsely chopped walnuts

1   cup chopped mixed candied fruits

1   teaspoon anise seeds, crushed

1½   cups milk

¼   cup sugar

3   tablespoons butter

2   packages active dry yeast

¼   teaspoon sugar

2   slightly beaten eggs

1   egg

1 In a very large bowl combine 4 cups of the flour, the raisins, walnuts, candied fruits, anise seeds, and 1½ teaspoons salt. Set aside.

2 In a medium saucepan combine milk, the ¼ cup sugar, and butter. Cook and stir over medium heat until sugar is dissolved and milk is steaming. Do not boil. Remove from heat. Let stand until cooled to lukewarm (105°F to 115°F). In a small bowl combine ½ cup warm water (105°F to 115°F), the yeast, and ¼ teaspoon sugar. Let stand about 5 minutes.

3 Make a well in the center of the flour mixture; add milk mixture, yeast mixture, and the 2 eggs. Using a wooden spoon, stir until well mixed. Stir in as much of the remaining flour as you can with a wooden spoon. Turn out onto a floured surface. Knead in enough remaining flour to make a moderately stiff dough that is smooth and elastic (6 to 8 minutes total).

4 Place dough in a greased bowl, turning once to grease surface. Cover; let rise in a warm place until double in size (1 to 1¼ hours). Punch down dough. Cover and let rise again until double in size (45 to 60 minutes). Punch down dough; cover and let rest for 10 minutes.

5 Preheat oven to 350°F. Grease two 9×5×3-inch loaf pans; set aside. Divide dough in half. Shape into loaves. Place in prepared pans. Cover and let rise until nearly double in size (30 to 45 minutes). In a small bowl beat the 1 egg with 1 tablespoon water. Brush top of loaves with egg mixture. Bake for 45 to 50 minutes or until bread sounds hollow when lightly tapped. Immediately remove bread from pans. Cool on wire racks.

Per serving: 216 cal., 6 g total fat (2 g sat. fat), 31 mg chol., 172 mg sodium, 36 g carbo., 2 g fiber, 6 g pro.

PREP:
40 minutes

RISE:
1 hour
+ 45 minutes + 30 minutes

BAKE:
45 minutes

OVEN:
350°F

MAKES:
2 loaves (24 servings)

Homemade bread topped with a layer of thinly sliced garlic makes this cheesy broiled bread a cut above ordinary garlic breads.

PESTO-GARLIC BREAD

PREP:
45 minutes

RISE:
30 minutes + 30 minutes

BAKE:
10 minutes + 10 minutes

COOL:
30 minutes

BROIL:
2 minutes

OVEN:
400°F

MAKES:
*4 bread rounds
(8 to 10 servings per round)*

2	cups warm water (105°F to 115°F)
2	packages active dry yeast
2	tablespoons sugar
5¾	to 6¼ cups all-purpose flour
2	teaspoons salt
2	tablespoons olive oil
⅔	cup purchased basil pesto
6	to 8 cloves garlic, very thinly sliced
1½	cups shredded Italian four-cheese blend or shredded mozzarella cheese (6 ounces)

1 In a medium bowl whisk together the water, yeast, and sugar. Let stand about 10 minutes or until foamy.

2 Meanwhile, in a large bowl combine 5 cups of the flour and the salt. Make a well in the center of the flour mixture. Pour yeast mixture and olive oil into the well. Stir with a wooden spoon until combined. When mixture becomes too difficult to stir, use floured hands to mix. Turn out dough onto a lightly floured surface. Knead in enough of the remaining flour to make a stiff dough that is smooth and elastic (12 to 15 minutes total).

3 Shape dough into a ball and place in a large greased bowl, turning once to grease surface. Cover and let rise in a warm place until doubled (about 30 minutes). Punch down dough. Divide dough in half. Cover; let rest for 10 minutes.

4 Meanwhile, lightly grease two large baking sheets. Shape dough by gently pulling each portion into a ball, tucking edges under. Place on prepared baking sheets. Flatten each dough round to about 6 inches in diameter. Cover and let rise in a warm place until nearly double (about 30 minutes).

5 Preheat oven to 400°F. Bake bread for 10 minutes. Cover with foil to prevent overbrowning; bake for 10 to 15 minutes more or until bread sounds hollow when lightly tapped. Cool on a wire rack for at least 30 minutes.

6 Preheat broiler. With a long serrated knife, split each loaf in half horizontally. Brush cut side of each bread round evenly with pesto. Top each round evenly with garlic slices. Sprinkle with cheese. Place rounds on baking sheets; broil 4 to 5 inches from the heat for 2 to 3 minutes or until cheese is melted and starts to brown.

Per serving: 135 cal., 6 g total fat (1 g sat. fat), 4 mg chol., 219 mg sodium, 16 g carbo., 0 g fiber, 4 g pro.

These attractive mini breadsticks get their authentic flavor from toasted pine nuts and Parmesan cheese.

GARLIC-CHEESE TWISTS

¼   cup butter or margarine, softened

2   cloves garlic, minced

½   teaspoon dried Italian seasoning, crushed

1   16-ounce loaf frozen bread dough, thawed

2   tablespoons pine nuts, toasted

½   cup finely shredded Parmesan cheese (2 ounces)
    Milk

1 Grease baking sheets; set aside. In a small bowl stir together butter, garlic, and Italian seasoning. Set aside.

2 On a lightly floured surface, roll bread dough into a 12-inch square. (If dough is too elastic, let rest for 5 to 10 minutes before rolling.) Spread butter mixture evenly over dough. Sprinkle with pine nuts, pressing into dough slightly. Sprinkle with cheese.

3 Fold dough into thirds. With a sharp knife or pastry wheel, cut dough crosswise into twenty-four ½-inch-wide strips. Twist each strip once; pinch ends to seal.

4 Place twists about 2 inches apart on prepared baking sheets. Cover and chill for 6 to 24 hours.

5 Preheat oven to 375°F. Lightly brush twists with milk. Bake for 15 to 18 minutes or until golden brown. Serve warm.

Per twist: 81 cal., 4 g total fat (2 g sat. fat), 7 mg chol., 154 mg sodium, 10 g carbo., 0 g fiber, 2 g pro.

PREP:
25 minutes

CHILL:
6 to 24 hours

BAKE:
15 minutes

OVEN:
375°F

MAKES:
24 twists

Serve these savory muffins alongside a steaming bowl of vegetable soup.

ASIAGO TOMATO~MUSHROOM MUFFINS

PREP:
25 minutes

BAKE:
18 minutes

COOL:
5 minutes

OVEN:
400°F

MAKES:
12 muffins

¼ cup oil-packed dried tomatoes

Olive oil

1 cup fresh mushrooms, coarsely chopped

1¾ cups all-purpose flour

½ cup finely shredded Asiago cheese or Romano cheese (2 ounces)

2 tablespoons sugar

2 teaspoons baking powder

½ teaspoon garlic salt

¼ teaspoon baking soda

⅛ teaspoon black pepper

1 beaten egg

¾ cup milk

2 to 3 tablespoons finely shredded Asiago or Romano cheese (optional)

1 Preheat oven to 400°F. Grease twelve 2½-inch muffin cups or coat with nonstick cooking spray; set aside. Drain tomatoes, reserving oil. Chop tomatoes; set aside. Add enough additional olive oil to reserved oil to measure ⅓ cup total.

2 In a medium skillet cook mushrooms in 1 tablespoon of the oil about 5 minutes or until mushrooms are tender and most of the liquid has evaporated. Remove from heat; cool slightly.

3 In a medium bowl stir together flour, the ½ cup Asiago cheese, the sugar, baking powder, garlic salt, baking soda, and pepper. Make a well in the center of the flour mixture; set aside.

4 In a small bowl stir together egg, milk, and remaining oil. Stir in mushrooms and chopped tomatoes. Add egg mixture all at once to flour mixture. Stir just until moistened (batter should be lumpy). Spoon batter into prepared muffin cups, filling each two-thirds full. If desired, sprinkle with the 2 to 3 tablespoons Asiago cheese.

5 Bake for 18 to 20 minutes or until golden brown. Cool in muffin cups on a wire rack for 5 minutes. Remove from muffin cups; cool slightly on a wire rack. Serve warm.

Per muffin: 121 cal., 4 g total fat (2 g sat. fat), 24 mg chol., 177 mg sodium, 16 g carbo., 1 g fiber, 4 g pro.

It only takes three ingredients to whip up these Parmesan cheese-filled rolls. They're great for last-minute entertaining.

PARMESAN CORN BREAD SWIRLS

1   11½-ounce package (8) refrigerated corn bread twists

2   tablespoons bottled Italian salad dressing

⅓   cup finely shredded Parmesan or Romano cheese

1 Preheat oven to 400°F. Grease a baking sheet; set aside. Carefully unroll corn bread twist dough on a sheet of waxed paper. Brush dough lightly with Italian salad dressing; sprinkle with Parmesan or Romano cheese. Re-roll dough. Separate along perforations to make 8 rolls. Place the rolls, cut sides down, on prepared baking sheet.

2 Bake about 12 minutes or until golden brown. Serve warm.

Per swirl: 248 cal., 14 g total fat (6 g sat. fat), 16 mg chol., 730 mg sodium, 19 g carbo., 0 g fiber, 11 g pro.

PREP:
15 minutes

BAKE:
12 minutes

OVEN:
400°F

MAKES:
8 swirls

The simple herbed cheese and nut filling dresses up refrigerated crescent rolls.

CHEESE-GARLIC CRESCENTS

PREP:
15 minutes

BAKE:
11 minutes

OVEN:
375°F

MAKES:
8 crescents

1   8-ounce package (8) refrigerated crescent rolls

¼   cup semi-soft cheese with garlic and herbs

2   tablespoons finely chopped walnuts, toasted
     Nonstick cooking spray
     Milk

1   tablespoon seasoned fine dry bread crumbs

1 Preheat oven to 375°F. Unroll crescent rolls; divide into 8 triangles. In a small bowl stir together cheese and walnuts. Place a rounded measuring teaspoon of the cheese mixture near the center of the wide end of each crescent roll. Roll up, starting at the wide end.

2 Lightly coat a baking sheet with nonstick cooking spray; place rolls, point sides down, on the prepared baking sheet. Brush tops lightly with milk; sprinkle with bread crumbs.

3 Bake about 11 minutes or until bottoms are browned. Serve warm.

Per crescent: 141 cal., 10 g total fat (3 g sat. fat), 6 mg chol., 254 mg sodium, 12 g carbo., 0 g fiber, 3 g pro.

MEATS

For dinner tonight, make some surf and turf—Italian-style. Served on skewers, this shrimp-and-beef combo makes an easy, but impressive, main dish.

STEAK & SHRIMP SKEWERS

PREP:
35 minutes

CHILL:
30 minutes

BROIL:
10 minutes

MAKES:
6 servings

18	fresh or frozen peeled, deveined large shrimp with tails
2	tablespoons olive oil
¼	cup fine dry bread crumbs
1	teaspoon dried parsley
1	clove garlic, minced
⅛	teaspoon salt
⅛	teaspoon black pepper
1	pound beef tenderloin, cut into 1-inch cubes
4	teaspoons olive oil
1	teaspoon dried basil, oregano, and/or thyme, crushed
½	teaspoon salt
½	teaspoon black pepper

1 Thaw shrimp, if frozen. Rinse shrimp; pat dry with paper towels.

2 In a medium bowl toss shrimp with the 2 tablespoons olive oil. In a small bowl combine bread crumbs, parsley, garlic, the ⅛ teaspoon salt, and the ⅛ teaspoon pepper; add to shrimp. Toss to coat. Cover and chill for 30 minutes.

3 Meanwhile, in a medium bowl combine beef cubes, the 4 teaspoons olive oil, the basil, the ½ teaspoon salt, and the ½ teaspoon pepper. Toss meat to coat.

4 On six 12-inch metal skewers, alternately thread shrimp and beef, leaving a ¼-inch space between pieces.

5 Place skewers on the unheated rack of a broiler pan. Broil 4 to 5 inches from the heat about 10 minutes or until shrimp are opaque and meat is medium-rare doneness, turning once halfway through broiling.

Per serving: 258 cal., 14 g total fat (3 g sat. fat), 124 mg chol., 482 mg sodium, 4 g carbo., 0 g fiber, 28 g pro.

Cipollini onions are generally available only in the autumn. If you can't find them, boiling onions, which are about 1 inch in diameter, work well. For easy peeling, drop them in boiling water for 30 seconds.

BEEF KABOBS WITH ORZO

2	tablespoons olive oil
12	cipollini onions or boiling onions, peeled and ends trimmed
12	medium-size fresh cremini mushrooms
1½	pounds boneless beef sirloin steak, cut into 1½-inch cubes
1	large red sweet pepper, cut into 12 pieces
1	8-ounce bottle clear Italian salad dressing
1	recipe Herbed Orzo

PREP:
50 minutes

MARINATE:
6 to 24 hours

GRILL:
12 minutes

MAKES:
4 servings

1 In a large skillet heat olive oil over medium heat. Arrange onions in an even layer in hot oil; cook for 4 to 6 minutes or until browned and just tender, turning once (do not stir). Reduce heat; add mushrooms. Cover and cook for 3 to 5 minutes or until mushrooms are almost tender. Transfer onions and mushrooms to a dish; set aside until cool.

2 Set a large resealable plastic bag in a shallow dish; add onions, mushrooms, beef, and sweet pepper to bag. Pour salad dressing over mixture. Seal bag; turn to coat vegetables and meat. Marinate in the refrigerator for 6 to 24 hours, turning bag occasionally.

3 Drain vegetables and meat, reserving marinade. On four 12- to 14-inch metal skewers, thread beef and vegetables, leaving a ¼-inch space between pieces. Transfer reserved marinade to a saucepan; bring to boiling. Set aside.

4 Place kabobs on the rack of an uncovered grill directly over medium coals. Grill for 12 to 14 minutes or until medium doneness, turning occasionally and brushing with some of the hot marinade during the last 2 minutes of grilling. Serve with Herbed Orzo. Pass remaining hot marinade.

HERBED ORZO: Prepare 1 cup orzo (rosamarina) pasta according to package directions; drain. Stir in 2 tablespoons olive oil and 1 tablespoon snipped fresh herb (such as oregano, marjoram, and/or thyme). Season to taste with salt and black pepper. If desired, sprinkle with freshly grated Parmigiano-Reggiano cheese.

Per serving: 701 cal., 38 g total fat (7 g sat. fat), 103 mg chol., 1,102 mg sodium, 46 g carbo., 3 g fiber, 44 g pro.

Put this beef and vegetable dish together in the skillet, then sit back and relax while it slowly simmers on the range top.

SAUCY BEEF & VEGETABLE SKILLET

PREP:
25 minutes

COOK:
1¼ hours

MAKES:
4 servings

1 pound boneless beef round steak

Salt

Black pepper

1 tablespoon olive oil

2 cups sliced fresh mushrooms

1 large onion, chopped

1 large green sweet pepper, chopped

1 stalk celery, chopped

2 cloves garlic, minced

1 14½-ounce can diced tomatoes, undrained

½ teaspoon dried basil, crushed, or 2 teaspoons snipped fresh basil

¼ teaspoon dried oregano, crushed, or 1 teaspoon snipped fresh oregano

⅛ to ¼ teaspoon crushed red pepper

2 tablespoons grated Parmesan cheese

Hot cooked pasta (optional)

1 Trim fat from meat. Cut meat into 4 serving-size pieces. Season meat with salt and black pepper. In a large skillet cook meat in hot oil until brown, turning to brown evenly. Remove meat from skillet; set aside.

2 Add mushrooms, onion, sweet pepper, celery, and garlic to skillet. Cook until vegetables are nearly tender. Stir in undrained tomatoes, dried herbs (if using), and crushed red pepper. Return meat to skillet, spooning vegetable mixture over meat. Cover and simmer about 1¼ hours or until meat is tender, stirring occasionally. Stir in fresh herbs (if using).

3 Using a slotted spoon, transfer meat to a serving platter. Cook vegetable mixture, uncovered, over medium heat until slightly thickened or until vegetable mixture is the desired consistency. Spoon the vegetable mixture over meat and sprinkle with Parmesan cheese. If desired, serve with hot cooked pasta.

Per serving: 245 cal., 8 g total fat (2 g sat. fat), 66 mg chol., 351 mg sodium, 13 g carbo., 2 g fiber, 30 g pro.

If you think meat loaf takes too long to make, this recipe will change your mind. Making mini loaves cuts down considerably on the baking time.

INDIVIDUAL SICILIAN MEAT LOAVES

1	beaten egg
1	14-ounce jar garlic and onion pasta sauce (1¾ cups)
¼	cup seasoned fine dry bread crumbs
¼	teaspoon salt
¼	teaspoon black pepper
12	ounces ground beef
2	ounces mozzarella cheese
4	thin slices prosciutto or cooked ham (about 2 ounces)
1	9-ounce package refrigerated plain or spinach fettuccine

PREP:
20 minutes

BAKE:
20 minutes

OVEN:
400°F

MAKES:
4 servings

1 Preheat oven to 400°F. In a medium bowl beat egg with a whisk. Stir in ¼ cup of the pasta sauce, the fine dry bread crumbs, salt, and pepper. Add ground beef; mix well.

2 Cut mozzarella cheese into four logs, each measuring approximately 2¼x¾x½ inches. Wrap a slice of prosciutto or ham around each cheese log. Shape one-fourth of the ground beef mixture around each cheese log to form a loaf. Flatten each meat loaf to 1½ inch thickness. Place the four meat loaves in a shallow baking pan.

3 Bake loaves about 20 minutes or until meat is done (160°F).*

4 Meanwhile, cook pasta according to package directions. In a small saucepan heat remaining pasta sauce over medium heat until bubbly.

5 Arrange meat loaves on hot cooked pasta. Spoon sauce over loaves.

Per serving: 651 cal., 31 g total fat (12 g sat. fat), 173 mg chol., 1,132 mg sodium, 55 g carbo., 3 g fiber, 31 g pro.

*NOTE: The internal color of a meat loaf is not a reliable doneness indicator. A beef or pork loaf cooked to 160°F is safe, regardless of color. To measure the doneness of this meat loaf, insert an instant-read thermometer into the center of the meat (not the cheese).

Spaghetti forms the crust for this family-pleasing main-dish pie. For extra-easy crust forming, use a large wooden spoon to press the spaghetti onto the bottom and up the side of the pie plate.

SPAGHETTI PIE

PREP:
30 minutes

BAKE:
20 minutes

OVEN:
350°F

MAKES:
6 servings

4   ounces dried spaghetti

1   tablespoon butter or margarine

1   beaten egg

¼   cup grated Parmesan cheese

8   ounces ground beef

1   medium onion, chopped

1   small green sweet pepper, chopped

1   clove garlic, minced

½   teaspoon fennel seeds, crushed

1   8-ounce can tomato sauce

1   teaspoon dried oregano, crushed

    Nonstick cooking spray

1   cup cottage cheese, drained

½   cup shredded mozzarella cheese (2 ounces)

1 Preheat oven to 350°F. Cook spaghetti according to package directions. Drain well. Return spaghetti to hot pan. Stir butter into hot pasta until melted. Stir in egg and Parmesan cheese; set aside.

2 Meanwhile, in a medium skillet cook ground beef, onion, sweet pepper, garlic, and fennel seeds until meat is brown and onion is tender. Drain off fat. Stir tomato sauce and oregano into beef mixture in skillet; heat through.

3 Coat a 9-inch pie plate with nonstick cooking spray. Press spaghetti mixture onto bottom and up side of pie plate to form a crust. Spread cottage cheese on the crust, spreading it up the side. Spread meat mixture over cottage cheese. Sprinkle with shredded mozzarella cheese.

4 Bake for 20 to 25 minutes or until bubbly and heated through. To serve, cut into wedges.

Per serving: 270 cal., 11 g total fat (6 g sat. fat), 76 mg chol., 500 mg sodium, 20 g carbo., 1 g fiber, 21 g pro.

A scrumptious filling of cream cheese, spinach, and Italian sausage peaks out from marinara-and cheese-covered manicotti in this baked delight.

CANNELLONI

1	8-ounce package dried manicotti shells (14 shells)
8	ounces lean ground beef or bulk Italian sausage
1	cup chopped onion
1	8-ounce package cream cheese, softened
2	beaten eggs
1	10-ounce package frozen chopped spinach, thawed and well drained
1½	cups soft bread crumbs (2 slices bread)
¾	cup shredded mozzarella cheese (3 ounces)
2½	cups Marinara Sauce (see recipe, page 259) or purchased spaghetti sauce or marinara sauce
2	tablespoons grated Parmesan cheese

PREP:
40 minutes

BAKE:
30 minutes

OVEN:
350°F

MAKES:
7 servings

1 Cook manicotti according to package directions. Drain well. Arrange manicotti in a single layer on a piece of greased foil; let stand until cool.

2 Meanwhile, for filling, in a large skillet cook ground beef and onion until meat is brown and onion is tender. Drain off fat. Remove from heat.

3 Stir softened cream cheese and eggs into meat mixture in skillet. Stir in drained spinach, bread crumbs, and mozzarella cheese.

4 Preheat oven to 350°F. Using a small spoon, spoon filling into manicotti shells. Arrange filled shells in a 3-quart rectangular baking dish. Pour Marinara Sauce over the filled shells. Sprinkle with Parmesan cheese.

5 Bake about 30 minutes or until heated through.

Per serving: 482 cal., 27 g total fat (12 g sat. fat), 127 mg chol., 494 mg sodium, 40 g carbo., 4 g fiber, 21 g pro.

This recipe calls for Old-Fashioned Meatballs. If you're crunched for time, try it with your favorite frozen meatballs.

BEEF & SWEET PEPPER PASTA

START TO FINISH:
35 minutes

MAKES:
6 servings

8   ounces dried fettuccine or pappardelle pasta

1   tablespoon olive oil or cooking oil

1   medium fennel bulb, trimmed and cut into thin bite-size strips

1   medium onion, quartered and thinly sliced

2   medium carrots, thinly bias sliced

2   cloves garlic, minced

1   recipe Old-Fashioned Meatballs (see recipe, page 127)

1   26-ounce jar spicy red pepper pasta sauce or mushroom and ripe olive pasta sauce

     Salt

     Black pepper

4   ounces fontina cheese or mozzarella cheese, shredded (1 cup)

½   cup finely shredded Parmesan cheese or Romano cheese (2 ounces)

1 Cook pasta according to package directions just until tender. Drain well. Return pasta to hot saucepan; cover and keep warm.

2 Meanwhile, in a large skillet heat oil over medium heat. Add fennel, onion, carrots, and garlic; cook about 7 minutes or until vegetables are tender. Add vegetable mixture, Old-Fashioned Meatballs, and pasta sauce to pasta; toss to coat. Heat through. Season to taste with salt and pepper. Top individual servings with the fontina cheese and Parmesan cheese.

Per serving: 521 cal., 22 g total fat (9 g sat. fat), 115 mg chol., 907 mg sodium, 45 g carbo., 4 g fiber, 32 g pro.

These spectacular meatballs are chock-full of delicious Italian ingredients. Serve them with your favorite pasta sauce over spaghetti or in meatball sandwiches.

OLD-FASHIONED MEATBALLS

1 egg

¾ cup soft bread crumbs (1 slice)

¼ cup grated Parmesan cheese

¼ cup finely chopped onion

2 tablespoons snipped fresh parsley

1 to 2 cloves garlic, minced

1 teaspoon dried Italian seasoning or ½ teaspoon dried rosemary, crushed

¼ teaspoon salt

¼ teaspoon black pepper

1 pound lean ground beef

PREP:
25 minutes

BAKE:
15 minutes

OVEN:
350°F

MAKES:
4 to 6 servings

1 Preheat oven to 350°F. In a large bowl beat egg with a fork; stir in bread crumbs, Parmesan cheese, onion, parsley, garlic, Italian seasoning or rosemary, salt, and pepper. Add ground beef; mix well. Shape into 28 meatballs, each about 1½ inches in diameter.

2 Arrange meatballs in a 15×10×1-inch baking pan. Bake for 15 to 20 minutes or until done (160°F).* Drain off fat.

Per serving: 253 cal., 14 g total fat (6 g sat. fat), 129 mg chol., 339 mg sodium, 6 g carbo., 1 g fiber, 25 g pro.

*NOTE: The internal color of a meatball is not a reliable doneness indicator. Beef meatballs cooked to 160°F are safe, regardless of color. To measure the doneness of a meatball, insert an instant-read thermometer into the center of the meatball.

TEST KITCHEN TIP: To cook meatballs in a skillet, prepare as directed through step 1. In a large skillet melt 1 tablespoon butter over medium heat. Cook meatballs, half at a time, in hot butter about 10 minutes or until done (160°F),* turning to brown evenly. Use a slotted spoon to remove meatballs from skillet.

A medley of ground beef and sweet pepper over a layer of spinach, ricotta, and mozzarella cheese—all contained in a flaky pastry shell—is irresistibly delicious.

BEEF & SPINACH PIE

PREP:
20 minutes

BAKE:
30 minutes

STAND:
10 minutes

OVEN:
350°F

MAKES:
8 servings

12 ounces lean ground beef

¾ cup chopped red and/or yellow sweet pepper

1 clove garlic, minced

1 cup water

1 6-ounce can Italian-style tomato paste

1 4-ounce can (drained weight) sliced mushrooms, drained

½ teaspoon dried Italian seasoning, crushed

1 10-ounce package frozen chopped spinach, thawed and well drained

¾ cup shredded mozzarella cheese (3 ounces)

⅔ cup light or regular ricotta cheese

½ teaspoon salt

1 baked 9-inch pastry shell*

1 Preheat oven to 350°F. In a large skillet cook beef, sweet pepper, and garlic until meat is brown and sweet pepper is tender. Stir in the water, tomato paste, mushrooms, and Italian seasoning. Bring to boiling; reduce heat. Cover and simmer for 10 minutes.

2 Meanwhile, in a medium bowl stir together spinach, ¼ cup of the mozzarella cheese, the ricotta cheese, and salt. Spoon spinach mixture into baked pastry shell. Top with meat mixture. Cover edge of pastry with foil to prevent overbrowning.

3 Bake for 30 to 35 minutes or until heated through. Remove foil. Top with remaining ½ cup mozzarella cheese. Let stand for 10 minutes before serving.

Per serving: 237 cal., 12 g total fat (4 g sat. fat), 38 mg chol., 635 mg sodium, 16 g carbo., 2 g fiber, 15 g pro.

*NOTE: For a baked pastry shell, bake one 9-inch frozen unbaked deep-dish pastry shell according to package directions. Or prepare and bake 1 folded refrigerated unbaked piecrust (half of a 15-ounce package) according to package directions.

If you're a wine enthusiast, this is a great recipe to try. Serve the same wine with dinner that you use to make the tomato sauce.

SPAGHETTI & PORCINI MEATBALLS

2½ ounces dried porcini mushrooms (2½ cups), well drained

1 cup finely chopped onion

2 cloves garlic, minced

2 teaspoons snipped fresh thyme

1 beaten egg

¼ cup fine dry bread crumbs

1 tablespoon Cabernet Sauvignon or dry red wine

1 pound ground beef or ground veal

3 tablespoons olive oil

4 cups chopped, peeled plum tomatoes (10 to 12 tomatoes)

1 cup Cabernet Sauvignon or dry red wine

2 tablespoons snipped fresh parsley

2 tablespoons snipped fresh thyme

1 teaspoon sugar

1 to 2 tablespoons Cabernet Sauvignon or dry red wine

Hot cooked spaghetti or fettuccine

1 In a medium bowl combine dried mushrooms and enough boiling water to cover. Let stand for 30 minutes; drain. Rinse mushrooms under running water. Drain well, squeezing out excess liquid. Set aside ½ cup of the mushrooms for the sauce. Finely chop remaining mushrooms.

2 Combine chopped mushrooms, ¾ cup of the onion, garlic, the 2 teaspoons thyme, egg, crumbs, the 1 tablespoon wine, and ½ teaspoon salt. Add ground beef; mix well. Shape into 18 meatballs.

3 In a very large skillet heat olive oil over medium-high heat. Add meatballs; cook about 8 minutes or until browned, turning occasionally to brown evenly. Transfer meatballs to a plate. Drain fat from skillet.

4 Add remaining ¼ cup onion, the tomatoes, the 1 cup wine, the parsley, the 2 tablespoons thyme, the sugar, ¼ teaspoon pepper, and the reserved ½ cup mushrooms to the hot skillet; stir well. Bring to boiling; reduce heat. Add the meatballs; simmer, uncovered, about 30 minutes or until desired consistency, gently stirring occasionally to keep meatballs moistened. Splash with the 1 to 2 tablespoons wine just before serving. Serve sauce and meatballs over hot cooked spaghetti. Season to taste with additional salt and black pepper.

Per serving: 549 cal., 19 g total fat (5 g sat. fat), 83 mg chol., 374 mg sodium, 64 g carbo., 5 g fiber, 26 g pro.

PREP:
35 minutes

STAND:
30 minutes

COOK:
8 minutes + 30 minutes

MAKES:
6 servings

You can have a satisfying dinner whenever you like if you keep the ingredients for this baked ("al forno" in Italian) dish on hand. Try kalamata or niçoise olives for an interesting flavor punch.

BAKED PENNE WITH MEAT SAUCE

PREP:
30 minutes

BAKE:
15 minutes + 5 minutes

OVEN:
375°F

MAKES:
6 servings

8	ounces dried penne pasta
1	14-ounce can whole Italian-style tomatoes, undrained
½	of a 6-ounce can (⅓ cup) Italian-style tomato paste
¼	cup dry red wine or tomato juice
½	teaspoon sugar
½	teaspoon dried oregano, crushed, or 2 teaspoons snipped fresh oregano
¼	teaspoon black pepper
1	pound lean ground beef
½	cup chopped onion
¼	cup sliced pitted ripe olives
½	cup shredded reduced-fat mozzarella cheese (2 ounces)

1 Preheat oven to 375°F. Cook pasta according to package directions. Drain well.

2 Meanwhile, in a blender or food processor combine undrained tomatoes, tomato paste, wine or tomato juice, sugar, dried oregano (if using), and pepper. Cover and blend or process until smooth. Set aside.

3 In a large skillet cook ground beef and onion until meat is brown. Drain off fat. Stir tomato mixture into meat mixture in skillet. Bring to boiling; reduce heat. Cover and simmer for 10 minutes. Stir in cooked pasta, fresh oregano (if using), and olives.

4 Divide the pasta mixture among six 10- to 12-ounce individual casseroles. Bake, covered, for 15 minutes. (Or spoon all of the pasta mixture into a 2-quart casserole. Bake, covered, for 30 minutes.) Sprinkle with mozzarella cheese. Bake, uncovered, about 5 minutes more or until cheese is melted.

Per serving: 339 cal., 11 g total fat (4 g sat. fat), 59 mg chol., 349 mg sodium, 33 g carbo., 3 g fiber, 24 g pro.

These messy, but tasty, sandwiches are a hit with children. Crisp carrot sticks make a healthful and sure-to-please side dish.

SLOPPY JOES ITALIAN-STYLE

12	ounces lean ground beef
1	8-ounce can tomato sauce
1	tablespoon dried minced onion
¼	teaspoon dried oregano, crushed
¼	teaspoon dried basil, crushed
8	3-inch hard rolls
1	cup shredded mozzarella cheese (4 ounces)
¼	cup grated Parmesan cheese

PREP:
30 minutes

BAKE:
20 minutes

OVEN:
400°F

MAKES:
8 servings

1 Preheat oven to 400°F. In a large skillet cook ground beef until brown. Drain off fat. Stir tomato sauce, dried minced onion, oregano, and basil into beef in skillet. Bring to boiling; reduce heat. Cover and simmer for 15 minutes.

2 Meanwhile, cut a thin slice from the top of each roll; set tops of rolls aside. Scoop out insides of rolls, leaving ½-inch-thick shells. Set shells aside. Reserve scooped-out bread for another use.

3 Divide beef mixture evenly among roll shells. Top with mozzarella and Parmesan cheese. Cover with roll tops. Wrap each roll in foil. Place on a large baking sheet. Bake about 20 minutes or until heated through.

Per serving: 291 cal., 9 g total fat (4 g sat. fat), 38 mg chol., 580 mg sodium, 32 g carbo., 2 g fiber, 18 g pro.

This old-time favorite includes a thick, full-bodied meat sauce known in Italy as a "ragu."

BEEFY SPAGHETTI CASSEROLE

PREP:
30 minutes

BAKE:
40 minutes

STAND:
5 minutes

OVEN:
350°F

MAKES:
4 to 6 servings

8   ounces dried spaghetti

8   ounces ground beef

½   cup chopped onion

½   cup chopped green sweet pepper

1   14½-ounce can diced tomatoes, undrained

1   10¾-ounce can condensed tomato soup

½   teaspoon black pepper

2   cups shredded cheddar cheese (8 ounces)

4   slices bacon, crisp-cooked, drained, and crumbled

1 Preheat oven to 350°F. Cook spaghetti according to package directions; drain and set aside.

2 In a large skillet cook and stir ground beef, onion, and sweet pepper until beef is brown; drain off fat. Stir undrained tomatoes, tomato soup, and black pepper into meat mixture in skillet. Bring just to boiling. Add 1½ cups of the shredded cheese, stirring until melted.

3 Grease a 2-quart casserole; set aside. Add cooked spaghetti and the bacon to the tomato mixture; toss to combine. Transfer mixture to prepared casserole.

4 Bake, covered, about 40 minutes or until bubbly and heated through. Uncover; sprinkle with remaining ½ cup cheese. Let stand for 5 to 10 minutes or until cheese is melted.

Per serving: 675 cal., 31 g total fat (16 g sat. fat), 100 mg chol., 1,007 mg sodium, 61 g carbo., 3 g fiber, 35 g pro.

Try these sophisticated basil-scented burgers at your next picnic or grill-out. They're sure to be a big hit!

ITALIAN-STYLE BURGERS

½	cup fine dry bread crumbs
½	cup finely chopped onion
⅓	cup milk
2	tablespoons grated Parmesan cheese
1	tablespoon dried basil, crushed
½	teaspoon garlic salt
¼	teaspoon black pepper
1½	pounds lean ground beef
8	slices provolone cheese
8	kaiser rolls with sesame seeds, split and toasted
	Lettuce (optional)
	Yellow and/or red tomato slices (optional)
	Purchased pasta sauce, warmed (optional)

1 In a medium bowl stir together bread crumbs, onion, milk, Parmesan cheese, basil, garlic salt, and pepper. Add meat; mix well. Shape meat mixture into eight ¾-inch-thick patties. Place patties in a shallow container. Cover and chill for 1 hour.

2 Place patties on the rack of an uncovered grill directly over medium coals. Grill for 14 to 18 minutes or until done (160°F),* turning once halfway through grilling and topping each burger with a cheese slice for the last 1 minute of grilling.

3 Serve burgers on rolls. If desired, top with lettuce, tomatoes, and/or pasta sauce.

Per serving: 464 cal., 22 g total fat (10 g sat. fat), 74 mg chol., 823 mg sodium, 36 g carbo., 2 g fiber, 29 g pro.

*NOTE: The internal color of a burger is not a reliable doneness indicator. A beef patty cooked to 160°F is safe, regardless of color. To measure the doneness of a patty, insert an instant-read thermometer through the side of the patty to a depth of 2 to 3 inches.

PREP:
15 minutes

CHILL:
1 hour

GRILL:
14 minutes

MAKES:
8 servings

Store-bought refrigerated crescent rolls make this baked dish indulgent and delicious, and also easy and fun to make.

CRESCENT CASSEROLE

PREP:
25 minutes

BAKE:
20 minutes

OVEN:
375°F

MAKES:
4 to 6 servings

1	pound lean ground beef
¼	cup chopped onion
1	cup purchased spaghetti sauce
1½	cups shredded mozzarella or Monterey Jack cheese (6 ounces)
½	cup dairy sour cream
1	4-ounce package (4) refrigerated crescent rolls
1	tablespoon butter or margarine, melted
¼	cup grated Parmesan cheese

1 Preheat oven to 375°F. In a large skillet cook ground beef and onion until meat is brown. Drain off fat. Stir spaghetti sauce into meat mixture in skillet; heat through. Spread meat mixture in an ungreased 2-quart casserole.

2 Meanwhile, in a medium bowl combine mozzarella cheese and sour cream; spoon over meat mixture in casserole.

3 Unroll crescent rolls; separate into triangles. Place triangles over the cheese layer. Brush with melted butter; sprinkle with Parmesan cheese. Bake for 20 to 25 minutes or until top is deep golden brown.

Per serving: 553 cal., 37 g total fat (18 g sat. fat), 127 mg chol., 946 mg sodium, 20 g carbo., 2 g fiber, 35 g pro.

This time-tested dish brings together meatballs, tomatoes, and pasta—three Italian favorites. Be sure to pass plenty of freshly grated Parmesan cheese so diners can sprinkle it on.

SPAGHETTI & MEATBALLS

1	large onion, finely chopped
1	carrot, finely chopped
1	stalk celery, finely chopped
3	large cloves garlic, minced
2	tablespoons olive oil
2	15-ounce cans tomato sauce
1	cup dry red wine
3	tablespoons finely snipped fresh parsley
10	fresh basil leaves, torn
1	tablespoon dried Italian seasoning, crushed
1	tablespoon tomato paste
1	teaspoon sugar
½	teaspoon crushed red pepper (optional)
3	bay leaves
1	recipe Beef-Sausage Meatballs
	Hot cooked spaghetti

1 In a 4-quart Dutch oven cook onion, carrot, celery, and garlic in hot oil about 15 minutes or until tender, stirring occasionally. Stir in 1 cup water, the tomato sauce, red wine, parsley, basil, Italian seasoning, tomato paste, sugar, crushed red pepper (if desired), and bay leaves.

2 Bring sauce to boiling; reduce heat. Simmer sauce, uncovered, for 45 to 60 minutes or until desired consistency, stirring occasionally. Discard bay leaves. Season to taste with salt and pepper.

3 Gently drop Beef-Sausage Meatballs, one at a time, into sauce; stir gently. Cover and cook about 30 minutes or until meatballs are done (160°F).* Serve sauce and meatballs over hot cooked spaghetti.

BEEF-SAUSAGE MEATBALLS: In a large bowl combine ¼ cup milk; 1 slightly beaten egg; ½ cup fine dry bread crumbs; ¼ cup finely snipped fresh parsley; ¼ cup freshly grated Parmesan cheese (1 ounce); 1 teaspoon dried Italian seasoning, crushed; ½ teaspoon salt; and ¼ teaspoon freshly ground black pepper. Add 1 pound ground beef and 12 ounces bulk Italian sausage; mix well. Form into meatballs, each about 1½ inches in diameter. In a large skillet heat 2 tablespoons olive oil over medium heat. Add meatballs; cook about 10 minutes or until browned, turning occasionally.

Per serving: 757 cal., 34 g total fat (11 g sat. fat), 129 mg chol., 1,681 mg sodium, 65 g carbo., 4 g fiber, 36 g pro.

PREP:
35 minutes

COOK:
15 minutes + 45 minutes + 30 minutes

MAKES:
6 to 8 servings

*NOTE: The internal color of a meatball is not a reliable doneness indicator. A beef or sausage meatball cooked to 160°F is safe, regardless of color. To measure the doneness of a meatball, insert an instant-read thermometer into the center of the meatball.

For a more mellow version of this savory pie, use ground beef. If you're in the mood for something with a little more kick, use Italian sausage.

MORE-THAN-PIZZA PIE

PREP:
20 minutes

BAKE:
25 minutes

OVEN:
425°F

MAKES:
6 servings

1	15-ounce package folded refrigerated unbaked piecrusts (2 crusts)
1	pound ground beef or bulk Italian sausage
2	8-ounce cans pizza sauce
1	10-ounce package frozen chopped spinach, thawed and well drained
2	eggs
1	cup ricotta cheese or cottage cheese
½	cup grated Parmesan cheese
½	teaspoon dried Italian seasoning, crushed

1 Preheat oven to 425°F. Let piecrusts stand at room temperature for 15 minutes as directed on package.

2 Meanwhile, for meat filling, in a large skillet cook meat until brown. Drain off fat. Stir pizza sauce and spinach into meat in skillet. Set aside.

3 In a medium bowl beat eggs with a fork; stir in ricotta cheese, Parmesan cheese, and Italian seasoning. Line a 9-inch pie plate with one of the piecrusts. Spoon ricotta mixture into crust. Top with meat filling. Place remaining piecrust over meat filling. Seal and flute edge. Cut slits in top crust to allow steam to escape.

4 Bake about 25 minutes or until crust is golden brown.

Per serving: 715 cal., 48 g total fat (20 g sat. fat), 173 mg chol., 844 mg sodium, 43 g carbo., 1 g fiber, 26 g pro.

Mafalda is a curly-edged pasta that looks like a slim lasagna noodle. It is available in long strips or short pieces.

MEATBALLS & MAFALDA

1½   cups dried mafalda (mini lasagna) noodles* (about 4 ounces)

1   14½-ounce can Italian-style stewed tomatoes, undrained

1   8-ounce can tomato sauce

¼   cup dry red wine

2   tablespoons dry onion soup mix

½   teaspoon dried oregano, crushed

     Dash black pepper

16   frozen Italian-style cooked meatballs (½ ounce each)

½   cup shredded mozzarella cheese (2 ounces)

1 Preheat oven to 350°F. Cook mafalda according to package directions; drain. Meanwhile, in a large saucepan combine undrained stewed tomatoes, tomato sauce, red wine, dry onion soup mix, oregano, and pepper. Stir in meatballs. Bring mixture to boiling over medium heat. Stir in cooked mafalda.

2 Spoon mixture into an ungreased 1½-quart casserole. Bake, covered, for 20 minutes. Sprinkle with cheese. Bake, uncovered, about 5 minutes more or until cheese melts.

Per serving: 389 cal., 16 g total fat (7 g sat. fat), 45 mg chol., 1,308 mg sodium, 39 g carbo., 4 g fiber, 18 g pro.

*NOTE: If you purchase the longer mafalda pasta, break into 1- to 1½-inch pieces before measuring.

PREP:
25 minutes

BAKE:
20 minutes + 5 minutes

OVEN:
350°F

MAKES:
4 servings

Who doesn't love baked pasta? This satisfying recipe calls for all the best ingredients—luscious cheese, tangy tomato sauce, and hearty meatballs.

THREE-CHEESE MEATBALL CASSEROLE

PREP:
30 minutes

BAKE:
30 minutes + 10 minutes + 5 minutes

OVEN:
350°F

MAKES:
8 to 10 servings

16   ounces dried cut ziti or penne pasta

1   26-ounce jar tomato-base pasta sauce

1   16-ounce package frozen Italian-style cooked meatballs (32), thawed

1   15-ounce can Italian-style tomato sauce

1   15-ounce carton ricotta cheese

½   cup grated Parmesan cheese

2   cups shredded mozzarella cheese (8 ounces)

1 Preheat oven to 350°F. Cook pasta according to package directions. Drain well. Return pasta to hot saucepan. Stir in pasta sauce, meatballs, and tomato sauce. Transfer to a 3-quart rectangular baking dish. Bake, covered, for 30 minutes.

2 Meanwhile, in a small bowl combine ricotta cheese and Parmesan cheese. Uncover pasta mixture and spoon ricotta mixture in mounds over pasta mixture. Cover loosely; bake about 10 minutes more or until heated through. Top with mozzarella cheese. Bake, uncovered, for 5 minutes more.

Per serving: 611 cal., 28 g total fat (14 g sat. fat), 86 mg chol., 1,441 mg sodium, 57 g carbo., 7 g fiber, 33 g pro.

This grilled delight makes an eyecatching presentation. For an elegant twist to the recipe, use pine nuts instead of almonds.

SPINACH PORK SPIRALS

1   12- to 16-ounce pork tenderloin

1½   cups loosely packed fresh spinach leaves

⅓   cup ricotta cheese

¼   cup finely shredded mozzarella cheese (1 ounce)

¼   cup chopped almonds, toasted

3   tablespoons bottled clear Italian salad dressing

2   tablespoons finely shredded Parmesan cheese

1   tablespoon olive oil

   Black pepper

PREP:
25 minutes

GRILL:
30 minutes

STAND:
10 minutes

MAKES:
4 servings

1 Trim fat from pork. Using a sharp knife, make a lengthwise cut down the center of the pork tenderloin, cutting to within ½ inch of the other side. Spread meat open. Place knife in the "v" of the first cut. With the knife positioned horizontal to the cut surface, cut away from the first cut to within ½ inch of the other side of the meat. Repeat on opposite side of the "v." Spread these sections open to lay meat flat. Place meat between two pieces of plastic wrap. Working from the center to the edges, pound lightly with the flat side of a meat mallet to form an 11×7-inch rectangle. Fold in the narrow ends as necessary to make an even rectangle. Remove plastic wrap.

2 Remove stems from spinach leaves. Layer leaves on top of pounded side of pork, leaving a 1-inch-wide space along one of the long sides. In a small bowl combine the ricotta, mozzarella cheese, almonds, 2 tablespoons of the salad dressing, and the Parmesan cheese. Spread ricotta mixture over spinach leaves. Roll up pork, beginning at a long side. Using 100%-cotton string, tie at 1½-inch intervals. Brush all surfaces of meat with the olive oil; sprinkle with pepper.

3 Prepare grill for indirect grilling. Test for medium-high heat above the pan. Place meat on the grill rack over drip pan. Cover and grill for 30 to 40 minutes or until done (160°F) and juices run clear, brushing with the remaining 1 tablespoon salad dressing during the last 10 minutes of grilling. Transfer meat to serving platter; cover with foil and let stand for 10 minutes before slicing. Remove strings from pork. Slice pork to serve.

Per serving: 333 cal., 21 g total fat (7 g sat. fat), 82 mg chol., 568 mg sodium, 5 g carbo., 1 g fiber, 30 g pro.

Choose fennel bulbs that are smooth and firm, without cracks or brown spots. The stalks should be crisp, and the leaves should be bright green and fresh looking.

PORK MEDALLIONS WITH FENNEL & PANCETTA

START TO FINISH:
30 minutes

MAKES:
4 servings

1   12-ounce pork tenderloin

¼   cup all-purpose flour

   Dash salt

   Dash black pepper

2   tablespoons olive oil

2   ounces pancetta or bacon, chopped

2   fennel bulbs, trimmed* and sliced crosswise

1   small onion, thinly sliced

2   cloves garlic, minced

2   tablespoons lemon juice

½   cup whipping cream

2   tablespoons snipped fresh flat-leaf parsley

1 Trim fat from meat. Cut meat crosswise into 1-inch-thick slices. Place each slice between two pieces of plastic wrap. Pound meat lightly with the flat side of a meat mallet to ¼-inch thickness. Remove plastic wrap. In a shallow dish combine flour, salt, and pepper. Dip meat slices in flour mixture to coat.

2 In a heavy very large skillet heat olive oil over high heat. Cook meat, half at a time, in hot oil for 2 to 3 minutes or until meat is slightly pink in center, turning once. (Add more oil during cooking, if necessary.) Remove meat from skillet; set aside.

3 For sauce, in the same skillet cook pancetta over medium-high heat until crisp. Add fennel, onion, and garlic; cook for 3 to 5 minutes or until crisp-tender. Add lemon juice; stir in whipping cream. Bring to boiling; return meat to skillet. Cook until meat is heated through and sauce is slightly thickened.

4 Transfer meat to a serving platter. Spoon sauce over meat. Sprinkle with parsley.

Per serving: 367 cal., 25 g total fat (10 g sat. fat), 106 mg chol., 375 mg sodium, 13 g carbo., 2 g fiber, 22 g pro.

*NOTE: Cut off and discard upper stalks of fennel bulb. Remove any wilted outer layers of stalks. Wash fennel and cut in half lengthwise. Remove core and discard.

This recipe calls for fennel seeds and a fennel bulb. Fennel seeds lend a zesty licorice flavor to the roast, while the bulb pieces caramelize during baking, sweetening the vegetable mixture.

ITALIAN PORK ROAST

2	tablespoons fennel seeds, crushed
2	tablespoons dried parsley, crushed
4	teaspoons dried Italian seasoning, crushed
1½	teaspoons garlic salt
1	teaspoon black pepper
1	3½- to 4-pound boneless pork shoulder roast
1	tablespoon cooking oil
¾	cup water
8	carrots, quartered
8	small potatoes, peeled
1	large fennel bulb, trimmed* and cut into wedges
½	cup cold water
¼	cup all-purpose flour
	Salt
	Black pepper

1 Preheat oven to 325°F. In a small bowl combine fennel seeds, dried parsley, Italian seasoning, garlic salt, and the 1 teaspoon pepper; set aside. Untie pork roast, if necessary, and unroll. Trim fat from meat. Sprinkle fennel seed mixture evenly over meat; rub in with your fingers. Retie roast, if necessary, with 100%-cotton-kitchen string. In an oven-going 5- to 6-quart Dutch oven brown pork in hot oil, turning to brown on all sides. Drain off fat.

2 Carefully pour the ¾ cup water over meat. Cover and roast for 1½ hours. Arrange carrots, potatoes, and fennel wedges around roast in Dutch oven. Cover and roast for 50 to 60 minutes more or until meat and vegetables are tender, adding additional water if necessary. Transfer meat to a serving platter; cover with foil. Using a slotted spoon, transfer vegetables to a serving bowl; cover and keep warm.

3 For gravy, strain cooking juices into a 2-cup glass measuring cup. Skim fat from juices; measure juices. If necessary, add enough water to measure 1½ cups total liquid. Return juices to Dutch oven. Cook over medium-high heat until bubbly. Combine the ½ cup cold water and the flour, stirring until smooth. Gradually add flour mixture to the hot pan juices, whisking until smooth and bubbly. Cook and stir for 1 minute more. Season to taste with salt and additional pepper. Serve gravy with roast.

Per serving: 431 cal., 14 g total fat (4 g sat. fat), 128 mg chol., 441 mg sodium, 32 g carbo., 5 g fiber, 43 g pro.

*NOTE: Cut off and discard upper stalks of fennel bulb. Remove any wilted outer layers of stalks. Wash fennel and cut lengthwise into quarters. Remove core and discard.

PREP:
45 minutes

ROAST:
1½ hours + 50 minutes

OVEN:
325°F

MAKES:
8 servings

This one-skillet recipe features winter squash and zucchini. Make this hearty dish for your family on a chilly autumn day.

PORK CHOP & SQUASH SKILLET

START TO FINISH:
30 minutes

MAKES:
4 servings

1	pound boneless pork sirloin chops, cut ½ inch thick
2	tablespoons all-purpose flour
½	teaspoon salt
½	teaspoon black pepper
2	tablespoons olive oil
1	pound winter squash (such as butternut or banana), peeled, seeded, and cut into 1-inch cubes (2 cups)
1	medium onion, cut into thin wedges
1	tablespoon snipped fresh oregano or 1 teaspoon dried oregano, crushed
¼	cup chicken broth
¼	cup orange juice
2	medium zucchini, quartered lengthwise and cut into 1-inch pieces (about 2½ cups)

1 Trim fat from pork; if necessary, cut pork into four serving-size portions. Sprinkle both sides of each portion with flour, salt, and pepper.

2 In a large skillet heat olive oil over medium-high heat. Brown pork in hot oil for 4 minutes, turning once. Add winter squash and onion; sprinkle with dried oregano, if using. Pour chicken broth and orange juice over vegetables and meat. Bring to boiling; reduce heat. Cover and simmer for 10 minutes.

3 Add zucchini. Cover and cook about 5 minutes more or until pork is tender and no longer pink. Transfer pork to a serving platter.

4 Stir fresh oregano, if using, into vegetables. Serve vegetables with pork.

Per serving: 276 cal., 12 g total fat (3 g sat. fat), 71 mg chol., 417 mg sodium, 17 g carbo., 2 g fiber, 26 g pro.

These zesty pork meatballs, seasoned with chili sauce, are served over a bed of hot noodles for a satisfying, stick-to-the-ribs meal.

FEISTY PORK MEATBALLS

Nonstick cooking spray

1 tablespoon finely chopped, drained canned whole cherry pepper (1 pepper) or pepperoncini salad peppers

¼ cup bottled chili sauce

¼ cup seasoned fine dry bread crumbs

2 tablespoons finely chopped onion

1 tablespoon grated Parmesan cheese or Romano cheese

1½ teaspoons fennel seeds, crushed

1 pound very lean ground pork

1 26- or 27-ounce jar chunky-style pasta sauce

¼ cup chopped, drained canned whole cherry peppers (4 peppers) or pepperoncini salad peppers

Hot cooked wide noodles

1 Preheat oven to 350°F. Lightly coat a 15×10×1 inch baking pan with nonstick cooking spray; set aside. In a large bowl combine the 1 tablespoon finely chopped pepper, the chili sauce, bread crumbs, onion, cheese, and fennel seeds. Add pork; mix well. Shape pork mixture into 36 meatballs. Place in prepared baking pan.

2 Bake, uncovered, for 20 to 25 minutes or until done (160°F).* Remove from oven; drain off fat.

3 Meanwhile, in a medium saucepan heat the pasta sauce until bubbly. Add baked meatballs and the ¼ cup chopped peppers; heat through. Serve over hot cooked noodles.

Per serving: 294 cal., 9 g total fat (3 g sat. fat), 62 mg chol., 993 mg sodium, 38 g carbo., 2 g fiber, 16 g pro.

*NOTE: The internal color of a meatball is not a reliable doneness indicator. Pork meatballs cooked to 160°F are safe, regardless of color. To measure the doneness of a meatball, insert an instant-read thermometer into the center of the meatball.

PREP:
20 minutes

BAKE:
20 minutes

OVEN:
350°F

MAKES:
6 servings

A slightly spicy green olive topper accents these Italian herb-infused grilled burgers.

OLIVE-TOPPED PORK BURGERS

PREP:
15 minutes

GRILL:
14 minutes + 1 minute

MAKES:
4 servings

1	pound ground pork
1¼	teaspoons dried Italian seasoning, crushed
¼	teaspoon salt
¼	teaspoon black pepper
2	ounces fontina cheese or mozzarella cheese, thinly sliced
½	cup pitted green olives, coarsely chopped
1	teaspoon olive oil
	Dash crushed red pepper

1 In a large bowl combine ground pork, 1 teaspoon of the Italian seasoning, the salt, and black pepper; mix well. Form mixture into four ¾-inch-thick patties.

2 Place patties on the rack of an uncovered grill directly over medium coals. Grill for 14 to 18 minutes or until done (160°F)* and juices run clear, turning once halfway through grilling. Top burgers with cheese. Grill for 1 to 2 minutes more or until cheese begins to melt.

3 Meanwhile, in a small bowl combine olives, olive oil, crushed red pepper, and remaining ¼ teaspoon Italian seasoning. Serve burgers with olive mixture.

Per serving: 219 cal., 16 g total fat (7 g sat. fat), 69 mg chol., 706 mg sodium, 1 g carbo., 0 g fiber, 18 g pro.

*NOTE: The internal color of a burger is not a reliable doneness indicator. A pork patty cooked to 160°F is safe, regardless of color. To measure the doneness of a patty, insert an instant-read thermometer through the side of the patty to a depth of 2 to 3 inches.

Your family will be delightfully surprised when they bite into these Italian-style cheese-stuffed pork sausage burgers.

PROVOLONE-STUFFED BURGERS

¾ cup shredded provolone cheese or mozzarella cheese (2 ounces)

3 tablespoons tomato paste

2 tablespoons snipped fresh basil or oregano or 2 teaspoons dried basil or oregano, crushed

1 clove garlic, minced

1½ pounds bulk pork sausage

2 tablespoons finely shredded Parmesan cheese

PREP:
25 minutes

GRILL:
20 minutes

MAKES:
4 servings

1 In a small bowl combine provolone, tomato paste, basil, and garlic. Shape pork sausage into eight ¼-inch-thick patties. Divide cheese mixture evenly among 4 of the patties, placing cheese mixture in center of each patty and leaving a ½-inch border around the filling. Top with remaining patties; press edges to seal.

2 Prepare grill for indirect grilling. Test for medium heat above drip pan. Place burgers on grill rack over drip pan. Cover and grill for 20 to 24 minutes or until meat is done (160°F),* sprinkling Parmesan cheese over burgers for the last minute of grilling.

Per serving: 673 cal., 55 g total fat (21 g sat. fat), 149 mg chol., 1,556 mg sodium, 4 g carbo., 0 g fiber, 38 g pro.

*NOTE: The internal color of a burger is not a reliable doneness indicator. A pork sausage patty cooked to 160°F is safe, regardless of color. To measure the doneness of a patty, insert an instant-read thermometer through the side of the patty to a depth of 2 to 3 inches.

Visit the Italian market in your town—most larger communities have one—for fresh, locally made Italian sausage. This recipe uses the sweet version, but hot sausage makes a great alternative for spicy food lovers.

TOMATO-PEPPER SAUCE WITH SAUSAGES

START TO FINISH:
35 minutes

MAKES:
6 servings

1 pound sweet Italian sausage links, cut into ½-inch pieces

2 tablespoons olive oil

1 yellow sweet pepper, cut into bite-size strips

1 red sweet pepper, cut into bite-size strips

1 cup chopped onion

2 cloves garlic, minced

½ cup dry red wine

1 28-ounce can Italian plum tomatoes in puree, undrained, crushed

3 tablespoons tomato paste

1 teaspoon sugar

Salt

Black pepper

Hot cooked pasta

1 In a 4-quart Dutch oven cook sausage pieces until brown, stirring occasionally. Remove from Dutch oven; set aside. Discard drippings.

2 Heat olive oil in same Dutch oven over medium heat. Add sweet peppers, onion, and garlic. Cook about 5 minutes or until tender, stirring occasionally. Carefully add wine. Bring to boiling; reduce heat. Simmer, uncovered, about 5 minutes or until wine is nearly evaporated, Stir in undrained tomatoes, tomato paste, sugar, and cooked sausage pieces. Bring sauce to boiling, stirring to mix well; reduce heat. Simmer, uncovered, about 10 minutes or until sauce is desired consistency, stirring occasionally. Season to taste with salt and black pepper. Serve sauce over hot cooked pasta.

Per serving: 560 cal., 22 g total fat (8 g sat. fat), 51 mg chol., 496 mg sodium, 60 g carbo., 5 g fiber, 20 g pro.

Smoked sausage combines with roasted red peppers for a smoky-sweet flavor. The sausage is already cooked when you buy it, making this pasta bake a breeze to prepare.

SMOKED SAUSAGE PASTA BAKE

12 ounces dried cavatelli or rotini pasta

1 26- to 28-ounce jar spicy tomato pasta sauce

6 ounces cooked smoked sausage, halved lengthwise and sliced

¾ cup bottled roasted red sweet peppers, drained and coarsely chopped

1 cup shredded provolone cheese or mozzarella cheese (4 ounces)

PREP:
25 minutes

BAKE:
15 minutes

OVEN:
375°F

MAKES:
4 servings

1 Preheat oven to 375°F. Cook the pasta according to package directions; drain well. Return pasta to pan. Stir pasta sauce, sausage, and roasted peppers into pasta, tossing gently to coat.

2 Spoon pasta mixture into four greased 14- to 16-ounce individual casseroles. Sprinkle with cheese. Bake for 15 to 20 minutes or until cheese is melted and pasta mixture is heated through.

Per serving: 654 cal., 25 g total fat (12 g sat. fat), 38 mg chol., 995 mg sodium, 77 g carbo., 6 g fiber, 26 g pro.

Served with pasta and the melange of colorful vegetables, these kabobs are real show-stoppers!

GRILLED MEATBALL KABOBS

PREP:
40 minutes

SOAK:
1 hour

GRILL:
15 minutes

MAKES:
6 servings

1 medium onion, cut into thin wedges

1 medium green sweet pepper, cut into bite-size strips

1 medium zucchini, cut into 1-inch pieces

½ of a small eggplant, peeled and cut into 1-inch pieces

⅓ cup olive oil

¼ cup balsamic vinegar

3 cloves garlic, minced

¾ teaspoon dried Italian seasoning, crushed

1 recipe Sausage-Beef Meatballs

8 ounces dried linguine or fettuccini

1 Soak six 12-inch wooden skewers in water for 1 hour. Tear off a 36×18-inch piece of heavy foil; fold in half to form an 18-inch square.

2 In a large bowl combine onion, sweet pepper, zucchini, and eggplant. In a small bowl whisk together olive oil, balsamic vinegar, garlic, Italian seasoning, ¾ teaspoon salt, and ½ teaspoon black pepper. Pour half of the oil mixture over vegetables. Reserve remaining oil mixture. Place vegetable mixture in center of foil. Bring up two opposite edges of foil; seal with a double fold. Fold remaining edges together to completely enclose vegetables, leaving space for steam to build. Thread Sausage-Beef Meatballs onto skewers, leaving a ¼-inch space between meatballs.

3 Prepare grill for indirect grilling. Test for medium heat above the drip pan. Place vegetable packet directly over coals. Place skewers on grill rack over drip pan. Cover and grill for 15 to 20 minutes or until meatballs are cooked through and vegetables are tender, turning vegetable packet once. (Remove kabobs and vegetables as they are done.)

4 Meanwhile, cook pasta according to package directions. Drain pasta; return to hot saucepan. Carefully open vegetable packet; add to pasta along with reserved oil mixture. Toss to combine. Serve with kabobs.

SAUSAGE-BEEF MEATBALLS: In a large bowl beat 1 egg with a fork; stir in 1 slightly beaten egg, ⅓ cup seasoned fine dry bread crumbs, ¼ cup grated Parmesan cheese, 2 tablespoons snipped fresh flat-leaf parsley, 2 teaspoons dried Italian seasoning, ¼ teaspoon salt, and ¼ teaspoon garlic powder. Add 12 ounces bulk hot or sweet Italian sausage and 8 ounces lean ground beef; mix well. Form meat mixture into 30 meatballs.

Per serving: 563 cal., 31 g total fat (9 g sat. fat), 100 mg chol., 947 mg sodium, 43 g carbo., 3 g fiber, 24 g pro.

Vary the spiciness of this elegant dish by the type of sausage you use. Mild sausage will appeal to youngsters, while hot sausage will please those who like their food with plenty of zip.

SAUSAGE & PORCINI BOLOGNESE

8	cups water
2¼	teaspoons salt
1	ounce dried porcini mushrooms
1	bunch escarole, core removed, or 8 cups fresh spinach
12	ounces bulk pork sausage
½	cup chopped onion
6	cloves garlic, minced
1	tablespoon snipped fresh sage
⅓	cup dry white wine
¾	cup beef broth
½	cup purchased chunky marinara sauce
1	tablespoon snipped fresh parsley
1	tablespoon olive oil
¼	teaspoon freshly ground black pepper
2	9-ounce packages refrigerated fettuccine
⅓	cup coarsely shaved Parmesan cheese

START TO FINISH:
50 minutes

MAKES:
6 servings

1 In a 4-quart Dutch oven bring the 8 cups water and 2 teaspoons of the salt to boiling. Place mushrooms in a small bowl; add 1 cup of the boiling water. Let stand for 15 minutes. Meanwhile, add escarole or spinach to the remaining boiling water. Return water to boiling; immediately drain greens in a colander and rinse with cold water. Drain well, pressing out excess liquid; coarsely chop greens and set aside. Drain mushrooms, reserving 2 tablespoons of the soaking liquid. Chop the mushrooms; set mushrooms and reserved soaking liquid aside.

2 In a large skillet cook sausage, onion, garlic, and sage until meat is browned, stirring to break up sausage. Drain off fat. Stir in wine and reserved mushroom liquid. Bring to boiling; reduce heat. Boil gently, uncovered, about 7 minutes or until most of the liquid is evaporated. Add broth, marinara sauce, parsley, olive oil, pepper, and remaining ¼ teaspoon salt. Bring to boiling; reduce heat. Simmer, uncovered, for 2 minutes.

3 Meanwhile, cook pasta according to package directions. Drain pasta, reserving ¼ cup of the pasta cooking water. Return pasta to hot pan. Cover and keep warm. Add reserved pasta cooking water, chopped mushrooms, and cooked escarole or spinach to sausage mixture. Heat through; spoon over hot cooked pasta. Toss before serving. Top with Parmesan cheese.

Per serving: 480 cal., 17 g total fat (6 g sat. fat), 130 mg chol., 776 mg sodium, 56 g carbo., 5 g fiber, 22 g pro.

If you're a die-hard pizza fan, this is the sandwich for you. Beef-and-Italian-sausage patties, topped with grilled pepper strips, mozzarella cheese, and spaghetti sauce are packaged into a hearty kaiser roll.

SAUSAGE PIZZA SANDWICHES

PREP:
25 minutes

GRILL:
10 minutes

MAKES:
8 servings

1	egg
1¼	cups purchased meatless spaghetti sauce
½	cup fine dry bread crumbs
⅓	cup chopped onion
1	teaspoon dried basil or oregano, crushed
2	cloves garlic, minced
1	pound lean ground beef
1	pound bulk Italian sausage
2	medium green, yellow, and/or red sweet peppers, cut into rings and halved
1	tablespoon olive oil or cooking oil
8	kaiser rolls, split and toasted
1	6-ounce package sliced mozzarella cheese (8 slices)

1 In a large bowl beat egg and ¼ cup of the spaghetti sauce with a whisk. Stir in bread crumbs, onion, basil, and garlic. Add beef and sausage; mix well. Shape meat mixture into eight ½-inch-thick patties.

2 Tear off a 36×12-inch piece of heavy foil; fold in half to make an 18×12-inch rectangle. Place sweet pepper strips in center of foil; drizzle with oil. Bring up two opposite edges of foil and seal with a double fold; fold in remaining ends to enclose the peppers, leaving space for steam to build.

3 Place patties and foil packet on the rack of an uncovered grill directly over medium coals. Grill for 10 to 13 minutes or until patties are done (160°F)* and peppers are tender, turning patties and foil packet once halfway through grilling.

4 Meanwhile, heat remaining 1 cup spaghetti sauce. Place patties on bottom halves of rolls; top with pepper strips and cheese. Spoon some of the heated spaghetti sauce over patties. Top with roll tops. Pass any remaining spaghetti sauce.

Per serving: 583 cal., 29 g total fat (11 g sat. fat), 117 mg chol., 1,146 mg sodium, 44 g carbo., 3 g fiber, 31 g pro.

*NOTE: The internal color of a burger is not a reliable doneness indicator. A beef or pork patty cooked to 160°F is safe, regardless of color. To measure the doneness of a patty, insert an instant-read thermometer through the side of the patty to a depth of 2 to 3 inches.

Italian sausage and kalamata olives are what give this dish an Italian flair. Use turkey sausage for a lower-fat version of the recipe.

TUSCAN MAC 'N' CHEESE

8   ounces Italian sausage or uncooked turkey Italian sausage (remove casing, if present)

8   ounces dried gemelli pasta or elbow macaroni (2 cups), cooked and drained

1   8-ounce package cream cheese, cut into cubes and softened

4   ounces crusty Italian bread, cut into 1-inch cubes (about 2 cups)

1   cup pitted kalamata olives, halved

1   cup shredded mozzarella cheese (4 ounces)

1   tablespoon butter or margarine

1   tablespoon all-purpose flour

1   tablespoon snipped fresh sage or 1 teaspoon dried leaf sage, crushed

1   teaspoon snipped fresh thyme or ¼ teaspoon dried thyme, crushed

½   teaspoon salt

⅛   teaspoon cayenne pepper

1½ cups milk

1   medium tomato, sliced

2   ounces shredded Asiago, Parmesan, or Romano cheese (½ cup)

PREP:
45 minutes

BAKE:
35 minutes + 15 minutes

STAND:
15 minutes

OVEN:
350°F

MAKES:
6 to 8 servings

1 Preheat oven to 350°F. In a medium skillet cook sausage until brown. Drain off fat. In a very large bowl combine sausage, cooked pasta, cream cheese, bread cubes, olives, and mozzarella cheese. Set aside.

2 In a medium saucepan melt butter over medium heat. Stir in flour, sage, thyme, salt, and cayenne pepper. Add milk all at once. Cook and stir until slightly thickened and bubbly. Pour sauce over pasta mixture. Stir gently.

3 Transfer mixture to a 2-quart casserole. Bake, covered, for 35 minutes. Top with tomato slices and Asiago cheese. Bake, uncovered, about 15 minutes more or until heated through. Let stand for 15 minutes before serving.

Per serving: 637 cal., 39 g total fat (19 g sat. fat), 101 mg chol., 1,187 mg sodium, 46 g carbo., 3 g fiber, 24 g pro.

Make this savory pie on a cold winter day. It's a great way to warm up your family.

SPINACH-SAUSAGE PIE

PREP:
40 minutes

BAKE:
40 minutes

COOL:
20 minutes

OVEN:
350°F

MAKES:
10 servings

1½ pounds bulk Italian sausage

1 cup chopped red sweet pepper

1 medium onion, chopped

2 cloves garlic, minced

1 16-ounce package hot roll mix

5 eggs

3 cups shredded mozzarella cheese or provolone cheese (12 ounces)

½ of a 15-ounce carton ricotta cheese (about 1 cup)

½ of a 10-ounce package frozen chopped spinach, thawed and well drained

2 4-ounce cans (drained weight) sliced mushrooms, drained

1 egg

1 tablespoon water

1 tablespoon shredded Parmesan cheese

1 In large skillet cook sausage, sweet pepper, onion, and garlic over medium heat until meat is brown. Drain off fat. Drain mixture on paper towels.

2 Preheat oven to 350°F. Prepare hot roll mix according to package directions through kneading step. Cover; let dough rest for 5 minutes.

3 In a large bowl beat the 5 eggs. Stir in 1 cup of the mozzarella cheese, the ricotta cheese, and drained spinach. Stir in meat mixture and mushrooms.

4 Grease bottom and side of a 9-inch springform pan. On lightly floured surface, roll three-fourths of the dough into a 15-inch circle; fit circle into bottom and press up side of springform pan. Sprinkle bottom with ½ cup of the mozzarella cheese. Spoon meat mixture over cheese. Sprinkle with remaining 1½ cups mozzarella cheese; press lightly into meat mixture.

5 Roll remaining dough into a 9-inch circle; place on top of meat-cheese mixture. Fold edge of bottom dough over top dough; pinch to seal.

6 In small bowl combine the 1 egg and the water; beat with a whisk. Brush egg-water mixture over top of pie; allow to dry for 5 minutes. Sprinkle with Parmesan cheese.

7 Bake for 40 to 45 minutes or until golden brown. Cool in springform pan on wire rack for 20 minutes. Using a small spatula, loosen pie from side of springform pan; remove side of pan. Cut pie into wedges.

Per serving: 597 cal., 32 g total fat (14 g sat. fat), 233 mg chol., 1,070 mg sodium, 40 g carbo., 1 g fiber, 31 g pro.

A vibrant mixture of spicy Italian sausage, mushrooms, and onions is mellowed out by rich and creamy polenta in this family-pleasing casserole.

SAUSAGE-POLENTA CASSEROLE

2½	cups chicken broth
3	tablespoons butter or margarine
2	cups milk
1½	cups quick-cooking polenta mix
1	3-ounce package cream cheese, cut up
1	cup shredded mozzarella cheese or provolone cheese (4 ounces)
½	cup finely shredded or grated Parmesan cheese
12	ounces bulk Italian sausage
1	cup fresh mushrooms, quartered
1	medium onion, cut into thin wedges
2	cloves garlic, minced
2	cups purchased pasta sauce

PREP:
45 minutes

BAKE:
20 minutes

OVEN:
400°F

MAKES:
8 servings

1 Preheat oven to 400°F. Lightly grease a 3-quart rectangular baking dish; set aside.

2 In a large saucepan bring chicken broth and butter to boiling. Meanwhile, stir together milk and dry polenta mix. Add polenta mixture to boiling broth. Cook and stir until bubbly; cook and stir for 3 to 5 minutes more or until very thick. Remove from heat. Stir in cream cheese, ¾ cup of the mozzarella cheese, and ¼ cup of the Parmesan cheese until well mixed. Spread two-thirds of the polenta mixture in the prepared baking dish; set aside.

3 In a large skillet cook sausage, mushrooms, onion, and garlic until meat is brown and onion is tender; drain off fat. Stir pasta sauce into sausage mixture in skillet; heat through. Spoon sausage mixture over polenta in dish, spreading evenly. Dollop remaining polenta mixture on top of sauce; sprinkle with the remaining ¼ cup mozzarella cheese and remaining ¼ cup Parmesan cheese.

4 Bake, uncovered, about 20 minutes or until heated through and top is lightly golden brown.

Per serving: 583 cal., 34 g total fat (18 g sat. fat), 92 mg chol., 1,933 mg sodium, 37 g carbo., 4 g fiber, 31 g pro.

Roasted red peppers give this hearty sausage lasagna a flavor that's sure to please.

RED PEPPER LASAGNA

PREP:
50 minutes

BAKE:
35 minutes

STAND:
20 minutes

OVEN:
350°F

MAKES:
8 servings

1	tablespoon olive oil
1	12-ounce jar roasted red sweet peppers, drained and cut into bite-size strips
1	28-ounce can crushed tomatoes
½	cup snipped fresh basil
4	cloves garlic, minced
¾	teaspoon black pepper
½	teaspoon salt
8	ounces bulk Italian sausage, browned and drained
⅓	cup butter or margarine
⅓	cup all-purpose flour
½	teaspoon ground nutmeg
½	teaspoon salt
3	cups milk
12	no-boil lasagna noodles
1¼	cups finely shredded Parmesan cheese (5 ounces)

1 Preheat oven to 350°F. For red pepper sauce, in a large saucepan heat olive oil over medium heat. Add pepper strips; cook for 1 minute. Stir in crushed tomatoes, basil, garlic, black pepper, and ½ teaspoon salt. Bring to boiling; reduce heat. Simmer, uncovered, for 20 minutes, stirring often. Stir in cooked sausage. Set aside to cool.

2 For white sauce, in a medium saucepan melt butter over medium heat. Stir in flour, nutmeg, and ½ teaspoon salt until smooth. Add milk all at once. Cook and stir until thickened and bubbly. Set aside to cool.

3 To assemble, grease the bottom of a 3-quart rectangular baking dish. Cover bottom of dish with three of the lasagna noodles. Spread about 1 cup of the red pepper sauce over the lasagna noodles in baking dish. Top with ¾ cup of the white sauce, spreading evenly; sprinkle with about ¼ cup of the Parmesan cheese. Repeat three more times. Be sure the top layer of noodles is completely covered with sauce. Sprinkle with the remaining Parmesan cheese.

4 Bake for 35 to 40 minutes or until bubbly and light brown on top. Let stand for 20 minutes before serving.

Per serving: 399 cal., 22 g total fat (11 g sat. fat), 56 mg chol., 883 mg sodium, 33 g carbo., 3 g fiber, 17 g pro.

This home-style casserole is full of favorite Italian ingredients—marinara sauce, mushrooms, onion, green sweet pepper, pepperoni, and, of course, oodles of cheese!

PEPPERONI-PENNE BAKE

Nonstick cooking spray

3 cups dried penne pasta

1 cup sliced fresh mushrooms

1 large onion, thinly sliced and quartered

2 medium green or red sweet peppers, cut into thin, bite-size strips

6 ounces sliced pepperoni or Canadian-style bacon, cut up

6 cloves garlic, minced

1 tablespoon olive oil or cooking oil

1 26- to 29-ounce jar (3 cups) marinara pasta sauce

1¼ cups shredded Italian-blend cheese (5 ounces)

1 Preheat oven to 350°F. Lightly coat a 3-quart rectangular baking dish with nonstick cooking spray; set dish aside. Cook pasta according to package directions; drain well. Return pasta to hot saucepan.

2 Meanwhile, in a large skillet cook mushrooms, onion, sweet peppers, pepperoni, and garlic in hot oil for 3 minutes. Add vegetable mixture and marinara sauce to pasta; toss to coat. Spread pasta mixture evenly in prepared baking dish.

3 Bake, covered, about 25 minutes or until heated through. Sprinkle with cheese. Bake, uncovered, about 5 minutes more or until cheese is melted.

Per serving: 373 cal., 17 g total fat (6 g sat. fat), 27 mg chol., 905 mg sodium, 40 g carbo., 3 g fiber, 16 g pro.

PREP:
25 minutes

BAKE:
25 minutes + 5 minutes

OVEN:
350°F

MAKES:
8 servings

This luscious tomato sauce is delightful over a hefty serving of "gnocchi," Italian for dumplings. Gnocchi can be made from either potatoes or flour. This recipe calls for the potato variety.

CREAMY TOMATO SAUCE

START TO FINISH:
35 minutes

MAKES:
4 servings

3	ounces pancetta or bacon, finely chopped
2	cups sliced fresh mushrooms
½	cup pine nuts
1	tablespoon butter or margarine
1½	cups whipping cream
¼	teaspoon coarsely ground black pepper
2	medium tomatoes or 4 plum tomatoes, peeled, seeded, and chopped (about 1¾ cups)
1	16-ounce package potato gnocchi
½	cup freshly grated Parmesan cheese
	Coarsely ground black pepper (optional)
	Freshly grated Parmesan cheese (optional)

1 In a large skillet cook and stir pancetta just until golden brown. Remove from skillet; drain off fat.

2 In the same skillet cook mushrooms and pine nuts in hot butter until mushrooms are tender and pine nuts are golden brown. Return pancetta to skillet. Stir in whipping cream and the ¼ teaspoon pepper. Bring to boiling; reduce heat. Boil gently, uncovered, over medium heat about 7 minutes or until mixture thickens slightly. Stir in chopped tomatoes.

3 Meanwhile, cook gnocchi according to package directions. Toss hot cooked gnocchi with the ½ cup Parmesan cheese. Add to tomato mixture; toss lightly to coat. If desired, sprinkle with additional pepper and Parmesan cheese.

Per serving: 746 cal., 57 g total fat (28 g sat. fat), 155 mg chol., 1,124 mg sodium, 47 g carbo., 1 g fiber, 20 g pro.

Fresh fava beans resemble very large lima beans. Each bean has a tough outer skin that must be removed before eating. This recipe calls for canned fava beans, whose pods and skins have already been removed.

FUSILLI WITH PROSCIUTTO & BEANS

12	ounces fusilli pasta
1	recipe Herbed Garlic Butter
1	19-ounce can fava beans or cannellini beans (white kidney beans), rinsed and drained
2	cups grape tomatoes or halved cherry tomatoes
4	ounces thinly sliced prosciutto, torn into bite-size pieces
¼	cup coarsely shredded pecorino Toscano cheese, pecorino Romano cheese, or grated Parmesan cheese (1 ounce)
1½	cups loosely packed torn arugula or watercress
3	tablespoons snipped fresh chives
	Coarse salt
	Black pepper
	Coarsely shredded pecorino Toscano cheese, pecorino Romano cheese, or grated Parmesan cheese

START TO FINISH:
25 minutes

MAKES:
8 servings

1 In a 4-quart Dutch oven bring about 3 quarts lightly salted water to boiling. Add pasta to water and cook according to package directions. Just before draining pasta, remove ½ cup of the pasta cooking water and set aside. Drain pasta; return to warm Dutch oven.

2 Immediately add Herbed Garlic Butter to pasta along with fava beans, tomatoes, prosciutto, and the ¼ cup cheese. Tossing constantly over low heat, gradually add ⅓ to ½ cup of the reserved cooking liquid as the butter and cheese melt and form a sauce. Add the arugula and chives; toss again. Season to taste with coarse salt and pepper.

3 Serve immediately. Pass additional cheese.

HERBED GARLIC BUTTER: In a small bowl stir together ⅓ cup butter, softened; 4 cloves garlic, minced; 2 teaspoons snipped fresh thyme; 1 teaspoon lemon juice; and ¼ teaspoon black pepper. Cover tightly and refrigerate until ready to use.

Per serving: 331 cal., 12 g total fat (6 g sat. fat), 74 mg chol., 722 mg sodium, 41 g carbo., 8 g fiber, 15 g pro.

Prosciutto may seem expensive, but a little goes a long way for big flavor in a dish. If you have any extra, wrap pieces around pear slices or cooked shrimp for elegant appetizers.

PASTA WITH PROSCIUTTO

START TO FINISH:
30 minutes

MAKES:
4 servings

6   ounces dried angel hair pasta
2   tablespoons olive oil
1   tablespoon butter or margarine
4   cloves garlic, minced
8   ounces fresh mushrooms, sliced (3 cups)
1   medium red onion, thinly sliced
4   ounces thinly sliced prosciutto, cut into ¾-inch-wide strips
4   ounces fresh spinach, torn (3 cups loosely packed)
⅓   cup finely shredded Parmesan cheese
¼   teaspoon salt
¼   teaspoon freshly ground black pepper
    Parmesan cheese curls or finely shredded Parmesan cheese (optional)

1 Cook pasta according to package directions. Drain well. Return to hot pan; cover and keep warm.

2 Meanwhile, in a very large skillet heat olive oil and butter over medium heat until butter is melted. Add garlic; cook for 30 seconds. Add mushrooms, red onion, and prosciutto. Cook over medium-high heat for 4 to 5 minutes or until mushrooms and onion are tender, stirring occasionally. Add spinach to skillet; remove from heat. Add cooked pasta, the ⅓ cup Parmesan cheese, the salt, and pepper. Toss well.

3 If desired, sprinkle with additional Parmesan cheese.

Per serving: 368 cal., 16 g total fat (5 g sat. fat), 32 mg chol., 1,066 mg sodium, 39 g carbo., 3 g fiber, 19 g pro.

Cavatappi, or corkscrew pasta, provides an ideal base for this chunky sauce. For an extra bit of authenticity, substitute prosciutto, a salt-cured dry Italian ham, for the cooked ham.

CAVATAPPI WITH TOMATOES & HAM

1	medium onion, cut into ¼-inch-thick slices
12	red and/or yellow cherry and/or pear tomatoes, halved
8	ounces dried cavatappi or gemelli pasta
¼	teaspoon crushed red pepper (optional)
4	ounces thinly sliced cooked ham, cut into strips
3	tablespoons thinly sliced fresh basil
2	tablespoons garlic-flavor olive oil or regular olive oil
	Arugula leaves (optional)

START TO FINISH:
30 minutes

MAKES:
4 servings

1 Preheat broiler. Place onion slices on the unheated foil-lined rack of a broiler pan. Broil onions 4 inches from heat for 5 minutes. Add tomato halves to pan; broil about 5 minutes more or until edges are browned.

2 Meanwhile, cook pasta according to package directions, adding crushed red pepper to water (if desired). Drain well. Return pasta to hot saucepan; cover and keep warm.

3 Cut up onion slices. Toss onion pieces and tomato halves with pasta, ham, basil, and olive oil. If desired, garnish with arugula leaves.

Per serving: 341 cal., 11 g total fat (2 g sat. fat), 16 mg chol., 381 mg sodium, 47 g carbo., 2 g fiber, 13 g pro.

Cremini mushrooms, also referred to as baby portobellos, give this lasagna a woodsy flavor, while whipping cream and wine make it decadent.

HAM & CHEESE LASAGNA

PREP:
1 hour

BAKE:
50 minutes

STAND:
20 minutes

OVEN:
350°F

MAKES:
12 servings

2 tablespoons olive oil

1 large onion, chopped

4 stalks celery, thinly sliced

4 carrots, chopped

2 cloves garlic, minced

3 cups sliced fresh cremini mushrooms or other small brown mushrooms (8 ounces)

2 cups cubed cooked ham

2 cups whipping cream

1 14½-ounce can diced tomatoes with basil, garlic, and oregano, undrained

½ cup water

¼ cup dry red wine

   Salt

   Black pepper

1½ cups shredded Swiss cheese (6 ounces)

1 cup grated Parmesan cheese

12 no-boil lasagna noodles

1 Preheat oven to 350°F. For sauce, in a 12-inch skillet or Dutch oven heat oil over medium heat. Add onion, celery, carrots, and garlic; cook about 10 minutes or just until vegetables are tender. Add mushrooms and ham. Cook for 10 minutes, stirring occasionally. Stir in whipping cream, undrained tomatoes, the water, and wine. Bring to boiling; reduce heat. Simmer, uncovered, for 5 minutes. Season to taste with salt and pepper.

2 In a medium bowl combine cheeses. Spoon 1½ cups of the sauce into a 3-quart rectangular baking dish. Sprinkle with ⅔ cup of the cheese mixture. Top with four of the lasagna noodles, overlapping as needed. Repeat twice. Spoon on remaining sauce and sprinkle with remaining cheese mixture. Cover tightly with foil.

3 Bake about 50 minutes or until heated through and noodles are tender when pierced with a fork. Let stand, covered, for 20 minutes before serving.

Per serving: 376 cal., 25 g total fat (14 g sat. fat), 86 mg chol., 671 mg sodium, 22 g carbo., 2 g fiber, 15 g pro.

Balsamic vinegar and Dijon mustard give this smash-hit entrée intense flavor—perfect for a special weekend dinner.

BALSAMIC-MARINATED LEG OF LAMB

1   5- to 6-pound leg of lamb, boned, rolled, and tied

4   to 6 cloves garlic, sliced

⅔   cup balsamic vinegar

½   cup olive oil

2   tablespoons Dijon-style mustard

1   tablespoon sugar

2   teaspoons dried basil, crushed

4   cloves garlic, minced

1   teaspoon salt

½   teaspoon black pepper

PREP:
25 minutes

MARINATE:
8 to 24 hours

ROAST:
2 hours

STAND:
15 minutes

OVEN:
325°F

MAKES:
12 servings

1 Cut 1-inch-wide pockets into lamb at 3-inch intervals. Place a slice of garlic in each of the pockets. For marinade, in a small bowl combine balsamic vinegar, olive oil, mustard, sugar, basil, minced garlic, salt, and pepper. Place lamb in a large resealable plastic bag set in a large bowl. Pour marinade over lamb. Seal bag; turn to coat lamb. Marinate in the refrigerator for 8 to 24 hours, turning occasionally.

2 Preheat oven to 325°F. Drain lamb, discarding marinade. Place lamb on rack in shallow roasting pan. Insert a meat thermometer into the thickest portion of the meat. Roast for 2 to 2½ hours or until thermometer registers 140°F. Cover and let stand for 15 minutes before carving. Temperature of the meat after standing should be 145°F.

3 Remove strings. Thinly slice lamb; transfer to a serving platter.

Per serving: 215 cal., 10 g total fat (2 g sat. fat), 83 mg chol., 188 mg sodium, 3 g carbo., 0 g fiber, 27 g pro.

Rosemary and red wine are key flavors in the marinade for these delicious lamb chops. Serve two per person. They're packed full of flavor, but are quite small.

ROSEMARY LAMB CHOPS

PREP:
25 minutes

MARINATE:
2 to 24 hours

GRILL:
12 minutes

MAKES:
6 servings

6   lamb chops, cut about 1 inch thick (about 1¾ pounds total)

¾   cup dry red wine

3   tablespoons finely snipped fresh rosemary

2   cloves garlic, minced

1   tablespoon balsamic vinegar

½   teaspoon coarsely ground black pepper

¼   teaspoon salt

Salt

Coarsely ground black pepper

1   tablespoon butter

Fresh rosemary sprigs

1 Trim fat from chops. Place chops in a resealable plastic bag set in a shallow dish. Add wine, 2 tablespoons of the snipped rosemary, the garlic, balsamic vinegar, the ½ teaspoon pepper, and the ¼ teaspoon salt. Seal bag; turn to coat chops. Marinate in the refrigerator for 2 to 24 hours, turning bag occasionally.

2 Drain chops, reserving marinade. Place lamb chops on rack of an uncovered grill directly over medium coals. Grill until desired doneness, turning once halfway through grilling. Allow 12 to 14 minutes for medium-rare doneness (145°F) or 15 to 17 minutes for medium doneness (160°F). Season to taste with additional salt and pepper.

3 Meanwhile, strain reserved marinade into a small saucepan; discard solids. Simmer, uncovered, over medium heat about 5 minutes or until reduced to ⅓ cup. Add butter and the remaining 1 tablespoon snipped rosemary; cook for 1 minute. Serve with the chops. Top with rosemary sprigs.

Per serving: 134 cal., 7 g total fat (3 g sat. fat), 43 mg chol., 154 mg sodium, 1 g carbo., 0 g fiber, 11 g pro.

Savory lamb pieces and cannellini beans are the stars in this thick, hearty stew served on a bed of pasta. You're in for a deliciously wholesome meal.

LAMB & BEANS WITH PASTA

1	pound lamb stew meat, cut into 1-inch cubes
1	tablespoon olive oil
2	14½-ounce cans diced tomatoes with garlic and onion, undrained
1	cup water
½	cup dry red wine or beef broth
1	tablespoon snipped fresh rosemary or 1 teaspoon dried rosemary, crushed
8	ounces dried rigatoni or farfalle pasta
1	19-ounce can cannellini beans (white kidney beans), rinsed and drained
⅓	cup freshly grated Parmesan cheese

1 In a large saucepan brown meat, half at a time, in hot olive oil. Drain off fat. Return all meat to saucepan. Stir in undrained tomatoes, the water, wine, and dried rosemary (if using). Bring to boiling; reduce heat. Cover and simmer about 1 hour or until meat is tender. Uncover and boil gently about 15 minutes more or until desired consistency.

2 Meanwhile, cook pasta according to package directions. Drain. Stir beans and fresh rosemary (if using) into meat mixture; heat through. Serve meat mixture over pasta. Sprinkle with Parmesan cheese.

Per serving: 598 cal., 12 g total fat (3 g sat. fat), 76 mg chol., 1,475 mg sodium, 81 g carbo., 11 g fiber, 47 g pro.

PREP:
20 minutes

COOK:
1 hour + 15 minutes

MAKES:
4 servings

Baked Italian classics, such as lasagna, have inspired numerous "melting-pot dishes." This layered pasta dish is full of ingredients such as cinnamon and feta cheese that are favored by Greek cooks.

GREEK-STYLE LASAGNA

PREP:
45 minutes

BAKE:
35 minutes

STAND:
10 minutes

OVEN:
350°F

MAKES:
12 servings

9   dried lasagna noodles

1   pound ground lamb or beef

1   medium onion, chopped

2   cloves garlic, minced

1   8-ounce can tomato sauce

¼   cup dry red wine or beef broth

1   teaspoon dried oregano, crushed

¼   teaspoon ground cinnamon

1   beaten egg

3   tablespoons butter or margarine

3   tablespoons all-purpose flour

¼   teaspoon black pepper

1¾   cups milk

½   cup grated Parmesan cheese

2   beaten eggs

1   2¼-ounce can sliced pitted ripe olives, drained

8   ounces feta cheese, crumbled

8   ounces white cheddar cheese, shredded (2 cups)

1 Preheat oven to 350°F. Cook lasagna noodles according to package directions; drain and rinse. In a large skillet cook meat, onion, and garlic until meat is brown. Drain off fat. Stir tomato sauce, wine, oregano, and cinnamon into meat mixture in skillet. Heat to boiling; reduce heat. Simmer, uncovered, for 10 minutes. Gradually stir meat mixture into the 1 beaten egg; set aside.

2 In a medium saucepan melt butter; stir in flour and pepper. Add milk. Cook and stir until thickened and bubbly; cook and stir for 1 minute more. Stir in ¼ cup of the Parmesan cheese; set aside. In a small bowl combine the 2 eggs and the remaining ¼ cup Parmesan cheese.

3 To assemble, spread 2 tablespoons of the cheese sauce in a 3-quart rectangular baking dish. Top with 3 noodles, one-third of the meat sauce, one-third of the remaining cheese sauce, and one-third of the olives. Drizzle with one-third of the egg-Parmesan mixture; sprinkle with one-third of each of the cheeses. Repeat layers twice.

4 Bake for 35 to 40 minutes or until hot in the center. Let stand for 10 minutes before serving.

Per serving: 372 cal., 22 g total fat (12 g sat. fat), 128 mg chol., 588 mg sodium, 21 g carbo., 1 g fiber, 21 g pro.

POULTRY & FISH

With just a handful of ingredients, this recipe is a snap to prepare. Ginger adds flavor notes to the sweet pesto mixture.

ROAST CHICKEN WITH FRUIT & PESTO

PREP:
20 minutes

ROAST:
1¾ hours

STAND:
15 minutes

OVEN:
325°F

MAKES:
10 servings

1 cup apricot or peach preserves

½ cup snipped dried apricots or peaches

¼ teaspoon ground ginger

⅔ cup purchased basil pesto

1 5- to 6-pound whole roasting chicken

1 Preheat oven to 325°F. In a medium bowl stir together preserves, apricots, and ginger. Place ⅓ cup of the preserves mixture in a small bowl; stir in pesto and set aside. Set aside remaining preserves mixture for sauce.

2 On one side of chicken, slip your fingers between the skin and breast meat of the chicken, forming a pocket; repeat on other side of chicken. Spoon some of the preserves-pesto mixture under the skin and spread over the breast meat. Spread some of the preserves-pesto mixture into the neck cavity. Pull neck skin to back; fasten with a small skewer. Spread some of the preserves-pesto mixture into the body cavity. Rub remaining preserves-pesto mixture over outside of chicken. Tuck drumsticks under the band of skin that crosses the tail. (If there is no band, tie drumsticks to the tail.) Twist the wing tips under the back.

3 Place chicken, breast side up, on a rack in a shallow roasting pan. Insert an oven-going meat thermometer into the center of an inside thigh muscle, making sure the bulb does not touch bone. Roast, uncovered, for 1¾ to 2½ hours or until drumsticks move easily in their sockets, chicken is no longer pink, and meat thermometer registers 180°F. When the bird is two-thirds done, cut the band of skin or string between the drumsticks so the thighs cook evenly. Transfer chicken to a serving platter. Let stand for 15 minutes before carving.

4 Meanwhile, for sauce, in a small saucepan heat the reserved preserves mixture over low heat until preserves have melted and heated through. Serve sauce with sliced chicken.

Per serving: 565 cal., 36 g total fat (7 g sat. fat), 121 mg chol., 224 mg sodium, 29 g carbo., 1 g fiber, 30 g pro.

The under-the-skin rub in this recipe works like a marinade, adding lots of extra Italian flavor to the chicken as it roasts.

ROASTED ITALIAN CHICKEN

2   tablespoons balsamic vinegar

2   tablespoons olive oil

2   tablespoons snipped fresh oregano or 2 teaspoons dried oregano, crushed

2   tablespoons snipped fresh basil or 2 teaspoons dried basil, crushed

1   tablespoon lemon juice

1   tablespoon snipped fresh thyme or 1 teaspoon dried thyme, crushed

1   teaspoon salt

1   teaspoon coarsely ground black pepper

4   cloves garlic, minced

1   3- to 3½-pound whole broiler-fryer chicken

PREP:
20 minutes

ROAST:
1 hour + 15 minutes

STAND:
10 minutes

OVEN:
375°F

MAKES:
6 servings

1 Preheat oven to 375°F. In a small bowl whisk together balsamic vinegar, olive oil, oregano, basil, lemon juice, thyme, salt, pepper, and garlic. Divide vinegar mixture in half and set aside.

2 On one side of the chicken, slip your fingers between the skin and breast meat of the chicken, forming a pocket; repeat on other side of chicken. Divide one portion of the herb mixture between pockets.

3 Tie drumsticks to the tail. Twist the wing tips under the back. Place chicken, breast side up, on a rack in a shallow roasting pan. Insert an oven-going meat thermometer into the center of an inside thigh muscle, making sure the bulb does not touch bone.

4 Roast, uncovered, for 1 hour. Cut string between chicken drumsticks. Brush chicken with remaining portion of herb mixture. Roast for 15 to 30 minutes more or until drumsticks move easily in their sockets, chicken is no longer pink, and meat thermometer registers 180°F. Transfer chicken to a serving platter. Cover with foil; let stand for 10 minutes before carving.

Per serving: 376 cal., 27 g total fat (7 g sat. fat), 115 mg chol., 476 mg sodium, 3 g carbo., 0 g fiber, 29 g pro.

Gremolata, made from parsley, lemon peel, and garlic, is a seasoning mixture often used as a garnish. Add the anchovy for a more robust flavor.

GREMOLATA ROTISSERIE CHICKEN

PREP:
40 minutes

GRILL:
1 hour (on spit)

STAND:
10 minutes

MAKES:
8 to 10 servings

½   cup butter, softened

3   tablespoons finely chopped fresh parsley

6   cloves garlic, minced

1   tablespoon finely shredded lemon peel

1   anchovy fillet, finely chopped (optional)

2   3- to 3½-pound whole broiler-fryer chickens

1 For gremolata butter, in a small bowl stir together butter, parsley, garlic, lemon peel, and anchovy (if desired); set aside.

2 Remove the neck and giblets from chickens. Working with one chicken, start at the neck on one side of the breast and slip your fingers between skin and meat, loosening the skin as you work toward the tail end. Once your entire hand is under the skin, free the skin around the thigh and leg area up to, but not around, the tip of the drumstick. Repeat on the other side of the breast. Rub half of the gremolata butter under the skin over entire surface. Skewer the neck skin to the back. Repeat with remaining chicken. Sprinkle surfaces and cavities of chickens with salt and pepper.

3 To secure chickens on a spit rod, place one holding fork on rod, tines toward point. Insert rod through one of the chickens, neck end first, pressing tines of holding fork firmly into breast meat. To tie wings, slip a 24-inch piece of 100%-cotton string under back of chicken; bring ends of string to front, looping around each wing tip. Tie in center of breast, leaving equal string ends. To tie legs, slip a 24-inch piece of string under tail. Loop string around tail, then around crossed legs. Tie very tightly to hold bird securely on spit, again leaving string ends. Pull together the strings attached to wings and legs; tie tightly. Trim any excess string. Place second holding fork on rod, tines toward the chicken; press tines of holding fork firmly into thigh meat. Adjust forks and tighten screws. Repeat with remaining chicken on the same rod. Test balance, making adjustments as necessary.

4 Prepare grill for indirect grilling. Test for medium heat above the drip pan. Attach spit; turn on the motor and lower the grill hood. Let the chickens rotate over drip pan for 1 to 1¼ hours or until chicken is no longer pink and drumsticks move easily (180°F in thigh muscle).

5 Remove chickens from spit. Cover with foil; let stand for 10 minutes before carving.

Per serving: 628 cal., 50 g total fat (18 g sat. fat), 209 mg chol., 216 mg sodium, 1 g carbo., 0 g fiber, 42 g pro.

Use pitted kalamata olives for this recipe. If you can't find pesto seasoning, mix together 1 teaspoon dried basil, ¹/₄ teaspoon garlic powder, and a dash each of salt and black pepper.

TUSCAN CHICKEN

2	tablespoons olive oil
2	to 2½ pounds meaty chicken pieces (breast halves, thighs, and drumsticks)
1¼	teaspoons dried pesto seasoning
½	cup pitted kalamata olives
½	cup dry white wine or chicken broth

1 In a 12-inch skillet heat olive oil over medium heat. Add chicken; cook for 15 minutes, turning to brown evenly. Reduce heat. Drain off fat. Sprinkle pesto seasoning evenly over chicken.

2 Add olives. Pour white wine over all. Cover tightly and cook for 25 minutes. Uncover and cook for 5 to 10 minutes more or until chicken is no longer pink (170°F for breasts; 180°F for thighs and drumsticks).

Per serving: 334 cal., 18 g total fat (4 g sat. fat), 104 mg chol., 280 mg sodium, 2 g carbo., 1 g fiber, 34 g pro.

PREP:
20 minutes

COOK:
25 minutes + 5 minutes

MAKES:
4 servings

Tarragon, known for its strong aniselike flavor, complements the sweet roasted cherry tomatoes and shallots in this recipe.

ROAST TARRAGON CHICKEN

PREP:
20 minutes

ROAST:
35 minutes + 10 minutes

OVEN:
375°F

MAKES:
6 servings

2½	to 3 pounds meaty chicken pieces (breast halves, thighs, and drumsticks)
3	tablespoons olive oil
2½	teaspoons dried tarragon, crushed
2	cloves garlic, minced
½	teaspoon salt
½	teaspoon coarsely ground black pepper
1	pound cherry tomatoes
8	small shallots
	Fresh tarragon leaves (optional)

1 Preheat oven to 375°F. If desired, skin chicken pieces; set aside.

2 In a medium bowl stir together olive oil, dried tarragon, garlic, salt, and pepper. Add cherry tomatoes and shallots; toss gently to coat. Use a slotted spoon to remove cherry tomatoes and shallots from bowl, reserving the oil mixture.

3 Place chicken in a single layer in a shallow roasting pan. Add shallots to roasting pan; set cherry tomatoes aside. Brush chicken with the reserved oil mixture. Discard any remaining oil mixture.

4 Roast chicken and shallots for 35 minutes. Add cherry tomatoes; roast for 10 to 12 minutes more or until chicken is tender and no longer pink (170°F for breasts; 180°F for thighs and drumsticks) and vegetables are tender. If desired, garnish with fresh tarragon leaves.

Per serving: 309 cal., 17 g total fat (4 g sat. fat), 86 mg chol., 277 mg sodium, 8 g carbo., 1 g fiber, 29 g pro.

Whip up the marinade and begin marinating the chicken breasts a day ahead. They'll be ready for the grill when you are.

WINE & ITALIAN HERB MARINATED CHICKEN

4	to 6 medium chicken breast halves with skin and bones (2 to 3 pounds total)
1½	cups dry white wine
½	cup olive oil
1	tablespoon dried Italian seasoning, crushed
4	cloves garlic, minced

1 If desired, remove skin from chicken. Place chicken in a resealable plastic bag set in a shallow dish. In a small bowl combine wine, olive oil, Italian seasoning, and garlic. Pour over chicken. Seal bag; turn to coat chicken. Marinate in the refrigerator for 8 to 24 hours, turning bag occasionally.

2 Drain chicken, reserving marinade. Prepare grill for indirect grilling. Test for medium heat above drip pan. Place chicken, bone sides up, on grill rack over drip pan. Cover and grill for 50 to 60 minutes or until chicken is no longer pink (170°F), turning and brushing once with reserved marinade halfway through grilling. Discard any remaining marinade.

Per serving: 462 cal., 29 g total fat (7 g sat. fat), 135 mg chol., 108 mg sodium, 1 g carbo., 0 g fiber, 41 g pro.

PREP:
15 minutes

MARINATE:
8 to 24 hours

GRILL:
50 minutes

MAKES:
4 to 6 servings

This dish is perfect for a dinner party. When your guests slice into these golden-roasted chicken breasts, they'll be pleasantly surprised when a creamy goat cheese filling oozes out.

ARTICHOKE-CHÈVRE STUFFED CHICKEN BREASTS

PREP:
45 minutes

BAKE:
40 minutes

OVEN:
350°F

MAKES:
8 servings

¼   cup olive oil

2   teaspoons dried thyme, crushed

¼   teaspoon crushed red pepper

2   6-ounce jars marinated artichoke hearts, drained and chopped

4   ounces prosciutto, cut into thin strips

3   cloves garlic, minced

6   ounces goat cheese (chèvre)

8   large chicken breast halves with skin and bone (4 to 5 pounds total)

    Salt

    Black pepper

1 For filling, in a medium skillet heat 2 tablespoons of the olive oil over medium heat. Add thyme and crushed red pepper; cook for 1 minute. Stir in artichokes, prosciutto, and garlic. Cook and stir for 4 minutes. Remove from heat; stir in goat cheese until melted. Cool filling completely.

2 Cut a horizontal pocket into each chicken breast half by cutting from one side almost to, but not through, the other side. Stuff pockets with cooled filling. Use wooden picks to close pockets to keep in filling. Sprinkle with salt and black pepper.

3 Preheat oven to 350°F. In a large nonstick skillet heat the remaining 2 tablespoons olive oil over medium-high heat. Brown chicken breasts, a few at a time, in hot oil. Transfer chicken to a large baking dish. Bake for 40 to 45 minutes or until no longer pink (170°F). Remove wooden picks before serving.

Per serving: 485 cal., 30 g total fat (9 g sat. fat), 135 mg chol., 720 mg sodium, 5 g carbo., 0 g fiber, 47 g pro.

Purchased pesto makes this recipe a breeze. Serve these flavor-packed chicken breasts on a bed of your favorite pasta.

PESTO-STUFFED CHICKEN BREASTS

4   chicken breast halves with skin and bone
     (about 2 pounds total)

½   cup bottled roasted red sweet peppers,
     drained and chopped

⅓   cup purchased basil pesto

2   tablespoons finely shredded Parmesan cheese

     Salt

     Black pepper

1   tablespoon butter

1 Preheat oven to 375°F. Lightly grease a 2-quart rectangular baking dish; set aside. Using your fingers, gently separate chicken skin from the meat of the breasts along rib edge.

2 For stuffing, in a small bowl combine roasted red peppers, pesto, and Parmesan cheese. Spoon a rounded tablespoon of the stuffing between the skin and meat of each chicken breast. Sprinkle stuffed chicken breasts with salt and pepper.

3 Place stuffed chicken breasts, bone sides down, in prepared baking dish. Drizzle with melted butter. Bake for 45 to 55 minutes or until chicken is no longer pink (170°F).

Per serving: 486 cal., 33 g total fat (7 g sat. fat), 127 mg chol., 381 mg sodium, 5 g carbo., 0 g fiber, 41 g pro.

PREP:
20 minutes

BAKE:
45 minutes

OVEN:
375°F

MAKES:
4 servings

The acidic combination of white wine, white wine vinegar, and lemon juice gives the chicken breasts a tangy kick. To complete the meal, serve this dish with pasta and a salad.

BAKED CHICKEN BREASTS

PREP:
20 minutes

MARINATE:
2 to 6 hours

BAKE:
45 minutes

BROIL:
4 minutes

OVEN:
375°F

MAKES:
4 servings

4   chicken breast halves with skin and bone (about 2 pounds total)
½   cup dry white wine
¼   cup olive oil
2   tablespoons white wine vinegar
2   tablespoons water
1   tablespoon lemon juice
1   tablespoon dried Italian seasoning, crushed
3   cloves garlic, minced
¼   teaspoon salt
¼   teaspoon black pepper
      Salt
      Black pepper
⅓   cup finely shredded Parmesan cheese

1 Skin chicken, if desired. Place chicken in a large resealable plastic bag set in a shallow bowl. For marinade, in a small bowl combine dry white wine, olive oil, white wine vinegar, the water, lemon juice, Italian seasoning, garlic, the ¼ teaspoon salt, and the ¼ teaspoon pepper. Pour marinade over chicken. Seal bag; turn to coat chicken. Marinate in the refrigerator for 2 to 6 hours, turning bag occasionally.

2 Preheat oven to 375°F. Drain chicken, discarding marinade. Sprinkle chicken with additional salt and pepper. Arrange chicken in a shallow baking pan. Bake for 45 to 55 minutes or until chicken is tender and no longer pink (170°F). Sprinkle with Parmesan cheese. Broil 4 to 5 inches from heat about 4 minutes or until cheese is melted and beginning to brown.

Per serving: 402 cal., 24 g total fat (6 g sat. fat), 120 mg chol., 350 mg sodium, 1 g carbo., 0 g fiber, 40 g pro.

Keep boneless chicken breasts on hand in the freezer so you can make this zesty chicken and rice dish often.

CHICKEN WITH CHUNKY VEGETABLE SAUCE

2 tablespoons all-purpose flour

4 skinless, boneless chicken breast halves (about 1¼ pounds total)

1 tablespoon olive oil

1 cup finely chopped onion

2 cloves garlic, minced

1 14½-ounce can diced tomatoes, undrained

1 14-ounce can artichoke hearts, drained and halved

⅓ cup chicken broth

1 tablespoon snipped fresh oregano or 1 teaspoon dried oregano, crushed

Dash black pepper

2 teaspoons drained capers or 2 tablespoons chopped pitted ripe olives

2 cups hot cooked rice

Pitted ripe olives (optional)

PREP:
20 minutes

COOK:
10 minutes

MAKES:
4 servings

1 Place flour in a shallow dish. Dip chicken in flour to coat. Set aside.

2 In a large skillet heat olive oil over medium heat. Add onion; cook for 3 minutes. Stir in garlic; push onion mixture to side of skillet. Add chicken. Cook about 4 minutes or until chicken is brown, turning once. Add undrained tomatoes, artichokes, chicken broth, dried oregano (if using), and pepper; stir just to combine.

3 Bring to boiling; reduce heat. Cover and simmer about 10 minutes or until chicken is tender and no longer pink (170°F). Remove chicken; cover and keep warm.

4 Simmer tomato mixture, uncovered, about 3 minutes or until reduced to desired consistency. Stir in capers and fresh oregano (if using). Serve chicken over hot cooked rice. Top with tomato mixture. If desired, garnish with ripe olives.

Per serving: 379 cal., 6 g total fat (1 g sat. fat), 82 mg chol., 685 mg sodium, 39 g carbo., 4 g fiber, 38 g pro.

These chicken breasts are dressed up with a rosemary-accented vegetable medley that's sure to delight everyone at the table.

CHICKEN WITH ROSEMARY VEGETABLES

START TO FINISH:
30 minutes

MAKES:
4 servings

4	skinless, boneless chicken breast halves (about 1¼ pounds total)
½	teaspoon lemon-pepper seasoning
2	tablespoons olive oil
2	cloves garlic, minced
2	medium zucchini and/or yellow summer squash, cut into ¼-inch-thick slices (about 2½ cups)
½	cup apple juice or apple cider
2	teaspoons snipped fresh rosemary or ½ teaspoon dried rosemary, crushed
4	ounces refrigerated spinach or plain linguine
2	tablespoons dry white wine
2	teaspoons cornstarch
12	cherry tomatoes, halved

1 Sprinkle chicken with lemon-pepper seasoning. In a large skillet heat olive oil over medium heat. Add chicken; cook for 8 to 10 minutes or until chicken is tender and no longer pink (170°F), turning once. Transfer chicken to a platter; cover and keep warm.

2 Add garlic to skillet; cook for 15 seconds. Add zucchini, apple juice, and rosemary. Bring to boiling; reduce heat. Cover and simmer for 2 minutes.

3 Meanwhile, cook pasta according to package directions; drain. In a small bowl combine wine and cornstarch; add to zucchini mixture in skillet. Cook and stir until thickened and bubbly; cook for 2 minutes more. Stir in halved, cherry tomatoes. Serve vegetables and pasta with chicken.

Per serving: 455 cal., 11 g total fat (2 g sat. fat), 132 mg chol., 294 mg sodium, 44 g carbo., 5 g fiber, 43 g pro.

Similar to chicken Parmesan, this delectable recipe requires less cheese and calls for tomatoes, basil, and roasted sweet peppers for a lighter, fresher take on the classic.

CHICKEN & PENNE WITH ROASTED RED PEPPERS

1	pound skinless, boneless chicken breast halves
½	cup seasoned fine dry bread crumbs
2	tablespoons grated Parmesan or Romano cheese
1	egg
1	tablespoon water
⅔	cup chicken broth
2	teaspoons cornstarch
8	ounces dried penne pasta (3 cups)
2	tablespoons olive oil
2	cloves garlic, minced
3	plum tomatoes, seeded and chopped (about 1 cup)
1	cup bottled roasted red sweet peppers, cut into thin strips
2	tablespoons dry white wine
2	tablespoons snipped fresh basil
2	tablespoons grated Parmesan or Romano cheese

START TO FINISH:
35 minutes

MAKES:
4 servings

1 Halve each chicken breast half lengthwise. In a shallow bowl combine bread crumbs and 2 tablespoons Parmesan cheese. In another shallow bowl beat together egg and the water. Dip each chicken piece into egg mixture, then into crumb mixture, turning to coat all sides. Set chicken aside.

2 In a small bowl stir together chicken broth and cornstarch; set aside.

3 Cook pasta according to package directions; drain.

4 Meanwhile, in a 12-inch skillet heat olive oil over medium-high heat. Add chicken; reduce heat to medium. Cook for 8 to 12 minutes or until chicken is tender and no longer pink, turning once. Remove from skillet; cover and keep warm.

5 Add garlic to skillet; cook and stir for 1 minute. Carefully add broth mixture; cook and stir until thickened and bubbly. Stir in tomatoes, pepper strips, wine, and basil; cook for 1 minute more. Toss mixture with drained pasta and 2 tablespoons Parmesan or Romano cheese; arrange chicken on top.

Per serving: 526 cal., 13 g total fat (3 g sat. fat), 123 mg chol., 709 mg sodium, 59 g carbo., 3 g fiber, 40 g pro.

Use fresh basil if you can get it. It will give the sauce a brighter, more intense flavor than dried basil.

CHICKEN WITH BASIL CREAM SAUCE

PREP:
15 minutes

BAKE:
20 minutes

OVEN:
400°F

MAKES:
4 servings

¼   cup fine dry bread crumbs

1   tablespoon snipped fresh basil or ¾ teaspoon
    dried basil, crushed

⅛   teaspoon black pepper

⅛   teaspoon paprika

1   tablespoon butter or margarine, melted

4   skinless, boneless chicken breast halves
    (about 1¼ pounds total)

⅔   cup milk

2   teaspoons all-purpose flour

¾   teaspoon instant chicken bouillon granules

1 Preheat oven to 400°F. In a small bowl stir together bread crumbs, 2 teaspoons of the fresh basil or ½ teaspoon of the dried basil, the pepper, and paprika. Add melted butter; toss to coat.

2 Arrange chicken in a 2-quart rectangular baking dish. Sprinkle chicken pieces with the crumb mixture, pressing onto the chicken to coat. Bake for 20 to 25 minutes or until no longer pink (170°F).

3 Meanwhile, in a small saucepan stir together milk, flour, bouillon granules, and remaining ¼ teaspoon dried basil (if using) until combined. Cook and stir until thickened and bubbly. Cook and stir for 1 minute more. Stir in remaining 1 teaspoon fresh basil (if using). Serve over chicken.

Per serving: 237 cal., 6 g total fat (3 g sat. fat), 93 mg chol., 459 mg sodium, 8 g carbo., 0 g fiber, 35 g pro.

In this baked dish, chicken breasts are rolled up with mozzarella cheese and a lively mix of Italian flavors. Brushing the chicken with sherry intensifies the flavor.

CHICKEN-MOZZARELLA ROLLUPS

4	teaspoons olive oil or cooking oil
¼	cup chopped onion
4	skinless, boneless chicken breast halves (about 1¼ pounds total)
4	mozzarella cheese slices (3 ounces)
½	teaspoon garlic powder
¼	teaspoon black pepper
2	tablespoons dry sherry or chicken broth
⅓	cup fine dry bread crumbs
2	tablespoons grated Romano cheese
½	teaspoon dried oregano, crushed
½	teaspoon onion salt
2	tablespoons butter, melted
2	cups purchased tomato base pasta sauce
	Hot cooked fettuccine (optional)

PREP:
30 minutes

BAKE:
20 minutes

OVEN:
375°F

MAKES:
4 servings

1 Preheat oven to 375°F. In a small saucepan heat 1 teaspoon of the oil over medium heat. Add onion; cook for 3 to 5 minutes or until tender.

2 Place each chicken breast half, boned side down, between 2 pieces of plastic wrap. Pound lightly with the flat side of a meat mallet into a rectangle about ⅛ inch thick. Remove plastic wrap. Brush tops of chicken breast halves with remaining 3 teaspoons oil. On boned side of each breast half, place a slice of mozzarella and one-fourth of the cooked onion.

3 In a small bowl combine garlic powder and pepper; sprinkle evenly over cheese and onion on chicken breast halves.

4 Fold in sides and bottom of chicken breast halves; roll up each piece into a spiral, pressing edges to seal. Brush chicken rolls with sherry. In a shallow bowl combine bread crumbs, Romano cheese, oregano, and onion salt. Roll chicken rolls in bread crumb mixture to coat. Place in a greased 2-quart rectangular baking dish. Drizzle with melted butter.

5 Bake for 20 to 25 minutes or until chicken is no longer pink. Meanwhile, in a medium saucepan cook and stir the pasta sauce over medium heat until heated through. Serve chicken rolls with warmed pasta sauce and, if desired, hot cooked pasta.

Per serving: 426 cal., 19 g total fat (8 g sat. fat), 117 mg chol., 1,300 mg sodium, 19 g carbo., 4 g fiber, 42 g pro.

Saltimbocca means "jump into the mouth" in Italian. Although it usually refers to a dish made with veal, this version features tender chicken breasts stuffed with a savory pesto, prosciutto, and fontina cheese filling.

POLLO SALTIMBOCCA CON PESTO

PREP:
45 minutes

COOK:
20 minutes

MAKES:
8 servings

8 skinless, boneless chicken breast halves (about 2½ pounds total)

1 recipe Basil-Walnut Pesto

8 very thin slices fontina cheese (6 ounces)

8 very thin slices prosciutto

   Salt

   Black pepper

1 tablespoon olive oil

½ cup dry white wine

½ cup whipping cream

1 Place a chicken breast half between two pieces of plastic wrap. Using the flat side of a meat mallet, pound meat lightly into a rectangle about ¼ inch thick. Remove plastic wrap. Repeat with remaining chicken. Set aside 2 tablespoons of the Basil-Walnut Pesto for the sauce. Divide remaining pesto among chicken pieces, spreading evenly. Place a slice of cheese and a slice of prosciutto on each chicken piece. Fold in bottom and sides; roll up. Secure with wooden toothpicks.

2 Place chicken rolls in a very large skillet. Sprinkle with salt and pepper. Add olive oil to skillet. Cook chicken over medium-high heat about 5 minutes or until golden brown, turning to brown evenly. Reduce heat to medium-low. Slowly add wine. Cover and cook chicken about 20 minutes more or until no longer pink (170°F).

3 For pesto-cream sauce, in a small bowl beat whipping cream with an electric mixer on medium speed until cream is soft and thick (about the consistency of a thin mayonnaise). Fold in reserved 2 tablespoons pesto.

4 To serve, remove toothpicks from chicken. Serve chicken with pesto-cream sauce.

BASIL-WALNUT PESTO: In a food processor or blender combine 8 cloves garlic, 1 cup lightly packed fresh flat-leaf parsley, 1 cup lightly packed fresh basil leaves, ⅓ cup olive oil, 2 tablespoons chopped walnuts, 2 tablespoons freshly grated Parmesan cheese, ¼ teaspoon salt, and dash black pepper. Cover and process or blend until smooth.

Per serving: 442 cal., 27 g total fat (10 g sat. fat), 138 mg chol., 754 mg sodium, 3 g carbo., 0 g fiber, 44 g pro.

Marsala, a fortified wine made in Sicily, has a rich smoky flavor. It's made in three styles—dry, semisweet, and sweet. This recipe calls for the dry variety.

CHICKEN WITH MARSALA SAUCE

START TO FINISH:
35 minutes

MAKES:
4 servings

4	skinless, boneless chicken breast halves (about 1¼ pounds total)
½	teaspoon salt
⅛	teaspoon black pepper
3	tablespoons butter or margarine
3	cups sliced fresh mushrooms
1	10¾-ounce can condensed cream of mushroom or golden mushroom soup
¼	cup dry Marsala
½	teaspoon dried thyme, crushed

1 Place a chicken breast half between two pieces of plastic wrap. Using the flat side of a meat mallet, pound chicken lightly to about ¼-inch thickness. Remove plastic wrap. Repeat with remaining chicken breast halves. Sprinkle chicken pieces with salt and pepper.

2 In a 12-inch skillet melt 2 tablespoons of the butter over medium heat. Add chicken; cook 5 to 6 minutes or until chicken is no longer pink, turning once. Transfer chicken to a serving platter; cover and keep warm.

3 Add remaining 1 tablespoon butter to the same skillet. Add mushrooms; cook and stir about 5 minutes or until mushrooms are tender.

4 Stir in cream of mushroom or golden mushroom soup, Marsala, and thyme. Cook and stir until heated through. Spoon mushroom mixture over chicken.

Per serving: 351 cal., 18 g total fat (8 g sat. fat), 107 mg chol., 992 mg sodium, 8 g carbo., 1 g fiber, 37 g pro.

A medley of vegetables and sauteed chicken, layered with a ricotta-spinach mixture, will make this unique lasagna a smash hit with your family.

VEGETABLE-CHICKEN LASAGNA

PREP:
40 minutes

BAKE:
35 minutes + 5 minutes

STAND:
10 minutes

OVEN:
350°F

MAKES:
8 to 10 servings

1	15-ounce carton ricotta cheese
1	10-ounce package frozen chopped spinach, thawed and well drained
1	slightly beaten egg
2	teaspoons dried Italian seasoning, crushed
1	tablespoon olive oil
1	pound skinless, boneless chicken breast halves, cut into ½-inch pieces
8	ounces fresh mushrooms, sliced
1	medium onion, chopped
2	cloves garlic, minced
2	14½-ounce cans diced tomatoes with basil, garlic, and oregano, undrained
1	8-ounce can tomato sauce
4	carrots, peeled and shredded (about 2 cups)
9	dried lasagna noodles
	Nonstick cooking spray
2	cups shredded mozzarella cheese (8 ounces)
¼	cup grated Parmesan cheese

1 Preheat oven to 350°F. In a small bowl combine ricotta cheese, spinach, egg, and 1 teaspoon of the Italian seasoning. Cover and chill.

2 In a large skillet heat oil over medium heat. Add chicken, mushrooms, onion, garlic, and the remaining 1 teaspoon Italian seasoning; cook for 5 to 7 minutes or until chicken is golden brown. Stir in undrained tomatoes, tomato sauce, carrots, and ½ teaspoon black pepper. Bring to boiling; reduce heat. Simmer, uncovered, for 15 to 20 minutes or until mixture is slightly thickened, stirring occasionally. Meanwhile, cook lasagna noodles according to package directions. Drain; rinse with cold water. Drain well.

3 Coat a 3-quart rectangular baking dish with nonstick cooking spray. Place three of the lasagna noodles in prepared dish. Spread half of the ricotta mixture over noodles. Spread one-third of the sauce over the ricotta; sprinkle with ½ cup of the mozzarella cheese and 1 tablespoon of the Parmesan cheese. Repeat layers, ending with noodles. Spoon remaining sauce over the top. Sprinkle with the remaining mozzarella and Parmesan cheese. Bake, covered, for 35 minutes. Uncover and bake for 5 to 10 minutes more or until cheese is melted and bubbly. Let stand for 10 minutes.

Per serving: 438 cal., 18 g total fat (9 g sat. fat), 111 mg chol., 1,033 mg sodium, 35 g carbo., 3 g fiber, 34 g pro.

Osso buco is a dish in which the meat, traditionally veal rather than the chicken in this version, is braised in a tomatoey wine sauce. Carrots, celery, and onions also are classic ingredients.

COUNTRY-STYLE CHICKEN OSSO BUCO

1	ounce dried porcini mushrooms
4	ounces thick-sliced pancetta or bacon, chopped
2	tablespoons olive oil
2½	to 3 pounds bone-in chicken thighs and drumsticks, skinned
2	cups fresh cremini or other mushrooms, quartered
1	cup finely chopped carrot
1	cup sliced celery
1	cup chopped onion
4	cloves garlic, minced
2	14½-ounce cans petite diced tomatoes, undrained
½	cup dry white wine
1	fresh thyme sprig
1	bay leaf
8	ounces dried linguine or spaghetti
¼	cup finely shredded Parmesan cheese
2	tablespoons snipped fresh basil or oregano
1	teaspoon finely shredded lemon peel

PREP:
30 minutes

SOAK:
20 minutes

COOK:
35 minutes + 10 minutes

MAKES:
4 to 6 servings

1 Rinse and drain dried mushrooms. Soak in ½ cup warm water for 20 minutes. Drain mushrooms, reserving liquid. Chop mushrooms; set aside. Strain liquid; set aside. In a very large skillet cook pancetta until crisp. Drain on paper towels; discard drippings. Cover pancetta; chill.

2 Add olive oil to skillet and heat over medium-high heat. Add chicken pieces; cook about 10 minutes or until browned, turning to brown evenly (add more oil during cooking, if necessary.) Remove chicken from skillet.

3 Add fresh mushrooms, carrot, celery, onion, and garlic to skillet. Cook and stir about 5 minutes or until almost tender. Add undrained tomatoes, wine, thyme, bay leaf, and reserved soaked mushrooms and liquid. Bring to boiling. Return chicken to skillet. Reduce heat to low. Cover; simmer for 35 to 40 minutes or until chicken is no longer pink (180°F). Remove chicken from skillet; keep warm. Simmer sauce, uncovered, about 10 minutes or until desired consistency. Discard bay leaf.

4 Meanwhile, cook pasta according to package directions; drain. In a small bowl combine Parmesan cheese, basil, lemon peel, and pancetta. Divide pasta among four warm pasta bowls. Top with chicken pieces; spoon on sauce and vegetable mixture. Sprinkle with cheese mixture.

Per serving: 896 cal., 42 g total fat (12 g sat. fat), 195 mg chol., 1,362 mg sodium, 67 g carbo., 7 g fiber, 56 g pro.

Pancetta, kalamata olives, and goat cheese are the ingredients that make this Mediterranean dish unforgettable. Orzo, rice-shaped pasta, rounds out the dish.

CHICKEN THIGHS & ORZO

PREP:
20 minutes

COOK:
25 minutes

MAKES:
6 servings

1   4-ounce package pancetta, chopped, or 4 slices bacon, chopped

Olive oil (optional)

6   bone-in chicken thighs (about 2¼ pounds total), skinned

2   14½-ounce cans diced tomatoes with garlic and onion, undrained

1   cup dried orzo pasta

1   cup water

2   cloves garlic, minced

⅓   cup pitted kalamata olives

¼   cup snipped fresh basil

1   6-ounce bag prewashed baby spinach leaves

3   ounces goat cheese with basil and roasted garlic, crumbled (about ⅓ cup)

1 In a 5- to 6-quart Dutch oven cook pancetta until browned. Remove pancetta, reserving 2 tablespoons drippings in Dutch oven (add olive oil if necessary to equal 2 tablespoons fat). Drain pancetta on paper towels; set aside. Cook chicken in drippings about 10 minutes or until light brown, turning to brown evenly; drain off fat.

2 Add undrained tomatoes, uncooked orzo, the water, and garlic to chicken in Dutch oven. Bring to boiling; reduce heat. Cover and simmer for 25 to 30 minutes or until chicken is no longer pink (180°F) and orzo is tender. If necessary, cook, uncovered, for 2 to 3 minutes or until sauce is desired consistency. Stir in pancetta, olives, and basil; heat through. Divide spinach among six plates. Top with chicken, orzo mixture, and cheese.

Per serving: 395 cal., 18 g total fat (5 g sat. fat), 77 mg chol., 1,229 mg sodium, 32 g carbo., 2 g fiber, 26 g pro.

A creamy white wine-and-mushroom sauce gives this old-fashioned dish an elegant touch.

CHICKEN, PASTA & MUSHROOMS

1	tablespoon olive oil
4	skinless, boneless chicken thighs (about 1 to 1¼ pounds total)
	Salt
	Black pepper
2	cups thinly sliced fresh mushrooms (such as button, chanterelle, and/or shiitake)
1	large onion, chopped
2	cloves garlic, minced
2	bay leaves
¾	cup chicken broth
¾	cup dry white wine or chicken broth
2	teaspoons snipped fresh thyme or ½ teaspoon dried thyme, crushed
¼	teaspoon salt
⅔	cup half-and-half or light cream
2	tablespoons all-purpose flour
8	ounces dried lemon-pepper or plain linguine or penne pasta

PREP:
25 minutes

COOK:
30 minutes

MAKES:
4 servings

1 In a large saucepan heat the olive oil over medium heat. Add chicken thighs; cook for 6 to 8 minutes or until browned, turning to brown evenly. Sprinkle lightly with salt and pepper. Transfer chicken to a plate.

2 In same saucepan combine mushrooms, onion, and garlic; cook for 5 minutes, stirring occasionally. Return chicken to saucepan. Add bay leaves, chicken broth, wine, thyme, and ¼ teaspoon salt. Bring to boiling; reduce heat. Cover and simmer gently for 30 minutes. Remove chicken; cover and keep warm. Discard bay leaves.

3 In small bowl whisk half-and-half and flour together until smooth. Add to liquid in saucepan. Cook and stir until thickened and bubbly; cook and stir for 1 minute more. Season to taste with additional pepper. Meanwhile, cook pasta according to the package directions.

4 To serve, drain pasta; place in a serving dish and top with chicken. Spoon half-and-half mixture over chicken and pasta.

Per serving: 489 cal., 12 g total fat (4 g sat. fat), 81 mg chol., 772 mg sodium, 52 g carbo., 2 g fiber, 37 g pro.

Cacciatore means "hunter" in Italian. Some say this dish was devised by clever cooks when hunters came home from the hunt empty-handed.

BAKED CHICKEN CACCIATORE

PREP:
20 minutes

BAKE:
20 minutes + 10 minutes

OVEN:
375°F

MAKES:
4 servings

8   skinless, boneless chicken thighs (about 2 pounds total)
1   tablespoon olive oil
1   teaspoon dried oregano, crushed
¼   teaspoon black pepper
3   cups sliced fresh mushrooms
1   large green sweet pepper, cut into ½-inch-wide strips
1   medium onion, chopped
1   10¾-ounce can condensed tomato soup
1   tablespoon snipped fresh parsley
    Hot cooked mashed potatoes (optional)

1 Preheat oven to 375°F. In a very large oven-going skillet brown chicken in hot olive oil, turning to brown evenly. Drain off fat. Sprinkle browned chicken with oregano and black pepper. Add mushrooms, sweet pepper, and onion to skillet. Cover and bake for 20 minutes.

2 Stir in tomato soup. Bake, uncovered, about 10 minutes more or until chicken is no longer pink (180°F) and vegetables are crisp-tender. Sprinkle with parsley. If desired, serve with mashed potatoes.

Per serving: 285 cal., 10 g total fat (2 g sat. fat), 115 mg chol., 587 mg sodium, 18 g carbo., 3 g fiber, 31 g pro.

To make a lattice crust for these individual pizza pies, begin by laying strips in the middle of each filled baking dish and work your way to the edges, cutting or piecing the strips of pastry to fit.

UPSIDE-DOWN PIZZA PIE

1   14½-ounce can diced tomatoes with basil, garlic, and oregano, undrained

2   cups cubed cooked chicken (about 10 ounces)

1½ cups quartered fresh mushrooms
(such as brown or button)

1   8-ounce can pizza sauce

1   cup shredded 4-cheese pizza blend (4 ounces)

¼   cup grated Parmesan cheese

1   11-ounce package (12) refrigerated breadsticks

Milk

1   tablespoon grated Parmesan cheese

Desired toppings
(such as sliced green onions, snipped fresh chives, sliced pitted black or green olives, chopped sweet green or yellow pepper, and/or shredded 4-cheese pizza blend)

PREP:
30 minutes

BAKE:
25 minutes

STAND:
5 minutes

OVEN:
375°F

MAKES:
4 servings

1 Preheat oven to 375°F. Grease four 12- to 16-ounce individual baking dishes; set aside. In a medium bowl stir together undrained tomatoes, chicken, mushrooms, and pizza sauce. Spoon chicken mixture into prepared baking dishes. Sprinkle the 1 cup 4-cheese pizza blend evenly over chicken mixture. Sprinkle with the ¼ cup Parmesan cheese.

2 Unroll breadstick dough. Separate dough along perforations to form 12 strips. Weave dough strips over filling to form a lattice crust on each baking dish. Depending on the width of your bowls, you may need to cut dough strips to length or piece strips together.

3 Brush dough strips with a little milk. Sprinkle with the 1 tablespoon Parmesan cheese. Bake about 25 minutes or until breadsticks are golden brown and filling is bubbly. Remove from oven. Let stand for 5 minutes before serving. Serve in baking dishes or loosen edges and invert onto dinner plates; remove dishes. Sprinkle with desired toppings.

Per serving: 562 cal., 20 g total fat (8 g sat. fat), 88 mg chol., 1,865 mg sodium, 52 g carbo., 3 g fiber, 40 g pro.

Italian and Mexican cuisines intertwine in this delightful dish. Chicken seasoned with Italian flavors and dried tomatoes is wrapped in flour tortillas for a great easy-to-prepare meal.

ITALIAN-STYLE ENCHILADAS

PREP:
20 minutes

BAKE:
25 minutes

OVEN:
350°F

MAKES:
6 servings

3 cups shredded cooked chicken (about 1 pound)

6 oil-packed dried tomato halves, drained and finely chopped

2 cups shredded mozzarella or Monterey Jack cheese (8 ounces)

4 green onions, sliced

Nonstick cooking spray

2 15-ounce containers refrigerated tomato-basil or marinara pasta sauce

12 6-inch flour tortillas

Dairy sour cream (optional)

Sliced green onions (optional)

1 Preheat oven to 350°F. In a large bowl toss together chicken, tomatoes, 1 cup of the cheese, and the 4 sliced green onions. Coat a 3-quart rectangular baking dish with nonstick cooking spray. Spread 3 tablespoons of the pasta sauce over bottom of prepared baking dish.

2 To assemble enchiladas, spoon about ¼ cup of the chicken mixture just below the center of one tortilla. Roll up tortilla and place seam side down in baking dish. Repeat with remaining chicken mixture and tortillas. Pour remaining pasta sauce over enchiladas. Sprinkle with remaining 1 cup cheese.

3 Bake, covered, for 25 to 30 minutes or until heated through and cheese melts. If desired, garnish with sour cream and additional green onions.

Per serving: 537 cal., 22 g total fat (8 g sat. fat), 82 mg chol., 1,090 mg sodium, 47 g carbo., 6 g fiber, 37 g pro.

Because this recipe calls for chicken that has already been cooked, try these stuffed peppers next time you have leftover chicken in the refrigerator.

GREEN PEPPER RISOTTO

4	small or 2 large green, red, orange, and/or yellow sweet peppers
	Salt
	Black pepper
3	ounces Parmesan or Romano cheese
½	cup Arborio or long grain white rice
1¼	cups chicken broth
1	cup 1-inch pieces asparagus or fresh broccoli florets
1	cup cubed cooked chicken (5 ounces)
2	teaspoons snipped fresh tarragon or oregano or ½ teaspoon dried tarragon or oregano, crushed
¼	cup whipping cream
¼	cup chopped walnuts or pine nuts, toasted

START TO FINISH:
30 minutes

MAKES:
4 servings

1 Cut tops off small sweet peppers or halve large sweet peppers lengthwise (remove and discard stems). Remove and discard seeds and membranes. In a 4-quart Dutch oven immerse sweet peppers in a large amount of boiling water for 3 minutes. Remove and drain, cut sides down, on paper towels. Place, cut sides up, in a serving dish. Sprinkle lightly with salt and black pepper; set aside.

2 Using a vegetable peeler, shave 1 ounce of the Parmesan cheese into thin strips. Finely shred or grate the remaining Parmesan cheese. Set aside.

3 Meanwhile, in a 2-quart saucepan combine uncooked rice and chicken broth. Bring to boiling; reduce heat. Cover and simmer for 15 minutes.

4 Stir asparagus or broccoli, cooked chicken, and herb into rice. Cover and cook for 5 minutes more. Stir in whipping cream, shredded or grated Parmesan cheese, and nuts. Spoon into cooked sweet pepper halves. Top with shaved Parmesan cheese.

Per serving: 338 cal., 19 g total fat (8 g sat. fat), 68 mg chol., 772 mg sodium, 20 g carbo., 2 g fiber, 22 g pro.

The word "piccata" refers to an Italian dish, traditionally made with veal, in which the meat—in this case turkey—is floured, quickly sautéed, and then doused with a lemony sauce.

TURKEY PICCATA WITH FETTUCCINE

START TO FINISH:
30 minutes

MAKES:
4 servings

6   ounces dried fettuccine or linguine
¼   cup all-purpose flour
½   teaspoon lemon-pepper seasoning or black pepper
2   turkey breast tenderloins (about 1 pound total)
2   tablespoons olive oil or cooking oil
⅓   cup dry white wine
2   tablespoons lemon juice
2   tablespoons water
½   teaspoon instant chicken bouillon granules
1   tablespoon capers, rinsed and drained (optional)
2   tablespoons snipped fresh parsley
     Lemon wedges (optional)

1 Cook pasta according to package directions; drain. Meanwhile, in a small bowl stir together flour and lemon-pepper seasoning; set aside.

2 Cut each turkey tenderloin crosswise into ½-inch-thick slices. Dip slices in flour mixture to coat.

3 In a large skillet heat oil over medium-high heat. Add turkey; cook for 6 to 10 minutes or until light golden brown and no longer pink (170°F), turning once. Remove turkey from skillet; cover and keep warm.

4 For sauce, add wine, lemon juice, the water, and bouillon granules to skillet, scraping up crusty bits from bottom of skillet. If desired, stir in capers. Bring to boiling; reduce heat. Simmer, uncovered, for 2 minutes. Remove from heat; stir in parsley.

5 To serve, divide pasta among four dinner plates. Arrange turkey pieces on pasta. Spoon sauce over all. If desired, serve with lemon wedges.

Per serving: 377 cal., 9 g total fat (2 g sat. fat), 68 mg chol., 301 mg sodium, 36 g carbo., 1 g fiber, 33 g pro.

Spinach adds a garden-fresh note to these delicate turkey patties.

MEDITERRANEAN TURKEY BURGERS

1	pound uncooked ground turkey
½	cup crushed rich round crackers (about 13 crackers)
½	of a 10-ounce package frozen chopped spinach, thawed and well drained
⅓	cup chopped onion
2	tablespoons Dijon-style mustard
¼	teaspoon salt
4	ounces drained fresh mozzarella cheese or mozzarella cheese, cut into 4 slices
¼	cup bottled roasted red sweet peppers, drained and cut into strips
4	white or wheat kaiser rolls, split and toasted

PREP:
15 minutes

GRILL:
14 minutes + 2 minutes

MAKES:
4 servings

1 In a large bowl combine turkey, crushed crackers, spinach, onion, mustard, and salt. Shape mixture into four ¾-inch-thick patties. If necessary, cover and chill for 30 minutes or until firm.

2 Place patties on the rack of an uncovered grill directly over medium coals. Grill for 14 to 18 minutes or until done (165°F),* turning once halfway through grilling time.

3 Top burgers with mozzarella and roasted red pepper strips. Grill for 2 to 3 minutes more or until cheese melts. Serve burgers on rolls.

Per serving: 492 cal., 20 g total fat (8 g sat. fat), 110 mg chol., 965 mg sodium, 41 g carbo., 3 g fiber, 34 g pro.

*NOTE: The internal color of a burger is not a reliable doneness indicator. A turkey patty cooked to 165°F is safe, regardless of color. To measure the doneness of a patty, insert an instant-read thermometer through the side of the patty to a depth of 2 to 3 inches.

The egg helps bind the ground turkey mixture together as the burgers cook. Use seasoned bread crumbs for added flavor.

PROVOLONE-TURKEY BURGERS

PREP:
20 minutes

BROIL:
10 minutes + 30 seconds

MAKES:
4 servings

1   egg

¼   cup seasoned fine dry bread crumbs

¼   teaspoon salt

1   pound uncooked ground turkey

4   slices provolone or mozzarella cheese (4 ounces)

4   kaiser rolls or hamburger buns, split and toasted
    Fresh basil leaves or shredded lettuce

¼   cup dried tomato-flavored light mayonnaise dressing

1 Preheat broiler. In a large bowl beat egg with a fork; stir in bread crumbs and salt. Add ground turkey; mix well. Shape into four ½-inch-thick patties.

2 Grease the unheated rack of a broiler pan. Place patties on prepared rack. Broil 3 to 4 inches from the heat for 10 to 12 minutes or until done (165°F),* turning once halfway through broiling time. Top patties with cheese slices; broil about 30 seconds more or until cheese melts.

3 Serve patties on rolls topped with basil leaves or shredded lettuce and mayonnaise dressing.

Per serving: 531 cal., 26 g total fat (9 g sat. fat), 172 mg chol., 1,087 mg sodium, 37 g carbo., 1 g fiber, 35 g pro.

*NOTE: The internal color of a burger is not a reliable doneness indicator. A turkey patty cooked to 165°F is safe, regardless of color. To measure the doneness of a patty, insert an instant-read thermometer through the side of the patty to a depth of 2 to 3 inches.

Light smoked turkey sausage is a lower-fat alternative to regular smoked sausage. The already-cooked polenta browns in minutes for a quick and healthful family dinner.

SAUSAGE & VEGETABLES WITH POLENTA

1   tablespoon olive oil

1   1-pound tube refrigerated cooked polenta, cut crosswise into 12 slices and quartered

8   ounces light smoked turkey sausage, halved lengthwise and cut into ½-inch-thick slices

2   medium red, green, and/or yellow sweet peppers, cut into bite-size pieces

1   medium onion, cut into bite-size pieces

1   cup sliced fresh mushrooms

½   cup purchased tomato-based pasta sauce

1 In 12-inch nonstick skillet heat olive oil over medium heat. Add polenta in a single layer; cook for 10 to 12 minutes or until lightly browned, turning occasionally. Remove from skillet; keep warm.

2 Add sausage, sweet peppers, onion, and mushrooms to skillet. Cook and stir until sausage is brown and vegetables are crisp-tender. Stir in pasta sauce. Add polenta; gently toss to combine ingredients. Heat through.

Per serving: 260 cal., 9 g total fat (2 g sat. fat), 38 mg chol., 1,088 mg sodium, 32 g carbo., 5 g fiber, 14 g pro.

START TO FINISH:
35 minutes

MAKES:
4 servings

A perfect way to use leftover Thanksgiving turkey, this version of the classic dish is super quick, thanks to the use of cooked turkey and ready-to-serve canned soup.

SHORTCUT TURKEY TETRAZZINI

PREP:
20 minutes

BAKE:
12 minutes

OVEN:
425°F

MAKES:
4 servings

Nonstick cooking spray

6 ounces dried spaghetti

1 19-ounce can ready-to-serve chunky creamy chicken with mushroom soup

6 ounces cooked turkey breast, chopped (about 1 cup)

½ cup finely shredded Parmesan cheese (2 ounces)

2 tablespoons sliced almonds

1 Preheat oven to 425°F. Lightly coat a 2-quart square baking dish with nonstick cooking spray; set aside. Cook spaghetti according to the package directions; drain well and return to hot pan. Stir in chicken with mushroom soup, turkey, and half of the cheese; heat through.

2 Transfer spaghetti mixture to baking dish. Sprinkle with almonds and remaining cheese. Bake for 12 to 15 minutes or until top is golden brown.

Per serving: 413 cal., 13 g total fat (5 g sat. fat), 59 mg chol., 752 mg sodium, 43 g carbo., 2 g fiber, 28 g pro.

Orange roughy is a firm, mild fish with white flesh. If it is not available at your supermarket, any white fish, such as cod or tilapia, will work just fine.

ORANGE ROUGHY WITH PUTTANESCA SAUCE

1   pound fresh or frozen skinless orange roughy
    or other white fish fillets

1   teaspoon dried oregano, crushed

½   teaspoon coarsely ground black pepper

1   tablespoon olive oil

4   medium plum tomatoes, chopped (about 1⅓ cups)

1   small onion, cut into thin wedges

½   of a 2¼-ounce can sliced ripe olives, drained (¼ cup)

¼   cup dry white wine or chicken broth

1   tablespoon capers, drained

2   cloves garlic, minced

    Hot cooked orzo pasta (rosamarina) (optional)

1 Thaw fish, if frozen. Rinse fish; pat dry with paper towels. Measure thickness of fish. Cut fish into four portions. Sprinkle fish with half of the oregano and half of the pepper.

2 In a large skillet heat olive oil over medium heat. Add fish, seasoned sides down; cook for 2 minutes, turning once. Add tomatoes, onion, olives, wine, capers, garlic, and the remaining oregano and pepper. Bring to boiling; reduce heat. Cover; simmer for 4 to 6 minutes per ½-inch thickness of fish or until fish flakes easily when tested with a fork.

3 Using a slotted spoon, transfer fish to serving platter. Boil wine mixture, uncovered, for 1½ to 2 minutes or until slightly thickened. Spoon over fish. If desired, serve with hot cooked orzo.

Per serving: 152 cal., 6 g total fat (1 g sat. fat), 23 mg chol., 211 mg sodium, 5 g carbo., 2 g fiber, 18 g pro.

START TO FINISH:
30 minutes

MAKES:
4 servings

For real Italian flavor, use canned tuna packed in olive oil (called genova tonna) for this recipe. Look for it in Italian specialty food stores.

TUNA, FENNEL & ROTINI CASSEROLE

PREP:
20 minutes

BAKE:
20 minutes

OVEN:
375°F

MAKES:
6 servings

1½ cups dried rotini pasta

2 tablespoons butter or margarine

¾ cup seasoned croutons, slightly crushed

2 cups sliced fennel (about 2 small fennel bulbs)

1 10-ounce container refrigerated light Alfredo sauce

2 tablespoons capers, rinsed and drained (optional)

2 6-ounce cans firm-chunk tuna (packed in oil), drained and broken up

1 Preheat oven to 375°F. Cook pasta according to package directions; drain.

2 Meanwhile, in a medium saucepan melt butter over medium heat. In a small bowl combine croutons with 1 tablespoon of the melted butter; toss to coat.

3 Add fennel to the remaining butter in saucepan. Cover and cook for 6 to 8 minutes or just until fennel is tender, stirring occasionally. Stir in cooked pasta, Alfredo sauce, and, if desired, drained capers. Fold in drained tuna.

4 Transfer tuna mixture to a 1½-quart casserole. Top with croutons. Bake about 20 minutes or until heated through.

Per serving: 306 cal., 11 g total fat (6 g sat. fat), 44 mg chol., 527 mg sodium, 29 g carbo., 9 g fiber, 20 g pro.

Take advantage of the peeled and deveined fresh or frozen shrimp at the grocery store. It's a great timesaver! For this recipe, you'll need to purchase about 12 ounces peeled, deveined shrimp.

TOMATO BISQUE SHRIMP OVER PENNE

1	pound fresh or frozen medium shrimp
2	tablespoons butter or margarine
2	cups sliced fresh mushrooms
½	cup chopped onion
½	cup chopped green sweet pepper
2	cloves garlic, minced
1	10¾-ounce can condensed tomato bisque soup
⅔	cup water
½	teaspoon dried Italian seasoning, crushed
	Hot cooked penne or rotini pasta
	Shredded or grated Parmesan cheese (optional)

START TO FINISH:
40 minutes

MAKES:
6 servings

1 Thaw shrimp, if frozen. Peel and devein shrimp. Rinse shrimp; pat dry with paper towels. Set aside.

2 In a large skillet melt butter over medium heat. Add mushrooms, onion, sweet pepper, and garlic; cook about 5 minutes or until vegetables are tender. Stir in tomato bisque soup, the water, and Italian seasoning. Bring to boiling; reduce heat. Cover and simmer for 10 minutes.

3 Add shrimp to skillet; cook for 3 to 4 minutes or until shrimp are opaque. Serve with hot cooked pasta. If desired, top individual servings with Parmesan cheese.

Per serving: 269 cal., 7 g total fat (4 g sat. fat), 98 mg chol., 510 mg sodium, 34 g carbo., 2 g fiber, 17 g pro.

Fennel and shrimp are complemented by a tangy orange sauce. Orange slices dress up the dish.

LINGUINE WITH FENNEL & SHRIMP

START TO FINISH:
30 minutes

MAKES:
4 servings

12 ounces fresh or frozen peeled and deveined shrimp

8 ounces dried plain, spinach, or tomato-basil linguine or fettuccine

1 tablespoon olive oil or cooking oil

1 medium fennel bulb, trimmed* and sliced crosswise

1 cup chicken broth

¼ cup orange juice

1 tablespoon cornstarch

2 oranges, peeled, halved lengthwise, and sliced

2 green onions, thinly sliced

1 Thaw shrimp, if frozen. Rinse shrimp; pat dry with paper towels. Set aside.

2 Cook pasta according to package directions, adding shrimp for the last 3 minutes of cooking or until shrimp are opaque and pasta is tender but still firm. Drain well. Return pasta and shrimp to hot saucepan; cover and keep warm.

3 Meanwhile, for sauce, in a medium saucepan heat oil over medium heat. Add fennel; cook for 3 to 5 minutes or until crisp-tender. In a small bowl stir together chicken broth, orange juice, and cornstarch. Add broth mixture to fennel in saucepan. Cook and stir until thickened and bubbly. Cook and stir for 2 minutes more. Gently stir in orange slices. Heat through.

4 Pour sauce over pasta mixture; toss gently to coat. Transfer to a warm serving dish. Sprinkle with green onions.

Per serving: 392 cal., 6 g total fat (1 g sat. fat), 130 mg chol., 386 mg sodium, 57 g carbo., 4 g fiber, 26 g pro.

*NOTE: Cut off and discard upper stalks of fennel bulb. Remove any wilted outer layers of stalks. Wash fennel and cut in half lengthwise. Remove core and discard.

A magnificent garlic cream sauce gives this baked dish intense flavor, while a sprinkling of Monterey Jack cheese with jalapeños gives it a spicy kick.

SHRIMP FETTUCCINE

1	pound fresh or frozen medium shrimp in shells
¼	cup butter or margarine
2	to 3 teaspoons garlic powder
8	ounces dried fettuccine
½	cup whipping cream
½	cup grated Parmesan cheese
4	ounces Monterey Jack cheese with jalapeño chile peppers, shredded (1 cup)
2	tablespoons snipped fresh parsley

PREP:
35 minutes

BAKE:
10 minutes

OVEN:
350°F

MAKES:
4 servings

1 Preheat oven to 350°F. Grease a 2-quart casserole; set aside. Thaw shrimp, if frozen. Peel and devein shrimp. Rinse shrimp; pat dry with paper towels. In a large skillet heat butter over medium-high heat. Add shrimp and garlic powder. Cook, stirring frequently, for 1 to 3 minutes or until shrimp are opaque. Set aside.

2 Cook fettuccine according to package directions; drain. Return fettuccine to hot pan; add whipping cream and Parmesan cheese. Toss over medium heat until cheese has melted. Remove from heat. Add shrimp mixture; toss to combine.

3 Spoon shrimp-pasta mixture into prepared casserole. Sprinkle with Monterey Jack cheese and parsley. Bake for 10 to 15 minutes or until heated through and cheese on top is melted.

Per serving: 660 cal., 36 g total fat (22 g sat. fat), 235 mg chol., 508 mg sodium, 46 g carbo., 2 g fiber, 36 g pro.

These mouthwatering shrimp packets are full of zesty Italian flavors. And because all the ingredients are folded up in parchment paper or foil, cleanup is a breeze.

MEDITERRANEAN SHRIMP PACKETS

PREP:
25 minutes

BAKE:
25 minutes

OVEN:
425°F

MAKES:
4 servings

8   ounces fresh or frozen peeled and deveined medium shrimp with tails

1   cup quick-cooking couscous

1   cup boiling water

2   small zucchini and/or yellow summer squash, halved lengthwise and thinly sliced

1   small red, yellow, or green sweet pepper, cut into bite-size strips

1   9-ounce package frozen artichoke hearts, thawed

¼   teaspoon coarsely ground black pepper

⅛   teaspoon salt

½   cup bottled Italian salad dressing

¼   cup thinly sliced fresh basil or fresh spinach

1 Preheat oven to 425°F. Thaw shrimp, if frozen. Rinse shrimp; pat dry with paper towels. Set aside. Cut four 16×12-inch pieces of parchment or use precut sheets. (Or tear off four 24×8-inch pieces heavy foil. Fold each piece in half to make four 18×12-inch pieces.)

2 In a small saucepan combine couscous and boiling water; cover and let stand for 5 minutes. Divide couscous mixture, shrimp, squash, sweet pepper, and artichokes evenly among the parchment or foil pieces. Sprinkle with black pepper and salt. Drizzle with salad dressing.

3 Bring together two opposite edges of each parchment or foil piece; seal with a double fold. Fold remaining ends to completely enclose the food, allowing space for steam to build. Place the packets in a single layer on a baking pan.

4 Bake about 25 minutes or until shrimp are opaque (carefully open a packet to check). Carefully open packets and sprinkle shrimp mixture with basil or spinach.

Per serving: 364 cal., 10 g total fat (2 g sat. fat), 86 mg chol., 696 mg sodium, 48 g carbo., 7 g fiber, 20 g pro.

Dried Italian seasoning allows you to add a variety of Italian herbs—usually basil, rosemary, oregano, and thyme—in just one measure. What a great timesaver!

SHRIMP ITALIAN

8	ounces fresh or frozen cooked, peeled, and deveined medium shrimp
½	cup chopped onion
1	tablespoon butter or margarine
1	10¾-ounce can condensed cream of shrimp or cream of mushroom soup
⅔	cup half-and-half or light cream
1	4-ounce can (drained weight) sliced mushrooms, drained
⅓	cup grated Parmesan cheese
1	teaspoon dried Italian seasoning, crushed
4	ounces dried penne or gemelli pasta (about 1 cup), cooked and drained
3	tablespoons grated Parmesan cheese

PREP:
25 minutes

BAKE:
40 minutes

OVEN:
350°F

MAKES:
4 to 6 servings

1 Preheat oven to 350°F. Thaw shrimp, if frozen. Rinse shrimp; pat dry with paper towels. In a medium saucepan cook onion in hot butter until tender. Stir in shrimp, cream of shrimp soup, half-and-half, mushrooms, the ⅓ cup Parmesan cheese, and the Italian seasoning. Stir in cooked pasta. Spoon into a 1½-quart casserole. Sprinkle with the 3 tablespoons Parmesan cheese.

2 Bake about 40 minutes or until heated through.

Per serving: 365 cal., 16 g total fat (8 g sat. fat), 154 mg chol., 1,036 mg sodium, 32 g carbo., 3 g fiber, 23 g pro.

This irresistible lasagna, made with cream cheese and cottage cheese rather than ricotta, oozes with luscious seafood-packed layers.

SEAFOOD LASAGNA

PREP:
40 minutes

BAKE:
45 minutes

STAND:
10 minutes

OVEN:
350°F

MAKES:
12 servings

12   ounces fresh or frozen cooked, peeled, and deveined shrimp, halved lengthwise

8   dried lasagna noodles

1   cup chopped onion

2   tablespoons butter or margarine

1   3-ounce package cream cheese, softened and cut up

1   12-ounce carton cream-style cottage cheese

1   beaten egg

2   teaspoons dried basil, crushed

¼   teaspoon salt

⅛   teaspoon black pepper

2   10¾-ounce cans condensed cream of mushroom soup

⅓   cup milk

1   6½-ounce can crabmeat, drained, flaked, and cartilage removed

¼   cup finely shredded Parmesan cheese (1 ounce)

1 Preheat oven to 350°F. Grease a 3-quart rectangular baking dish; set aside.

2 Thaw shrimp, if frozen. Rinse shrimp; pat dry with paper towels. Cook lasagna noodles according to package directions; drain. Arrange four of the noodles in the bottom of prepared baking dish. Set aside.

3 In a medium skillet cook onion in hot butter until tender. Remove from heat. Add cream cheese and stir until melted. Stir in cottage cheese, egg, basil, salt, and pepper. Spread half of the cheese mixture over the noodles.

4 In a large bowl combine cream of mushroom soup and milk; stir in shrimp and crabmeat. Spread half of the shrimp mixture over cheese layer. Repeat layers. Sprinkle with Parmesan cheese.

5 Bake about 45 minutes or until an instant-read thermometer inserted in center registers 170°F. Let stand for 10 to 15 minutes before serving.

Per serving: 243 cal., 11 g total fat (5 g sat. fat), 112 mg chol., 720 mg sodium, 18 g carbo., 1 g fiber, 17 g pro.

If you're too busy to shop during the work week, keep these five ingredients on hand and you can make this tasty recipe at your convenience.

CRAB & SPINACH PASTA WITH FONTINA

8   ounces dried bow-tie pasta (3½ cups)

1   10-ounce package frozen chopped spinach, thawed and well drained

2   6- to 6½-ounce cans crabmeat, drained, flaked, and cartilage removed

1   26-ounce jar tomato-based pasta sauce

1½ cups shredded fontina cheese (6 ounces)

1 Preheat oven to 375°F. Cook pasta according to package directions; drain. Meanwhile, in a medium bowl combine spinach and crabmeat.

2 Cover bottom of a 2-quart square baking dish with 1 cup of the pasta sauce. Top with cooked pasta. Top pasta evenly with crab mixture. Sprinkle with ¾ cup of the cheese. Top with remaining sauce. Sprinkle with remaining ¾ cup cheese.

3 Bake for 30 to 35 minutes or until sauce is bubbly around edges and cheese is slightly golden brown. Let stand for 10 minutes before serving.

Per serving: 376 cal., 11 g total fat (6 g sat. fat), 83 mg chol., 1,061 mg sodium, 45 g carbo., 5 g fiber, 27 g pro.

PREP:
30 minutes

BAKE:
30 minutes

STAND:
10 minutes

OVEN:
375°F

MAKES:
6 servings

Asparagus adds crisp flavor and texture, while Brie cheese makes this lobster dish extra elegant.

LOBSTER LASAGNA

PREP:
40 minutes

BAKE:
20 minutes + 5 minutes

STAND:
5 minutes

OVEN:
475°F/400°F

MAKES:
6 servings

1	pound fresh asparagus
1	tablespoon olive oil
4	ounces no-boil lasagna noodles
2	tablespoons butter or margarine
2	tablespoons all-purpose flour
¾	cup chicken broth
⅛	teaspoon ground white pepper
1	4½-ounce round Brie cheese, peeled and cubed
2	tablespoons dry sherry (optional)
1¼	cups chopped cooked lobster meat or one 6- or 8-ounce package flake-style imitation lobster
⅓	cup grated Parmesan cheese
½	cup chopped tomato

1 Preheat oven to 475°F. Snap off and discard woody bases from asparagus. If desired, scrape off scales. Cut asparagus into 2-inch-long pieces. Place in a 13×9×2-inch baking pan; toss with olive oil. Bake, uncovered, for 5 to 10 minutes or until crisp-tender; cool.

2 Meanwhile, separate lasagna noodles and soak in water for 15 minutes; drain. Reduce oven temperature to 400°F.

3 In a small saucepan melt butter over medium heat; stir in flour. Cook and stir about 2 minutes or until flour is lightly browned. Stir in chicken broth and white pepper; cook and stir until thickened and bubbly. Reduce heat to low. Stir in Brie until melted. If desired, stir in sherry.

4 Grease a 2-quart square baking dish; place one-third of the lasagna noodles in bottom of dish, folding or trimming as necessary to fit. Top with ⅓ cup of the sauce, half of the asparagus, half of the lobster, and a sprinkle of the Parmesan cheese.

5 Repeat layers with another one-third of the noodles, ⅓ cup of the sauce, remaining asparagus, remaining lobster, and a sprinkle of the Parmesan cheese. Top with remaining lasagna noodles, chopped tomato, remaining sauce, and remaining Parmesan cheese. Cover and bake in the 400°F oven for 20 minutes. Uncover and bake for 5 to 10 minutes more or until bubbly. Let stand for 5 minutes before serving.

Per serving: 263 cal., 14 g total fat (7 g sat. fat), 57 mg chol., 466 mg sodium, 18 g carbo., 1 g fiber, 16 g pro.

If lobster is not available, try this recipe with another kind of seafood such as shrimp, scallops, or cod. The recipe calls for cooked seafood so precook whatever type you choose to use.

LOBSTER MANICOTTI WITH CHIVE CREAM SAUCE

12	dried manicotti shells
1	tablespoon butter or margarine
1	tablespoon all-purpose flour
1¼	cups milk
1	8-ounce tub cream cheese with chive and onion
¼	cup grated Romano or Parmesan cheese
12	ounces chopped cooked lobster or chunk-style imitation lobster (about 2⅔ cups)
1	10-ounce package frozen chopped broccoli, thawed and well drained
½	of a 7-ounce jar roasted red sweet peppers, drained and chopped, or one 4-ounce jar diced pimiento, drained
¼	teaspoon black pepper
	Paprika

PREP:
45 minutes

BAKE:
30 minutes

OVEN:
350°F

MAKES:
6 servings

1 Cook the manicotti shells according to package directions. Drain; rinse with cold water. Drain again.

2 Meanwhile, for cheese sauce, in a medium saucepan melt butter over medium heat. Add flour and stir until combined. Add 1 cup of the milk. Cook and stir until mixture is thickened and bubbly. Turn heat to low. Gradually add cream cheese, stirring until smooth. Stir in Romano cheese.

3 Preheat oven to 350°F. For filling, in a medium bowl combine ¾ cup of the cheese sauce, the lobster, broccoli, roasted sweet peppers, and black pepper. Using a small spoon, carefully fill each manicotti shell with about ⅓ cup of the filling. Arrange filled shells in an ungreased 3-quart rectangular baking dish. Stir the remaining ¼ cup milk into the remaining cheese sauce; pour over the shells. Sprinkle with paprika.

4 Bake, covered, for 30 to 40 minutes or until heated through.

Per serving: 386 cal., 17 g total fat (11 g sat. fat), 90 mg chol., 471 mg sodium, 34 g carbo., 2 g fiber, 21 g pro.

Because so much of Italy is bounded by water, clams are popular in many Italian dishes. If you can't find whole baby canned clams, use chopped clams instead.

PASTA WITH RED CLAM SAUCE

PREP:
15 minutes

COOK:
30 minutes

MAKES:
4 servings

1	tablespoon olive oil or cooking oil
3	cloves garlic, minced
⅛	to ¼ teaspoon crushed red pepper
⅛	teaspoon coarsely ground black pepper
2	14½-ounce cans diced tomatoes, undrained
1	10-ounce can whole baby clams
1	tablespoon snipped fresh basil or 1 teaspoon dried basil, crushed
½	teaspoon anchovy paste (optional)
2	tablespoons snipped fresh parsley
8	ounces dried mostaccioli or cavatelli pasta (about 1½ cups)

1 For sauce, in a large skillet heat oil over medium heat. Add garlic; cook for 30 seconds. Add crushed red pepper and black pepper. Cook and stir for 30 seconds more. Remove from heat.

2 Drain one can of the tomatoes; set aside. Drain clams, reserving juice. Set clams aside. Add drained tomatoes, undrained tomatoes, reserved clam juice, dried basil (if using), and anchovy paste (if desired) to mixture in skillet. Bring to boiling. Boil gently about 30 minutes or until desired consistency. Stir in clams, fresh basil (if using), and parsley; heat through.

3 Meanwhile, cook pasta according to package directions. Drain well. Serve sauce over pasta.

Per serving: 320 cal., 4 g total fat (1 g sat. fat), 11 mg chol., 543 mg sodium, 56 g carbo., 2 g fiber, 12 g pro.

MEATLESS PASTA MAIN DISHES

Kalamata olives and fresh basil are the robust ingredients that make this vegetarian dish a true delight.

ARTICHOKE & OLIVE SAUCE

PREP:
25 minutes

COOK:
20 minutes

MAKES:
4 servings

10	ounces dried rotini or small shell macaroni
1	tablespoon olive oil
1½	cups sliced onion
2	cloves garlic, thinly sliced
½	teaspoon salt
¼	teaspoon black pepper
1	14-ounce can artichoke hearts, drained and quartered
½	cup pitted kalamata olives, halved
½	cup whipping cream
½	cup grated Asiago or pecorino Romano cheese
1	6-ounce package prewashed baby spinach
¼	cup snipped fresh basil or parsley
	Grated Asiago or pecorino Romano cheese

1 Cook pasta according to package directions. Drain well. Return to hot pan; cover and keep warm.

2 Meanwhile, for sauce, in a very large skillet heat olive oil over medium-low heat. Add onion, garlic, salt, and pepper; cook about 10 minutes or until very tender, stirring occasionally.

3 Add artichoke hearts and olives. Cook for 3 minutes, stirring occasionally. Add whipping cream. Bring just to boiling; reduce heat. Simmer, uncovered, about 3 minutes or until slightly thickened. Stir in the ½ cup grated cheese. Add spinach and basil or parsley; toss just until spinach is wilted.

4 Serve sauce over pasta. Top with additional grated cheese.

Per serving: 541 cal., 24 g total fat (11 g sat. fat), 56 mg chol., 999 mg sodium, 65 g carbo., 7 g fiber, 16 g pro.

Nutmeg and allspice enhance the flavor of many cheese sauces. A dash of each gives this baked dish outstanding flavor.

TRIPLE-CHEESE MACARONI

¼ cup butter or margarine

1 cup milk

½ teaspoon salt

⅛ teaspoon ground nutmeg

⅛ teaspoon ground allspice

⅛ teaspoon freshly ground black pepper

Dash cayenne pepper

8 ounces dried whole wheat or regular small shell macaroni, elbow macaroni, or wagon wheel macaroni (ruote)

4 ounces sharp white cheddar cheese or sharp cheddar cheese, shredded (1 cup)

4 ounces fontina, Monterey Jack, or Gouda cheese, shredded (1 cup)

3 eggs

½ cup dairy sour cream

¼ cup grated Asiago, Parmesan, or Romano cheese

¼ cup fine dry bread crumbs

Tomato wedges (optional)

PREP:
30 minutes

BAKE:
30 minutes

STAND:
5 minutes

OVEN:
350°F

MAKES:
4 servings

1 Preheat oven to 350°F. In a small saucepan melt butter over medium heat. Add milk, salt, nutmeg, allspice, black pepper, and cayenne pepper. Cook and stir until heated through. Remove from heat; set aside to cool.

2 Meanwhile, cook macaroni according to package directions. Set aside ¼ cup of the hot pasta water. Drain the pasta in a colander. Immediately place drained pasta in a large bowl. (Should have 4 cups cooked pasta.) Drizzle the reserved pasta water over the drained pasta. While pasta is still hot, stir in the cheddar and fontina cheeses.

3 Whisk eggs and sour cream into milk mixture in saucepan. Stir sour cream mixture into pasta mixture. Transfer mixture to a 2-quart casserole. In a small bowl combine Asiago cheese and bread crumbs. Sprinkle bread crumb mixture over top of pasta mixture. Bake, uncovered, for 30 to 40 minutes or until heated through. Let stand for 5 minutes before serving. If desired, garnish with tomato wedges.

Per serving: 719 cal., 44 g total fat (26 g sat. fat), 275 mg chol., 1,125 mg sodium, 53 g carbo., 5 g fiber, 33 g pro.

Walnuts give this cheese-stuffed pasta bake an unexpected and satisfying crunch. Experiment with different kinds of nuts, such as almonds or pine nuts.

CHEESE & NUT STUFFED SHELLS

PREP:
45 minutes

BAKE:
45 minutes

OVEN:
350°F

MAKES:
6 servings

24	dried jumbo shell macaroni*
2	eggs
1	15-ounce carton ricotta cheese
1½	cups shredded mozzarella cheese (6 ounces)
1	cup shredded Parmesan cheese (4 ounces)
1	cup chopped walnuts
1	tablespoon snipped fresh parsley
½	teaspoon salt
¼	teaspoon black pepper
⅛	teaspoon ground nutmeg
1	26-ounce jar thick-and-chunky pasta sauce (2¾ cups)

1 Cook pasta shells according to package directions. Drain shells; rinse with cold water and drain well. Set shells in a single layer on a sheet of foil. Preheat oven to 350°F.

2 Meanwhile, for filling, in a large bowl beat eggs with a whisk; stir in ricotta cheese, 1 cup of the mozzarella cheese, ¾ cup of the Parmesan cheese, the walnuts, parsley, salt, pepper, and nutmeg.

3 Spread 1 cup of the pasta sauce in the bottom of a 3-quart baking dish. Spoon a heaping tablespoon of the filling into each cooked pasta shell. Arrange filled shells in the baking dish. Pour remaining sauce over shells. Sprinkle with the remaining ½ cup mozzarella cheese and ¼ cup Parmesan cheese. Bake, covered, about 45 minutes or until heated through.

Per serving: 549 cal., 32 g total fat (12 g sat. fat), 132 mg chol., 1,072 mg sodium, 36 g carbo., 4 g fiber, 30 g pro.

*NOTE: Cook a few extra shells to replace any that tear during cooking.

Intensely flavored portobello and shiitake mushrooms and reduced red wine make the sauce richly flavored and extra fragrant.

FETTUCCINE WITH WILD MUSHROOM SAUCE

4   4-ounce fresh portobello mushrooms

5   ounces fresh shiitake mushrooms

2   tablespoons olive oil

2   cloves garlic, thinly sliced

¾   cup dry red wine

1   14½-ounce can diced tomatoes, drained

¼   cup beef broth

2   tablespoons butter or margarine

2   9-ounce packages refrigerated fettuccine

    Salt

    Freshly ground black pepper

1   to 2 ounces Parmesan cheese, coarsely grated

START TO FINISH:
40 minutes

MAKES:
4 to 6 servings

1 Remove stems and gills from the portobello mushrooms; slice mushrooms. Discard stems from shiitake mushrooms; halve mushrooms. Set aside.

2 In a large skillet heat 1 tablespoon of the olive oil over medium heat. Add sliced portobellos; cook and stir for 3 to 5 minutes or until tender. Use a slotted spoon to transfer portobello mushrooms to a large bowl. Add shiitake mushrooms to hot skillet; cook and stir about 3 minutes or until tender. Transfer to the bowl.

3 Add remaining 1 tablespoon olive oil and the garlic to hot skillet; cook and stir for 1 minute. Carefully add red wine; simmer, uncovered, for 2 to 3 minutes or until reduced by about half.

4 Add drained tomatoes and broth. Simmer, uncovered, for 3 minutes. Add mushroom mixture, including any liquid that has accumulated. Cook for 5 to 7 minutes more or until liquid is thick. Stir in butter.

5 Meanwhile, cook fettuccine according to package directions.

6 Toss fettuccine with mushroom sauce. Season to taste with salt and freshly ground black pepper. Top with Parmesan cheese.

Per serving: 616 cal., 20 g total fat (8 g sat. fat), 103 mg chol., 572 mg sodium, 83 g carbo., 5 g fiber, 23 g pro.

A colorful melange of fresh veggies, savory herbs, and a light and creamy sauce results in a delicate, yet substantial, main dish.

GARDEN-SPECIAL PRIMAVERA

START TO FINISH:
45 minutes

MAKES:
6 servings

6   ounces fresh wax or green beans, cut into 2-inch pieces

½   cup bias-sliced carrot

6   ounces fresh asparagus, trimmed and cut into 2-inch pieces

1   cup broccoli or cauliflower florets

12   ounces dried fettuccine, linguine, vermicelli, or spaghetti

1   small red and/or yellow sweet pepper, cut into bite-size strips

1   small zucchini, halved lengthwise and sliced (1 cup)

2   tablespoons butter or margarine

1   small onion, cut into thin wedges

2   cloves garlic, minced

¾   cup vegetable broth or chicken broth

¾   cup whipping cream

2   tablespoons all-purpose flour

½   cup finely shredded Parmesan cheese (2 ounces)

2   green onions, thinly sliced

2   tablespoons snipped fresh basil or 2 teaspoons dried basil, crushed

1 In a covered large saucepan cook beans and carrot in a small amount of boiling salted water for 10 minutes. Add asparagus and broccoli or cauliflower. Return to boiling; reduce heat. Cover and cook about 5 minutes more or until vegetables are crisp-tender. Drain.

2 Meanwhile, in a large saucepan cook pasta according to package directions, adding sweet pepper and zucchini for the last 3 minutes of cooking (vegetables should be crisp-tender). Drain and return mixture to the hot saucepan. Add the bean mixture to the saucepan. Cover and keep warm while preparing sauce.

3 For sauce, in a medium saucepan melt butter over medium heat. Add onion and garlic; cook for 5 to 8 minutes or until tender. Stir in broth. Bring to boiling; reduce heat. In a small bowl stir together whipping cream and flour. Add cream mixture to broth mixture in saucepan. Cook and stir until thickened and bubbly. Stir in Parmesan cheese, the green onions, and basil. Cook and stir for 1 minute more. Pour sauce over pasta and vegetables. Toss gently to coat.

Per serving: 421 cal., 18 g total fat (11 g sat. fat), 56 mg chol., 288 mg sodium, 53 g carbo., 4 g fiber, 13 g pro.

Pappardelle means "gulp down" in Italian. The name makes it a very suitable pasta for the mouthwatering roasted tomato sauce.

PAPPARDELLE ALLA PEPOLINO

12   ounces dried pappardelle, mafalda, or fettuccine

2   tablespoons olive oil

1   clove garlic, minced

1   8-ounce can tomato sauce

1   tablespoon snipped fresh thyme

¼   teaspoon crushed red pepper

1   recipe Roasted Tomatoes

¼   teaspoon freshly ground black pepper

Salt

Black pepper

¼   cup coarsely shaved pecorino Romano or Parmesan cheese*

1 In a large saucepan cook pasta according to package directions; drain and set aside.

2 In the same saucepan heat olive oil over medium heat. Add garlic; cook and stir for 30 seconds. Stir in tomato sauce, half of the thyme, and the crushed red pepper. Bring to boiling; reduce heat. Simmer, uncovered, for 2 minutes.

3 Add cooked pasta, Roasted Tomatoes, black pepper, and remaining thyme. Heat through. Season to taste with salt and black pepper. Transfer to a serving dish. Sprinkle with cheese.

ROASTED TOMATOES: Preheat oven to 450°F. Line a 15×10×1-inch baking pan with foil. Halve 8 plum tomatoes; place tomatoes, cut sides up, on the prepared baking pan. Drizzle with 1 tablespoon olive oil; sprinkle with salt and black pepper. Roast, uncovered, for 20 to 25 minutes or until bottoms of the tomatoes are dark brown. Remove from pan; carefully halve each piece.

Per serving: 468 cal., 14 g total fat (2 g sat. fat), 4 mg chol., 496 mg sodium, 72 g carbo., 4 g fiber, 14 g pro.

*NOTE: To shave cheese into strips, draw a vegetable peeler across a block of cheese.

START TO FINISH:
40 minutes

OVEN:
450°F

MAKES:
4 servings

If Asiago cheese is difficult to find at your supermarket, substitute shredded Parmesan cheese.

RIGATONI & VEGETABLES ALFREDO

START TO FINISH:
30 minutes

MAKES:
4 servings

6   ounces dried rigatoni or mostaccioli pasta

1   small eggplant, peeled, if desired, and cut into ¾-inch pieces (about 12 ounces)

1   medium onion, chopped

2   tablespoons cooking oil

1   medium zucchini or yellow summer squash, quartered lengthwise and cut into ½-inch pieces

1   10-ounce container refrigerated light Alfredo sauce

½   teaspoon garlic salt

2   medium tomatoes, seeded and chopped

½   cup shredded Asiago cheese (2 ounces)

1   tablespoon snipped fresh basil

1 Cook pasta according to package directions. Drain well. Return to hot pan; cover and keep warm.

2 Meanwhile, in a very large skillet cook eggplant and onion in hot oil for 5 minutes. Add zucchini; cook for 2 to 3 minutes more or until zucchini is crisp-tender. Stir in Alfredo sauce, garlic salt, and cooked pasta; heat through.

3 Transfer pasta mixture to a serving dish. Top with chopped tomatoes, Asiago cheese, and basil.

Per serving: 472 cal., 23 g total fat (11 g sat. fat), 47 mg chol., 920 mg sodium, 51 g carbo., 5 g fiber, 16 g pro.

If you don't have a round springform pan, make the lasagna in a 13×9×2-inch baking pan, layering the pasta in traditional lasagna fashion. The layers will be a little more shallow, so the lasagna will bake more quickly.

PESTO LASAGNA PIE

12   dried regular or whole wheat lasagna noodles

1   slightly beaten egg

1   15-ounce carton ricotta cheese

1   8-ounce package shredded Italian blend cheese or mozzarella cheese (2 cups)

     Nonstick cooking spray

2   cups chopped fresh spinach

1   recipe Lemon-Parsley Pesto or 1 cup purchased pesto

1½   cups thinly sliced fresh mushrooms

1   28-ounce can whole Italian-style tomatoes, drained, sliced

1 Preheat oven to 375°F. Cook lasagna noodles according to package directions. Drain lasagna noodles; rinse with cold water and drain well. Lay lasagna noodles in a single layer on a sheet of foil.

2 In a medium bowl combine, egg, ricotta cheese, 1 cup of the shredded cheese, ¼ teaspoon salt, and ¼ teaspoon black pepper; set aside.

3 To assemble pie, lightly coat a 9-inch springform pan with nonstick cooking spray. Arrange four of the lasagna noodles in the bottom of the pan, trimming and overlapping as necessary to cover bottom of pan with one layer of noodles. Top with spinach. Spoon half of the ricotta cheese mixture over spinach, spreading evenly. Spoon one-third of the Lemon-Parsley Pesto over ricotta layer, spreading evenly. Top with another layer of lasagna noodles, trimming to fit. Top with mushrooms. Spread remaining ricotta cheese mixture over mushrooms. Spread half of the remaining Lemon-Parsley Pesto over ricotta layer. Top with another layer of lasagna noodles and remaining Lemon-Parsley Pesto. Top with tomatoes.

4 Place springform pan in a foil-lined shallow baking pan. Bake, covered, for 45 minutes. Uncover and sprinkle with remaining 1 cup Italian blend cheese. Bake, uncovered, about 15 minutes more or until cheese is melted and lasagna is heated through. Cover and let stand on a wire rack for 20 minutes before serving. Carefully remove side of springform pan.

LEMON-PARSLEY PESTO: In a food processor combine 4 cups fresh spinach leaves; ½ cup fresh flat-leaf parsley; ⅓ cup grated Parmesan or Romano cheese; ⅓ cup pine nuts, toasted; 2 cloves garlic, quartered; 2 tablespoons olive oil; 2 teaspoons shredded lemon peel; 2 tablespoons lemon juice; and ¼ teaspoon salt. Cover and process until nearly smooth.

Per serving: 418 cal., 23 g total fat (10 g sat. fat), 76 mg chol., 577 mg sodium, 32 g carbo., 2 g fiber, 23 g pro.

PREP:
50 minutes

BAKE:
45 minutes + 15 minutes

STAND:
20 minutes

OVEN:
375°F

MAKES:
8 to 10 servings

Heating onions until their natural sugars turn brown results in caramelized onions.
The process produces the star flavor in this dish.

CARAMELIZED ONIONS & GARLIC WITH CAVATELLI

PREP:
20 minutes

COOK:
21 minutes

MAKES:
4 servings

10   ounces dried cavatelli or other medium-size pasta (about 2 cups)

1   tablespoon olive oil

2   medium onions, sliced

1   teaspoon sugar

1   medium zucchini, halved lengthwise and sliced

4   cloves garlic, minced

2   tablespoons water

2   tablespoons balsamic vinegar

¼   cup pine nuts or chopped walnuts, toasted

1   tablespoon snipped fresh thyme

Salt

Freshly ground black pepper

1 Cook pasta according to package directions. Drain well. Return to hot pan; cover and keep warm.

2 Meanwhile, in a heavy large skillet heat olive oil over medium-low heat. Add onions; cover and cook for 13 to 15 minutes or until onions are tender, stirring occasionally. Uncover; add sugar. Cook and stir over medium-high heat for 4 to 5 minutes more or until onions are golden brown.

3 Add zucchini and garlic. Cook and stir for 2 minutes. Stir in the water and balsamic vinegar; cook for 2 to 3 minutes more or until zucchini is crisp-tender.

4 In a large bowl toss together warm pasta, onion mixture, nuts, and thyme. Season to taste with salt and freshly ground black pepper.

Per serving: 386 cal., 10 g total fat (1 g sat. fat), 0 mg chol., 97 mg sodium, 64 g carbo., 3 g fiber, 12 g pro.

Nutty Gruyère, grainy ricotta, and tangy goat cheese mesh delightfully for an outstanding flavor combination.

THREE-CHEESE LASAGNA

2	medium eggplants (2 pounds total), chopped (11 cups)
2	large red onions, halved crosswise and thickly sliced
2	cloves garlic, minced
1	cup snipped fresh basil
¼	cup olive oil
12	dried lasagna noodles
8	ounces Gruyère cheese, finely shredded (2 cups)
1	15-ounce carton ricotta cheese
12	ounces goat cheese (chèvre)
1	cup whipping cream
2	eggs
½	teaspoon salt
½	teaspoon black pepper
¼	teaspoon crushed red pepper
2	teaspoons finely shredded lemon peel

PREP:
50 minutes

BAKE:
20 minutes + 15 minutes

STAND:
15 minutes

OVEN:
450°F/375°F

MAKES:
12 servings

1 Preheat oven to 450°F. In a roasting pan combine eggplant, onions, and garlic. Add ½ cup of the basil and the oil; toss to coat. Roast, uncovered, for 30 to 35 minutes or until vegetables are very tender, stirring once; set aside.

2 Meanwhile, cook lasagna noodles according to package directions. Drain lasagna noodles; rinse with cold water and drain well. Lay noodles in a single layer on a sheet of foil.

3 For filling, in a food processor combine 1½ cups of the Gruyère cheese, the ricotta cheese, goat cheese, whipping cream, eggs, salt, black pepper, and crushed red pepper. Cover and process just until combined.

4 Reduce oven temperature to 375°F. Spread one-third of the eggplant mixture evenly in the bottom of a 3-quart rectangular baking dish. Layer with four of the lasagna noodles and one-third of the filling. Repeat layers twice, starting with eggplant and ending with filling. Sprinkle with remaining ½ cup Gruyère cheese.

5 Cover with nonstick foil. Bake for 20 minutes; uncover and bake for 15 to 20 minutes more or until heated through. Let stand for 15 minutes before serving. Sprinkle top with the remaining ½ cup basil and the lemon peel.

Per serving: 439 cal., 30 g total fat (16 g sat. fat), 114 mg chol., 315 mg sodium, 23 g carbo., 3 g fiber, 20 g pro.

A great way to pack lots of vegetables into one dish, this layered delight makes a satisfying family meal. Add interest by using a variety of mushrooms including cremini, button, and shiitake.

VEGETARIAN LASAGNA

PREP:
40 minutes

BAKE:
30 minutes

STAND:
10 minutes

OVEN:
350°F

MAKES:
8 to 10 servings

3	tablespoons olive oil
1	9-ounce package frozen artichoke hearts, thawed, quartered
2	tablespoons dry white wine
1½	pounds fresh asparagus, trimmed and cut into bite-size pieces
1	cup chopped carrot
4	shallots, finely chopped (½ cup)
3	cloves garlic, minced
3	cups fresh mushrooms, quartered
1	cup chopped zucchini
½	cup loose-pack frozen peas, thawed
6	tablespoons butter or margarine
½	cup all-purpose flour
4	cups milk
2	small bay leaves
9	dried lasagna noodles (prepared as in step 1, page 219)
½	cup snipped fresh basil
½	cup snipped fresh parsley
1	cup finely shredded Parmesan cheese (4 ounces)

1 In a large skillet heat 1 tablespoon of the oil over medium heat. Add artichokes; cook and stir for 5 minutes. Add wine; cook and stir for 1 minute. Transfer to a bowl. In a covered large saucepan cook asparagus and carrot in boiling water for 2 minutes; drain. In the same skillet cook shallots and garlic in remaining oil until tender. Add asparagus, carrot, mushrooms, zucchini, and peas; cook and stir 5 minutes more.

2 Preheat oven to 350°F. In the large saucepan melt butter over medium heat; stir in flour until smooth. Cook and stir about 2 minutes or until mixture begins to brown. Stir in milk all at once. Add bay leaves. Cook and stir until thickened and bubbly. Discard bay leaves. Stir in zucchini mixture, artichokes, ¾ teaspoon salt, and ¼ teaspoon black pepper.

3 Arrange three lasagna noodles in a greased 3-quart rectangular baking dish. Spoon one-third of the vegetable mixture over noodles; sprinkle with ¼ cup basil, ¼ cup parsley, and ⅓ cup Parmesan cheese. Repeat the layers. Top with remaining noodles, vegetable mixture, and Parmesan. Bake about 30 minutes or until golden brown. Let stand 10 minutes.

Per serving: 392 cal., 20 g total fat (10 g sat. fat), 40 mg chol., 538 mg sodium, 38 g carbo., 5 g fiber, 15 g pro.

Canned artichoke hearts, frozen spinach, and store-bought pasta sauce make this meal-in-a-dish a snap to prepare.

ARTICHOKE-SPINACH LASAGNA

9 dried lasagna noodles

Nonstick cooking spray

1 medium onion, chopped

4 cloves garlic, minced

1 cup vegetable broth or chicken broth

1 tablespoon snipped fresh rosemary

2 14-ounce cans artichoke hearts, drained and coarsely chopped

2 10-ounce packages frozen chopped spinach, thawed and well drained

1 26- to 28-ounce jar meatless tomato-based pasta sauce

3 cups shredded mozzarella cheese (12 ounces)

1 4-ounce package crumbled herb and garlic feta cheese

PREP:
30 minutes

BAKE:
40 minutes + 15 minutes

STAND:
10 minutes

OVEN:
375°F

MAKES:
8 servings

1 Preheat oven to 375°F. Cook lasagna noodles according to package directions. Drain lasagna noodles; rinse with cold water and drain well. Lay noodles in a single layer on a sheet of foil.

2 Meanwhile, lightly coat an unheated large skillet with nonstick cooking spray. Preheat over medium heat. Add onion and garlic; cook for 3 minutes. Stir in broth and rosemary; bring to boiling. Stir in artichoke hearts and spinach; remove from heat.

3 Lightly coat a 3-quart rectangular baking dish with nonstick cooking spray. Spread ½ cup of the pasta sauce evenly in bottom of dish. Arrange three of the lasagna noodles over the sauce. Layer with half of the spinach mixture and sprinkle with ¾ cup of the mozzarella cheese. Spoon ¾ cup of the sauce over the cheese. Sprinkle the feta cheese over the sauce. Repeat layers with three more noodles, remaining spinach mixture, ¾ cup of the mozzarella cheese, and ¾ cup of the pasta sauce. Top with remaining three lasagna noodles. Spoon remaining pasta sauce over the top. Sprinkle with remaining 1½ cups mozzarella cheese.

4 Cover and bake for 40 minutes. Uncover and bake about 15 minutes more or until heated through. Let stand for 10 minutes before serving.

Per serving: 322 cal., 11 g total fat (7 g sat. fat), 37 mg chol., 1,145 mg sodium, 38 g carbo., 7 g fiber, 21 g pro.

MAKE-AHEAD DIRECTIONS: Prepare lasagna as directed through step 3. Cover baking dish with plastic wrap, then foil; refrigerate for up to 24 hours. To serve, preheat oven to 375°F; remove plastic wrap from baking dish. Bake, covered with foil, for 45 minutes. Uncover and bake for 20 to 25 minutes more or until heated through. Let stand for 10 minutes before serving.

The roasted red sweet peppers add a dose of sweetness to the sauce, and the ricotta cheese makes the whole veggie-filled dish creamy and luscious.

ROASTED PEPPER LASAGNA

PREP:
35 minutes

BAKE:
20 minutes + 15 minutes

STAND:
15 minutes

OVEN:
375°F

MAKES:
6 servings

1 10¾-ounce can condensed tomato soup

1 7-ounce jar roasted red sweet peppers, drained

1 teaspoon dried oregano, crushed

2 cloves garlic, minced

Nonstick cooking spray

1 tablespoon olive oil

2 cups coarsely chopped zucchini and/or yellow summer squash

2 cups sliced fresh mushrooms

1 medium onion, chopped

1 15-ounce carton ricotta cheese

¼ cup finely shredded or grated Parmesan cheese

¼ teaspoon black pepper

6 no-boil lasagna noodles

1 cup shredded mozzarella cheese (4 ounces)

1 Preheat oven to 375°F. For red pepper sauce, in a blender combine tomato soup, roasted red peppers, oregano, and garlic. Cover and blend until nearly smooth; set aside. Coat a 2-quart square baking dish with nonstick cooking spray; set aside.

2 In a large skillet heat oil over medium heat. Add zucchini, mushrooms, and onion; cook about 6 minutes or until zucchini is tender. Drain well. In a small bowl stir together ricotta cheese, Parmesan cheese, and black pepper.

3 To assemble, spread about ¼ cup of the red pepper sauce evenly in the bottom of the prepared dish. Top with two of the lasagna noodles. Top with one-third of the ricotta mixture, one-third of the vegetable mixture, one-third of the remaining red pepper sauce, and one-third of the mozzarella cheese. Repeat layers twice.

4 Bake, covered, for 20 minutes. Uncover and bake for 15 to 20 minutes more or until heated through. Let stand for 15 minutes before serving.

Per serving: 396 cal., 21 g total fat (2 g sat. fat), 63 mg chol., 837 mg sodium, 26 g carbo., 3 g fiber, 26 g pro.

When purchasing asparagus, look for firm, bright green stalks with tight tips. If you're using the asparagus later, store it with the spears standing upright in a jar with about an inch of water.

FETTUCCINE WITH ASPARAGUS, TOMATOES & PESTO

8	ounces fresh asparagus spears
12	ounces dried fettuccine
1	tablespoon olive oil
1	medium onion, cut into thin wedges
4	cloves garlic, minced
¼	teaspoon black pepper
8	plum tomatoes, seeded and chopped (about 2⅔ cups)
½	cup dry white wine
¼	teaspoon salt
¼	cup purchased basil pesto
⅓	cup shredded fresh basil (optional)
	Shredded or grated Parmesan cheese (optional)

START TO FINISH:
35 minutes

MAKES:
4 servings

1 Snap off and discard woody bases from asparagus. Bias-slice asparagus into 1- to 1½-inch-long pieces; set aside.

2 Cook pasta according to package directions. Drain well. Return pasta to hot saucepan; cover and keep warm.

3 Meanwhile, in a large skillet heat olive oil over medium heat. Add onion, garlic, and pepper; cook for 3 minutes, stirring constantly. Add tomatoes; cook for 3 minutes more, stirring often.

4 Add asparagus, wine, and salt. Cook about 5 minutes or until asparagus is crisp-tender. Add asparagus mixture and pesto to pasta; toss gently to coat. Transfer to a warm serving dish. If desired, sprinkle with fresh basil and serve with Parmesan cheese.

Per serving: 524 cal., 15 g total fat (1 g sat. fat), 2 mg chol., 276 mg sodium, 77 g carbo., 5 g fiber, 15 g pro.

Bring out your pasta machine to roll the homemade dough into thin, long sheets. If you don't have a pasta machine, use dried lasagna noodles to make cheese-filled rollups.

FREE-FORM BASIL LASAGNA

PREP:
1 hour

BAKE:
30 minutes

OVEN:
350°F

MAKES:
5 servings

1	cup all-purpose flour
1/8	teaspoon salt
1	egg
2	tablespoons water
1	teaspoon olive oil
8	ounces fresh mozzarella cheese, cubed
6	ounces fontina cheese, shredded
1/2	cup ricotta cheese
1/2	cup finely shredded Parmesan cheese (2 ounces)
1/2	cup snipped fresh basil or 1/4 cup snipped fresh oregano or sage
1/8	teaspoon freshly ground black pepper
2 1/4	cups purchased meatless spaghetti sauce

1 For pasta,* in a medium bowl combine flour and salt. In a small bowl beat together egg, the water, and olive oil. Pour egg mixture all at once into flour mixture. Stir until combined. Knead dough on a lightly floured surface until smooth and elastic (8 to 10 minutes total). Cover and let the dough rest for 10 minutes.

2 Meanwhile, for filling, in a large bowl stir together cheeses, desired herb, and pepper; set aside.

3 Preheat oven to 350°F. Divide pasta dough into five pieces. Using a pasta machine according to manufacturer's directions, roll each piece of pasta dough into thin, long sheets (about 15×4 1/2 inches). Trim each pasta sheet to a 12×4-inch rectangle. Place about 2/3 cup of the cheese filling on each pasta sheet and spread evenly over sheet, leaving about a 1-inch border along the long sides. Fold in long edges to overlap filling slightly. With sides in place, roll up from a short side. Place filled pasta sheets in individual au gratin dishes. Top each filled roll with about 1/2 cup of the spaghetti sauce, being sure to cover all edges of the pasta to prevent edges from drying out.

4 Bake about 30 minutes or until sauce is bubbly.

Per serving: 516 cal., 31 g total fat (17 g sat. fat), 136 mg chol., 1,180 mg sodium, 31 g carbo., 4 g fiber, 29 g pro.

*TEST KITCHEN TIP:
If you prefer, use 10 dried lasagna noodles instead of making fresh pasta. Cook lasagna noodles according to package directions; drain well and cool. Prepare filling as directed in step 2. Spread about 1/3 cup of the filling on each noodle; roll up from a short side and place two lasagna noodles, seam sides down, in each au gratin dish. Cover with sauce, being sure to cover edges of the pasta to prevent edges from drying out. Bake as directed in step 4.

Stacked with fresh vegetables, three cheeses, and aromatic herbs, this lasagna looks as wonderful as it tastes. If you like, garnish the lasagna with fresh rosemary sprigs and cherry tomatoes.

MILE-HIGH MEATLESS LASAGNA PIE

2	tablespoons olive oil
3	medium carrots, finely chopped
1	medium zucchini, finely chopped (2 cups)
4	cloves garlic, minced
3	cups sliced fresh mushrooms (8 ounces)
2	6-ounce packages prewashed baby spinach
2	tablespoons snipped fresh basil
1	beaten egg
1	15-ounce carton ricotta cheese
⅓	cup finely shredded Parmesan cheese
1	26-ounce jar tomato-and-basil pasta sauce (2½ cups)
14	dried lasagna noodles (prepared as in step 1 on page 219)
2	cups shredded fontina or mozzarella cheese (8 ounces)

PREP:
50 minutes

BAKE:
1 hour

STAND:
15 minutes

OVEN:
375°F

MAKES:
10 servings

1 Preheat oven to 375°F. In a large skillet heat 1 tablespoon of the oil over medium-high heat. Add carrots, zucchini, and half of the garlic. Cook and stir about 5 minutes or until crisp-tender. Transfer to a bowl. Heat remaining oil in same skillet. Add mushrooms and remaining garlic. Cook and stir about 5 minutes or until tender. Gradually add spinach. Cook and stir for 1 to 2 minutes or until spinach is wilted. Using a slotted spoon, transfer spinach mixture to medium bowl; stir in basil. In a bowl combine, egg, ricotta, Parmesan, ½ teaspoon salt, and ¼ teaspoon black pepper.

2 To assemble pie, spread ½ cup of the pasta sauce in the bottom of a 9-inch springform pan. Arrange three to four of the lasagna noodles over the sauce, trimming and overlapping as necessary to cover sauce with one layer. Top with half of the spinach mixture. Top with half of the ricotta mixture. Top with another layer of noodles. Spread with half of the remaining pasta sauce. Top with all of the zucchini-carrot mixture. Sprinkle with half of the fontina cheese. Top with another layer of the lasagna noodles. Layer with remaining spinach mixture and ricotta mixture. Top with another layer of noodles and remaining sauce (you may have extra noodles). Gently press down pie with the back of a spatula.

3 Place springform pan on a foil-lined baking sheet. Bake about 1 hour or until heated through, topping with remaining fontina cheese for the last 15 minutes of baking. Cover and let stand on a wire rack for 15 minutes before serving. Carefully remove side of springform pan.

Per serving: 450 cal., 23 g total fat (12 g sat. fat), 82 mg chol., 966 mg sodium, 37 g carbo., 7 g fiber, 26 g pro.

Use tricolor pappardelle pasta for extra presentation points. Raisins give this dish an enjoyable touch of sweetness.

PAPPARDELLE WITH SPINACH & RED ONIONS

START TO FINISH:
30 minutes

MAKES:
4 servings

8 ounces dried tri-color (spinach, beet, and egg) or plain pappardelle or fettuccine

2 tablespoons butter or margarine

4 cloves garlic, minced

2 medium red onions, cut into thin wedges

¾ cup vegetable broth or chicken broth

¼ teaspoon salt

¼ teaspoon cracked black pepper

2 6-ounce packages prewashed baby spinach

½ cup golden raisins

1 4-ounce log semi-soft goat cheese, crumbled

½ cup coarsely chopped walnuts, toasted

1 teaspoon finely shredded lemon peel

   Salt

   Cracked black pepper

1 In a large Dutch oven cook pasta in lightly salted boiling water according to package directions. Drain well. Return pasta to hot Dutch oven; cover and keep warm.

2 Meanwhile, in a very large skillet melt butter over medium heat. Add garlic; cook and stir for 30 seconds. Add onion wedges; reduce heat to medium-low. Cover and cook about 15 minutes or until onion wedges are very tender, stirring occasionally.

3 Add broth, the ¼ teaspoon salt, and the ¼ teaspoon cracked pepper to onions in skillet. Bring to boiling; reduce heat to medium. Boil gently, uncovered, for 2 minutes. Add spinach in batches to onion mixture, stirring just until spinach wilts. Remove from heat; stir in raisins.

4 Toss spinach mixture with hot pasta in Dutch oven. Transfer to a warm serving dish. Sprinkle with goat cheese, walnuts, and lemon peel. Season to taste with additional salt and cracked pepper. Serve immediately.

Per serving: 547 cal., 23 g total fat (9 g sat. fat), 28 mg chol., 624 mg sodium, 72 g carbo., 8 g fiber, 19 g pro.

Fennel, a stalk vegetable with a mild licorice flavor, is in greatest supply during the winter. Try this hearty, delicious recipe the next time the cold wind blows into your neighborhood.

PENNE WITH FENNEL

6	ounces dried penne pasta
1	tablespoon olive oil or cooking oil
3	cloves garlic, minced
¼	teaspoon crushed red pepper
2	medium fennel bulbs, trimmed* and cut into thin bite-size strips
1	large red or green sweet pepper, cut into thin bite-size strips
1	15-ounce can Great Northern beans, rinsed and drained
2	teaspoons snipped fresh thyme
	Freshly ground black pepper

1 In a large saucepan cook pasta according to package directions. Drain well. Return pasta to hot saucepan; cover and keep warm.

2 Meanwhile, in a large skillet heat oil over medium-high heat. Add garlic and crushed red pepper; cook for 30 seconds. Add fennel; cook and stir for 5 minutes. Add sweet pepper strips; cook for 3 minutes more. Add beans and thyme; cook about 2 minutes or until hot.

3 Add fennel mixture to pasta; toss gently to combine. Season to taste with freshly ground black pepper.

Per serving: 350 cal., 5 g total fat (1 g sat. fat), 0 mg chol., 36 mg sodium, 63 g carbo., 9 g fiber, 15 g pro.

*NOTE: Cut off and discard upper stalks of fennel bulbs. Remove any wilted outer layers of stalks. Wash fennel and cut lengthwise into quarters. Remove core and discard.

START TO FINISH:
35 minutes

MAKES:
4 servings

The Italian flag colors of red, white, and green are well represented in this dish with tomatoes, fresh greens, and pasta. A sure delight for any Italian food lover!

PASTA ROSA-VERDE

START TO FINISH:
30 minutes

MAKES:
4 servings

8 ounces dried cut ziti or mostaccioli pasta (about 3 cups)

1 tablespoon olive oil

1 medium onion, thinly sliced

4 to 6 medium tomatoes, seeded and coarsely chopped (3 cups)

2 cloves garlic, minced

1 teaspoon salt

½ teaspoon black pepper

⅛ to ¼ teaspoon crushed red pepper (optional)

3 cups arugula, watercress, and/or fresh spinach, coarsely chopped

¼ cup pine nuts or slivered almonds, toasted

2 tablespoons crumbled Gorgonzola or other blue cheese

❶ Cook pasta according to package directions. Drain well. Return pasta to hot pan; cover and keep warm.

❷ Meanwhile, in a large skillet heat olive oil over medium heat. Add onion; cook until tender. Add tomatoes, garlic, salt, black pepper, and, if desired, crushed red pepper. Cook and stir over medium-high heat about 2 minutes or until the tomatoes are warm and release some of their juices. Stir in arugula; heat just until wilted.

❸ To serve, divide pasta among four bowls. Top with tomato mixture. Sprinkle with nuts and cheese.

Per serving: 348 cal., 11 g total fat (2 g sat. fat), 3 mg chol., 659 mg sodium, 53 g carbo., 4 g fiber, 12 g pro.

Ripe olives, complemented here by feta cheese and yogurt, give this dish a distinct Mediterranean flair. Visit an Italian food store to find a selection of ripe olives.

ROTINI-BEAN BAKE

12	ounces dried rotini pasta
½	cup bottled balsamic vinaigrette
1	pound plum tomatoes, coarsely chopped
1	15-ounce can cannellini beans (white kidney beans) or garbanzo beans (chickpeas), rinsed and drained
8	ounces feta cheese, crumbled
1	cup coarsely chopped pitted ripe olives
½	cup seasoned fine dry bread crumbs
1	8-ounce carton plain low-fat yogurt
¾	cup milk
⅓	cup grated Parmesan cheese
1	tablespoon all-purpose flour

PREP:
40 minutes

BAKE:
25 minutes + 10 minutes

STAND:
10 minutes

OVEN:
375°F

MAKES:
8 servings

1 Preheat oven to 375°F. Lightly grease a 3-quart rectangular baking dish; set aside. Cook pasta according to package directions. Drain. In a very large bowl combine vinaigrette and pasta; toss to coat. Stir in tomatoes, beans, feta cheese, and olives.

2 Sprinkle ¼ cup of the bread crumbs in prepared dish. Spoon pasta mixture into dish. In a medium bowl stir together yogurt, milk, Parmesan cheese, and flour until smooth. Pour yogurt mixture evenly over pasta mixture. Sprinkle top with remaining ¼ cup bread crumbs.

3 Bake, covered, for 25 minutes. Uncover and bake for 10 to 15 minutes more or until heated through and top is lightly browned. Let stand for 10 minutes before serving.

Per serving: 425 cal., 15 g total fat (6 g sat. fat), 31 mg chol., 1,045 mg sodium, 57 g carbo., 6 g fiber, 19 g pro.

Packed full of vitamins with broccoli and roasted red peppers, this layered masterpiece makes a delicious family meal.

BROCCOLI LASAGNA

PREP:
45 minutes

BAKE:
20 minutes + 10 minutes

STAND:
10 minutes

OVEN:
425°F

MAKES:
10 servings

2 bunches broccoli, trimmed and cut up (about 8 cups)

1 15-ounce carton ricotta cheese

¼ cup grated Parmesan cheese

1 slightly beaten egg

2 tablespoons snipped fresh parsley

1 12-ounce jar roasted red sweet peppers, drained

¼ cup butter or margarine

¼ cup all-purpose flour

2 cloves garlic, minced

3 cups milk

½ teaspoon dried basil, crushed

Nonstick cooking spray

12 dried lasagna noodles (prepared as in step 1, page 219)

2 cups shredded Monterey Jack cheese (8 ounces)

3 tablespoons grated Parmesan cheese

1 Preheat oven to 425°F. Place a steamer basket in a 4-quart Dutch oven. Add water to just below bottom of steamer basket; bring to boiling. Add broccoli. Cover; reduce heat. Steam for 4 to 5 minutes or until crisp-tender. Meanwhile, in a small bowl stir together ricotta cheese, the ¼ cup Parmesan cheese, the egg, and parsley; set aside.

2 For sauce, in a blender or food processor blend or process the roasted red peppers until almost smooth; set aside. In a large skillet melt butter over medium heat. Stir in flour and garlic. Cook and stir for 1 minute. Gradually add milk and pureed peppers. Cook and stir until thickened and bubbly. Stir in ½ teaspoon salt, basil, and ¼ teaspoon black pepper.

3 Lightly coat a 3-quart rectangular baking dish with nonstick cooking spray. Spread ¾ cup of the sauce in prepared dish. Arrange three of the lasagna noodles over sauce. Carefully spread one-third of the ricotta mixture over noodles. Top with one-third of the broccoli; sprinkle with ½ cup of the Monterey Jack cheese. Repeat layers two more times. Top with remaining noodles. Spoon remaining sauce over the top.

4 Bake, covered, for 20 minutes. Uncover; sprinkle with remaining ½ cup Monterey Jack cheese and the 3 tablespoons Parmesan. Bake about 10 minutes more or until heated through. Let stand for 10 minutes.

Per serving: 406 cal., 21 g total fat (13 g sat. fat), 84 mg chol., 460 mg sodium, 34 g carbo., 3 g fiber, 21 g pro.

PIZZA & SANDWICHES

A springform pan works well for this recipe. It allows you to remove the side of the pan to expose the crust for a show-stopping presentation.

CHICAGO-STYLE DEEP-DISH PIZZA

PREP:
40 minutes

RISE:
50 minutes + 30 minutes

BAKE:
45 minutes

COOL:
10 minutes

OVEN:
375°F

MAKES:
6 to 8 servings

*TEST KITCHEN TIP:
If you like, substitute 1 teaspoon dried oregano, crushed, and 1 teaspoon dried basil, crushed, for the fresh herbs.

Olive oil or cooking oil

Cornmeal

1 package active dry yeast

3 to 3½ cups all-purpose flour

⅓ cup cooking oil

6 ounces bulk mild Italian sausage

1 14½-ounce can diced tomatoes, drained

1 tablespoon snipped fresh oregano*

1 tablespoon snipped fresh basil*

12 ounces sliced mozzarella cheese

¼ cup grated Parmesan cheese or Romano cheese

❶ Generously grease a 10-inch springform pan with oil. Sprinkle bottom with cornmeal. Dissolve yeast in 1 cup warm water (120°F to 130°F). Let stand for 5 minutes. Stir in 1½ cups of the flour, the ⅓ cup oil, and ½ teaspoon salt. Beat with electric mixer on low speed for 30 seconds, scraping bowl. Beat for 2 minutes on high speed, scraping side of bowl. Using a wooden spoon, stir in as much of the remaining flour as you can.

❷ Turn out dough onto a lightly floured surface. Knead in enough of the remaining flour to make a moderately stiff dough that is smooth and elastic (6 to 8 minutes total). Shape dough into a ball. Place in a lightly greased bowl, turning once to grease surface. Cover; let rise in a warm place until double (50 to 60 minutes). Punch down. Cover; let rest for 5 minutes.

❸ Turn dough into prepared pan. Using oiled hands, press and spread the dough evenly over bottom and 1½ inches up the side of the pan. Cover; let rise in a warm place until nearly double (30 to 35 minutes).

❹ Preheat oven to 375°F. In a medium skillet cook sausage until browned. Drain off fat. Remove sausage from skillet; pat dry with paper towels. Wipe out skillet with paper towels. Return sausage to skillet. Stir in drained tomatoes, oregano, and basil. Cook and stir until heated through. To assemble pizza, layer mozzarella cheese on dough. Top with meat mixture and Parmesan cheese.

❺ Bake for 45 to 55 minutes or until edges of crust are crisp and golden brown and filling is hot. If necessary to prevent overbrowning, cover crust with foil for the last 10 minutes of baking. Cool on a wire rack for 10 minutes. Remove side of springform pan. Cut into wedges.

Per serving: 621 cal., 34 g total fat (13 g sat. fat), 67 mg chol., 871 mg sodium, 50 g carbo., 2 g fiber, 25 g pro.

If you've never tried making pizza on the grill, you're in for a treat. For convenience, have all your pizza toppings ready in advance so you can quickly layer them on the partially cooked crusts.

GRILLED ROASTED GARLIC & SAUSAGE PIZZAS

1	package active dry yeast
2	tablespoons cornmeal
1	teaspoon olive oil
	Dash sugar
2½	to 2¾ cups all-purpose flour
	Cornmeal
1	pound bulk Italian sausage
2	cups sliced fresh mushrooms
1	8-ounce can pizza sauce
2	heads garlic, roasted*
1	medium green sweet pepper, cut into thin bite-size strips
2	cups shredded provolone cheese (8 ounces)
2	plum tomatoes, sliced and quartered

1 In a large bowl dissolve yeast in 1 cup warm water (105°F to 115°F). Let stand for 5 minutes. Stir in the 2 tablespoons cornmeal, the olive oil, sugar, and ½ teaspoon salt. Using a wooden spoon, stir in as much flour as you can.

2 Turn out dough onto a lightly floured surface. Knead in enough of the remaining flour to make a moderately stiff dough that is smooth and elastic (about 6 minutes total). Shape dough into two balls. Cover; let rest for 10 minutes. Line 2 baking sheets with waxed paper; sprinkle each with additional cornmeal. Roll each dough portion into a 10-inch circle. Transfer each circle to a prepared baking sheet. Cover dough; set aside.

3 In a large skillet cook sausage and mushrooms until sausage is brown; drain well and set aside.

4 Use the waxed paper to carefully invert each dough circle onto the rack of an uncovered grill directly over medium coals; remove paper. Grill for 1 to 2 minutes or until dough is puffed in some places, starting to become firm, and bottom is lightly browned. Remove crusts from grill; turn crusts browned sides up.

5 Spread browned side of each crust with half of the pizza sauce; top each with half of the sausage mixture, half of the roasted garlic cloves, half of the sweet pepper strips, half of the provolone cheese, and half of the tomato slices. Return crusts to grill. Cover and grill about 2 minutes more or until cheese is melted and bottom crust is browned and crisp.

Per serving: 946 cal., 46 g total fat (21 g sat. fat), 115 mg chol., 1,654 mg sodium, 81 g carbo., 5 g fiber, 44 g pro.

PREP:
25 minutes

GRILL:
35 minutes (garlic)
1 minute + 2 minutes

MAKES:
4 to 6 servings

*TEST KITCHEN TIP!
To roast garlic, cut off the top ½ inch from each of two garlic heads. Leaving heads whole, remove loose, papery outer layers of skin. Place garlic heads, cut sides up, in center of a 10-inch square of heavy foil. Brush sides and tops of heads with olive oil. Bring up two opposite edges of foil and seal with a double fold. Fold remaining edges together to completely enclose the garlic, leaving space for steam to build. Place packet on the rack of an uncovered grill directly over medium coals. Grill about 35 minutes or until garlic heads feel soft when packet is squeezed, turning packets occasionally. Remove from grill; cool. Squeeze garlic cloves from skins, leaving cloves intact. Discard skins.

If you prefer, use 3 cups shredded pizza cheese in place of the mix of provolone, Asiago, and mozzarella cheeses.

GARLIC & BASIL PIZZAS

PREP:
45 minutes

RISE:
45 minutes (dough)

BAKE:
8 minutes

OVEN:
450°F

MAKES:
six (8- to 9-inch) pizzas

1   recipe Garlic-Basil Pizza Dough
    Cornmeal
1   cup bottled roasted red sweet peppers
½   cup snipped fresh basil or 2 teaspoons dried basil, crushed
1   tablespoon olive oil
1   clove garlic, minced
4   ounces provolone or fontina cheese, shredded (1 cup)
4   ounces Asiago or Romano cheese, shredded (1 cup)
1   cup shredded mozzarella or Swiss cheese (4 ounces)
6   ounces thinly sliced Italian cappacola, Genoa salami, salami, pepperoni, summer sausage, or prosciutto, cut into thin strips; 1 cup cubed cooked ham or Canadian-style bacon; or 1 pound bulk Italian sausage, cooked and drained

1 Preheat the oven to 450°F. Divide Garlic-Basil Pizza Dough into six portions. Cover; let rest for 10 minutes. Grease three very large baking sheets; dust with cornmeal. On each baking sheet, roll two dough portions into two circles 8 to 9 inches in diameter. Add more cornmeal as needed.

2 Cut roasted peppers into ¼-inch-wide strips. In a small bowl combine roasted peppers, basil, the 1 tablespoon olive oil, and the garlic. In a medium bowl toss together provolone, Asiago, and mozzarella cheeses.

3 Spread some of the roasted pepper mixture evenly over each crust. Top with some of the meat. Sprinkle with some of the cheese mixture. Bake pizzas, two at a time, for 8 to 10 minutes or until cheese is bubbly and crusts are golden brown. Cut into wedges. Serve while hot.

GARLIC-BASIL PIZZA DOUGH: In a large bowl combine 1 cup all-purpose flour; 2 packages active dry yeast; 2 cloves garlic, minced; 1 tablespoon snipped fresh basil or 1 teaspoon dried basil, crushed; and ½ teaspoon salt. Add 1 cup warm water (120°F to 130°F); 3 tablespoons olive oil; and 1 tablespoon honey. Beat on low speed of an electric mixer for 30 seconds, scraping bowl constantly. Beat for 3 minutes on medium speed. Stir in 1½ cups whole wheat flour. Turn out on a lightly floured surface. Knead in enough all-purpose flour (¼ to ½ cup) to make a moderately stiff dough that is smooth and elastic (6 to 8 minutes total). Place in a lightly greased bowl, turning once. Cover; let rise in a warm place until double in size (45 to 60 minutes). Punch dough. Turn out onto a lightly floured surface.

Per serving: 676 cal., 42 g total fat (15 g sat. fat), 71 mg chol., 1,200 mg sodium, 51 g carbo., 6 g fiber, 27 g pro.

This deep-dish delight is baked in an ovenproof skillet instead of on a pizza pan to allow the pizza toppings to be piled extra high.

DEEP-DISH PIZZA

Nonstick cooking spray

2 13.8-ounce packages refrigerated pizza dough (each for 1 crust)

¼ cup olive oil

1½ cups sliced red onion

2 cloves garlic, minced

1 10-ounce package frozen chopped spinach, thawed and well drained

½ teaspoon salt

¼ teaspoon black pepper

1 cup ricotta cheese

1¼ cups shredded 4-cheese pizza blend (5 ounces)

2 tablespoons snipped fresh flat-leaf parsley

¼ teaspoon crushed red pepper (optional)

4 plum tomatoes, thinly sliced

1 Preheat oven to 425°F. Lightly coat a 12-inch cast-iron or heavy oven-going skillet with nonstick cooking spray. Unroll one package of the pizza dough; gently pull into a circle. Place dough in prepared skillet; press dough into bottom and halfway up side of skillet. Bake for 5 minutes; remove from oven. Dough will have puffed slightly.

2 Meanwhile, in a large skillet heat 2 tablespoons of the olive oil over medium heat. Add red onion and garlic; cook about 5 minutes or until tender. Add spinach, ¼ teaspoon of the salt, and the black pepper. Cook and stir for 1 minute more. Remove from heat; set aside.

3 In a small bowl combine ricotta cheese, ¼ cup of the pizza cheese, the parsley, crushed red pepper, and the remaining ¼ teaspoon salt. Spoon spinach mixture evenly over bottom of partially baked crust.

4 Spread ricotta mixture over spinach layer. Top with tomatoes; drizzle with 1 tablespoon of the remaining olive oil. Sprinkle with ¾ cup of the remaining pizza cheese. Unroll remaining pizza dough; shape into a 12- to 13-inch circle. Lay dough round on layers in skillet. Brush with remaining 1 tablespoon olive oil. Bake for 15 to 20 minutes or until top is golden brown. Top with remaining ¼ cup pizza cheese. Bake for 2 to 3 minutes or until cheese is melted. Let stand for 10 minutes before serving.

Per serving: 443 cal., 18 g total fat (7 g sat. fat), 28 mg chol., 882 mg sodium, 52 g carbo., 3 g fiber, 18 g pro.

PREP:
35 minutes

BAKE:
5 minutes + 15 minutes + 2 minutes

STAND:
10 minutes

OVEN:
425°F

MAKES:
8 servings

Salsa serves as the tomato sauce in this Tex-Mex version of the classic Italian-style pizza. For added kick, use shredded Monterey Jack cheese with jalapeño chile peppers.

PEPPY PEPPERONI PIZZA

PREP:
20 minutes

BAKE:
18 minutes

OVEN:
425°F

MAKES:
6 servings

1   13.8-ounce package refrigerated pizza dough (for 1 crust)

1   8-ounce package shredded Monterey Jack cheese (2 cups)

1   cup purchased salsa

1   4-ounce can (drained weight) sliced mushrooms, drained

½   of a 3½-ounce package sliced pepperoni

1 Preheat oven to 425°F. Grease a baking sheet; roll pizza dough into a 15×10-inch rectangle on prepared baking sheet. Build up edges of dough slightly. Sprinkle 1½ cups of the Monterey Jack cheese over the dough. Spoon salsa evenly over cheese. Top with mushrooms and pepperoni. Sprinkle with remaining ½ cup cheese.

2 Bake for 18 to 20 minutes or until crust is golden brown and cheese melts.

Per serving: 313 cal., 16 g total fat (8 g sat. fat), 40 mg chol., 719 mg sodium, 27 g carbo., 2 g fiber, 15 g pro.

Refrigerated dough makes this favorite pizza a cinch to prepare. If you have extra time, use sliced fresh mushrooms instead of canned.

SAUSAGE PIZZA

1   13.8-ounce package refrigerated pizza dough
     (for 1 crust)

8   ounces bulk Italian sausage

½   of a medium green sweet pepper,
     cut into thin strips

1   8-ounce can pizza sauce

1   4-ounce can (drained weight) sliced mushrooms,
     drained

1   8-ounce package shredded pizza cheese
     (2 cups)

1 Preheat oven to 425°F. Grease a 12-inch pizza pan; press pizza dough into prepared pan, building up side. Bake for 5 minutes.

2 Meanwhile, in a medium skillet cook sausage and sweet pepper until sausage is brown. Drain off fat. Stir pizza sauce and mushrooms into sausage mixture in skillet.

3 Sprinkle half of the cheese on the crust. Spoon sausage mixture over cheese. Top with remaining cheese. Bake for 10 to 15 minutes or until cheese is bubbly. Let stand for 5 minutes before serving.

Per serving: 394 cal., 20 g total fat (9 g sat. fat), 53 mg chol., 980 mg sodium, 29 g carbo., 2 g fiber, 20 g pro.

PREP:
25 minutes

BAKE:
10 minutes

STAND:
5 minutes

OVEN:
425°F

MAKES:
6 servings

Sicilians are big fans of escarole—a mild, leafy variety of endive. Added during the last two minutes of baking, it wilts to perfection.

SICILIAN-STYLE PIZZA

PREP:
15 minutes

BAKE:
8 minutes + 2 minutes

OVEN:
425°F

MAKES:
4 servings

1   16-ounce Italian bread shell (such as Boboli brand)

3   medium red and/or yellow tomatoes, thinly sliced

4   ounces fresh mozzarella or buffalo mozzarella cheese, thinly sliced

⅓   cup halved pitted ripe olives

1   tablespoon olive oil

1   cup coarsely chopped escarole or curly endive

¼   cup shredded pecorino Romano or Parmesan cheese (1 ounce)

Freshly ground black pepper

1 Preheat oven to 425°F. Place bread shell on an ungreased baking sheet or pizza pan. Top bread shell with tomatoes, mozzarella cheese, and olives. Drizzle olive oil over all.

2 Bake pizza for 8 minutes. Carefully sprinkle with escarole. Bake for 2 minutes more. To serve, sprinkle Romano cheese and freshly ground black pepper over pizza.

Per serving: 460 cal., 20 g total fat (5 g sat. fat), 31 mg chol., 936 mg sodium, 53 g carbo., 3 g fiber, 21 g pro.

Goat cheese, often called chèvre, makes this pizza rich and creamy.

PEASANT PIZZA WITH GOAT CHEESE

1   14-ounce Italian bread shell (such as Boboli brand)

2   ounces cream cheese, softened

2   ounces semi-soft goat cheese (chèvre)

1   to 2 tablespoons milk

1   tablespoon snipped fresh basil or 1 teaspoon dried basil, crushed

1   clove garlic, minced

⅛   teaspoon black pepper

3   plum tomatoes, chopped (about 1 cup)

1   small yellow, orange, or green sweet pepper, chopped

2   to 3 tablespoons olive oil

1 Preheat oven to 400°F. Place bread shell on a baking sheet.

2 In a small bowl stir together cream cheese, goat cheese, and enough of the milk to make cheese mixture a spreading consistency. Stir in basil, garlic, and black pepper. Spread cheese mixture over the bread shell. Spread chopped tomatoes and sweet pepper over the cheese mixture. Drizzle olive oil over all.

3 Bake for 15 to 20 minutes or until heated through.

Per serving: 289 cal., 14 g total fat (4 g sat. fat), 18 mg chol., 428 mg sodium, 32 g carbo., 2 g fiber, 11 g pro.

PREP:
10 minutes

BAKE:
15 minutes

OVEN:
400°F

MAKES:
6 servings

Purchased tomato pesto serves as the tomato sauce in this pizza, giving it a fresh, zesty flavor. Precooked chicken breast makes it easy to prepare.

MUSHROOM-TOMATO PESTO PIZZA

PREP:
15 minutes

BAKE:
10 minutes

OVEN:
400°F

MAKES:
4 servings

1   12-inch Italian bread shell (such as Boboli brand)

½   cup purchased dried tomato pesto

1   cup shredded 4-cheese pizza blend (4 ounces)

1   6-ounce package refrigerated Italian-seasoned cooked chicken breast strips

1½   cups sliced fresh mushrooms (such as shiitake, cremini, and/or button)

1 Preheat oven to 400°F. Place the bread shell on a 12-inch pizza pan. Spread pesto over bread shell. Sprinkle with half of the cheese. Top with chicken strips and mushrooms. Sprinkle with the remaining cheese. Bake for 10 to 15 minutes or until pizza is heated through and cheese is melted.

Per serving: 585 cal., 24 g total fat (8 g sat. fat), 55 mg chol., 1,382 mg sodium, 64 g carbo., 4 g fiber, 33 g pro.

No need to prepare pizza dough. Work-saving Italian bread shells make a tasty substitute.

GRILLED EGGPLANT & PEPPER PIZZAS

4	ounces soft goat cheese (chèvre)
¼	cup purchased dried tomato pesto or basil pesto
2	medium green, red, and/or yellow sweet peppers
8	½-inch-thick slices eggplant (1 medium)
2	tablespoons olive oil
	Salt
	Black pepper
2	6-inch Italian bread shells (such as Boboli brand)

PREP:
20 minutes

GRILL:
8 minutes

MAKES:
4 servings

1 In a small bowl stir together goat cheese and pesto; set aside.

2 Cut sweet peppers lengthwise into quarters. Remove and discard stems, seeds, and membranes. Brush peppers and eggplant slices lightly with some of the olive oil. Sprinkle vegetables lightly with salt and black pepper. Brush tops of bread shells with remaining olive oil.

3 Place sweet pepper quarters, eggplant slices, and bread shells on the rack of an uncovered grill directly over medium coals. Grill bread shells for 2 to 3 minutes or until toasted, turning once halfway through grilling. Grill eggplant slices for 6 to 8 minutes or until tender, turning once halfway through grilling. Grill sweet pepper quarters for 8 to 10 minutes or until softened and slightly charred, turning once halfway through grilling. Remove bread shells and vegetables from grill as they are done. Coarsely chop vegetables and set aside.

4 Spread goat cheese mixture evenly onto bread shells. Top bread shells with grilled vegetables. To serve, cut each bread shell into quarters.

Per serving: 370 cal., 21 g total fat (6 g sat. fat), 17 mg chol., 663 mg sodium, 34 g carbo., 5 g fiber, 14 g pro.

Eggs and asparagus are a winning combination. Make them into a pizza and you're in for a unique, yet delicious dinner.

EGG & ASPARAGUS PIZZA

START TO FINISH:
30 minutes

OVEN:
450°F

MAKES:
6 servings

1   12-inch Italian bread shell (such as Boboli brand)

6   eggs

⅓   cup milk

2   teaspoons snipped fresh tarragon or oregano

⅛   teaspoon salt

⅛   teaspoon black pepper

2   tablespoons butter or margarine

1   cup asparagus bias-sliced into 1-inch pieces

1   clove garlic, minced

1   large tomato, chopped

2   tablespoons finely shredded Parmesan cheese

1 Preheat oven to 450°F. Place bread shell on a 12-inch pizza pan. Bake for 8 to 10 minutes or until heated through.

2 Meanwhile, in a medium bowl combine eggs, milk, tarragon or oregano, salt, and pepper; beat with a whisk or rotary beater until well mixed. Set aside.

3 In a large skillet heat butter over medium heat. Add asparagus and garlic; cook for 3 minutes. Pour egg mixture over asparagus mixture in skillet. Cook, without stirring, until egg mixture begins to set on the bottom and around the edge.

4 With a spatula or large spoon, lift and fold the partially cooked egg mixture so that the uncooked portion flows underneath. Continue cooking for 2 to 3 minutes more or until egg mixture is cooked through but is still slightly moist. Remove from heat.

5 Spoon scrambled egg mixture onto warm bread shell. Sprinkle with tomato and Parmesan cheese. Bake for 2 minutes. Serve immediately.

Per serving: 332 cal., 14 g total fat (4 g sat. fat), 227 mg chol., 595 mg sodium, 36 g carbo., 2 g fiber, 17 g pro.

Orange peel and juice make the pesto for this pizza go beyond the ordinary. Add a variety of fresh vegetables and you end up with a delicious melding of flavors.

SAN FRANCISCO PIZZA

⅓	cup slivered almonds, toasted
1½	cups firmly packed fresh spinach leaves
1	cup firmly packed fresh parsley sprigs
½	cup firmly packed fresh basil leaves
½	cup olive oil
½	cup grated Parmesan cheese
1	teaspoon finely shredded orange peel
¼	cup orange juice
¼	teaspoon salt
¼	teaspoon black pepper
2	12-inch purchased Italian flatbreads (focaccia) or Italian bread shells (such as Boboli brand)
1	cup chopped red sweet pepper
⅓	cup chopped seeded tomato
½	cup red onion cut into thin wedges
½	teaspoon crushed red pepper
1	cup grated Parmesan cheese

PREP:
40 minutes

BAKE:
12 minutes

OVEN:
400°F

MAKES:
12 to 16 servings

1 For pesto, place almonds in a food processor or blender. Cover and process or blend until finely chopped. Add spinach, parsley, and basil; cover. With the machine running, gradually add olive oil in a thin, steady stream, processing or blending until the mixture is combined and slightly chunky. (If using a blender, stop occasionally, scrape side, and push mixture into blades. The blender produces a smoother mixture than the food processor.) Add the ½ cup Parmesan cheese, the orange peel, orange juice, salt, and black pepper. Cover and process or blend just until combined.

2 Preheat oven to 400°F. Place each bread on a baking sheet or 12-inch pizza pan. Spread pesto over breads. Top with sweet pepper, tomato, red onion, and crushed red pepper. Sprinkle with the 1 cup Parmesan cheese. Bake for 12 to 15 minutes or until heated through.

Per serving: 342 cal., 17 g total fat (5 g sat. fat), 13 mg chol., 207 mg sodium, 36 g carbo., 4 g fiber, 13 g pro.

MAKE-AHEAD DIRECTIONS: Prepare the pesto as directed in step 1. Transfer to an airtight container; seal. Chill in the refrigerator for up to 1 week or freeze for up to 3 months.

Classic Pizza Margherita was created in 1889 to honor Queen Margherita. This version relies on focaccia rather than a homemade crust but maintains the traditional red, white, and green toppings.

PIZZA MARGHERITA

START TO FINISH:
25 minutes

OVEN:
425°F

MAKES:
4 servings

4	6- to 7-inch purchased Italian flatbreads (focaccia) or prebaked pizza crusts
1½	cups shredded 4-cheese pizza blend (6 ounces)
4	plum tomatoes or 2 medium tomatoes, thinly sliced
2	to 3 teaspoons olive oil
½	cup finely shredded fresh basil
¼	cup pine nuts (optional)

1 Preheat oven to 425°F. Place flatbreads or pizza crusts on a very large baking sheet. Bake for 5 minutes. Remove from oven; sprinkle with cheese. Arrange tomato slices on top. Drizzle tomatoes with olive oil. Top with basil. If desired, sprinkle with pine nuts.

2 Bake for 10 minutes more. Serve immediately.

Per serving: 369 cal., 15 g total fat (9 g sat. fat), 30 mg chol., 631 mg sodium, 41 g carbo., 5 g fiber, 19 g pro.

Whole wheat pita bread rounds provide the crust for these healthful miniature pizzas.

EASY VEGGIE PIZZA

2   large whole wheat pita bread rounds
    Nonstick cooking spray

½   cup assorted cut-up fresh vegetables
    (such as small broccoli or cauliflower florets,
    chopped red sweet pepper, sliced fresh mushrooms,
    and/or finely chopped carrot)

¼   cup pizza sauce

¼   cup shredded mozzarella cheese (1 ounce)

1 Preheat oven to 400°F. Place pita bread on a baking sheet. Bake for 5 minutes.

2 Meanwhile, coat an unheated small skillet with nonstick cooking spray. Preheat over medium heat. Add vegetables; cook and stir until crisp-tender.

3 Spread pizza sauce onto pita bread rounds; sprinkle with cooked vegetables and mozzarella cheese. Bake for 8 to 10 minutes more or until light brown. Cut each round in half and serve warm.

Per serving: 235 cal., 5 g total fat (2 g sat. fat), 11 mg chol., 602 mg sodium, 39 g carbo., 5 g fiber, 11 g pro.

PREP:
15 minutes

BAKE:
8 minutes

OVEN:
400°F

MAKES:
2 servings

This kid-pleasing recipe uses a loaf of French bread as the crust, making it easy and convenient to prepare. Try it at your child's next sleepover or party; you'll be amazed at how fast it is devoured.

PIZZA BY THE YARD

PREP:
20 minutes

BROIL:
1 minute

BAKE:
8 minutes

OVEN:
350°F

MAKES:
6 servings

1	16-ounce loaf unsliced French bread
1	pound lean ground beef
1	6-ounce can tomato paste
¼	cup water
¼	cup sliced green onions
¼	cup chopped pitted ripe olives
½	teaspoon dried oregano, crushed
½	teaspoon salt
⅛	teaspoon black pepper
⅓	cup grated Parmesan cheese
2	medium tomatoes, sliced
1	medium green sweet pepper, cut into rings
1	cup shredded American cheese (4 ounces)

1 Preheat broiler. Cut bread in half horizontally. Place bread halves, cut sides up, on the unheated rack of a broiler pan. Broil 4 inches from the heat about 1 minute or until lightly toasted. Transfer to a very large cookie sheet. Set aside. Set oven temperature to 350°F.

2 In a large skillet cook ground beef until brown. Drain off fat. Stir tomato paste, the water, green onions, olives, oregano, salt, and black pepper into ground beef in skillet. Cook and stir over medium heat until heated through. Remove from heat; stir in Parmesan cheese. Divide ground beef mixture between bread halves. Top with tomato slices, sweet pepper rings, and American cheese. Bake for 8 to 10 minutes or until cheese is melted. Serve immediately.

Per serving: 545 cal., 26 g total fat (11 g sat. fat), 81 mg chol., 1,413 mg sodium, 49 g carbo., 5 g fiber, 29 g pro.

Semolina is a type of wheat flour, usually used to make pasta. It can be found in the baking aisle of your supermarket. If you can't find it, use quick-cooking polenta.

TOMATO POLENTA PIZZA

3	cups milk
1½	cups semolina pasta flour or quick-cooking polenta mix
2	beaten eggs
½	cup finely shredded Asiago or Parmesan cheese (2 ounces)
¼	teaspoon salt
⅛	teaspoon black pepper
	Nonstick cooking spray
4	plum tomatoes, very thinly sliced
1	cup shredded mozzarella cheese (4 ounces)
2	tablespoons snipped fresh basil and/or oregano

PREP:
25 minutes

CHILL:
2 to 24 hours

BAKE:
20 minutes

OVEN:
400°F

MAKES:
6 servings

1 In a large saucepan bring milk just to boiling over medium heat. Sprinkle semolina flour over milk, stirring constantly. Cook and stir for 2 minutes (mixture will be very stiff). Remove from heat; cool for 5 minutes. Stir in eggs, Asiago cheese, salt, and black pepper.

2 Coat a 12-inch pizza pan with nonstick cooking spray. Spread semolina mixture in the prepared pizza pan. Cover and chill for 2 to 24 hours.

3 Preheat oven to 400°F. Arrange tomato slices over semolina mixture. Top with mozzarella cheese. Bake about 20 minutes or until cheese is melted and beginning to brown. Sprinkle with basil and/or oregano. Serve immediately.

Per serving: 345 cal., 12 g total fat (7 g sat. fat), 105 mg chol., 395 mg sodium, 39 g carbo., 2 g fiber, 18 g pro.

Purchased refrigerated pizza dough makes these turnover delights a quick and easy solution for dinner on a busy night.

BEEF-VEGETABLE CALZONES

PREP:
25 minutes

BAKE:
12 minutes

STAND:
5 minutes

OVEN:
425°F

MAKES:
6 calzones

8   ounces lean ground beef

½   cup sliced fresh mushrooms

¼   cup chopped green sweet pepper

1   cup shredded mozzarella cheese (4 ounces)

⅓   cup purchased pizza sauce

1   13.8-ounce package refrigerated pizza dough

1   tablespoon milk

     Grated Parmesan cheese (optional)

     Purchased pizza sauce, warmed (optional)

1 Preheat oven to 425°F. Grease a large baking sheet; set aside. In a medium skillet cook ground beef, mushrooms, and sweet pepper until meat is brown; drain well. Stir in mozzarella cheese and the ⅓ cup pizza sauce.

2 Unroll pizza dough. On a lightly floured surface, roll or stretch pizza dough into a 15×10-inch rectangle. Cut dough into six 5-inch squares. Divide meat mixture among squares, positioning it on one half of each square. Brush dough edges with water. Fold dough over filling to form rectangles or triangles, stretching dough as needed. Seal edges by pressing with the tines of a fork.

3 Place calzones on a prepared baking sheet. Prick tops with a fork to allow steam to escape. Brush with milk. If desired, sprinkle with Parmesan cheese. Bake for 12 to 15 minutes or until golden brown. Let stand for 5 minutes before serving. If desired, serve with warmed pizza sauce.

Per calzone: 265 cal., 11 g total fat (4 g sat. fat), 39 mg chol., 417 mg sodium, 26 g carbo., 1 g fiber, 15 g pro.

This flavor-packed sandwich is chock-full of peppy Italian ingredients. Jalapeño-stuffed olives add a hint of heat.

ARTICHOKE-BEEF MELTS

1	6½-ounce jar marinated artichoke hearts
1	cup purchased roasted red sweet peppers, drained and cut into strips
⅔	cup jalapeño-stuffed olives, sliced
1	medium red onion, thinly sliced and separated into rings
1	tablespoon snipped fresh parsley
1	small clove garlic, minced
⅛	teaspoon dried oregano, crushed
⅛	teaspoon ground cumin
1	pound thinly sliced roast beef or pork (purchase from the deli or use leftover)
8	ounces sliced provolone cheese
4	4-inch-long pieces Italian-style bread (ciabatta) or hoagie buns, split horizontally
4	teaspoons olive oil

PREP:
30 minutes

MARINATE:
2 to 24 hours

COOK:
8 minutes per batch

MAKES:
8 sandwiches

1 Drain artichokes, reserving marinade. Slice artichokes. In a small bowl combine artichokes, reserved marinade, roasted red peppers, olives, red onion, parsley, garlic, oregano, and cumin. Cover and marinate in the refrigerator for 2 to 24 hours, stirring occasionally.

2 Drain artichoke mixture. Divide artichoke mixture, roast beef, and provolone cheese among bottom halves of bread pieces. Replace top halves of bread. Cut each in half diagonally (to make 8 sandwiches total).

3 Coat a 12-inch skillet with 2 teaspoons of the olive oil. Heat skillet over medium heat for 2 to 3 minutes or until hot. Add four of the sandwiches. Cover sandwiches with foil; place a large heavy skillet on sandwiches to weight them down.

4 Cook for 8 to 10 minutes or until heated through, turning sandwiches once and replacing foil and weight. (If sandwiches brown too quickly, reduce heat to medium-low.) Remove from skillet; cover and keep warm. Repeat with remaining olive oil and sandwiches.

Per sandwich: 362 cal., 20 g total fat (8 g sat. fat), 64 mg chol., 793 mg sodium, 20 g carbo., 1 g fiber, 26 g pro.

Thanks to store-bought cooked beef roast au jus, this sandwich is super quick to put together. Prosciutto and pepperoncini peppers give it a distinctive Italian flavor.

ITALIAN PO BOY

START TO FINISH:
30 minutes

MAKES:
4 servings

2 ounces prosciutto (about 4 slices)

2 cups shredded lettuce

8 pepperoncini, chopped

1 17-ounce package refrigerated cooked beef roast au jus

1 round flat country Italian bread loaf, halved horizontally*

4 slices provolone cheese (4 ounces)

¼ cup bottled clear Italian salad dressing

1 In a large skillet cook prosciutto over medium heat about 6 minutes or until browned, turning once. Remove from heat; set aside.

2 In a small bowl combine shredded lettuce and pepperoncini.

3 Heat roast beef in microwave oven according to package directions. Remove meat from juices, reserving juices; shred meat. Brush cut sides of the bread with some of the reserved juices. Arrange meat on bottom half of the bread. Top with provolone cheese, prosciutto, and lettuce mixture. Drizzle with dressing. Add top of bread. Cut into wedges to serve. Serve with any remaining juices.

Per serving: 651 cal., 25 g total fat (11 g sat. fat), 93 mg chol., 2,180 mg sodium, 63 g carbo., 3 g fiber, 44 g pro.

*NOTE: If the bread is too tall, remove a 1- to 2-inch-thick slice from the center, so that the top of the bread is 1 inch thick. The bread you slice off can be used to make croutons or bread crumbs.

Panini, which means "small bread" in Italian, refers to sandwich-size bread or a roll. Here the panini are filled with a flavorful mixture of frozen meatballs and pizza sauce.

SHORTCUT MEATBALL PANINI

16   frozen Italian-style cooked meatballs
    (about 1 pound)

1   15-ounce can pizza sauce

4   Italian rolls or hoagie buns

4   slices provolone cheese

1   cup loosely packed large fresh basil
    or spinach leaves

PREP:
20 minutes

BROIL:
1 minute + 1 minute

MAKES:
4 servings

1 Preheat the broiler. In a large saucepan combine meatballs and pizza sauce. Cover and cook over medium-low heat about 10 minutes or until heated through, stirring occasionally.

2 Cut a thin slice from the top of each roll; hollow out each roll leaving a ¼- to ½-inch-thick shell. (Discard or save bread from rolls for another use). Place hollowed-out rolls and roll tops, cut sides up, on a baking sheet. Broil 3 to 4 inches from the heat for 1 to 2 minutes or until lightly toasted. Remove roll tops from baking sheet.

3 Spoon meatballs and sauce into toasted rolls. Top with provolone cheese. Broil about 1 minute more or until cheese is melted. To serve, arrange basil or spinach leaves on top of cheese and replace roll tops.

Per serving: 740 cal., 38 g total fat (18 g sat. fat), 98 mg chol., 1,570 mg sodium, 63 g carbo., 8 g fiber, 36 g pro.

Focaccia bread can be found plain or topped with various Italian ingredients such as garlic, rosemary, or sweet peppers. Any one works delightfully for this recipe, so choose the flavor that best suits your family.

SALAMI-HAM SANDWICHES

PREP:
20 minutes

BROIL:
1 minute

MAKES:
6 sandwiches

1   9- to 10- inch Italian flat bread (focaccia),
    1 to 2 inches thick

¼   cup bottled creamy garlic salad dressing

4   ounces thinly sliced hard salami

2   plum tomatoes, thinly sliced

4   ounces thinly sliced provolone cheese

1   cup bottled roasted red sweet peppers, drained

4   ounces thinly sliced cooked ham

4   romaine leaves or 1 cup fresh baby spinach

1 Preheat broiler. Carefully split bread in half horizontally. Place bread, cut sides up, on the unheated rack of a broiler pan. Broil 4 to 5 inches from the heat about 1 minute or until toasted.

2 Spread bottom half of the bread with salad dressing. Layer remaining ingredients on the bread in the following order: salami, tomatoes, provolone cheese, sweet peppers, ham, and romaine. Add top half of the bread. Cut into 6 wedges. Use a 6-inch wooden skewer to secure each wedge.

Per sandwich: 345 cal., 18 g total fat (7 g sat. fat), 46 mg chol., 1,116 mg sodium, 31 g carbo., 3 g fiber, 19 g pro.

Cappacola is an Italian ham coated with peppery spices. It can be found at Italian delis and in some larger supermarkets. If you are unable to find it, substitute cured deli ham and a sprinkling of pepper.

GRILLED ITALIAN PANINI

1	16-ounce loaf unsliced ciabatta or Italian bread
6	ounces thinly sliced provolone cheese
¼	cup mayonnaise or salad dressing
1	tablespoon purchased basil pesto
4	ounces thinly sliced cappacola or cooked ham
4	ounces thinly sliced salami
1	recipe Red Onion Relish
1	cup arugula
1	tablespoon olive oil

PREP:
20 minutes

GRILL:
5 minutes + 3 minutes

MAKES:
4 servings

1 Carefully trim off and discard the top crust of the bread to make a flat surface. Turn bread over; trim off and discard bottom crust. Cut remaining bread horizontally into two ½-inch-thick slices.

2 Place half of the provolone cheese on one slice of bread. In a small bowl stir together mayonnaise and pesto; spread over cheese. Layer with cappacola, salami, Red Onion Relish, arugula, and remaining cheese. Top with the other slice of bread. Brush both sides of panini with olive oil.

3 Place panini on the greased grill rack of an uncovered grill directly over medium coals. Put a 13×9×2-inch baking pan on top of panini; weight it down with several baking potatoes or a brick. Grill about 5 minutes or until lightly browned. Use hot pads to remove baking pan. Use a spatula to carefully turn panini over. Place baking pan back on panini; grill about 3 minutes more or until cheese is melted.

RED ONION RELISH: In a small bowl combine 1 medium red onion, halved and thinly sliced; 2 tablespoons olive oil; 1 tablespoon red wine vinegar; and 1 teaspoon snipped fresh oregano. Season to taste with salt and black pepper. Cover and let stand at room temperature for up to 2 hours.

Per serving: 840 cal., 51 g total fat (15 g sat. fat), 77 mg chol., 2,118 mg sodium, 62 g carbo., 4 g fiber, 33 g pro.

Formaggio means "cheese" in Italian. Both Scamorza and provolone are mild-flavored cow's milk cheeses. Scamorza will give the sandwiches a slightly nutty flavor, while provolone will provide a hint of smokiness.

GRILLED FORMAGGIO SANDWICHES

PREP:
20 minutes

COOK:
6 minutes

MAKES:
4 sandwiches

4   teaspoons butter, margarine, or olive oil

4   wedges Italian flat bread (focaccia) (about 1 inch thick), split in half horizontally*

8   ounces Scamorza or provolone cheese, thinly sliced

12   to 16 fresh spinach leaves, washed and patted dry

4   slices bacon or turkey bacon, halved, crisp-cooked, and drained

1 For each sandwich, spread 1 teaspoon of the butter on uncut sides of each wedge of bread. Divide Scamorza cheese evenly among the unbuttered sides of the focaccia wedge bottoms. Place three or four spinach leaves and two half-slices bacon on each cheese-topped wedge. Top with wedge tops.

2 Place sandwiches in a large skillet or on a griddle. Cook over medium-high heat for 6 to 8 minutes or until the cheese is melted and the bread is golden brown, turning once.

Per serving: 510 cal., 24 g total fat (13 g sat. fat), 64 mg chol., 576 mg sodium, 50 g carbo., 4 g fiber, 26 g pro.

*NOTE: If using thin focaccia bread, use two unsplit wedges to make each sandwich.

Save the oil drained from the dried tomatoes to brush on the dough before baking. The coating of oil helps the calzones bake to an even golden brown.

HERO CALZONES

2 tablespoons cornmeal

⅓ cup snipped oil-packed dried tomatoes

1 cup chopped cooked meat
(such as smoked turkey, smoked sausage,
cooked chicken, ham, and/or pepperoni)

⅓ cup chopped pitted ripe olives

1½ cups shredded mozzarella cheese (6 ounces)

1 13.8-ounce package refrigerated pizza dough

Finely shredded or grated Parmesan cheese

Cayenne pepper (optional)

Purchased pizza or pasta sauce, warmed

1 Preheat oven to 425°F. Lightly grease a large baking sheet and sprinkle with cornmeal; set aside. Drain dried tomatoes well, reserving oil; set aside. In a medium bowl combine cooked meat, olives, and tomatoes. Stir in mozzarella cheese.

2 Unroll pizza dough. On a lightly floured surface, roll or stretch pizza dough to a 14-inch square. Cut dough into four 7-inch squares. Divide meat mixture among squares, positioning it on one half of each square. Brush dough edges with water. Fold dough over filling to form rectangles or triangles, stretching dough as needed. Seal edges by pressing with the tines of a fork.

3 Place calzones on prepared baking sheet. Brush tops with reserved oil; sprinkle with Parmesan cheese and, if desired, cayenne pepper. Bake about 15 minutes or until golden brown. Serve warm with warmed pizza sauce.

Per calzone: 423 cal., 17 g total fat (7 g sat. fat), 54 mg chol., 1,095 mg sodium, 44 g carbo., 3 g fiber, 23 g pro.

PREP:
20 minutes

BAKE:
15 minutes

OVEN:
425°F

MAKES:
4 calzones

This recipe provides a great way to use leftover chicken or turkey. Purchased ingredients like pesto, marinated artichoke hearts, and roasted red peppers add a lot of flavor without a lot of work.

CHICKEN-PROSCIUTTO SANDWICHES

PREP:
15 minutes

BAKE:
8 minutes + 4 minutes

OVEN:
450°F

MAKES:
6 sandwiches

6   ½-inch-thick slices Italian bread

⅓   cup purchased basil pesto

3   ounces thinly sliced prosciutto

2½   cups cooked chicken or turkey cut into bite-size strips (about 12 ounces)

1   14-ounce can artichoke hearts, drained and thinly sliced

1   cup bottled roasted red sweet peppers, drained and cut into strips

1   to 1½ cups shredded provolone cheese (4 to 6 ounces)

1 Preheat oven to 450°F. Lightly spread bread slices with pesto. Layer on the bread in the following order: prosciutto, chicken strips, artichoke hearts, and roasted red peppers.

2 Line a large baking sheet with foil. Place sandwiches on prepared baking sheet. Cover loosely with foil. Bake about 8 minutes or until nearly heated through. Uncover and sprinkle with provolone cheese. Bake for 4 to 5 minutes more or until cheese is melted.

Per sandwich: 387 cal., 20 g total fat (6 g sat. fat), 67 mg chol., 855 mg sodium, 20 g carbo., 1 g fiber, 31 g pro.

Aromatic fresh basil gives the spread for these sandwiches an intense flavor.
Do not substitute dried basil—it simply will not create the same flavor.

ROASTED PEPPER-TURKEY SANDWICHES

⅓   cup fine dry bread crumbs

2   teaspoons dried Italian seasoning, crushed

2   turkey breast tenderloins (about 1 pound total)

2   teaspoons olive oil

2   tablespoons snipped fresh basil

¼   cup light mayonnaise or salad dressing

8   ½-inch-thick slices Italian bread, toasted

1   cup bottled roasted red and/or yellow sweet peppers, cut into thin strips

      Fresh basil leaves (optional)

1 In a large resealable plastic bag combine bread crumbs and Italian seasoning. Split each turkey breast tenderloin in half horizontally. Place a turkey tenderloin piece in the bag; seal and shake to coat. Repeat with remaining pieces.

2 In a 12-inch nonstick skillet heat olive oil over medium heat. Add turkey; cook about 10 minutes or until tender and no longer pink (170°F), turning once.

3 In a small bowl stir 1 tablespoon of the snipped basil into the mayonnaise. Spread mayonnaise mixture on one side of four of the bread slices. Top bread slices with turkey, sweet pepper strips, and the remaining 1 tablespoon snipped basil. If desired, garnish with basil leaves. Top with remaining bread slices.

Per sandwich: 399 cal., 11 g total fat (2 g sat. fat), 73 mg chol., 671 mg sodium, 40 g carbo., 3 g fiber, 33 g pro.

START TO FINISH:
20 minutes

MAKES:
4 sandwiches

This is the perfect sandwich for summer when fresh vegetables are at their very best.

ITALIAN VEGETABLE MELT

PREP:
30 minutes

BROIL:
2 minutes

MAKES:
4 servings

4	individual Italian loaves (each about 7 inches long)
¼	cup bottled clear Italian salad dressing
1	small onion, thinly sliced
1	small zucchini, halved lengthwise and sliced
1	small green sweet pepper, cut into thin strips
2	cloves garlic, minced
1	large tomato, seeded and chopped
3	cups shredded provolone or mozzarella cheese (12 ounces)
¼	cup grated Parmesan cheese

1 Preheat broiler. Split bread loaves in half horizontally. Place halves on large baking sheet, cut sides up.

2 In a 10-inch skillet heat salad dressing. Add onion, zucchini, sweet pepper, and garlic. Cook and stir for 3 to 5 minutes or until vegetables are crisp-tender. Stir in tomato. Sprinkle half of the provolone or mozzarella cheese on bottoms of bread halves. Spoon vegetable mixture over cheese; sprinkle with remaining provolone or mozzarella and the Parmesan cheese.

3 Broil 4 to 5 inches from the heat about 2 minutes or until cheese melts. Serve immediately.

Per serving: 693 cal., 32 g total fat (17 g sat. fat), 63 mg chol., 1,733 mg sodium, 65 g carbo., 4 g fiber, 35 g pro.

CLASSIC DISHES

8

This classic sauce begins with a basic Italian "soffrito," a mix of chopped onions, garlic, and various other vegetables sautéed in olive oil.

BASIC TOMATO SAUCE

PREP:
30 minutes

COOK:
30 minutes

MAKES:
2¾ cups

½   cup chopped onion

¼   cup olive oil

¼   cup shredded carrot

¼   cup chopped celery

2   to 4 cloves garlic, minced

3   pounds plum tomatoes, peeled, seeded, and chopped (about 4 cups), or two 28-ounce cans Italian plum tomatoes, drained and cut up

¼   teaspoon salt

¼   teaspoon black pepper

1   bay leaf

   Salt

   Black pepper

1 In a large saucepan cook onion in hot oil about 5 minutes or until tender, stirring occasionally. Add carrot, celery, and garlic. Cook about 5 minutes or until vegetables are golden brown, stirring occasionally.

2 Stir in tomatoes, the ¼ teaspoon salt, the ¼ teaspoon pepper, and the bay leaf. Bring to boiling; reduce heat. Simmer, uncovered, for 30 to 40 minutes or until sauce is thickened, stirring occasionally. Discard bay leaf. If desired, transfer sauce to a food processor or blender; cover and process or blend until smooth. (If using a blender, blend sauce half at a time.) Season to taste with additional salt and pepper.

Per ½ cup: 134 cal., 11 g total fat (2 g sat. fat), 0 mg chol., 192 mg sodium, 9 g carbo., 2 g fiber, 2 g pro.

TOMATO CREAM SAUCE: Prepare as directed, except stir ½ cup whipping cream into sauce after it is cooked (and pureed, if desired). Heat through, stirring constantly.

Per ½ cup: 180 cal., 17 g total fat (6 g sat. fat), 27 mg chol., 167 mg sodium, 8 g carbo., 2 g fiber, 2 g pro.

Marinara means "from the sea" in Italian. In the 16th century, it was made in Naples for the sailors returning home from sea. By now, it has become a favorite for topping pasta and a variety of main dishes.

MARINARA SAUCE

¼   cup olive oil

4   to 6 cloves garlic, minced

3   pounds plum tomatoes, peeled, seeded, and chopped (about 4 cups), or two 28-ounce cans Italian plum tomatoes, drained and chopped

½   teaspoon salt*

½   teaspoon black pepper

⅓   cup snipped fresh basil

1 In a 3-quart saucepan heat oil over medium heat. Add garlic; cook and stir for 1 minute. Stir in tomatoes, salt, and pepper. Reduce heat to medium-low. Cook, uncovered, for 15 to 20 minutes or until sauce is thickened and chunky, stirring occasionally. Stir in basil. Simmer for 5 minutes more. If desired, adjust seasonings to taste.

Per ½ cup: 109 cal., 9 g total fat (1 g sat. fat), 0 mg chol., 205 mg sodium, 6 g carbo., 2 g fiber, 1 g pro.

*NOTE: If using canned tomatoes, reduce salt to ¼ teaspoon.

PREP:
35 minutes

COOK:
15 minutes + 5 minutes

MAKES:
3 cups

A hearty brunch dish, this recipe calls for Italy's famous ham, prosciutto. If you can't find it, use two extra slices of bacon.

FETTUCCINE ALLA CARBONARA

START TO FINISH:
40 minutes

MAKES:
*3 main-dish servings or
6 side-dish servings*

2 tablespoons finely chopped onion

¼ cup unsalted butter

4 slices bacon, cut into ½-inch pieces and crisp-cooked

3 ounces prosciutto, sliced ⅛ inch thick and cut into ½-inch pieces

⅓ cup dry white wine

⅓ cup whipping cream

⅓ cup milk

1 slightly beaten egg yolk

2 tablespoons finely shredded Parmesan cheese

1 tablespoon snipped fresh parsley

1 9-ounce package refrigerated fettuccine

Finely shredded Parmesan cheese (optional)

Cracked black pepper (optional)

1 In a medium saucepan cook onion in hot butter about 5 minutes or just until tender. Stir in bacon and prosciutto. Cook and stir for 3 minutes more.

2 Carefully add white wine. Bring to boiling; reduce heat. Simmer, uncovered, for 5 minutes more, stirring occasionally. Add cream and milk; bring to a gentle boil.

3 Gradually add 1 cup of the hot cream mixture to egg yolk, stirring constantly. Stir egg yolk mixture into cream mixture in saucepan. Return to a gentle boil. Cook and stir for 2 minutes. Add 2 tablespoons Parmesan cheese and the parsley, stirring just until cheese melts.

4 Meanwhile, cook the fettuccine according to package directions; drain well. Pour the sauce over hot pasta. Toss to coat. If desired, sprinkle pasta with additional Parmesan cheese and cracked black pepper.

Per main-dish serving: 654 cal., 38 g total fat (21 g sat. fat), 274 mg chol., 1,115 mg sodium, 49 g carbo., 2 g fiber, 26 g pro.

Originating in Liguria, a coastal region of Italy, this versatile pesto can be used on everything from pasta and crostini to soups and sandwiches.

CLASSIC PESTO

⅓   to ½ cup olive oil

2   cups firmly packed fresh basil leaves (2½ ounces)

½   cup pine nuts

½   cup grated Parmesan or Romano cheese (2 ounces)

3   or 4 cloves garlic, peeled and quartered

¼   teaspoon salt

Black pepper

❶ In a food processor or blender combine ⅓ cup of the olive oil, the basil, pine nuts, Parmesan cheese, garlic, and salt. Cover and process or blend until nearly smooth, stopping and scraping side as necessary and adding enough of the remaining oil to make desired consistency. Season to taste with black pepper.

Per tablespoon: 92 cal., 9 g total fat (2 g sat. fat), 3 mg chol., 111 mg sodium, 2 g carbo., 0 g fiber, 3 g pro.

MAKE-AHEAD DIRECTIONS: Prepare as directed. Divide pesto into three portions. Place each portion in a small airtight container; seal. Refrigerate for 1 to 2 days or freeze for up to 3 months.

START TO FINISH:
20 minutes

MAKES:
about ¾ cup pesto

Many classic Italian recipes call for fruits of the sea, such as clams. If you use canned clams for this dish, reserve the drained juice. It can serve as part of the clam juice in the recipe.

LINGUINE IN WHITE CLAM SAUCE

PREP:
20 minutes

COOK:
10 minutes + 10 minutes

MAKES:
4 servings

8	ounces dried linguine
¼	cup butter
2	tablespoons cooking oil
2¼	cups sliced fresh mushrooms
¼	cup chopped onion
3	cloves garlic, minced
¾	cup bottled clam juice
1	pint fresh shucked clams, drained and chopped, or two 6½-ounce cans minced clams, drained
¾	cup dry white wine
¼	cup finely shredded Parmesan cheese (1 ounce)
2	tablespoons snipped fresh parsley

1 Cook the pasta according to package directions. Drain and return pasta to hot saucepan; cover and keep warm. Meanwhile, in a 10-inch skillet heat butter and oil over medium heat. Add mushrooms, onion, and garlic. Cook and stir about 5 minutes or until mushrooms are tender.

2 Add clam juice to mushroom mixture. Bring to boiling; reduce heat. Simmer, uncovered, for 10 minutes. Add clams and wine. Bring to boiling; reduce heat. Simmer, uncovered, for 10 minutes more, stirring occasionally.

3 Add clam mixture to pasta in the saucepan. Toss to coat. Transfer to serving dish. Sprinkle with Parmesan cheese and parsley.

Per serving: 529 cal., 24 g total fat (10 g sat. fat), 78 mg chol., 375 mg sodium, 49 g carbo., 2 g fiber, 26 g pro.

Arugula, an extremely popular salad green in Italy, adds a peppery mustard flavor to this dish.

VEAL CHOPS MILANESE-STYLE

2	8-ounce boneless veal loin chops or 1 pound pork tenderloin
4	eggs
1	cup all-purpose flour
1	teaspoon salt
¼	teaspoon black pepper
1	cup fine dry bread crumbs
3	tablespoons olive oil
1	teaspoon olive oil
2	cloves garlic, minced
1	5-ounce package baby arugula or fresh baby spinach (about 6 cups)

START TO FINISH:
35 minutes

MAKES:
4 servings

1 Cut veal chops in half. Place each half between 2 pieces of plastic wrap. Using the flat side of a meat mallet, pound meat lightly to an even ¼-inch thickness. Remove plastic wrap. (If using pork tenderloin, cut tenderloin into 8 pieces and pound, cut sides up, as directed for veal.)

2 In a shallow dish beat eggs with a fork. In another shallow dish combine flour, salt, and pepper. Place bread crumbs in a third shallow dish. Dip chops in eggs, then in flour mixture, and then in bread crumbs to coat.

3 In a 12-inch skillet heat the 3 tablespoons olive oil over medium heat. Cook chops, half at a time, in hot oil for 4 to 6 minutes or until golden brown, turning once. (If necessary, add more oil during cooking.) Transfer chops to a serving platter; cover and keep warm.

4 In the same skillet heat the 1 teaspoon olive oil over medium heat. Add garlic; cook and stir for 30 seconds. Add arugula; cook and stir about 1 minute or just until wilted. Spoon arugula on top of chops.

Per serving: 520 cal., 22 g total fat (4 g sat. fat), 302 mg chol., 1,470 mg sodium, 43 g carbo., 2 g fiber, 36 g pro.

Traditional old-world flavors come together for a truly memorable meal. Use your hands to evenly coat the tenderloin slices with the seasoning mixture.

AROMATIC PORK WITH BABY ZUCCHINI & FIGS

START TO FINISH:
35 minutes

MAKES:
4 servings

2	cloves garlic, minced
¾	teaspoon ground cumin
¾	teaspoon paprika
½	teaspoon whole black peppercorns, crushed
¼	teaspoon salt
12	ounces pork tenderloin, trimmed
½	cup water
6	ounces pearl onions, peeled and halved (about 1 dozen)
½	teaspoon cardamom pods, crushed
1	bay leaf
½	teaspoon salt
12	ounces baby zucchini, ends trimmed (about 2 dozen)
1	tablespoon olive oil
8	fresh figs, halved

1 In a small bowl combine garlic, cumin, paprika, peppercorns, and the ¼ teaspoon salt. Cut pork tenderloin crosswise into ¾-inch-thick slices. Sprinkle cumin mixture evenly over surfaces of pork tenderloin; rub in with your fingers. Set aside.

2 In a large nonstick skillet combine the water, onions, cardamom, bay leaf, and the ½ teaspoon salt. Bring to boiling over high heat; reduce heat. Cover and cook for 5 minutes. Add zucchini. Cover and cook for 3 to 4 minutes more or just until zucchini and onions are tender. Discard bay leaf. Transfer mixture to a bowl; cover and keep warm. Carefully wipe out skillet with paper towels.

3 In the skillet heat olive oil over medium-high heat. Add pork tenderloin slices. Cook about 6 minutes or just until pork is slightly pink in center, turning once. Remove from skillet; keep warm. Place figs in the skillet. Cook about 1 minute or just until heated through; set aside.

4 To serve, arrange pork tenderloin slices and figs on four dinner plates. Serve zucchini-onion mixture with pork and figs.

Per serving: 247 cal., 6 g total fat (1 g sat. fat), 50 mg chol., 475 mg sodium, 27 g carbo., 5 g fiber, 24 g pro.

This Italian-style meat loaf is packed full of mozzarella cheese, prosciutto, and Italian herbs. When sliced, it displays an attractive swirl for a dazzling presentation.

SICILIAN MEAT ROLL

2	eggs
¾	cup soft bread crumbs (1 slice)
½	cup tomato juice
2	tablespoons snipped fresh parsley
½	teaspoon dried oregano, crushed
¼	teaspoon salt
¼	teaspoon black pepper
1	small clove garlic, minced
2	pounds lean ground beef
6	ounces thinly sliced prosciutto
1½	cups shredded mozzarella cheese (6 ounces)

PREP:
25 minutes

BAKE:
65 minutes + 5 minutes

STAND:
10 minutes

OVEN:
350°F

MAKES:
8 servings

1 Preheat oven to 350°F. In a large bowl beat eggs with a fork. Stir in bread crumbs, tomato juice, parsley, oregano, salt, pepper, and garlic. Add ground beef; mix well.

2 On a large piece of foil, pat meat mixture into a 12×10-inch rectangle. Arrange the prosciutto slices on meat, leaving a ¾-inch border around all edges. Sprinkle 1¼ cups of the mozzarella cheese over the prosciutto. Starting from a short end, carefully roll up meat rectangle, using foil to lift; seal edges and ends. Place meat roll, seam side down, in a 13×9×2-inch baking pan.

3 Bake about 65 minutes or until an instant-read thermometer inserted in the center registers 160°F and juices run clear. (Center of meat roll will be pink due to prosciutto.) Sprinkle remaining ¼ cup mozzarella cheese over top of meat roll. Return to oven about 5 minutes or until cheese melts. Let stand for 10 to 15 minutes before slicing.

Per serving: 312 cal., 17 g total fat (7 g sat. fat), 152 mg chol., 878 mg sodium, 4 g carbo., 0 g fiber, 33 g pro.

Italian sausage and dried oregano make this dish sing with Italian flavors. Use a colorful combination of red, yellow, and green sweet peppers for a pumped-up presentation.

SALSICCIA WITH PEPPERS & POTATOES

START TO FINISH:
45 minutes

MAKES:
4 servings

2	tablespoons olive oil
4	uncooked mild Italian sausage links (about 1 pound)
½	cup water
3	large potatoes, peeled and thinly sliced
1	large green sweet pepper, cut into strips
1	medium onion, sliced and separated into rings
3	cloves garlic, minced
1	28-ounce can crushed tomatoes, undrained
2	teaspoons sugar
2	teaspoons dried oregano, crushed
¼	teaspoon salt
¼	teaspoon black pepper

1 In a very large skillet heat 1 tablespoon of the oil over medium heat. Add sausage links; cook about 5 minutes or until brown, turning frequently. Carefully add the water. Bring to boiling; reduce heat. Cover and simmer for 5 minutes. Uncover and cook sausages until liquid evaporates and sausages are cooked through (160°F), turning frequently. Watch carefully so that sausages do not burn. Drain sausages on paper towels.

2 In the same skillet heat remaining 1 tablespoon oil over medium heat. Add potatoes, sweet pepper, onion, and garlic. Cook for 10 to 15 minutes or just until potatoes are tender, turning mixture occasionally.

3 Stir in undrained tomatoes, sugar, oregano, salt, and black pepper. Return sausage links to skillet. Bring to boiling; reduce heat. Cover and simmer for 10 minutes.

Per serving: 680 cal., 43 g total fat (14 g sat. fat), 86 mg chol., 1,249 mg sodium, 53 g carbo., 8 g fiber, 24 g pro.

Italian sausage and tomatoes give this classic pasta dish a lively kick.
Whipping cream and mozzarella cheese make it rich and delicious.

SHELLS WITH ITALIAN SAUSAGE & MOZZARELLA

12	ounces bulk Italian sausage
1	large onion, chopped
4	cloves garlic, minced
1	28-ounce can tomatoes, undrained, cut up
2	to 3 tablespoons snipped fresh oregano or 2 teaspoons dried oregano, crushed
2	tablespoons tomato paste
2	bay leaves
1	teaspoon sugar
½	teaspoon salt
¼	teaspoon black pepper
½	cup whipping cream
6	ounces mozzarella cheese, cubed
10	ounces dried small shell macaroni

PREP:
30 minutes

COOK:
15 minutes + 5 minutes

MAKES:
5 servings

1 In a large saucepan or Dutch oven cook sausage, onion, and garlic until sausage is brown and onion is tender. Drain off fat.

2 Stir undrained tomatoes, dried oregano (if using), tomato paste, bay leaves, sugar, salt, and pepper into sausage mixture in Dutch oven. Bring to boiling; reduce heat. Cover and simmer for 15 minutes. Stir in whipping cream. Return to boiling; reduce heat. Simmer, uncovered, about 5 minutes more or until mixture is slightly thickened, stirring occasionally. Discard bay leaves. Stir mozzarella cheese and fresh oregano (if using) into tomato mixture. Cook and stir until cheese starts to melt.

3 Meanwhile, cook pasta according to package directions. Drain. Toss tomato mixture with pasta. Mixture will thicken as it stands.

Per serving: 629 cal., 31 g total fat (15 g sat. fat), 100 mg chol., 1,033 mg sodium, 57 g carbo., 4 g fiber, 28 g pro.

Sage, an herb native to the Mediterranean, complements the chicken in this recipe and gives the dish a distinctive earthy flavor.

CHICKEN ROMANA

PREP:
30 minutes

BAKE:
10 minutes + 5 minutes

OVEN:
375°F

MAKES:
4 servings

4 skinless, boneless chicken breast halves (about 1¼ pounds total)

12 fresh sage leaves

4 thin slices prosciutto (2 ounces)

½ cup seasoned fine dry bread crumbs

¼ teaspoon black pepper

2 tablespoons olive oil

½ cup shredded mozzarella cheese (2 ounces)

2 tablespoons grated Parmesan cheese

2 tablespoons butter

2 tablespoons all-purpose flour

1 cup beef broth

¼ cup dry white wine or 2 tablespoons lemon juice

1 teaspoon snipped fresh sage or ¼ teaspoon ground sage

Salt

Black pepper

1 Preheat oven to 375°F. Place a chicken breast half between 2 pieces of plastic wrap. Using the flat side of a meat mallet, pound chicken lightly to an even ¼-inch thickness. Remove plastic wrap. Place 3 sage leaves on chicken and top with a slice of prosciutto; return plastic wrap. Lightly pound prosciutto and sage leaves into chicken. Remove plastic wrap. Repeat with remaining chicken breast halves, sage leaves, and prosciutto.

2 Grease a 15×10×1-inch baking pan; set aside. In a shallow dish combine bread crumbs and the ¼ teaspoon pepper. Brush chicken generously with oil. Dip chicken in crumb mixture to coat. Place in prepared baking pan, prosciutto sides up.

3 Bake for 10 minutes. Sprinkle with mozzarella cheese and Parmesan cheese. Bake about 5 minutes more or until chicken is no longer pink and cheese is melted.

4 Meanwhile, for sauce, in a small saucepan melt butter; stir in flour. Add beef broth, wine or lemon juice, and snipped or ground sage. Cook and stir until thickened and bubbly. Cook and stir for 1 minute more. Season to taste with salt and additional black pepper. Serve sauce over chicken.

Per serving: 418 cal., 19 g total fat (7 g sat. fat), 116 mg chol., 1,083 mg sodium, 14 g carbo., 0 g fiber, 43 g pro.

Classic Italian ingredients, such as prosciutto and mushrooms, join forces with store-bought salad dressing for these easy and mouthwatering kabobs.

CHICKEN SPIEDINI

1¼ pounds chicken breast tenderloins

⅔ cup bottled sweet Italian salad dressing or clear Italian salad dressing

¾ cup seasoned fine dry bread crumbs

¾ cup halved fresh mushrooms

2 cloves garlic, minced

1 tablespoon butter

¼ cup coarsely chopped prosciutto

¾ cup shredded provolone or mozzarella cheese (3 ounces)

1 lemon, quartered

1 Place chicken in a resealable plastic bag set in a shallow dish. Pour salad dressing over chicken. Seal bag; turn to coat chicken. Marinate in the refrigerator for 2 to 24 hours, turning bag occasionally.

2 Drain chicken, discarding marinade. Place bread crumbs in a shallow dish. Dip chicken in bread crumbs to coat. On five or six long metal skewers, thread chicken, accordion-style, leaving a ¼-inch space between pieces.

3 Place skewers on the rack of an uncovered grill directly over medium coals. Grill for 10 to 12 minutes or until chicken is tender and no longer pink (170°F), turning once halfway through grilling.

4 Meanwhile, in a large skillet cook mushrooms and garlic in hot butter about 5 minutes or just until mushrooms are tender, stirring occasionally. Add prosciutto; cook and stir for 2 minutes more.

5 Remove chicken from skewers; arrange on a serving plate. Sprinkle chicken with half of the cheese. Spoon mushroom mixture over chicken. Sprinkle with remaining cheese. Squeeze lemon over individual servings.

Per serving: 424 cal., 18 g total fat (7 g sat. fat), 111 mg chol., 1,402 mg sodium, 20 g carbo., 0 g fiber, 45 g pro.

OVEN DIRECTIONS: Prepare as directed through step 2. Preheat oven to 375°F. Arrange skewers in a 15×10×1-inch baking pan. Bake about 15 minutes or until chicken is tender and no longer pink (170°F). Continue as directed in steps 4 and 5.

PREP:
30 minutes

MARINATE:
2 to 24 hours

GRILL:
10 minutes

MAKES:
4 servings

Four authentic Italian topping combinations produce a pizza that's sure to please everyone at the table.

FOUR SEASONS PIZZA

PREP:
30 minutes

STAND:
5 minutes + 10 minutes

RISE:
45 minutes

BAKE:
15 minutes

OVEN:
425°F

MAKES:
4 servings

1	teaspoon active dry yeast
1	teaspoon honey or sugar
⅔	cup warm water (105°F to 115°F)
1	cup all-purpose flour
¼	teaspoon salt
1	teaspoon olive oil
¾	to 1 cup semolina (ground durum wheat) or all-purpose flour
	Cornmeal
1	recipe Tomato-Basil Topping
1	recipe Fontina-Gorgonzola Topping
1	recipe Sausage-Cheese Topping
1	recipe Mushroom-Garlic Topping
	Olive oil (optional)

1 In a small bowl dissolve yeast and honey in the warm water. Let stand for 5 minutes.

2 In a large bowl combine the 1 cup all-purpose flour and the salt. Gradually stir in yeast mixture until combined. Add the 1 teaspoon olive oil, stirring to combine. Stir in as much of the semolina or all-purpose flour as you can.

3 Turn out dough onto a lightly floured surface. Knead in enough of the remaining semolina or flour to make a moderately stiff dough that is smooth and elastic (6 to 8 minutes total). Shape into a ball and place in a lightly greased bowl; turn once. Cover and let rise in a warm place until nearly double (45 to 60 minutes).

4 Preheat oven to 425°F. Punch down dough. Cover and let rest for 10 minutes. Place dough on a lightly floured surface. Remove about ½ cup of the dough; divide into six portions and roll each portion into a 9-inch-long rope. Twist together two of the ropes; repeat to make a total of three twisted ropes. Roll remaining dough into a 13×9-inch rectangle, building up edges slightly. Transfer dough to a large baking sheet that has been sprinkled with cornmeal.

5 Carefully place the twisted ropes of dough crosswise over the dough to make 4 equal sections. Top each section with a different topping, representing the four seasons.

6 Bake for 15 to 20 minutes or until crust is golden brown. If desired, drizzle with additional olive oil. Serve immediately.

FOUR SEASONS TOPPINGS

TOMATO-BASIL TOPPING: In a small bowl combine 2 teaspoons olive oil; 1 clove garlic, minced; and 1 teaspoon snipped fresh basil. Spread mixture on one section of Four Seasons Pizza. Top with 5 thin slices of plum tomato. After pizza is done, top with 2 teaspoons snipped fresh basil.

Per serving with Tomato-Basil Topping: 338 cal., 11 g total fat (1 g sat. fat), 0 mg chol., 151 mg sodium, 52 g carbo., 3 g fiber, 8 g pro.

FONTINA-GORGONZOLA TOPPING: Top Four Seasons Pizza section with ⅓ cup shredded fontina cheese and 2 tablespoons crumbled Gorgonzola cheese.

Per serving with Fontina-Gorgonzola Topping: 463 cal., 19 g total fat (12 g sat. fat), 63 mg chol., 686 mg sodium, 49 g carbo., 3 g fiber, 22 g pro.

SAUSAGE-CHEESE TOPPING: Spread one section Four Seasons Pizza with 2 tablespoons purchased marinara sauce. Top with ¼ cup cooked and well-drained bulk Italian sausage and ¼ cup shredded mozzarella cheese (1 ounce). Top with ¼ cup bottled roasted red sweet pepper strips.

Per serving with Sausage-Cheese Topping: 516 cal., 21 g total fat (8 g sat. fat), 49 mg chol., 1,030 mg sodium, 56 g carbo., 4 g fiber, 23 g pro.

MUSHROOM-GARLIC TOPPING: In a large skillet cook ½ cup thinly sliced fresh mushrooms and ¼ teaspoon minced garlic in 2 teaspoons hot olive oil until tender. Season to taste with salt and black pepper. Spread mushroom mixture on one section Four Seasons Pizza. Top with 2 tablespoons grated Parmesan cheese.

Per serving with Mushroom-Garlic Topping: 382 cal., 15 g total fat (3 g sat. fat), 9 mg chol., 594 mg sodium, 51 g carbo., 3 g fiber, 13 g pro.

TEST KITCHEN TIP!
Creating four individual pizzas is another way to enjoy this Italian classic. After the dough rests, shape it into four equal pieces and roll each piece into a 6-inch round. Add the toppings and bake as directed for 8 to 9 minutes.

Braising the fish, "pesce" in Italian, consists of cooking it in oil, then in liquid. This classic cooking method brings out the optimum flavor of the fish.

PESCE ITALIANO

START TO FINISH:
30 minutes

MAKES:
2 servings

2   fresh or frozen salmon, tuna, or swordfish steaks, ¾ inch thick (about 12 ounces total)

1   cup dried penne pasta (about 3 ounces)

1   teaspoon Creole seasoning

1   cup sliced fresh mushrooms

⅓   cup dry white wine

2   tablespoons purchased basil pesto

1   tablespoon lemon juice

2   teaspoons drained capers

1   tablespoon olive oil

   Fresh basil leaves (optional)

1 Thaw fish, if frozen. Rinse fish; pat dry with paper towels. Set aside.

2 In a large saucepan cook the pasta in a large amount of lightly salted boiling water for 4 minutes; drain and set aside. (Pasta will not be tender.)

3 Meanwhile, sprinkle both sides of each fish steak with the Creole seasoning; set aside. (If using a salt-free Creole seasoning, also sprinkle fish with ¼ teaspoon salt.) In a medium bowl combine the partially cooked pasta, the mushrooms, wine, pesto, lemon juice, and capers; set aside.

4 In a large skillet heat oil over medium-high heat. Add fish steaks. Cook for 1 minute; turn and cook for 1 minute more. Reduce heat to medium. Spoon pasta mixture around fish steaks in the skillet. Bring to boiling; reduce heat to medium. Cover and simmer for 6 to 9 minutes or just until fish flakes easily when tested with a fork. If desired, garnish individual servings with fresh basil leaves.

Per serving: 627 cal., 30 g total fat (5 g sat. fat), 109 mg chol., 352 mg sodium, 36 g carbo., 2 g fiber, 46 g pro.

CLASSIC DISHES

CLASSIC DISHES

**FOUR
SEASONS
PIZZA**

page 270

PESCE ITALIANO
page 272

CLASSIC DISHES

EGGPLANT PARMIGIANA

page 289

CHEESE POLENTA WITH TOMATO-BASIL SAUCE

page 290

CLASSIC DISHES

SICILIAN ARTICHOKES

page 293

CLASSIC RISOTTO WITH SPRING PEAS

page 294

TUSCAN
LAMB
CHOP
SKILLET
page 314

25-MINUTE MAIN DISHES

BALSAMIC CHICKEN & VEGETABLES

page 319

SCALLOPS WITH PARMESAN SAUCE

page 331

25-MINUTE MAIN DISHES

**TRATTORIA-
STYLE
SPINACH
FETTUCCINE**

page 337

**PASTA
WITH
RICOTTA &
VEGETABLES**

page 338

DESSERTS

WALNUT-CAPPUCCINO TORTE

page 372

PECAN WINE CAKE

page 373

DESSERTS

CORNMEAL-APPLE CAKE

page 374

DESSERTS

SPUMONI CHEESECAKE
page 379

COUNTRY PEAR & BLACKBERRY JAM CROSTATA
page 381

DESSERTS

ALMOND
PANNA
COTTA
WITH
MOCHA
SAUCE

page 383

DESSERTS

RICE PUDDING SOUFFLÉ WITH RASPBERRY SAUCE

page 385

FRUIT COMPOTE WITH LEMON CREAM

page 389

DESSERTS

NECTARINES WITH CHOCOLATE-HAZELNUT CREAM

page 390

PISTACHIO-LEMON GELATO

page 392

DESSERTS

FROZEN ORANGE SORBET TOWERS
page 394

DESSERTS

CANNOLI COOKIE STACKS

page 395

CAFFÈ MOCHA

page 399

This tasty recipe calls for eggplant and Parmesan cheese, two Italian favorites. It comes in handy when you have dinner guests who prefer meatless dishes.

EGGPLANT PARMIGIANA

1	small eggplant (12 ounces)
1	egg
1	tablespoon water
¼	cup all-purpose flour
2	tablespoons cooking oil
⅓	cup grated Parmesan cheese
1	cup purchased meatless spaghetti sauce
¾	cup shredded mozzarella cheese (3 ounces)

1 Preheat oven to 400°F. Wash and peel eggplant; cut crosswise into ½-inch-thick slices. In a shallow bowl whisk together egg and the water. Dip eggplant slices into egg mixture, then into flour, turning to coat both sides. In a large skillet cook eggplant, half at a time, in hot oil for 4 to 6 minutes or until golden brown, turning once. (If necessary, add additional oil during cooking.) Drain eggplant on paper towels.

2 Place eggplant slices in a single layer in a 2-quart rectangular baking dish. (If necessary, cut slices to fit.) Sprinkle with Parmesan cheese. Top with spaghetti sauce and mozzarella cheese. Bake for 10 to 12 minutes or until heated through.

Per serving: 269 cal., 18 g total fat (6 g sat. fat), 76 mg chol., 660 mg sodium, 17 g carbo., 3 g fiber, 12 g pro.

PREP:
25 minutes

BAKE:
10 minutes

OVEN:
400°F

MAKES:
4 servings

Polenta, made of cornmeal mush, is a staple of Northern Italy. If you're short on time, use the tubes of precooked, refrigerated polenta that you can find in the supermarket produce section. Just heat and serve with the homemade sauce.

CHEESE POLENTA WITH TOMATO-BASIL SAUCE

PREP:
40 minutes

COOL:
1 hour

CHILL:
3 to 24 hours

BAKE:
40 minutes

STAND:
10 minutes

OVEN:
350°F

MAKES:
6 servings

1½   cups shredded fontina or mozzarella cheese (6 ounces)

⅓   cup grated Parmesan or Romano cheese

2   tablespoons snipped fresh basil or 2 teaspoons dried basil, crushed

2¾   cups water

1   cup yellow cornmeal

1   cup cold water

½   teaspoon salt

1   recipe Tomato-Basil Sauce

Fresh basil leaves (optional)

1 Grease a 2-quart square baking dish; set aside. In a medium bowl stir together fontina cheese, Parmesan cheese, and the snipped or dried basil. Set aside.

2 For polenta, in a medium saucepan bring the 2¾ cups water to boiling. Meanwhile, in a medium bowl stir together cornmeal, the 1 cup cold water, and the salt. Slowly add cornmeal mixture to boiling water, stirring constantly. Cook and stir until mixture returns to boiling. Reduce heat to very low. Cook for 10 to 15 minutes or until mixture is very thick, stirring occasionally.

3 Immediately transfer one-third of the hot mixture to prepared baking dish. Sprinkle with half of the cheese mixture. Repeat layers, ending with the hot mixture. Cool for 1 hour. Cover with foil and chill 3 to 24 hours or until firm.

4 Preheat oven to 350°F. Uncover polenta; bake about 40 minutes or until lightly browned and heated through. Let stand for 10 minutes before serving. Serve with Tomato-Basil Sauce. If desired, garnish with basil leaves.

TOMATO-BASIL SAUCE: In a medium saucepan heat 2 tablespoons butter or margarine over medium heat. Add ¾ cup chopped onion and 2 cloves garlic, minced; cook until onion is tender. Carefully stir in two 14½-ounce cans whole Italian-style tomatoes, undrained, cut up; half of a 6-ounce can (⅓ cup) tomato paste; ½ teaspoon sugar; ¼ teaspoon salt; and ⅛ teaspoon black pepper. Bring to boiling; reduce heat. Simmer, uncovered, about 20 minutes or until desired consistency. Stir in ¼ cup snipped fresh basil or 1 tablespoon dried basil, crushed. Cook for 5 minutes more. Makes about 3⅓ cups sauce.

Per serving: 310 cal., 15 g total fat (9 g sat. fat), 47 mg chol., 969 mg sodium, 29 g carbo., 4 g fiber, 14 g pro.

Orzo—tiny, rice-shaped pasta—is a popular addition to many Italian soups. Dried tomatoes give the meatballs a pleasant tang.

ITALIAN WEDDING SOUP

1	large onion
3	oil-packed dried tomatoes, finely snipped
2	teaspoons dried Italian seasoning, crushed
1	pound lean ground beef
1	slightly beaten egg
¼	cup fine dry bread crumbs
¼	teaspoon salt
2	teaspoons olive oil
1	large fennel bulb
4	14-ounce cans chicken broth
6	cloves garlic, thinly sliced
½	teaspoon black pepper
¾	cup dried orzo pasta
5	cups shredded fresh spinach

PREP:
40 minutes

COOK:
10 minutes

MAKES:
6 servings

1 Finely chop one-third of the onion; thinly slice remaining onion. In a large bowl combine chopped onion, dried tomatoes, and 1 teaspoon of the Italian seasoning. Add ground beef, egg, bread crumbs, and salt; mix well. Shape into 12 meatballs. In a Dutch oven brown meatballs in hot olive oil. Carefully drain off fat.

2 Meanwhile, cut off and discard upper stalks of fennel, except if desired, save some of the feathery fennel leaves for a garnish. Remove any wilted outer layers; cut off a thin slice from fennel base. Cut fennel into thin wedges.

3 Add fennel, sliced onion, chicken broth, garlic, black pepper, and the remaining 1 teaspoon Italian seasoning to meatballs in Dutch oven. Bring to boiling; stir in uncooked orzo. Simmer, uncovered, for 10 to 15 minutes or until orzo is tender. Stir in spinach. If desired, garnish soup with reserved fennel leaves.

Per serving: 292 cal., 11 g total fat (3 g sat. fat), 86 mg chol., 1,352 mg sodium, 27 g carbo., 3 g fiber, 20 g pro.

SLOW-COOKER METHOD: Prepare as directed through step 2. After browning meatballs, place meatballs and sliced onion in a 5-quart slow cooker. Add fennel, broth, garlic, black pepper, and the remaining 1 teaspoon Italian seasoning. Cover and cook on low-heat setting for 8 to 10 hours or on high-heat setting for 4 to 5 hours. If using low-heat setting, turn to high-heat setting. Gently stir uncooked orzo into mixture in slow cooker. Cover and cook for 15 minutes more. Stir in spinach. If desired, garnish with reserved fennel leaves.

Top each bowl of this Italian vegetable soup with a sprinkling of slivered basil or spinach.

MINESTRONE

START TO FINISH:
30 minutes

MAKES:
4 servings

2	14-ounce cans chicken broth with Italian herbs
2	medium carrots, thinly sliced
½	cup dried ditalini (tiny thimbles) or tiny bow-tie pasta
1	medium zucchini, chopped (1¼ cups)
1	14½-ounce can diced tomatoes with onions and garlic, undrained
1	15- to 19-ounce can cannellini beans (white kidney beans) or navy beans, rinsed and drained
¼	cup slivered fresh basil or spinach
	Bottled hot pepper sauce (optional)

1 In a large saucepan combine broth and carrots. Bring to boiling; reduce heat. Cover and simmer for 5 minutes.

2 Stir in uncooked pasta. Simmer, uncovered, about 8 minutes or just until pasta is tender. Add zucchini, undrained tomatoes, and beans; heat through. Sprinkle individual servings with basil or spinach. If desired, pass bottled hot pepper sauce.

Per serving: 203 cal., 2 g total fat (0 g sat. fat), 0 mg chol., 1,328 mg sodium, 38 g carbo., 7 g fiber, 14 g pro.

If preparing fresh artichokes is new to you, this Sicilian favorite is a great place to start. Each one is brimming with a savory filling made from croutons, sweet peppers, and two cheeses.

SICILIAN ARTICHOKES

3 cups onion and/or garlic croutons

½ cup finely chopped red or yellow sweet pepper

½ cup shredded mozzarella cheese (2 ounces)

¼ cup finely shredded Parmesan cheese (1 ounce)

4 anchovy fillets, rinsed, patted dry, and finely chopped (optional)

2 tablespoons olive oil

1 tablespoon balsamic vinegar

1 tablespoon snipped fresh oregano or 1 teaspoon dried oregano, crushed

¼ teaspoon salt

¼ teaspoon freshly ground black pepper

¼ to ⅓ cup chicken broth

4 large artichokes (about 10 ounces each)

2 tablespoons lemon juice

PREP:
45 minutes

COOK:
25 minutes

MAKES:
4 servings

1 For filling, coarsely crush any large croutons. In a large bowl combine croutons, sweet pepper, mozzarella cheese, and Parmesan cheese. If desired, add anchovies. In a small bowl combine olive oil, balsamic vinegar, oregano, salt, and pepper; drizzle over crouton mixture. Toss to combine. Add enough of the chicken broth to moisten. Set aside.

2 Wash the artichokes; trim stems and remove loose outer leaves. Cut off 1 inch from top of each artichoke; using kitchen scissors, snip off the sharp leaf tips. Brush the cut edges with a little of the lemon juice. Whack the artichokes, point sides down, on a countertop and the centers will open to expose yellow center leaves and chokes. If necessary, use your fingers to pull the outer leaves away from the center leaves. Use a spoon to scoop out inner yellow leaves and fuzzy centers. Brush insides of artichokes with the remaining lemon juice. Spoon the filling into the artichokes, packing lightly.

3 Place artichokes, filling sides up, in a 4- to 5-quart stainless steel or enamel-coated Dutch oven. Add 1½ cups water to pan. Bring to boiling; reduce heat. Cover and simmer for 25 to 30 minutes or until an artichoke leaf pulls out easily. Carefully remove with tongs. Serve artichokes in shallow bowls.

Per serving: 418 cal., 16 g total fat (4 g sat. fat), 14 mg chol., 1,089 mg sodium, 55 g carbo., 19 g fiber, 24 g pro.

For classic risotto, the rice is cooked slowly, allowing the outside to become soft, while the inside remains firm. In the shortcut version of this recipe, the rice is uniformly tender and the risotto's texture is less creamy.

CLASSIC RISOTTO WITH SPRING PEAS

START TO FINISH:
35 minutes

MAKES:
4 to 6 servings

2	tablespoons olive oil
1	medium onion, chopped
2	cloves garlic, minced
1	cup Arborio rice
2	14-ounce cans vegetable broth or chicken broth (3½ cups)
1	cup loose-pack frozen tiny or regular-size peas
¼	cup coarsely shredded carrot
2	cups fresh spinach, shredded
¼	cup grated Parmesan cheese
1	tablespoon snipped fresh thyme

1 In a large saucepan heat olive oil over medium heat. Add onion and garlic; cook until onion is tender. Add the uncooked rice. Cook and stir about 5 minutes or until rice is golden brown.

2 Meanwhile, in a medium saucepan bring broth to boiling; reduce heat to keep broth simmering. Carefully add 1 cup of the broth to the rice mixture, stirring constantly. Continue to cook and stir over medium heat until liquid is absorbed. Add another 1 cup of the broth to the rice mixture, stirring constantly. Continue to cook and stir until liquid is absorbed. Add another 1 cup broth, ½ cup at a time, stirring constantly until the broth has been absorbed. (This should take 18 to 20 minutes total.)

3 Stir in remaining broth, the peas, and carrot. Cook and stir until rice is slightly firm (al dente) and creamy.

4 Stir in spinach, Parmesan cheese, and thyme; heat through. Serve immediately.

Per serving: 252 cal., 8 g total fat (2 g sat. fat), 4 mg chol., 912 mg sodium, 38 g carbo., 2 g fiber, 7 g pro.

SHORTCUT RISOTTO WITH SPRING PEAS: In a medium saucepan heat olive oil over medium heat. Add onion and garlic; cook until onion is tender. Add uncooked rice. Cook and stir for 2 minutes. Carefully stir in the broth. Bring to boiling; reduce heat. Cover and simmer for 20 minutes (do not lift cover). Remove from heat. Stir in peas and carrot. Cover and let stand for 5 minutes. Rice should be just tender and the mixture should be slightly creamy. (If necessary, stir in a little water to reach desired consistency.) Stir in spinach, Parmesan cheese, and thyme; heat through. Serve immediately.

A distinctive fresh apple-and-dried fig filling gives this rustic Italian dessert an intriguing flavor.

CROSTATA

2	cups all-purpose flour
⅓	cup granulated sugar
1½	teaspoons baking powder
⅓	cup butter
1	egg
⅓	cup milk
1	teaspoon vanilla
4	cups peeled, thinly sliced cooking apples (such as Jonathan)
⅔	cup apricot or peach preserves
½	cup snipped dried Calimyrna (light) figs
	Milk
	Coarse sugar
	Whipped cream (optional)

PREP:
35 minutes

BAKE:
40 minutes

COOL:
45 minutes

OVEN:
375°F

MAKES:
12 servings

1 Preheat oven to 375°F. In a large bowl stir together flour, the ⅓ cup sugar, and the baking powder. Using a pastry blender, cut in butter until mixture resembles coarse crumbs. In a small bowl beat egg with a fork; stir in the ⅓ cup milk and the vanilla. Add egg mixture to flour mixture; mix well. Shape dough into a ball.

2 On a lightly floured surface, gently knead dough for 10 to 12 strokes or until smooth. Remove one-third of the dough; cover and set aside. Pat remaining dough onto the bottom and up the side of a 10- or 11-inch tart pan with removable bottom (use floured hands, if necessary). Line crust with a double thickness of foil. Bake for 8 minutes. Remove foil. Bake for 4 to 5 minutes more or until lightly browned.

3 In another large bowl toss together apple slices, preserves, and figs. Spoon into the crust-lined pan.

4 On a lightly floured surface, roll reserved dough into a 10- to 11-inch circle. Cut into 12 wedges. Twist each wedge twice at the narrow end; arrange on apple mixture with the wide ends toward the edge. Brush dough with milk. Sprinkle with coarse sugar.

5 Bake, uncovered, for 40 to 45 minutes or until fruit is tender. If necessary to prevent overbrowning, cover loosely with foil for the last 5 to 10 minutes of baking. Cool in tart pan on a wire rack for 45 minutes. Remove side of tart pan before serving. Serve warm. If desired, serve with whipped cream.

Per serving: 238 cal., 6 g total fat (3 g sat. fat), 32 mg chol., 82 mg sodium, 44 g carbo., 2 g fiber, 3 g pro.

Layers of custard, fresh raspberries, and pound cake make this stacked dessert irresistible.

ZUPPA INGLESE

PREP:
1 hour

CHILL:
2 hours + 3 to 4 hours

MAKES:
8 servings

⅓ cup sugar

1 tablespoon cornstarch

⅛ teaspoon salt

1 cup milk

2 slightly beaten egg yolks

⅓ cup Marsala, cream sherry, or orange juice

⅓ cup water

¼ cup sugar

2 tablespoons orange liqueur or orange juice

1 cup whipping cream

1 10¾-ounce frozen loaf pound cake, thawed and cut into 15 slices

3 cups fresh raspberries

1 tablespoon sugar

1 For custard, in a medium saucepan stir together the ⅓ cup sugar, the cornstarch, and salt. Stir in milk. Cook and stir until thickened and bubbly. Cook and stir for 2 minutes more. Gradually stir half of the hot mixture into egg yolks; return to remaining hot mixture in saucepan. Cook and stir until bubbly. Cook and stir for 2 minutes more. Remove from heat. Stir in Marsala. Transfer to a medium bowl; cover surface with plastic wrap. Chill about 2 hours (do not stir while chilling) or until completely cooled.

2 Meanwhile, for syrup, in a small saucepan combine the water and the ¼ cup sugar. Cook over medium heat until boiling, stirring to dissolve sugar. Boil for 1 minute. Remove from heat; stir in orange liqueur. Cool.

3 In a chilled small mixing bowl beat ½ cup of the whipping cream with chilled beaters of an electric mixer on medium speed until soft peaks form (tips curl over). Gently fold into cooled custard.

4 In the bottom of a 2-quart soufflé dish or trifle dish arrange five of the cake slices, cutting to fit as necessary. Drizzle with about one-third of the syrup. Spoon about half of the custard over cake; sprinkle with 1½ cups of the raspberries. Repeat layers of cake, syrup, custard, and raspberries. Top with remaining five cake slices and drizzle with remaining syrup. Cover and chill for 3 to 4 hours.

5 To serve, beat together remaining ½ cup whipping cream and the 1 tablespoon sugar until soft peaks form. Spoon on top of cake layer.

Per serving: 390 cal., 21 g total fat (12 g sat. fat), 179 mg chol., 216 mg sodium, 45 g carbo., 2 g fiber, 5 g pro.

Tiramisu, which means "pick me up" in Italian, contains layers of espresso-soaked ladyfingers, mascarpone cheese, and whipped cream.

TIRAMISU

½	cup sugar
½	cup water
2	tablespoons instant espresso coffee powder
1	tablespoon amaretto
1	tablespoon hazelnut liqueur
2	8-ounce cartons mascarpone cheese
¼	cup sugar
1	teaspoon vanilla
1½	cups whipping cream
3	tablespoons sugar
½	cup water
3	tablespoons dried egg whites*
⅓	cup sugar
2	3-ounce packages ladyfingers, split
2	tablespoons unsweetened cocoa powder

1 For syrup, in a small saucepan combine the ½ cup sugar, ½ cup water, and coffee powder. Cook over medium heat until boiling. Boil gently, uncovered, for 1 minute. Remove from heat; stir in amaretto and hazelnut liqueur. Cool.

2 In a medium bowl stir together mascarpone cheese, the ¼ cup sugar, and the vanilla. In a chilled medium bowl combine whipping cream and the 3 tablespoons sugar. Beat with chilled beaters of an electric mixer on medium speed until soft peaks form (tips curl). Fold ½ cup of the whipped cream mixture into the mascarpone mixture to lighten; set both mixtures aside. In another medium bowl combine ½ cup water and dried egg whites; beat according to package directions until stiff peaks form (tips stand straight), adding the ⅓ cup granulated sugar, 1 tablespoon at a time, while beating.

3 To assemble, arrange half of the ladyfinger halves in the bottom of a 9×9×2-inch baking pan. Brush with half of the syrup mixture. Spread with half of the mascarpone mixture, half of the whipped cream, and half of the egg white mixture. Sprinkle with half of the cocoa powder. Arrange the remaining ladyfingers on top of layers in pan. Brush with the remaining syrup mixture. Spread with the remaining mascarpone mixture, whipped cream, and egg white mixture. Sprinkle with the remaining cocoa powder. Cover and chill 4 to 24 hours before serving.

Per serving: 314 cal., 22 g total fat (13 g sat. fat), 106 mg chol., 56 mg sodium, 25 g carbo., 0 g fiber, 8 g pro.

PREP:
45 minutes

CHILL:
4 to 24 hours

MAKES:
16 servings

*TEST KITCHEN TIP.
Look for dried egg whites in the baking section of your supermarket.

The combination of cream cheese and butter makes a decadent frosting for this Italian classic. Chopped toasted pecans between the layers add a likable crunch and great depth of flavor.

ITALIAN CREAM CAKE

PREP:
45 minutes

BAKE:
35 minutes

OVEN:
350°F

MAKES:
16 servings

*TEST KITCHEN TIPS:

• If you prefer, you can use three 9×1½-inch round baking pans instead of the 8-inch pans. Bake cake layers about 25 minutes or until a wooden toothpick inserted near cake centers comes out clean.

• If you don't have three pans of the same size, divide two-thirds of the batter between two pans; bake, cool, and remove cakes from pans. Refrigerate remaining batter while cakes bake. Wash and dry one of the pans; grease and flour the pan. Bake remaining batter in prepared pan according to directions.

2	cups all-purpose flour
1	teaspoon baking soda
½	cup butter, softened
½	cup shortening
2	cups sugar
5	eggs, separated
1	teaspoon vanilla
1	cup buttermilk
1	cup flaked coconut
½	cup finely chopped pecans, toasted
1	recipe Cream Cheese Frosting
¾	cup chopped pecans, toasted

1 Preheat oven to 350°F. Grease and flour three 8×1½-inch round baking pans.* In a small bowl combine the 2 cups flour and baking soda.

2 In a very large bowl combine butter and shortening; beat with an electric mixer on medium to high speed for 30 seconds. Add sugar; beat until combined. Add egg yolks and vanilla; beat on medium speed until combined. Alternately add flour mixture and buttermilk, beating on low speed after each addition just until combined. Fold in coconut and the finely chopped pecans. Wash and dry beaters. In a medium bowl beat egg whites with electric mixer on high speed until stiff peaks form. Fold one-third of the egg whites into cake batter to lighten. Fold in remaining egg whites. Spread batter into prepared pans. Bake about 35 minutes or until a wooden toothpick inserted near cake centers comes out clean. Cool in pans on wire racks 10 minutes. Remove layers from pans; cool on racks.

3 Place a cake layer, bottom side up, on serving plate. Top with ½ cup Cream Cheese Frosting; sprinkle with ¼ cup of the chopped pecans. Top with second cake layer, bottom side down. Spread with another ½ cup of the frosting and sprinkle with another ¼ cup chopped pecans. Top with remaining cake layer, bottom side up; spread top and side with remaining frosting and sprinkle top with remaining pecans. Refrigerate.

CREAM CHEESE FROSTING: In a large bowl combine one 8-ounce package cream cheese, softened; ½ cup butter; and 2 teaspoons vanilla. Beat with an electric mixer on medium speed until smooth. Gradually add 5¾ cups powdered sugar, beating until smooth.

Per serving: 645 cal., 33 g total fat (15 g sat. fat), 111 mg chol., 259 mg sodium, 84 g carbo., 2 g fiber, 6 g pro.

In ancient times, figs—the star ingredient in these Italian cookies—were thought to bring peace and prosperity.

FIG COOKIES

2½   cups all-purpose flour

½   cup sugar

2½   teaspoons baking powder

½   cup butter

2   eggs

¼   cup milk

½   teaspoon vanilla

1   recipe Fig Filling

1   recipe Citrus Frosting

Small multicolored decorative candies

1 For dough, in a large bowl stir together flour, sugar, baking powder, and ¼ teaspoon salt. Cut in butter until mixture resembles coarse cornmeal. Beat eggs with a fork; stir in milk and vanilla. Stir milk mixture into flour mixture. Turn out dough onto a lightly floured surface; knead lightly with hands until a ball forms. Cover; chill for 30 minutes.

2 Preheat oven to 400°F. Grease cookie sheets or line with parchment paper. Divide the chilled dough into thirds. While working with one portion, refrigerate remaining dough. (Dough will be soft and a bit sticky.) On a well-floured work surface, roll dough to about ¹⁄₁₆-inch thickness. Cut dough with a 2¼- to 2½-inch round cookie cutter. Place about 1 teaspoon of the Fig Filling in the center of half of the dough rounds. Cover with remaining dough rounds. Press edges of dough around the filling; press with a fork to seal, dipping fork frequently in flour to prevent sticking. Place cookies on prepared cookie sheets.

3 Bake about 10 minutes or until cookies are light brown on edges. Transfer to wire rack; cool. Ice with Citrus Frosting; sprinkle with candies.

FIG FILLING: In a food processor process 2 ounces hazelnuts, toasted,* until finely chopped. Add 4 ounces dried figs, halved and stems removed; ¼ cup raisins; and 2 teaspoons shredded finely orange peel. Cover and process until fruit is coarsely chopped. In a small bowl whisk together ¼ cup honey, 2 tablespoons brandy, and ¼ teaspoon ground cinnamon until smooth. With food processor running, add honey mixture to fig mixture in a steady stream, processing until mixture is combined.

CITRUS FROSTING: In a bowl combine 1½ cups powdered sugar and 4 to 6 teaspoons lemon or orange juice until of drizzling consistency.

Per serving: 95 cal., 3 g total fat (1 g sat. fat), 15 mg chol., 45 mg sodium, 15 g carbo., 1 g fiber, 1 g pro.

PREP:
2 hours

BAKE:
10 minutes per batch

CHILL:
30 minutes

OVEN:
400°F

MAKES:
about 45 cookies

*TEST KITCHEN TIP:
To toast hazelnuts, preheat oven to 350°F. Spread nuts in a single layer in a shallow baking pan. Bake for 10 to 15 minutes or until light golden brown, watching carefully and stirring once or twice so the nuts don't burn. Cool slightly. Place the nuts on a clean kitchen towel, fold towel over top, and rub vigorously to remove skins.

Anici means anise in Italian. It gives these twice-baked cookies a sweet licorice flavor. Dip them in espresso for an authentic Italian flavor experience.

BISCOTTI D'ANICI

PREP:
30 minutes

BAKE:
20 minutes + 10 minutes + 10 minutes

COOL:
1 hour

OVEN:
375°F/325°F

MAKES:
about 40 cookies

½   cup butter, softened
1   cup sugar
1   tablespoon anise seeds, crushed
2½   teaspoons baking powder
3   eggs
3¼   cups all-purpose flour
1   tablespoon finely shredded lemon peel or orange peel

1 Preheat oven to 375°F. Lightly grease a cookie sheet; set aside.

2 In a large bowl beat butter with an electric mixer on medium speed for 30 seconds. Add sugar, anise seeds, and baking powder. Beat until combined, scraping side of bowl occasionally. Beat in eggs until combined. Beat in as much of the flour as you can with the mixer. Using a wooden spoon, stir in any remaining flour and the lemon peel.

3 Divide dough in half. Shape each half into an 11-inch-long roll. Place rolls 5 inches apart on prepared cookie sheet; flatten each one to a width of 2 inches.

4 Bake for 20 to 25 minutes or until lightly browned. Cool rolls on cookie sheet for 1 hour. Reduce oven temperature to 325°F. Transfer baked rolls to a cutting board. Using a serrated knife, cut each roll diagonally into ½-inch-thick slices. Place slices, cut sides down, on an ungreased cookie sheet.

5 Bake in the 325°F oven for 10 minutes. Turn slices over and bake for 10 to 15 minutes more or until dry and crisp (do not overbake). Transfer cookies to a wire rack and let cool.

TO BAKE AHEAD: Prepare as directed. Place cooled cookies in layers separated by waxed paper in an airtight container; cover. Store at room temperature for up to 3 days. (Or place cooled cookies in layers in a freezer container; cover. Freeze for up to 3 months.)

Per cookie: 79 cal., 3 g total fat (2 g sat. fat), 22 mg chol., 37 mg sodium, 12 g carbo., 0 g fiber, 1 g pro.

25-MINUTE MAIN DISHES

9

Balsamic vinegar, pine nuts, and fettuccine give this easy-fixing dish an Italian flair.

QUICK ITALIAN PEPPER STEAK

START TO FINISH:
25 minutes

MAKES:
4 or 5 servings

1   9-ounce package refrigerated fettuccine

12   ounces boneless beef top sirloin steak,
cut into thin bite-size strips

¼   teaspoon crushed red pepper

2   tablespoons olive oil

1   16-ounce package frozen (yellow, green, and red)
pepper and onion stir-fry vegetables, thawed
and well drained

2   tablespoons balsamic vinegar

1   14½-ounce can diced tomatoes with garlic, basil,
and oregano

2   tablespoons pine nuts, toasted (optional)

Crushed red pepper (optional)

1 Prepare pasta according to package directions. Drain well. Return to hot saucepan; cover and keep warm.

2 Meanwhile, in a medium bowl combine beef and the ¼ teaspoon crushed red pepper; set aside.

3 In a large skillet heat 1 tablespoon of the olive oil over medium heat; add thawed stir-fry vegetables. Stir-fry for 2 to 3 minutes or until crisp-tender. Carefully add balsamic vinegar; toss to coat. Remove from skillet. Cover and keep warm.

4 Heat remaining 1 tablespoon olive oil in the same skillet; add beef. Cook and stir for 2 to 3 minutes or until desired doneness. Add tomatoes; heat through.

5 Toss beef mixture with pasta and vegetables. Sprinkle with pine nuts. If desired, pass additional crushed red pepper.

Per serving: 433 cal., 12 g total fat (3 g sat. fat), 119 mg chol., 595 mg sodium, 52 g carbo., 3 g fiber, 29 g pro.

Dried Italian seasoning, garlic, and herb-seasoned diced tomatoes give this zesty pasta dish a rich, full flavor.

BEEF & VEGETABLES WITH FETTUCCINE

1	9-ounce package refrigerated fettuccine or linguine
12	ounces boneless beef sirloin steak
1	teaspoon dried Italian seasoning, crushed
1	tablespoon olive oil
1	medium onion, cut into thin wedges
2	teaspoons bottled minced garlic (4 cloves)
¼	teaspoon crushed red pepper
1	14½-ounce can diced tomatoes with basil, garlic, and oregano, undrained
1	cup purchased roasted red sweet peppers, drained and coarsely chopped
1	tablespoon balsamic vinegar
2	cups fresh baby spinach leaves
¼	cup finely shredded Parmesan cheese (1 ounce)

START TO FINISH:
25 minutes

MAKES:
4 servings

1 Cook pasta according to package directions. Drain well. Return pasta to hot pan. Using kitchen shears; snip pasta in a few places to break up the long pieces. Cover and keep warm. Meanwhile, trim fat from beef. Sprinkle beef with Italian seasoning; rub in with your fingers. Thinly slice meat across the grain.

2 In a large skillet heat olive oil over medium-high heat; add beef. Cook and stir for 3 to 4 minutes until desired doneness; remove from skillet using a slotted spoon. Add onion, garlic, and crushed red pepper to skillet. Cook about 5 minutes or until onion is tender, stirring occasionally.

3 Stir beef, undrained tomatoes, roasted red peppers, and balsamic vinegar into skillet. Heat through. Add beef mixture and spinach to hot pasta; toss to mix. Sprinkle with Parmesan cheese.

Per serving: 413 cal., 10 g total fat (3 g sat. fat), 123 mg chol., 687 mg sodium, 50 g carbo., 3 g fiber, 30 g pro.

Talk about a time-efficient recipe. While the pasta is cooking, you prepare the simple, no-fuss sauce. No baking required!

SKILLET LASAGNA

START TO FINISH:
25 minutes

MAKES:
6 servings

3 cups dried mafalda (mini lasagna) noodles (6 ounces)

12 ounces lean ground beef or bulk pork sausage

1 26- to 27¾-ounce jar tomato-base pasta sauce

1½ cups shredded mozzarella cheese (6 ounces)

¼ cup grated Parmesan cheese

1 Cook pasta according to package directions. Drain well.

2 Meanwhile, in a 10-inch nonstick skillet cook meat until brown. Drain off fat. Set meat aside. Wipe out skillet with paper towels.

3 Spread about half of the cooked pasta in the skillet. Cover with about half of the pasta sauce. Spoon cooked meat over sauce. Sprinkle with 1 cup of the mozzarella cheese. Top with remaining pasta and sauce. Sprinkle with remaining ½ cup mozzarella and the Parmesan cheese.

4 Cover and cook over medium heat for 5 to 7 minutes or until heated through and cheese melts. Remove skillet from heat. Let stand, covered, for 1 minute.

Per serving: 375 cal., 17 g total fat (6 g sat. fat), 50 mg chol., 1,046 mg sodium, 30 g carbo., 2 g fiber, 25 g pro.

In this recipe, two American favorites—pizza and hamburgers—come together in complete harmony.

PIZZA BURGERS

4   3¾-ounce purchased uncooked hamburger patties

4   ¾-inch-thick slices sourdough bread

1   cup purchased mushroom pasta sauce

1   cup shredded provolone or mozzarella cheese (4 ounces)

2   tablespoons thinly sliced fresh basil

1 Preheat broiler. Place hamburger patties on the unheated rack of a broiler pan. Broil 3 to 4 inches from heat for 10 to 12 minutes or until an instant-read thermometer inserted through side of patty into center registers 160°F; turn patties once during broiling. Add the bread slices to broiler pan for the last 2 to 3 minutes of broiling; turn once to toast evenly.

2 Meanwhile, in a medium saucepan heat pasta sauce over medium heat until heated through, stirring occasionally. Place one hamburger patty on each bread slice. Spoon pasta sauce over patties; sprinkle with cheese. Place on broiler rack. Return to broiler and broil 1 to 2 minutes more or until cheese is melted. Top with basil.

Per serving: 504 cal., 30 g total fat (13 g sat. fat), 96 mg chol., 815 mg sodium, 27 g carbo., 2 g fiber, 30 g pro.

START TO FINISH:
25 minutes

MAKES:
4 servings

Store-bought roasted red peppers, frozen tortellini, and Alfredo sauce are the secrets to this quick meal. Fresh basil gives it a fragrant, zesty finish.

TORTELLINI ALFREDO WITH ROASTED PEPPERS

START TO FINISH:
15 minutes

MAKES:
4 servings

1   16-ounce package frozen meat- or cheese-filled tortellini (4 cups)

1   cup bottled roasted red sweet peppers

1   10-ounce container refrigerated light Alfredo pasta sauce

¼   cup snipped fresh basil

Coarsely ground black pepper

❶ Cook tortellini according to package directions; drain well. Return tortellini to hot pan. Meanwhile, drain roasted peppers and cut into ½-inch-wide strips.

❷ Add Alfredo sauce and roasted peppers to pan with tortellini. Cook over medium heat until hot and bubbly. Stir in snipped basil. Season to taste with coarsely ground black pepper.

Per serving: 495 cal., 15 g total fat (6 g sat. fat), 98 mg chol., 1,150 mg sodium, 65 g carbo., 1 g fiber, 24 g pro.

The ravioli soak up the chicken broth and juice from the cherry tomatoes as they cook, giving this one-pan dish maximum flavor with minimum cleanup.

SAUCY ONE-PAN RAVIOLI

2	cups cherry tomatoes
½	teaspoon bottled minced garlic (1 clove)
¾	cup chicken broth
¼	teaspoon salt
¼	teaspoon black pepper
1	9-ounce package refrigerated ravioli
2	tablespoons snipped fresh basil
1	tablespoon snipped fresh flat-leaf parsley
¼	cup shredded Romano or Parmesan cheese (1 ounce)

1 In a blender or food processor combine cherry tomatoes and garlic. Cover and blend or process until smooth. Transfer to a large saucepan. Add chicken broth, salt, and pepper. Bring to boiling.

2 Add ravioli. Return to boiling; reduce heat. Cover and simmer for 6 to 8 minutes or just until pasta is tender, stirring gently once or twice. Stir in basil and parsley. Spoon onto plates; sprinkle with cheese.

Per serving: 502 cal., 21 g total fat (11 g sat. fat), 123 mg chol., 1,346 mg sodium, 56 g carbo., 3 g fiber, 25 g pro.

START TO FINISH:
15 minutes

MAKES:
2 servings

Pork chops have never tasted so juicy and delicious! The wine-accented vegetable mixture complements the meat.

BROILED PORK CHOPS WITH ITALIAN VEGETABLES

START TO FINISH:
20 minutes

MAKES:
4 servings

4   pork loin chops (bone-in), cut ½ inch thick (about 1½ pounds total)

     Salt

     Black pepper

     Nonstick cooking spray

1   16-ounce package frozen (yellow, green, and red) peppers and onion stir-fry vegetables

1½   cups bite-size strips zucchini and/or yellow summer squash

1   teaspoon dried Italian seasoning, crushed

½   teaspoon bottled minced garlic (1 clove)

¼   teaspoon salt

2   tablespoons dry white wine

1 Sprinkle pork chops with salt and pepper. Place chops on the unheated rack of a broiler pan. Broil 3 to 4 inches from the heat for 8 to 10 minutes or until chops are slightly pink in center and juices run clear (160°F).

2 Meanwhile, coat an unheated large skillet with nonstick cooking spray. Preheat skillet over medium-high heat. Add frozen stir-fry vegetables, zucchini, Italian seasoning, garlic, and the ¼ teaspoon salt. Cook and stir for 3 to 4 minutes or just until vegetables are tender. Add wine; cook and stir for 1 minute more. Serve chops with vegetable mixture.

Per serving: 187 cal., 5 g total fat (2 g sat. fat), 53 mg chol., 341 mg sodium, 9 g carbo., 2 g fiber, 23 g pro.

Italian sausage links, packed full of robust flavors, are a great convenience product. Because the meat's seasonings are so flavorful not much extra is needed.

SAUSAGE WITH BOW TIES & SWEET PEPPERS

8	ounces dried large bow tie pasta
12	ounces spicy Italian sausage links
2	medium red sweet peppers, cut into ¾-inch pieces
½	cup vegetable broth or beef broth
¼	teaspoon coarsely ground black pepper
¼	cup snipped fresh flat-leaf parsley

1 Cook pasta according to package directions. Drain well. Return pasta to hot pan; cover to keep warm.

2 Meanwhile, cut the sausage into 1-inch-thick pieces. In a large skillet cook sausage and sweet peppers over medium-high heat until sausage is browned. Drain off fat.

3 Stir broth and black pepper into mixture in skillet. Bring to boiling; reduce heat. Simmer, uncovered, for 5 minutes. Remove from heat. Pour over pasta; add parsley. Toss gently to coat. Transfer to a warm serving dish.

Per serving: 476 cal., 18 g total fat (6 g sat. fat), 94 mg chol., 713 mg sodium, 38 g carbo., 3 g fiber, 24 g pro.

START TO FINISH:
25 minutes

MAKES:
4 servings

Layers of flavor compose this unforgettable dish. A slice of baked polenta on a bed of mixed greens is crowned by sweet Italian sausages cooked in balsamic vinegar.

SAUSAGE & POLENTA WITH BALSAMIC VINAIGRETTE

START TO FINISH:
25 minutes

OVEN
400°F

MAKES:
4 servings

3　sweet Italian sausage links, each cut into four pieces (about 12 ounces)

½　of a 16-ounce tube refrigerated polenta (plain or flavored)

1　tablespoon olive oil

6　cups purchased Mediterranean- or Italian-blend torn mixed greens

½　cup apple juice or apple cider

¼　cup balsamic vinegar

2　tablespoons snipped dried tomato

¼　cup pine nuts or slivered almonds, toasted (optional)

1 Preheat oven to 400°F.

2 In a 10-inch skillet cook sausage pieces over medium heat for 5 minutes, turning to brown evenly. Meanwhile, cut polenta into ¼-inch-thick slices; cut each slice crosswise in half. Brush top of each polenta slice with olive oil. Arrange in a single layer on a baking sheet. Bake for 10 to 12 minutes or until golden brown, turning once.

3 Divide greens among four plates; set aside.

4 Remove sausage from skillet. Drain off fat. Wipe out skillet with paper towels. Return sausage pieces to skillet; add apple juice, balsamic vinegar, and dried tomato. Bring to boiling; reduce heat. Cover and simmer for 8 to 10 minutes or until sausage pieces are cooked through.

5 Arrange polenta slices on greens on plates. Add sausage pieces to plates; drizzle with balsamic mixture. If desired, sprinkle with nuts.

Per serving: 380 cal., 22 g total fat (8 g sat. fat), 57 mg chol., 741 mg sodium, 23 g carbo., 4 g fiber, 15 g pro.

Wedges of fennel give the sauce a sweet, licoricelike flavor, while Italian sausage links add a kick.

SAUSAGE & TOMATO SAUCED PASTA

8	ounces dried penne, fettuccine, linguine, or rotelle pasta
1	pound sweet or hot Italian sausage links, cut into 1-inch pieces
1½	cups water
2	medium fennel bulbs, cut into thin wedges (about 2 cups)
1	26-ounce jar tomato-based pasta sauce
⅓	cup water

START TO FINISH:
25 minutes

MAKES:
4 servings

1 Cook pasta according to package directions. Drain well. Return to hot saucepan; cover and keep warm.

2 Meanwhile, in a large skillet combine sausage and the 1½ cups water. Heat to boiling. Cook, uncovered, over high heat for 10 minutes; drain. Return sausage to skillet. Add fennel to sausage in skillet; cook for 3 to 4 minutes or until sausage is brown and fennel is crisp-tender. Add pasta sauce and the ⅓ cup water.* Bring to boiling; reduce heat. Cover and simmer for 5 minutes. Serve with pasta.

Per serving: 714 cal., 38 g total fat (13 g sat. fat), 86 mg chol., 1,474 mg sodium, 65 g carbo., 8 g fiber, 28 g pro.

*NOTE: Swirl the ⅓ cup water in the empty pasta sauce jar before adding it to the skillet to get every bit of sauce out of the jar.

Polenta, an Italian cornmeal mush, is surprisingly quick and easy to make. It provides a velvety contrast to Italian sausage links.

SAUSAGES WITH POLENTA

START TO FINISH:
25 minutes

MAKES:
6 servings

1   14-ounce can chicken broth

1   cup yellow cornmeal

2½   cups milk

¼   teaspoon freshly ground black pepper

⅓   cup finely shredded Parmesan cheese

4   sweet or hot Italian sausage links (about 1 pound)

½   cup water

1 For the polenta, in a large saucepan whisk together chicken broth and cornmeal. Whisk in milk and pepper. Cook and stir over medium heat until mixture boils and thickens. Reduce heat to low. Cook, stirring frequently, about 10 minutes or until very thick. Stir in Parmesan cheese.

2 Meanwhile, in a large skillet cook sausage links over medium-high heat until browned, turning to brown evenly. Carefully add the water to the skillet. Reduce heat to medium-low. Cover and cook for 5 minutes. Uncover; cook about 5 minutes more or until liquid evaporates and sausages are done (160°F),* turning to brown sausages evenly.

3 Slice each sausage into thirds. Serve sausage with polenta.

Per serving: 377 cal., 21 g total fat (9 g sat. fat), 63 mg chol., 935 mg sodium, 24 g carbo., 2 g fiber, 18 g pro.

*NOTE: The internal color of a sausage is not a reliable doneness indicator. A sausage cooked to 160°F is safe, regardless of color. To measure the doneness of a sausage, insert an instant-read thermometer from an end into the center of sausage.

Italian sausage, often flavored with fennel seeds and crushed red pepper, adds an unmatched punch to this dynamite meal.

PASTA WITH SPINACH & SAUSAGE

4	ounces sweet or hot Italian sausage links (remove casings, if present)
1	large leek, cut into ¼-inch-thick slices
1	teaspoon bottled minced garlic (2 cloves)
1	teaspoon olive oil
⅔	cup chicken broth
½	cup roasted red sweet peppers, drained and cut into thin, bite-size strips
8	cups torn fresh spinach
6	ounces dried bow-tie pasta
¼	cup finely shredded Parmesan cheese (1 ounce)
1	tablespoon dried basil, crushed

25 minutes

MAKES:
4 servings

1 Cut sausage lengthwise into quarters. In a skillet cook sausage over medium-high heat until cooked through. Drain off fat. Slice sausage into ¼-inch pieces.

2 In a large skillet cook leek and garlic in hot olive oil until leek is tender. Stir in sausage, chicken broth, and roasted red peppers. Bring to boiling; reduce heat. Add spinach. Cook, stirring frequently, for 1 to 2 minutes or just until spinach starts to wilt. Remove from heat.

3 Meanwhile, cook pasta according to package directions, except omit any oil or salt; drain. Return pasta to hot saucepan. Add spinach mixture, Parmesan cheese, and basil. Toss to coat. Serve immediately.

Per serving: 303 cal., 10 g total fat (4 g sat. fat), 23 mg chol., 505 mg sodium, 38 g carbo., 3 g fiber, 14 g pro.

In recent years, Americans have really taken to Tuscan-style cooking. Its stylish simplicity and quick-cooking techniques mesh well with a fast-paced lifestyle.

TUSCAN LAMB CHOP SKILLET

START TO FINISH:
25 minutes

MAKES:
4 servings

8	lamb rib chops, cut 1-inch thick (about 1½ pounds)
	Salt
	Black pepper
1	tablespoon olive oil
1½	teaspoons bottled minced garlic
1	15- to 19-ounce can cannellini beans (white kidney beans), rinsed and drained
1	14½-ounce can Italian-style stewed tomatoes, undrained
2	tablespoons balsamic vinegar
2	teaspoons dried rosemary, crushed
	Fresh rosemary sprigs (optional)

1 Trim fat from chops. Season chops with salt and pepper. In a very large skillet heat olive oil over medium heat. Add chops; cook about 8 minutes or until medium doneness (160°F), turning once. Transfer chops to a serving plate; keep warm.

2 Stir garlic into drippings in skillet. Cook and stir for 1 minute. Stir in beans, undrained tomatoes, balsamic vinegar, and dried rosemary. Bring to boiling; reduce heat. Simmer, uncovered, for 5 minutes.

3 Serve sauce over chops. If desired, garnish with rosemary sprigs.

Per serving: 266 cal., 11 g total fat (3 g sat. fat), 48 mg chol., 576 mg sodium, 24 g carbo., 6 g fiber, 22 g pro.

A savory blend of Parmesan cheese, rosemary, and bread crumbs creates a crispy golden coating for these chicken cutlets.

PARMESAN-CRUSTED CHICKEN CUTLETS

4   skinless, boneless chicken breast halves
     (about 1¼ pounds total)
¼   teaspoon salt
¼   teaspoon freshly ground black pepper
¾   cup fine dry bread crumbs
2   tablespoons freshly grated Parmesan cheese
1   tablespoon snipped fresh flat-leaf parsley
1   teaspoon snipped fresh rosemary
1   egg
1   egg white
2   tablespoons olive oil

PREP:
15 minutes

COOK:
10 minutes

MAKES:
4 servings

1 Place each chicken piece between two pieces of plastic wrap. Using the flat side of a meat mallet, pound lightly until ½ inch thick. Remove plastic wrap. Sprinkle chicken with salt and black pepper.

2 In a shallow dish combine bread crumbs, Parmesan cheese, parsley, and rosemary. In another shallow dish combine whole egg and egg white; beat with a fork. Dip chicken in beaten egg, then in crumb mixture to coat.

3 In a large skillet heat olive oil over medium-high heat. Add chicken and cook for 10 to 12 minutes or until chicken is no longer pink, turning once.

Per serving: 312 cal., 12 g total fat (3 g sat. fat), 137 mg chol., 698 mg sodium, 11 g carbo., 1 g fiber, 38 g pro.

Capers and minced garlic freshen up the flavor of bottled Italian salad dressing.
Next time, drizzle this tangy vinaigrette over grilled or broiled fish.

CHICKEN BREASTS WITH CAPER VINAIGRETTE

PREP:
10 minutes

GRILL:
12 minutes

MAKES:
4 servings

¼ cup oil-packed dried tomato strips

4 skinless, boneless chicken breast halves (about 1¼ pounds total)

¼ cup bottled Italian salad dressing

2 tablespoons capers, drained

½ teaspoon bottled minced garlic (1 clove)

¼ teaspoon black pepper

1 Drain tomato strips, reserving oil. Set tomato strips aside. Brush chicken with some of the reserved oil.

2 Place chicken on the rack of uncovered grill directly over medium coals. Grill for 12 to 15 minutes or until chicken is no longer pink (170°F), turning once and brushing with remaining reserved oil halfway through grilling.

3 Meanwhile, for vinaigrette, in a small bowl whisk together salad dressing, capers, garlic, and pepper.

4 Diagonally slice each chicken breast. Spoon vinaigrette over chicken. Top with tomato strips.

Per serving: 218 cal., 4 g total fat (1 g sat. fat), 99 mg chol., 447 mg sodium, 3 g carbo., 1 g fiber, 40 g pro.

This meal is quick, easy, healthful, and satisfying—perfect for the end of a busy work day.

BASIL & SPINACH CHICKEN SKILLET

2	tablespoons olive oil
1½	pounds skinless, boneless chicken breast halves, cut into thin bite-size strips
¼	teaspoon salt
⅛	teaspoon black pepper
1	14½-ounce can diced tomatoes with basil, garlic, and oregano, drained
2	tablespoons snipped fresh basil
1	10-ounce package prewashed spinach
1	cup shredded mozzarella cheese (4 ounces)

1 In a 12-inch skillet heat olive oil over medium-high heat. Add half of the chicken; cook until tender and no longer pink. Remove chicken. Cook remaining chicken in same skillet; drain off fat. Return all of the chicken to skillet. Sprinkle chicken with salt and pepper.

2 Add drained tomatoes and basil to skillet. Bring to boiling. Add spinach to skillet, half at a time, tossing with tongs just until wilted. Remove from heat. Sprinkle with cheese. Let stand for 3 to 5 minutes or until cheese melts.

Per serving: 380 cal., 14 g total fat (4 g sat. fat), 116 mg chol., 998 mg sodium, 12 g carbo., 2 g fiber, 50 g pro.

START TO FINISH:
25 minutes

MAKES:
4 to 6 servings

Refrigerated pasta helps make this delicious main dish speedy to prepare.

CHICKEN FETTUCCINE

START TO FINISH:
25 minutes

MAKES:
4 servings

1   9-ounce package refrigerated fettuccine or linguine

½   cup oil-packed dried tomato strips or pieces

1   large zucchini or yellow summer squash, halved lengthwise and sliced (about 2 cups)

8   ounces skinless, boneless chicken breast halves, cut into bite-size strips

½   cup finely shredded Parmesan, Romano, or Asiago cheese (2 ounces)

Freshly ground black pepper

Finely shredded Parmesan, Romano, or Asiago cheese (optional)

1 Use kitchen scissors to cut pasta in half. Cook in lightly salted boiling water according to package directions. Drain well. Return pasta to hot pan; cover and keep warm.

2 Meanwhile, drain tomato strips, reserving 2 tablespoons of the oil; set aside. In a large skillet heat 1 tablespoon of the reserved oil over medium-high heat. Add zucchini; cook and stir for 3 to 4 minutes or until crisp-tender. Remove from skillet. Turn heat to medium. Add remaining 1 tablespoon reserved oil to skillet. Add chicken; cook and stir for 2 to 3 minutes or until no longer pink. Add zucchini, chicken, tomato strips, and the ½ cup cheese to cooked pasta; toss gently to combine. Season to taste with black pepper. If desired, sprinkle individual servings with additional cheese.

Per serving: 325 cal., 8 g total fat (3 g sat. fat), 108 mg chol., 265 mg sodium, 39 g carbo., 3 g fiber, 26 g pro.

Balsamic means "like balsam," which is a thick and aromatic resin. The name refers to balsamic vinegar's syrupy body, intense aroma, and slight sweetness. It adds a distinctive flavor to any dish.

BALSAMIC CHICKEN & VEGETABLES

¼ cup bottled Italian salad dressing

2 tablespoons balsamic vinegar

1 tablespoon honey

⅛ to ¼ teaspoon crushed red pepper

2 tablespoons olive oil

12 ounces chicken breast tenderloins

1 10-ounce package frozen cut asparagus, thawed and well drained

1 cup purchased shredded carrot

1 small tomato, seeded and chopped

1 In a small bowl stir together salad dressing, balsamic vinegar, honey, and crushed red pepper. Set aside.

2 In a large skillet heat olive oil over medium-high heat. Add chicken; cook for 5 to 6 minutes or until chicken is tender and no longer pink, turning once. Transfer from skillet to a serving platter; cover and keep warm.

3 Add asparagus and carrot to skillet. Cook and stir for 3 to 4 minutes or until asparagus is crisp-tender; transfer to serving platter.

4 Stir dressing mixture; add to skillet. Cook and stir for 1 minute, scraping up browned bits. Drizzle over chicken and vegetables. Sprinkle with tomato.

Per serving: 271 cal., 15 g total fat (2 g sat. fat), 49 mg chol., 174 mg sodium, 12 g carbo., 2 g fiber, 22 g pro.

START TO FINISH:
25 minutes

MAKES:
4 servings

This easy-to-prepare meal is chock-full of healthful ingredients such as broccoli and sweet peppers. Parmesan cheese provides a great finishing touch.

PESTO PENNE WITH CHICKEN

START TO FINISH:
20 minutes

MAKES:
4 servings

8 ounces dried penne, mostaccioli, or bow-tie pasta (4 cups)

2 cups broccoli florets

1 7-ounce container basil pesto (about ¾ cup)

2½ cups purchased refrigerated cooked chicken strips or bite-size slices deli-roasted or leftover cooked chicken (about 12 ounces)

1 7-ounce jar roasted red sweet peppers, drained and cut into strips

¼ cup finely shredded Parmesan cheese (1 ounce)

Finely shredded Parmesan cheese (optional)

½ teaspoon black pepper

1 Cook pasta according to package directions, adding broccoli for the last 2 minutes of cooking. Drain, reserving ½ cup of the pasta cooking water. Return drained pasta and broccoli to saucepan.

2 In a small bowl combine pesto and the reserved pasta cooking water. Add chicken, roasted red peppers, and pesto mixture to pasta in saucepan. Toss gently to coat. Heat through over medium heat.

3 Add the ¼ cup Parmesan cheese to pasta mixture; toss to combine. Divide pasta among four warmed pasta bowls. If desired, sprinkle with additional Parmesan cheese. Sprinkle with black pepper. Serve immediately.

Per serving: 672 cal., 35 g total fat (7 g sat. fat), 93 mg chol., 857 mg sodium, 53 g carbo., 3 g fiber, 37 g pro.

Smoked turkey sausage melds with tangy stewed tomatoes for a satisfying smoky-sweet flavor. Beans and pasta make this dish extra hearty.

WHITE BEAN & SAUSAGE RIGATONI

8   ounces dried rigatoni pasta or medium shell pasta

1   15- to 19-ounce can cannellini beans
     (white kidney beans), Great Northern beans,
     or navy beans, rinsed and drained

1   14½-ounce can Italian-style stewed tomatoes,
     undrained, cut up

6   ounces cooked smoked turkey sausage, halved
     lengthwise and cut into ½-inch-thick slices

⅓   cup snipped fresh basil

1   ounce Asiago cheese, shaved or finely shredded
     (optional)

1 Cook pasta according to package directions, except omit any salt. Drain. Return pasta to hot saucepan; cover and keep warm.

2 Meanwhile, in a large saucepan combine drained beans, undrained tomatoes, and sausage; heat through. Add pasta and basil; toss gently to combine. If desired, sprinkle with cheese.

Per serving: 378 cal., 6 g total fat (1 g sat. fat), 29 mg chol., 760 mg sodium, 65 g carbo., 7 g fiber, 21 g pro.

START TO FINISH:
20 minutes

MAKES:
4 servings

Squash, red sweet pepper, and red onion add fresh accents to store-bought pasta sauce. Turkey Italian sausage adds delicious flavor.

SPICY TURKEY PASTA SAUCE

START TO FINISH:
25 minutes

MAKES:
4 servings

1   9-ounce package refrigerated fettuccine or linguine

8   ounces uncooked turkey Italian sausage
    (remove casings, if present)

1   cup cut-up pattypan squash or yellow summer squash

1   small red sweet pepper, cut into thin strips

¼   cup chopped red onion

1   14-ounce jar tomato-base pasta sauce

2   tablespoons shredded Parmesan cheese (optional)

❶ Cook pasta according to package directions. Drain. Return pasta to hot saucepan; cover and keep warm.

❷ Meanwhile, in a large skillet cook sausage, squash, sweet pepper, and onion over medium heat until sausage is brown; drain off fat. Stir pasta sauce into sausage mixture in skillet; heat through.

❸ Serve sausage mixture over pasta. If desired, sprinkle with Parmesan cheese.

Per serving: 350 cal., 10 g total fat (3 g sat. fat), 115 mg chol., 866 mg sodium, 49 g carbo., 5 g fiber, 20 g pro.

A handful of ingredients makes this time-efficient meal a breeze. Toasted pine nuts or almonds add a special touch.

POLENTA WITH TURKEY SAUSAGE FLORENTINE

1	9- or 10-ounce package frozen creamed spinach
8	ounces uncooked bulk turkey sausage
½	of a 16-ounce tube refrigerated cooked polenta with wild mushrooms, cut into ¾-inch-thick slices
1	tablespoon olive oil
2	tablespoons sliced almonds or pine nuts, toasted

1 Cook the spinach according to package directions. Meanwhile, in a medium skillet cook sausage until brown. Drain in a colander. In the same skillet cook polenta slices in hot olive oil about 6 minutes or until golden brown, turning once. Transfer polenta to serving plates.

2 Stir cooked sausage into hot creamed spinach; heat through and spoon on top of the polenta. Sprinkle with nuts.

Per serving: 607 cal., 41 g total fat (8 g sat. fat), 119 mg chol., 1,586 mg sodium, 33 g carbo., 6 g fiber, 28 g pro.

START TO FINISH:
25 minutes

MAKES:
2 servings

Light, delicately flavored fish fillets produce optimal results in this recipe. Try using orange roughy, cod, or haddock.

PIZZA-SAUCED FISH WITH SPINACH FETTUCCINE

START TO FINISH:
25 minutes

OVEN:
450°F

MAKES:
6 servings

1½ pounds fresh or frozen white fish fillets, ½ to ¾ inch thick

½ teaspoon lemon-pepper seasoning

Nonstick cooking spray

12 ounces dried spinach fettuccine

1 8-ounce package sliced fresh mushrooms

1 medium green sweet pepper, chopped

1 medium onion, chopped

2 teaspoons cooking oil

1 8-ounce can pizza sauce

½ cup shredded mozzarella cheese (2 ounces)

1 Thaw fish, if frozen. Rinse fish; pat dry with paper towels. Preheat oven to 450°F.

2 Cut the fish into six serving-size pieces. Sprinkle fish with lemon-pepper seasoning. Coat a 2-quart rectangular baking dish with nonstick cooking spray. Place fish in the prepared baking dish, tucking under any thin edges.

3 Bake until fish flakes easily when tested with a fork (allow 6 to 9 minutes per ½-inch thickness of fish). Drain off any liquid.

4 Meanwhile, cook fettuccine according to package directions. For sauce, in a medium saucepan cook mushrooms, sweet pepper, and onion in hot oil about 5 minutes or until tender, stirring occasionally. Add pizza sauce; heat through.

5 Serve fish on hot cooked fettuccine; spoon sauce over fish. Sprinkle with cheese.

Per serving: 388 cal., 7 g total fat (2 g sat. fat), 56 mg chol., 398 mg sodium, 48 g carbo., 3 g fiber, 32 g pro.

No need for lemon on this fish dish. Stewed tomatoes provide all the tangy kick you'll need.

ITALIAN-STYLE FISH

1½	pounds fresh or frozen white-fleshed fish fillets, ½ to 1 inch thick
¼	teaspoon salt
⅛	teaspoon black pepper
2	cups packaged sliced fresh mushrooms
1	tablespoon cooking oil
1	14½-ounce can Italian-style stewed tomatoes, undrained
1	10¾-ounce can condensed tomato bisque soup
⅛	teaspoon black pepper
⅓	cup finely shredded Parmesan cheese
	Hot cooked pasta

START TO FINISH:
20 minutes

MAKES:
6 servings

1 Thaw fish, if frozen. Rinse fish; pat dry with paper towels. If necessary, cut fish into six serving-size pieces. Measure thickness of fish. Place fish on the greased unheated rack of a broiler pan. Turn any thin portions under to make uniform thickness. Sprinkle with salt and ⅛ teaspoon pepper.

2 Broil about 4 inches from the heat until fish flakes easily when tested with a fork. (Allow 4 to 6 minutes per ½-inch thickness of fish. If fillets are 1 inch thick, turn once halfway through broiling.)

3 Meanwhile, for sauce, in a medium saucepan cook mushrooms in hot oil until tender. Stir in undrained tomatoes, tomato bisque soup, and ⅛ teaspoon pepper. Cook and stir over medium heat until heated through.

4 Spoon sauce over fish fillets. Sprinkle with Parmesan cheese. Serve with hot cooked pasta.

Per serving: 415 cal., 14 g total fat (6 g sat. fat), 71 mg chol., 1,218 mg sodium, 35 g carbo., 2 g fiber, 37 g pro.

Bottled Italian dressing, seasoned stewed tomatoes, and purchased picante sauce make the caponata (the sauce for this dish) a snap to make.

HALIBUT STEAKS WITH CAPONATA

START TO FINISH:
25 minutes

MAKES:
4 servings

4   6-ounce fresh or frozen halibut steaks, cut 1 inch thick

1   tablespoon bottled Italian salad dressing

1   14½-ounce can Italian-style stewed tomatoes, undrained

1   tablespoon olive oil

1   small eggplant, cut into ½-inch cubes (about 12 ounces)

⅔   cup coarsely chopped yellow and/or green sweet pepper

⅓   cup purchased picante sauce

¼   teaspoon bottled minced garlic

1   tablespoon balsamic vinegar

1 Thaw fish, if frozen. Rinse fish; pat dry with paper towels.

2 Preheat broiler. Brush fish with salad dressing. Place fish on greased unheated rack of a broiler pan. Broil about 4 inches from the heat for 8 to 12 minutes or until fish flakes easily when tested with a fork, turning once halfway through broiling.

3 Meanwhile, for caponata, cut up any large tomato pieces; set aside. In a large nonstick skillet heat olive oil over medium-high heat. Add eggplant; cook about 3 minutes or until golden brown, stirring occasionally. Stir in undrained tomatoes, sweet pepper, picante sauce, and garlic. Bring to boiling; reduce heat. Simmer, uncovered, for 4 to 5 minutes or until slightly thickened. Stir in balsamic vinegar. Serve caponata with fish.

Per serving: 309 cal., 9 g total fat (1 g sat. fat), 54 mg chol., 543 mg sodium, 16 g carbo., 3 g fiber, 38 g pro.

White wine, purchased pesto, and capers pep up the sauce in this dish. You'll be amazed at how fast everything comes together for the meal.

FISH WITH PESTO & WINE PASTA

4	fresh or frozen salmon or swordfish steaks, cut ¾ inch thick (1¼ pounds)
¼	teaspoon salt
¼	teaspoon black pepper
6	ounces dried penne pasta
2	cups packaged sliced fresh mushrooms
½	cup dry white wine
⅓	cup purchased basil pesto
2	tablespoons lemon juice
1	tablespoon drained capers
2	tablespoons olive oil or cooking oil

START TO FINISH:
25 minutes

MAKES:
4 servings

1 Thaw fish, if frozen. Rinse fish; pat dry with paper towels. Sprinkle both sides of each fish steak with salt and pepper. Set aside.

2 In a large saucepan cook pasta in a large amount of lightly salted boiling water for 4 minutes; drain and set aside (pasta will not be tender).

3 Meanwhile, in a large bowl combine mushrooms, wine, pesto, lemon juice, and capers. Stir in drained pasta. Set pasta mixture aside.

4 In a 12-inch skillet heat oil over medium-high heat. Add fish; cook for 2 minutes, carefully turning once. Reduce heat to medium.

5 Spoon pasta mixture around fish in skillet. Bring to boiling; reduce heat. Cover and simmer over medium heat for 6 to 9 minutes or until fish flakes easily when tested with a fork and pasta is tender.

Per serving: 597 cal., 31 g total fat (3 g sat. fat), 78 mg chol., 464 mg sodium, 38 g carbo., 2 g fiber, 39 g pro.

Because they cook so rapidly, fish fillets make a naturally quick meal. This recipe calls for ingredients often found on hand, making it extra convenient.

FISH FILLETS WITH ROASTED RED PEPPER SAUCE

START TO FINISH:
25 minutes

MAKES:
4 servings

1   pound fresh or frozen orange roughy or cod fillets, about ½ to ¾ inch thick

1   12-ounce jar roasted red sweet peppers, drained

1   teaspoon bottled minced garlic (2 cloves)

1   cup water

2   tablespoons tomato paste

1   tablespoon red wine vinegar

2   teaspoons dried basil, crushed

½   teaspoon sugar

⅛   teaspoon salt

     Dash cayenne pepper

1   lemon, sliced

¼   teaspoon salt

¼   teaspoon lemon-pepper seasoning

1 Thaw fish, if frozen. Rinse fish; pat dry with paper towels. Set aside.

2 For sauce, in a blender or food processor combine roasted peppers and garlic. Cover and blend or process until nearly smooth. Add ½ cup of the water, the tomato paste, red wine vinegar, basil, sugar, the ⅛ teaspoon salt, and the cayenne pepper. Cover; blend or process with several on-off turns until nearly smooth. Transfer to a small saucepan; cook over medium heat, stirring frequently, until heated through.

3 Meanwhile, measure thickness of fish. Cut fish into four portions. In a large skillet combine the remaining ½ cup water and half of the lemon slices; heat just until boiling. Carefully add fish. Return just to boiling; reduce heat. Cover and simmer until fish flakes easily when tested with a fork. (Allow 4 to 6 minutes per ½-inch thickness of fish.) Gently pat tops of fish portions dry with paper towels. Sprinkle fish with the ¼ teaspoon salt and lemon-pepper seasoning.

4 To serve, spoon some of the sauce onto four dinner plates. Place a fish portion on top of sauce on each plate. Top with remaining lemon slices.

Per serving: 109 cal., 1 g total fat (0 g sat. fat), 23 mg chol., 358 mg sodium, 7 g carbo., 2 g fiber, 18 g pro.

Try white albacore tuna in this recipe. It has a more delicate flavor than chunk light tuna.

TUNA & PASTA ALFREDO

START TO FINISH:
25 minutes

MAKES:
4 servings

3   cups dried mini lasagna, broken mafalda,
     or medium noodles

2   cups chopped broccoli

1   medium red sweet pepper, cut into thin strips

1   10-ounce container refrigerated light Alfredo sauce

¾   teaspoon dried dill, crushed

2   to 3 tablespoons milk (optional)

1   9½-ounce can tuna (water pack), drained and
     broken into chunks

1 In a large saucepan cook pasta according to package directions, adding broccoli and sweet pepper for the last 5 minutes of cooking. Drain well. Return pasta mixture to hot pan.

2 Stir Alfredo sauce and dill into pasta mixture in saucepan. If desired, stir in enough of the milk to make sauce desired consistency. Gently stir tuna into pasta mixture. Heat through.

Per serving: 545 cal., 12 g total fat (7 g sat. fat), 47 mg chol., 821 mg sodium, 78 g carbo., 4 g fiber, 30 g pro.

Invite some friends over for this seafood delight. It's so scrumptious, your guests will never guess how easy it was to prepare.

LINGUINE WITH GARLIC SHRIMP

START TO FINISH:
25 minutes

MAKES:
4 servings

1	9-ounce package refrigerated linguine or fettuccine
⅓	cup chicken broth
1	tablespoon cornstarch
½	teaspoon dried basil, crushed, or 1 tablespoon snipped fresh basil
2	cups packaged sliced fresh mushrooms
1	large yellow or green sweet pepper, chopped
2	tablespoons bottled minced garlic (12 cloves)
1	tablespoon olive oil
1	14½-ounce can Italian-style stewed tomatoes, undrained
8	ounces fresh or frozen peeled and deveined shrimp
¼	cup finely shredded Parmesan cheese (1 ounce)
	Fresh basil leaves (optional)

1 Cook pasta according to package directions; drain well. Return to hot pan; cover and keep warm.

2 In a small bowl combine chicken broth, cornstarch, and the dried or snipped basil; set aside.

3 In a large skillet cook mushrooms, sweet pepper, and garlic in hot olive oil about 3 minutes or just until tender. Add broth mixture and undrained tomatoes; cook and stir until bubbly. Add fresh or frozen shrimp; cover and simmer for 2 to 5 minutes or until shrimp are opaque.

4 Serve shrimp mixture over hot cooked pasta. Top with Parmesan cheese. If desired, garnish with fresh basil leaves.

Per serving: 381 cal., 10 g total fat (2 g sat. fat), 131 mg chol., 487 mg sodium, 50 g carbo., 3 g fiber, 24 g pro.

Hot, broiled sea scallops drizzled with a creamy sauce provide a pleasant contrast to the cool, mixed greens. The greens wilt just a bit, creating an interesting textural effect in this dish.

SCALLOPS WITH PARMESAN SAUCE

1   pound fresh or frozen large sea scallops

6   cups purchased Italian-blend torn mixed greens
    or prewashed baby spinach

4   small red and/or yellow tomatoes,
    cut into chunks or wedges

3   tablespoons butter or margarine

1   teaspoon bottled minced garlic (2 cloves)

¼   teaspoon cayenne pepper

1   tablespoon all-purpose flour

¾   cup half-and-half or light cream

⅓   cup grated Parmesan cheese

START TO FINISH:
25 minutes

MAKES:
4 servings

1 Thaw scallops, if frozen. Rinse scallops; pat dry with paper towels. Preheat broiler. Divide greens among four dinner plates. Arrange tomatoes on top of greens; set aside.

2 Place scallops on the unheated rack of a broiler pan; set aside. In a small saucepan melt butter; stir in garlic and cayenne pepper. Remove from heat. Brush half of the butter mixture on scallops. Broil scallops 4 inches from heat about 8 minutes or until opaque, turning once. (If desired, for easier turning, thread scallops on metal skewers before broiling.)

3 Meanwhile, for sauce, return saucepan to heat; stir flour into remaining butter mixture. Add half-and-half and Parmesan cheese; cook and stir until thickened and bubbly. Cook and stir for 1 minute more.

4 Arrange broiled scallops on top of greens and tomatoes on dinner plates; drizzle with sauce.

Per serving: 310 cal., 18 g total fat (11 g sat. fat), 85 mg chol., 464 mg sodium, 12 g carbo., 2 g fiber, 26 g pro.

Lobster makes this meal elegant. If you can't get lobster, cod or shrimp make great alternatives.

WHITE BEANS, PASTA SPIRALS & LOBSTER

START TO FINISH:
25 minutes

MAKES:
3 or 4 servings

8 ounces dried cavatappi, fusilli, or rotini pasta

1 15- to 19-ounce can cannellini beans (white kidney beans), rinsed and drained

½ cup chicken broth

1½ teaspoons bottled minced garlic (3 cloves)

1 tablespoon olive oil

6 plum tomatoes, coarsely chopped (about 2 cups)

12 ounces cooked lobster,* 12 ounces fresh or frozen cod fillets, cooked and cut into 1-inch pieces, or 12 ounces peeled cooked shrimp

½ cup snipped fresh flat-leaf parsley

½ to 1 teaspoon cracked black pepper

½ teaspoon salt

1 Cook pasta according to package directions. Drain and set aside.

2 In a blender or food processor combine ¾ cup of the drained beans and the chicken broth; cover and blend or process until smooth. Add to the saucepan used for cooking the pasta; bring to boiling. Return pasta to saucepan.

3 Meanwhile, in a large skillet cook garlic in 1 tablespoon hot olive oil for 1 minute. Add tomatoes; cook for 1 minute. Add remaining drained beans, the lobster, parsley, pepper, and salt. Heat through.

4 Add tomato mixture to hot pasta; toss to coat. Serve immediately.

Per serving: 602 cal., 9 g total fat (1 g sat. fat), 102 mg chol., 1,051 mg sodium, 87 g carbo., 10 g fiber, 49 g pro.

*NOTE: If cooked lobster is not available, cook 3 lobster tails; remove meat from shells and cut up. (To broil lobster, preheat broiler. Use a large knife to cut through top shell, cutting just to bottom shell; press lobster open. Place, cut side up, on unheated rack of a broiler pan. If desired, brush with melted butter. Broil 4 to 5 inches from heat for 12 to 15 minutes or until meat is opaque.)

Frozen peas, parsley, and basil give a burst of fresh flavor to the savory clam sauce.

WHITE CLAM SAUCE WITH SPAGHETTI

8	ounces dried spaghetti, linguine, or twisted spaghetti pasta
2	6½-ounce cans minced clams
1	medium onion, chopped
1	teaspoon bottled minced garlic
1	tablespoon olive oil
1	cup milk
⅓	cup all-purpose flour
½	teaspoon lemon-pepper seasoning
¼	teaspoon salt
½	cup loose-pack frozen peas
¼	cup snipped fresh parsley
¼	cup dry white wine or chicken broth
2	teaspoons snipped fresh basil or ⅓ teaspoon dried basil, crushed

START TO FINISH:
20 minutes

MAKES:
4 servings

1 Cook pasta according to package directions. Drain well. Return to hot pan; cover and keep warm.

2 Meanwhile, drain clams, reserving the liquid. Set clams aside. If necessary, add enough water or milk to the reserved liquid to measure 1 cup total liquid. Set aside.

3 For sauce, in a medium saucepan cook onion and garlic in hot olive oil until onion is tender. In a screw-top jar combine the 1 cup milk and the flour; cover and shake until smooth. Add milk mixture to saucepan along with lemon-pepper seasoning, salt, and the reserved clam liquid. Cook and stir over medium heat until thickened and bubbly. Cook and stir for 1 minute more. Stir in clams, peas, parsley, wine, and basil. Heat through.

4 Serve sauce over hot cooked pasta.

Per serving: 384 cal., 6 g total fat (1 g sat. fat), 24 mg chol., 364 mg sodium, 59 g carbo., 3 g fiber, 19 g pro.

You can prepare this no-fuss pasta dish in a hurry thanks to refrigerated tortellini and canned cannellini beans. The bean and pasta combo makes it really hearty!

CHEESE TORTELLINI WITH CANNELLINI BEAN SAUCE

START TO FINISH:
20 minutes

MAKES:
4 or 5 servings

2   9-ounce packages refrigerated cheese-filled tortellini

1⅓   cups thin strips red, yellow, and/or green sweet pepper

2   15-ounce cans cannellini beans (white kidney beans), rinsed and drained

1   cup milk

¼   cup finely shredded Parmesan cheese (1 ounce)

1   tablespoon snipped fresh oregano or 1 teaspoon dried oregano, crushed

¼   teaspoon salt

¼   teaspoon ground nutmeg

¼   teaspoon black pepper

Finely shredded Parmesan cheese (optional)

1 Cook the pasta according to package directions, adding the sweet peppers for the last 1 minute of cooking.

2 Meanwhile, for sauce, in a food processor or blender combine 1 can of the drained beans and the milk. Cover and process or blend until smooth.

3 Drain pasta mixture; return to pan. Add the bean mixture, remaining can of drained beans, the ¼ cup Parmesan cheese, the oregano, salt, nutmeg, and black pepper.

4 Cook and stir until heated through. If desired, sprinkle with additional Parmesan cheese.

Per serving: 576 cal., 12 g total fat (5 g sat. fat), 69 mg chol., 1,052 mg sodium, 93 g carbo., 11 g fiber, 36 g pro.

For a more intense flavor, use crimini mushrooms, also called baby bellas. They lend a robust, woodsy flavor to the sauce.

TORTELLINI WITH MUSHROOM MARINARA SAUCE

START TO FINISH:
20 minutes

MAKES:
4 servings

2   9-ounce packages refrigerated cheese- or meat-filled tortellini

2   cups sliced fresh crimini or button mushrooms

2   cloves garlic, minced

1   tablespoon snipped fresh oregano or 1 teaspoon dried oregano, crushed

2   tablespoons olive oil

2   14½-ounce cans diced tomatoes with basil, garlic, and oregano

¼   cup tomato paste

    Finely shredded Parmesan cheese

1 Cook tortellini according to package directions. Drain well. Return pasta to hot pan; cover and keep warm.

2 Meanwhile, for sauce, in a large skillet cook mushrooms, garlic, and oregano in hot olive oil until mushrooms are tender.

3 Sir in undrained tomatoes and tomato paste. Bring to boiling; reduce heat. Simmer, uncovered, for 2 to 3 minutes or until desired consistency.

4 To serve, spoon sauce over tortellini. Top with Parmesan cheese.

Per serving: 584 cal., 18 g total fat (5 g sat. fat), 64 mg chol., 1,623 mg sodium, 82 g carbo., 2 g fiber, 27 g pro.

This range-top version is just as satisfying as the classic baked casserole. Best of all, this one-skillet recipe makes for extra easy cleanup.

SKILLET EGGPLANT PARMIGIANA

START TO FINISH:
25 minutes

MAKES:
4 servings

1	medium eggplant (1 pound), peeled if desired
½	cup grated Parmesan cheese
¼	cup seasoned fine dry bread crumbs
1	egg
1	tablespoon water
2	tablespoons olive oil or cooking oil
1¼	cups purchased meatless spaghetti sauce
1	cup shredded mozzarella cheese (4 ounces)
¼	cup snipped fresh basil
2	tablespoons finely chopped walnuts

1 Cut eggplant into ¾-inch-thick slices. In a shallow dish combine ¼ cup of the Parmesan cheese and bread crumbs. In another shallow dish combine egg and the water; beat together with a fork. Dip eggplant slices into the egg mixture, then into the crumb mixture to coat.

2 In a 12-inch skillet heat oil over medium heat. Add eggplant; cook for 6 to 8 minutes or until golden brown, turning once. Add spaghetti sauce; sprinkle with mozzarella cheese and remaining ¼ cup Parmesan cheese. Reduce heat to medium-low. Cover and cook for 5 minutes.

3 Sprinkle basil and walnuts over eggplant.

Per serving: 295 cal., 20 g total fat (7 g sat. fat), 48 mg chol., 850 mg sodium, 18 g carbo., 5 g fiber, 15 g pro.

A trattoria is a family-run restaurant that serves up casual, simple fare like this pasta dish. Spiced feta cheese provides a bounty of flavor in one easy measure.

TRATTORIA-STYLE SPINACH FETTUCCINE

1	9-ounce package refrigerated spinach fettuccine
1	medium carrot
1	tablespoon olive oil
1	medium shallot or 2 green onions, chopped
4	red and/or yellow tomatoes, halved and sliced (2 cups)
¼	cup oil-packed dried tomatoes, drained and snipped
½	cup crumbled garlic and herb or peppercorn feta cheese (2 ounces)

START TO FINISH:
20 minutes

MAKES:
4 servings

1 Use kitchen shears to cut pasta strands in half. Cook pasta according to package directions. Drain well. Return pasta to hot pan; cover and keep warm.

2 Meanwhile, peel carrot. Using a sharp vegetable peeler, slice carrot lengthwise into wide, flat "ribbons." Set ribbons aside.

3 In a large skillet heat olive oil over medium heat. Add shallot or green onions; cook for 30 seconds. Stir in fresh tomatoes, dried tomatoes, and carrot ribbons. Cover and cook for 5 minutes, stirring once.

4 Spoon tomato mixture over cooked pasta; toss gently. Sprinkle individual servings with feta cheese.

Per serving: 311 cal., 11 g total fat (4 g sat. fat), 73 mg chol., 250 mg sodium, 44 g carbo., 2 g fiber, 13 g pro.

Serve this colorful pasta dish with crusty Italian bread. It's perfect for sopping up every last bit of the delicious sauce.

PASTA WITH RICOTTA & VEGETABLES

START TO FINISH:
25 minutes

MAKES:
4 servings

8	ounces dried cut ziti or penne pasta (about 3 cups)
2½	cups broccoli florets
1½	cups 1-inch pieces fresh asparagus or green beans
1	cup ricotta cheese
¼	cup snipped fresh basil
1	tablespoon snipped fresh thyme
1	tablespoon balsamic vinegar
1	tablespoon olive oil
½	teaspoon bottled minced garlic (1 clove)
½	teaspoon salt
½	teaspoon black pepper
1⅓	cups chopped, seeded red and/or yellow tomatoes
	Shaved Parmesan or Romano cheese
	Fresh thyme sprigs (optional)

1 Cook pasta according to package directions, adding green beans (if using) with pasta for the whole cooking time or adding broccoli and asparagus (if using) for the last 3 minutes of cooking. Drain well. Return to hot pan; cover and keep warm.

2 Meanwhile, in a large bowl combine ricotta cheese, basil, snipped thyme, balsamic vinegar, olive oil, garlic, salt, and pepper. Gently stir in tomatoes.

3 Add drained pasta mixture to tomato mixture; toss gently to combine. Top with Parmesan cheese. If desired, garnish with thyme sprigs.

Per serving: 432 cal., 15 g total fat (7 g sat. fat), 36 mg chol., 490 mg sodium, 56 g carbo., 5 g fiber, 21 g pro.

White wine intensifies the flavor of this dish. If you prefer not to cook with wine, use vegetable or chicken broth in place of the wine in the recipe.

MOSTACCIOLI WITH GREEN BEANS & TOMATOES

8	ounces dried mostaccioli pasta (about 3 cups)
6	ounces fresh green beans and/or wax beans, cut into 1-inch-long pieces (about 1½ cups)
1	tablespoon olive oil
½	cup chopped onion
1	teaspoon bottled minced garlic (2 cloves)
4	plum tomatoes, seeded and chopped (about 1⅓ cups)
⅓	cup dry white wine, vegetable broth, or chicken broth
¼	cup finely shredded Parmesan cheese (1 ounce)
1	tablespoon snipped fresh flat-leaf parsley
	Salt
	Freshly ground black pepper

START TO FINISH:
25 minutes

MAKES:
4 servings

1 In a large saucepan cook pasta and beans in a large amount of lightly salted boiling water for 10 to 12 minutes or until the pasta and beans are tender. Drain well. Return mixture to hot saucepan; cover and keep warm.

2 Meanwhile, in a medium saucepan heat oil over medium heat. Add onion and garlic; cook for 3 to 5 minutes or until onion is tender, stirring occasionally. Reduce heat to low. Add tomatoes and wine; cook for 2 minutes more, stirring frequently.

3 Add tomato mixture to pasta mixture; toss gently to combine. Transfer to a serving dish. Sprinkle with Parmesan cheese and parsley. Season to taste with salt and pepper.

Per serving: 308 cal., 6 g total fat (1 g sat. fat), 4 mg chol., 167 mg sodium, 50 g carbo., 4 g fiber, 11 g pro.

Three kinds of beans—red, lima, and green—make this wholesome meal colorful.
Instant rice and bottled spaghetti sauce make it easy and fast to prepare.

ITALIAN THREE-BEAN & RICE MEDLEY

START TO FINISH:
15 minutes

MAKES:
4 servings

1   15- to 15½-ounce can small red beans or red kidney beans, rinsed and drained

1   14½-ounce can diced tomatoes, undrained

1   cup loose-pack frozen baby lima beans

1   cup loose-pack frozen cut green beans

1   cup vegetable broth or chicken broth

¾   cup instant brown rice

½   teaspoon dried basil, crushed, or dried Italian seasoning, crushed

1   cup bottled meatless spaghetti sauce

1 In a large saucepan combine red beans or kidney beans, undrained diced tomatoes, lima beans, green beans, broth, uncooked brown rice, and basil or Italian seasoning. Bring to boiling; reduce heat. Cover and simmer for 5 minutes.

2 Stir in spaghetti sauce. Heat through.

Per serving: 282 cal., 3 g total fat (1 g sat. fat), 0 mg chol., 892 mg sodium, 55 g carbo., 12 g fiber, 14 g pro.

For garden-fresh flavor, make a stop at your local farmer's market to pick up the mushrooms, zucchini, onion, herbs, and tomatoes for this simple pasta dish.

FRESH TOMATO FUSILLI

8	ounces dried fusilli pasta (about 3 cups)
1	tablespoon butter
3	cups packaged sliced fresh mushrooms
1	small zucchini, halved lengthwise and cut crosswise into ¼-inch-thick slices (1 cup)
¼	cup chopped onion
1½	teaspoons bottled minced garlic (3 cloves)
1	tablespoon all-purpose flour
¾	cup half-and-half or light cream
2	tablespoons snipped fresh basil or 2 teaspoons dried basil, crushed
1	tablespoon snipped fresh oregano or 1 teaspoon dried oregano, crushed
½	teaspoon salt
2	cups red and/or yellow cherry tomatoes, halved
2	tablespoons dry white wine or 4 teaspoons lemon juice
¼	cup finely shredded Parmesan cheese (1 ounce)

START TO FINISH:
25 minutes

MAKES:
4 servings

1 Cook pasta according to package directions; drain. Return pasta to hot pan; cover and keep warm.

2 Meanwhile, for sauce, in a large skillet melt butter over medium heat. Add mushrooms, zucchini, onion, and garlic; cook about 5 minutes or until tender. Sprinkle flour over vegetable mixture; stir to combine. Add half-and-half, dried herbs (if using), and salt to vegetable mixture. Cook and stir over medium heat until thickened and bubbly. Cook and stir for 1 minute more. Remove from heat. Stir in cherry tomatoes, wine, and fresh herbs (if using). Pour over pasta; toss to coat.

3 Transfer to a warm serving dish. Sprinkle with Parmesan cheese.

Per serving: 376 cal., 12 g total fat (6 g sat. fat), 28 mg chol., 428 mg sodium, 54 g carbo., 4 g fiber, 14 g pro.

A terrific meatless dish, this one-skillet wonder combines ready-to-serve soup and instant rice for a delicious meal that comes together in no time.

PARMESAN RICE SKILLET

START TO FINISH:
20 minutes

MAKES:
4 servings

1   19-ounce can ready-to-serve tomato-basil soup

1   15- to 19-ounce can cannellini beans
    (white kidney beans), rinsed and drained

2   cups loose-pack frozen cut green beans

1   cup instant white rice

½   cup water

⅓   cup finely shredded Parmesan cheese

1 In a large skillet combine tomato-basil soup, drained cannellini beans, green beans, uncooked rice, and the water. Bring to boiling; reduce heat. Cover and simmer about 10 minutes or until rice and green beans are tender, stirring frequently.

2 Top individual servings with Parmesan cheese.

Per serving: 254 cal., 3 g total fat (1 g sat. fat), 8 mg chol., 674 mg sodium, 51 g carbo., 8 g fiber, 13 g pro.

SLOW-COOKER RECIPES

Before leaving home, take just 10 minutes to toss together the ingredients for these mouthwatering sandwiches, then turn on the slow cooker. You'll come home to Italian-seasoned beef, ready to be transformed into a delicious and fun family meal.

ITALIAN BEEF SANDWICHES

PREP:
10 minutes

COOK:
Low 10 hours, High 5 hours

MAKES:
10 to 12 sandwiches

1	4-pound boneless beef sirloin or rolled rump roast
½	cup water
1	0.7-ounce package Italian salad dressing mix
2	teaspoons dried Italian seasoning, crushed
½	to 1 teaspoon crushed red pepper
½	teaspoon garlic powder
10	to 12 kaiser rolls or other sandwich rolls, split, or 1 loaf French bread, split
	Bottled roasted red pepper strips (optional)

1 Trim fat from meat. Cut meat into 1-inch pieces. Place meat in a 3½- to 5-quart slow cooker. In a small bowl stir together the water, dry dressing mix, Italian seasoning, crushed red pepper, and garlic powder; pour over beef. Cover and cook on low-heat setting for 10 to 12 hours or on high-heat setting for 5 to 6 hours.

2 Remove meat with a slotted spoon. Using two forks, shred meat. Serve meat on rolls. If desired, top individual sandwiches with roasted red pepper strips. Drizzle with some of the cooking juices to moisten.

Per sandwich: 396 cal., 10 g total fat (3 g sat. fat), 104 mg chol., 642 mg sodium, 31 g carbo., 1 g fiber, 41 g pro.

Keep these ingredients on hand in your pantry and freezer and you can make a delicious, super-hearty soup—without a trip to the supermarket.

BEEF & PASTA SOUP

12	ounces boneless beef round steak, cut ¾ inch thick
1	16-ounce package loose-pack frozen zucchini, carrots, cauliflower, lima beans, and Italian beans
1	1¼-ounce envelope spaghetti sauce mix
3	cups water
1	14½-ounce can diced tomatoes with basil, oregano, and garlic, undrained
1	14-ounce can chicken broth
4	ounces dried gemelli pasta or medium shell macaroni
⅓	cup finely shredded Parmesan cheese

1 Trim fat from meat. Cut meat into ¾-inch pieces. In a 3½- or 4-quart slow cooker combine meat and frozen vegetables. Sprinkle with dry spaghetti sauce mix. Stir in the water, undrained tomatoes, and chicken broth.

2 Cover and cook on low-heat setting for 8 to 10 hours or on high-heat setting for 4 to 5 hours.

3 If using low-heat setting, turn to high-heat setting. Stir in uncooked pasta. Cover and cook about 30 minutes more or until pasta is tender. Sprinkle individual servings with Parmesan cheese.

Per serving: 227 cal., 3 g total fat (1 g sat. fat), 36 mg chol., 1,372 mg sodium, 29 g carbo., 3 g fiber, 19 g pro.

PREP:
15 minutes

COOK:
Low 8 hours, High 4 hours; plus 30 minutes on High

MAKES:
6 servings

You can use red or white wine—or beef broth—in this recipe. Choose red wine for a more intense, bold flavor. Choose white wine if you're looking for a lighter, tangy flavor. Or use extra beef broth if you prefer a nonalcoholic version.

WINE-SAUCED ROUND STEAK

PREP:
20 minutes

COOK:
Low 9 hours, High 4½ hours

MAKES:
6 servings

1½	pounds boneless beef bottom round steak
2	medium carrots, cut into ½-inch pieces
2	stalks celery, cut into ½-inch pieces
1	cup quartered fresh mushrooms
½	cup sliced green onions
1	14½-ounce can Italian-style stewed tomatoes, undrained
1	cup beef broth
½	cup dry red wine, white wine, or beef broth
3	tablespoons quick-cooking tapioca
1	teaspoon dried Italian seasoning, crushed
½	teaspoon salt
¼	teaspoon black pepper
1	bay leaf
3	cups hot cooked noodles

1 Trim fat from meat; cut meat into 1-inch cubes.

2 Transfer meat to a 3½- or 4-quart slow cooker. Add carrots, celery, mushrooms, green onions, undrained tomatoes, beef broth, wine, tapioca, Italian seasoning, salt, pepper, and bay leaf.

3 Cover and cook on low-heat setting for 9 to 10 hours or on high-heat setting for 4½ to 5 hours. Discard bay leaf. Serve over hot cooked noodles.

Per serving: 324 cal., 7 g total fat (2 g sat. fat), 83 mg chol., 552 mg sodium, 33 g carbo., 3 g fiber, 27 g pro.

To add more color to this satisfying fix-and-forget beef stew, use half of a red sweet pepper and half of a green sweet pepper.

BEEF & VEGETABLE STEW

1   2-pound boneless beef chuck pot roast

2   medium onions, cut into 1-inch chunks

1   large red sweet pepper, cut into ¾-inch pieces

1   14-ounce jar spaghetti sauce

1½   pounds zucchini, cut into ¾-inch chunks

    Salt

    Black pepper

1 Trim fat from roast. Cut roast into 1-inch cubes. In a 3½- or 4-quart slow cooker layer beef cubes, onions, and sweet pepper. Add spaghetti sauce. Cover and cook on low-heat setting for 9 to 10 hours or on high-heat setting for 5 hours.

2 If using low-heat setting, turn to high-heat setting. Stir in zucchini; cook about 1 hour more or until meat is tender. Season to taste with salt and black pepper.

Per serving: 350 cal., 15 g total fat (6 g sat. fat), 101 mg chol., 505 mg sodium, 20 g carbo., 3 g fiber, 32 g pro.

PREP:
15 minutes

COOK:
Low 9 hours, High 5 hours; plus 1 hour on High

MAKES:
6 to 8 servings

A great meal any night of the week, this recipe calls for fennel, which brings subtle, licorice-like notes to the pot of soup.

FENNEL-BEEF SOUP

PREP:
25 minutes

COOK:
Low 10 hours, High 5 hours

STAND:
15 minutes

MAKES:
8 servings

1   2- to 2½-pound boneless beef chuck pot roast

¼   teaspoon black pepper

1   tablespoon olive oil or cooking oil

2   14-ounce cans beef broth

1   26-ounce jar spaghetti sauce

2   small fennel bulbs, trimmed and thinly sliced

2   medium zucchini, halved lengthwise and thinly sliced (2½ cups)

½   cup shredded Parmesan cheese (2 ounces) (optional)

1 Trim fat from meat. Cut meat into 1-inch pieces. Sprinkle meat with pepper. In a large skillet cook meat, half at a time, in hot oil over medium heat until brown. Drain off fat. Place meat in a 4- to 5-quart slow cooker. Stir in beef broth, spaghetti sauce, and fennel.

2 Cover and cook on low-heat setting for 10 to 11 hours or on high-heat setting for 5 to 5½ hours.

3 Stir in zucchini. Turn off heat. Cover and let stand for 15 minutes before serving. If desired, top individual servings with Parmesan cheese.

Per serving: 218 cal., 7 g total fat (2 g sat. fat), 67 mg chol., 892 mg sodium, 14 g carbo., 3 g fiber, 27 g pro.

During the wintertime, you can always use another recipe for beef stew. This version features fennel and parsnips for an intriguing change of pace from celery and carrots. Spinach adds a touch of freshness at the end.

COUNTRY ITALIAN BEEF

2	pounds boneless beef chuck
3	medium parsnips, cut into 1-inch pieces
2	large onions, chopped
1	medium fennel bulb, trimmed and coarsely chopped (1 cup)
1	teaspoon dried rosemary, crushed
1	cup dry red wine or beef broth
1	6-ounce can tomato paste
¾	cup beef broth
2	tablespoons quick-cooking tapioca
1	teaspoon sugar
1	teaspoon salt
1	teaspoon finely shredded orange peel
⅓	teaspoon black pepper
4	cloves garlic, minced
3	cups torn fresh spinach
	Hot mashed potatoes (optional)

1 Trim fat from meat. Cut meat into 2-inch pieces. Set aside.

2 In a 3½- or 4-quart slow cooker combine parsnips, onions, and fennel. Add meat; sprinkle with rosemary.

3 In a small bowl combine wine, tomato paste, beef broth, tapioca, sugar, salt, orange peel, pepper, and garlic. Pour over mixture in slow cooker.

4 Cover and cook on low-heat setting for 8 to 10 hours or on high-heat setting for 4 to 5 hours.

5 Just before serving, stir in spinach. If desired, serve meat mixture with hot mashed potatoes.

Per serving: 336 cal., 6 g total fat (2 g sat. fat), 89 mg chol., 647 mg sodium, 28 g carbo., 10 g fiber, 36 g pro.

PREP:
25 minutes

COOK:
Low 8 hours, High 4 hours

MAKES:
6 servings

Putting foil strips under this simple meat loaf is the secret to easily lifting it out of the slow cooker and onto a serving platter for a no-fuss family meal.

PIZZA-SAUCED MEAT LOAF

PREP:
15 minutes

COOK:
Low 5 hours, High 2½ hours

STAND:
10 minutes

MAKES:
6 to 8 servings

1   beaten egg

1   8-ounce can pizza sauce

½   cup seasoned fine dry bread crumbs

2   pounds lean ground beef

¼   cup shredded Monterey Jack cheese, mozzarella cheese, or Parmesan cheese (1 ounce)

1 In a large bowl combine egg, ½ cup of the pizza sauce, and the bread crumbs. Add ground beef and mix well.

2 On waxed paper, shape meat mixture into a 6-inch round loaf. Crisscross three 18×2-inch foil strips on a dinner plate. Place meat loaf in center of strips. Bringing up foil strips, lift and transfer meat and foil to a 3½- or 4-quart slow cooker. Press meat away from side of cooker to avoid burning.

3 Cover and cook on low-heat setting for 5 to 6 hours or on high-heat setting for 2½ to 3 hours.

4 Using foil strips, carefully lift meat loaf from the cooker and transfer to a serving plate. Spoon remaining pizza sauce over meat; sprinkle with cheese. Let stand for 10 minutes before slicing.

Per serving: 327 cal., 17 g total fat (7 g sat. fat), 135 mg chol., 541 mg sodium, 11 g carbo., 1 g fiber, 31 g pro.

This make-ahead spaghetti sauce allows the intense flavors of the ingredients to slowly meld together as it cooks. You end up with a sauce that's a surefire crowd-pleaser.

SPAGHETTI SAUCE ITALIANO

1	pound lean ground beef
8	ounces bulk Italian sausage
1	28-ounce can diced tomatoes, undrained
2	6-ounce cans tomato paste
2	4½-ounce jars (drained weight) sliced mushrooms, drained
1	large onion, chopped
¾	cup chopped green sweet pepper
½	cup dry red wine or water
⅓	cup water
1	2¼-ounce can sliced pitted ripe olives, drained
2	teaspoons sugar
1½	teaspoons Worcestershire sauce
½	teaspoon salt
½	teaspoon chili powder
⅛	teaspoon black pepper
2	cloves garlic, minced
1	pound dried spaghetti
½	cup finely shredded Parmesan cheese (2 ounces)

PREP:
25 minutes

COOK:
Low 9 hours, High 4½ hours

MAKES:
8 servings

1 In a large skillet cook ground beef and sausage until meat is brown. Drain off fat.

2 Transfer meat mixture to a 3½- to 4½-quart slow cooker. Stir in undrained tomatoes, tomato paste, mushrooms, onion, sweet pepper, wine, the water, olives, sugar, Worcestershire sauce, salt, chili powder, black pepper, and garlic.

3 Cover and cook on low-heat setting for 9 to 10 hours or on high-heat setting for 4½ to 5 hours.

4 Cook spaghetti according to package directions. Drain well. Serve meat mixture over hot cooked spaghetti. Sprinkle individual servings with Parmesan cheese.

Per serving: 637 cal., 24 g total fat (11 g sat. fat), 79 mg chol., 1,359 mg sodium, 60 g carbo., 6 g fiber, 38 g pro.

Italian sausage and basil give this traditional Tex-Mex dish an Italian flair. Hot cooked rice, sour cream, and cheddar cheese cool the spiciness of the chili.

TWO-MEAT CHILI

PREP:
25 minutes

COOK:
Low 6 hours, High 3 hours

MAKES:
6 to 8 servings

1 pound lean ground beef

8 ounces bulk Italian sausage

1 large onion, chopped

1 cup chopped green sweet pepper

3 cloves garlic, minced

1 28-ounce can Italian-style tomatoes, undrained, cut up

1 15-ounce can garbanzo beans (chickpeas), rinsed and drained

1 15-ounce can light red kidney beans, rinsed and drained

1 cup water

3 tablespoons Worcestershire sauce

2 to 3 tablespoons chili powder

2 teaspoons dried basil, crushed

2 teaspoons dried oregano, crushed

½ teaspoon bottled hot pepper sauce (optional)

¼ teaspoon salt

Hot cooked rice

Shredded cheddar cheese

Dairy sour cream

1 In a large skillet cook ground beef, Italian sausage, onion, sweet pepper, and garlic until meat is brown and vegetables are tender. Drain off fat.

2 In a 3½- or 4-quart slow cooker combine meat mixture, undrained tomatoes, garbanzo beans, kidney beans, the water, Worcestershire sauce, chili powder, basil, oregano, bottled hot pepper sauce (if desired), and salt.

3 Cover and cook on low-heat setting for 6 to 8 hours or on high-heat setting for 3 to 4 hours.

4 Serve over hot cooked rice. Top with shredded cheddar cheese and sour cream.

Per serving: 436 cal., 20 g total fat (7 g sat. fat), 72 mg chol., 992 mg sodium, 36 g carbo., 10 g fiber, 29 g pro.

Two frozen ingredients—ravioli and meatballs—make this slow-cooked casserole super easy.
Add a quick sprinkle of Parmesan cheese and you have a spectacular meal.

SAUCY RAVIOLI WITH MEATBALLS

Nonstick cooking spray

2 26-ounce jars spaghetti sauce with mushrooms and onions

2 24-ounce packages frozen meat-filled ravioli

1 12-ounce package frozen cooked Italian meatballs, thawed

2 cups shredded mozzarella cheese (8 ounces)

½ cup finely shredded Parmesan cheese (2 ounces)

1 Lightly coat a 5½- or 6-quart slow cooker with nonstick cooking spray. Add 1 cup of the spaghetti sauce. Add one package of the frozen ravioli and the meatballs. Sprinkle with 1 cup of the mozzarella cheese. Top with remaining spaghetti sauce from first jar. Add remaining package of ravioli and remaining 1 cup mozzarella cheese. Pour spaghetti sauce from second jar over mixture in slow cooker.

2 Cover and cook on low-heat setting for 4½ to 5 hours or on high-heat setting for 2½ to 3 hours. Turn off slow cooker. Sprinkle with Parmesan cheese. Cover and let stand for 15 minutes before serving.

Per serving: 550 cal., 27 g total fat (6 g sat. fat), 124 mg chol., 1,479 mg sodium, 50 g carbo., 3 g fiber, 29 g pro.

PREP:
15 minutes

COOK:
Low 4½ hours, High 2½ hours

STAND:
15 minutes

MAKES:
12 servings

The savory flavors of fennel-infused roast and luscious mashed sweet potatoes make a winning combination.

FENNEL-CRUSTED PORK

PREP:
20 minutes

COOK:
Low 8 hours, High 4 hours

MAKES:
4 servings

1	teaspoon fennel seeds, crushed
½	teaspoon dried oregano, crushed
½	teaspoon garlic powder
½	teaspoon paprika
¼	teaspoon salt
¼	teaspoon black pepper
1	1½- to 2-pound boneless pork shoulder roast
1	pound sweet potatoes, peeled and cut into 1-inch pieces
1	cup chicken broth

1 In a small bowl combine fennel seeds, oregano, garlic powder, paprika, salt, and pepper. Trim fat from meat. Sprinkle fennel mixture evenly over meat; rub in with your fingers. If necessary, cut meat to fit into a 3½- or 4-quart slow cooker. Set aside.

2 Place sweet potatoes in the slow cooker. Add meat. Pour chicken broth over mixture in slow cooker.

3 Cover and cook on low-heat setting for 8 to 10 hours or on high-heat setting for 4 to 5 hours.

4 Remove meat from slow cooker; slice meat. Using a slotted spoon, transfer sweet potatoes to a medium bowl. Using a potato masher, mash sweet potatoes, adding enough of the cooking liquid to moisten. Serve meat with mashed sweet potatoes.

Per serving: 356 cal., 14 g total fat (5 g sat. fat), 115 mg chol., 525 mg sodium, 21 g carbo., 3 g fiber, 35 g pro.

Two kinds of pork—Italian sausage and cubed pork—give this stew exceptional flavor.

TOMATOEY PORK STEW

2 cups dry Great Northern beans

6 cups cold water

8 ounces bulk Italian sausage

1 pound lean boneless pork, cut into cubes

3 medium onions, coarsely chopped

3 medium carrots, cut into ½-inch pieces

3 cloves garlic, minced

3 cups water

1 teaspoon instant beef bouillon granules

½ teaspoon dried thyme, crushed

½ teaspoon dried oregano, crushed

⅓ cup tomato paste (½ of a 6-ounce can)

¼ cup dry red wine

¼ cup snipped fresh parsley

PREP:
30 minutes

STAND:
1 hour

COOK:
*Low 7 hours, High 3½ hours;
plus 15 minutes on High*

MAKES:
6 servings

1 Rinse beans; drain. In a large saucepan combine beans and the 6 cups water. Bring to boiling; reduce heat. Simmer, uncovered, for 10 minutes. Remove from heat. Cover and let stand for 1 hour. Drain and rinse beans. Transfer beans to a 4- to 5-quart slow cooker.

2 In a large skillet cook sausage over medium heat until brown. Drain off fat. Transfer sausage to slow cooker. In the same skillet cook pork cubes, half at a time, until cooked through. Drain off fat. Transfer pork cubes to slow cooker. Add onions, carrots, and garlic. Stir in the 3 cups water, the bouillon granules, thyme, and oregano.

3 Cover and cook on low-heat setting for 7 to 8 hours or on high-heat setting for 3½ to 4 hours.

4 If using low-heat setting, turn to high-heat setting. In a small bowl stir together tomato paste and wine. Stir wine mixture and parsley into mixture in slow cooker. Cover and cook for 15 minutes more.

Per serving: 473 cal., 13 g total fat (5 g sat. fat), 73 mg chol., 566 mg sodium, 49 g carbo., 15 g fiber, 37 g pro.

Artichoke hearts make this dish extra special, and lots of garlic makes it zesty and distinctive.

PASTA ALLA ITALIANO

PREP:
20 minutes

COOK:
Low 8 hours, High 4 hours

MAKES:
6 servings

1   pound bulk Italian sausage

1   large onion, chopped

6   cloves garlic, minced

1   28-ounce can crushed tomatoes, undrained

2   4½-ounce jars (drained weight)
    sliced mushrooms, drained

1   8- or 9-ounce package frozen artichoke hearts,
    thawed and cut up

1   cup tomato juice

½   cup dry red wine

1   tablespoon quick-cooking tapioca

½   teaspoon salt

½   teaspoon dried rosemary, crushed

¼   teaspoon black pepper
    Several dashes bottled hot pepper sauce

12 ounces dried rigatoni pasta or spaghetti
    Grated Parmesan cheese (optional)

1 In a large skillet cook Italian sausage, onion, and garlic until meat is brown and onion is tender. Drain off fat.

2 Transfer meat mixture to a 3½- or 4-quart slow cooker. Stir in undrained tomatoes, mushrooms, artichoke hearts, tomato juice, wine, tapioca, salt, rosemary, black pepper, and hot pepper sauce.

3 Cover and cook on low-heat setting for 8 to 10 hours or on high-heat setting for 4 to 5 hours.

4 Cook pasta according to package directions. Drain well. Serve meat mixture over hot cooked pasta. If desired, sprinkle individual servings with Parmesan cheese.

Per serving: 542 cal., 18 g total fat (7 g sat. fat), 51 mg chol., 1,101 mg sodium, 64 g carbo., 7 g fiber, 23 g pro.

Seasoned chicken broth and canned tomatoes with basil, oregano, and garlic fill this dish with Italian flavors. No extra seasonings are needed. Now how easy is that?

SAUSAGE STEW

1 pound bulk Italian sausage

2 14-ounce cans seasoned chicken broth with Italian herbs (3½ cups)

1 15- to 19-ounce can cannellini beans (white kidney beans), rinsed and drained

1 14½-ounce can diced tomatoes with basil, oregano, and garlic, undrained

1 9-ounce package refrigerated cheese-filled tortellini

Finely shredded Parmesan cheese (optional)

1 In a large skillet cook sausage over medium heat until brown. Drain off fat.

2 In a 3½- to 4½-quart slow cooker combine cooked sausage, broth, beans, and undrained tomatoes.

3 Cover and cook on low-heat setting for 5 to 6 hours or on high-heat setting for 2½ to 3 hours. Stir in uncooked pasta. Cover and cook on low-heat setting for 30 minutes more or on high-heat setting for 15 minutes more. If desired, sprinkle individual servings with Parmesan cheese.

Per serving: 441 cal., 20 g total fat (8 g sat. fat), 72 mg chol., 1,597 mg sodium, 40 g carbo., 5 g fiber, 24 g pro.

PREP:
15 minutes

COOK:
Low 5 hours plus 30 minutes, High 2½ hours plus 15 minutes

MAKES:
6 servings

It may sound unusual, but this version of lasagna makes the classic casserole easier than ever. Allowing it to cook for a long time helps the lasagna develop loads of flavor.

SLOW COOKER LASAGNA

PREP:
20 minutes

COOK:
Low 4 hours, High 2 hours

STAND:
15 minutes

MAKES:
8 to 10 servings

Nonstick cooking spray

1　pound bulk sweet Italian sausage

1　26-ounce jar chunky tomato, basil, and cheese pasta sauce

¾　cup water

12　no-boil lasagna noodles

1　15-ounce carton ricotta cheese

1　8-ounce package shredded Italian blend cheese (2 cups)

1 Lightly coat a 3½- or 4-quart slow cooker with nonstick cooking spray; set aside. In a large skillet cook sausage until brown. Drain off fat. Stir pasta sauce and the water into sausage in skillet.

2 Place ½ cup of the meat mixture in the bottom of the prepared cooker. Layer four of the uncooked noodles (break noodles to fit) on top the meat mixture. Top with one-third of the ricotta cheese, one-third of the remaining meat mixture, and one-third of the shredded cheese. Repeat layers twice, starting with noodles and ending with meat mixture. Set aside the remaining shredded cheese.

3 Cover and cook on low-heat setting for 4 to 6 hours or on high-heat setting for 2 to 3 hours.

4 Sprinkle with remaining shredded cheese. Cover and let stand for 15 minutes before serving.

Per serving: 497 cal., 30 g total fat (14 g sat. fat), 87 mg chol., 909 mg sodium, 26 g carbo., 1 g fiber, 26 g pro.

A touch of whipping cream just before serving makes this zesty tomato dish rich and creamy. It's sure to have your family or guests coming back for seconds.

PASTA WITH SPICY TOMATO-CREAM SAUCE

1   pound bulk hot Italian sausage

2   large onions, chopped

4   cloves garlic, minced

2   14½-ounce cans diced tomatoes, undrained

1   15-ounce can tomato sauce

3   tablespoons quick-cooking tapioca

2   teaspoons dried Italian seasoning, crushed

¼   teaspoon salt

¼   teaspoon black pepper

1   pound dried spaghetti

½   cup whipping cream

   Finely shredded or grated Parmesan cheese (optional)

   Snipped fresh parsley (optional)

PREP:
20 minutes

COOK:
Low 6 hours, High 3 hours

MAKES:
8 servings

1 In a large skillet cook Italian sausage, onions, and garlic until meat is brown and onions are tender. Drain off fat.

2 Transfer meat mixture to a 3½- or 4-quart slow cooker. Stir in undrained tomatoes, tomato sauce, tapioca, Italian seasoning, salt, and pepper.

3 Cover and cook on low-heat setting for 6 to 8 hours or on high-heat setting for 3 to 4 hours.

4 Cook spaghetti according to package directions. Drain well. Just before serving, stir whipping cream into meat mixture in slow cooker. Serve meat mixture over hot cooked spaghetti. If desired, sprinkle individual servings with Parmesan cheese and parsley.

Per serving: 517 cal., 24 g total fat (10 g sat. fat), 64 mg chol., 908 mg sodium, 56 g carbo., 4 g fiber, 17 g pro.

Bring the Tuscany region of Italy to your table with this hearty white bean soup. It's the perfect meal on a cold winter day.

TUSCAN HAM & BEAN SOUP

PREP:
25 minutes

COOK:
Low 6 hours, High 3 hours

MAKES:
8 servings

3	15-ounce cans small white beans, rinsed and drained
2½	cups cubed cooked ham (about 12 ounces)
3	medium carrots, chopped
2	stalks celery, thinly sliced
1	large onion, chopped
¼	teaspoon black pepper
2	14½-ounce cans diced tomatoes with basil, garlic, and herbs, undrained
2	14-ounce cans reduced-sodium chicken broth
8	cups torn fresh kale or spinach leaves
	Freshly shredded Parmesan cheese (optional)

1 In a 5- to 6-quart slow cooker combine beans, ham, carrots, celery, onion, and pepper. Stir in undrained tomatoes and chicken broth.

2 Cover and cook on low-heat setting for 6 to 8 hours or on high-heat setting for 3 to 4 hours. Just before serving, stir in kale or spinach. If desired, sprinkle individual servings with Parmesan cheese.

Per serving: 259 cal., 5 g total fat (1 g sat. fat), 24 mg chol., 1,615 mg sodium, 44 g carbo., 11 g fiber, 22 g pro.

This easy-to-make family dinner features cabbage and mushrooms, giving the dish old-world flavors. Tapioca thickens the sauce while it cooks.

EASY ITALIAN CHICKEN

½   of a medium head cabbage, cut into wedges
     (about 12 ounces)

1   medium onion, sliced and separated into rings (½ cup)

1   4½-ounce jar (drained weight) sliced mushrooms, drained

2   tablespoons quick-cooking tapioca

2   to 2½ pounds meaty chicken pieces
     (breast halves, thighs, and drumsticks), skinned

2   cups purchased meatless spaghetti sauce
     Grated Parmesan cheese

1 In a 3½- to 6-quart slow cooker combine cabbage wedges, onion, and mushrooms. Sprinkle tapioca over vegetables. Place chicken pieces on vegetables. Pour spaghetti sauce over chicken.

2 Cover and cook on low-heat setting for 6 to 7 hours or on high-heat setting for 3 to 3½ hours.

3 Transfer to a serving platter. Sprinkle with Parmesan cheese.

Per serving: 300 cal., 9 g total fat (3 g sat. fat), 94 mg chol., 662 mg sodium, 24 g carbo., 4 g fiber, 35 g pro.

PREP:
10 minutes

COOK:
Low 6 hours, High 3 hours

MAKES:
4 to 6 servings

This is the perfect recipe for a day when you don't think you have time to cook. Simply put three flavor-packed ingredients into your slow cooker, and you can be on your way in no time.

CHICKEN IN ROASTED GARLIC SAUCE

PREP:
15 minutes

COOK:
Low 6 hours, High 3 hours

MAKES:
4 servings

4 small chicken legs (thigh-drumstick piece)
   (2½ to 3 pounds total), skinned

1 26-ounce jar roasted garlic pasta sauce

1 16-ounce package frozen (yellow, green, and red) peppers
   and onion stir-fry vegetables

3 cups hot cooked noodles

⅓ cup shredded mozzarella cheese or finely shredded
   Parmesan cheese

1 Place chicken in a 3½- or 4-quart slow cooker. Add pasta sauce and frozen vegetables.

2 Cover and cook on low-heat setting for 6 to 7 hours or on high-heat setting for 3 to 3½ hours.

3 Serve chicken and vegetable mixture with hot cooked noodles. Sprinkle with mozzarella cheese.

Per serving: 500 cal., 12 g total fat (3 g sat. fat), 174 mg chol., 796 mg sodium, 52 g carbo., 6 g fiber, 45 g pro.

Cannellini beans, often called white kidney beans, have been an Italian staple for ages. They give this dish a true Italian touch.

CHICKEN WITH WHITE BEANS

1	large onion, chopped
2	medium carrots, chopped
1	stalk celery, thinly sliced
3	cloves garlic, minced
2	pounds skinless, boneless chicken thighs
¼	teaspoon salt
⅛	teaspoon black pepper
1	14½-ounce can diced tomatoes, undrained
½	cup chicken broth
½	cup dry white wine
1½	teaspoons dried Italian seasoning, crushed
1	15- or 19-ounce can cannellini beans (white kidney beans), rinsed and drained
	Grated Parmesan cheese

PREP:
20 minutes

COOK:
Low 6 hours, High 3 hours

STAND:
10 minutes

MAKES:
6 to 8 servings

1 In a 3½- or 4-quart slow cooker combine onion, carrots, celery, and garlic. Add chicken thighs; sprinkle with salt and pepper. In a medium bowl stir together undrained tomatoes, chicken broth, wine, and Italian seasoning. Pour over mixture in slow cooker.

2 Cover and cook on low-heat setting for 6 to 7 hours or on high-heat setting for 3 to 3½ hours. Remove liner from cooker, if possible, or turn off slow cooker. Stir cannellini beans into mixture in slow cooker. Cover and let stand for 10 minutes.

3 Using a slotted spoon, transfer chicken and vegetables to a serving dish, reserving cooking liquid. Drizzle chicken and vegetables with enough of the reserved cooking liquid to moisten. Sprinkle individual servings with Parmesan cheese.

Per serving: 296 cal., 7 g total fat (2 g sat. fat), 123 mg chol., 577 mg sodium, 19 g carbo., 5 g fiber, 37 g pro.

Italian-style tomatoes and tomato paste as well as Italian seasoning give this slow-cooked meal intense flavor. A sprinkling of Parmesan cheese adds the perfect finishing touch.

CHICKEN & FETTUCCINE

PREP:
15 minutes

COOK:
Low 5 hours, High 2½ hours

MAKES:
4 servings

1   9-ounce package frozen Italian-style green beans

1   cup fresh mushrooms, quartered

1   small onion, cut into ¼-inch-thick slices

12   ounces skinless, boneless chicken thighs, cut into
     1-inch pieces

1   14½-ounce can Italian-style stewed tomatoes, undrained

1   6-ounce can Italian-style tomato paste

1   teaspoon dried Italian seasoning, crushed

2   cloves garlic, minced

3   tablespoons finely shredded or grated Parmesan cheese

6   ounces dried fettuccine

1 In a 3½- or 4-quart slow cooker combine green beans, mushrooms, and onion. Place chicken pieces on vegetables.

2 In a small bowl combine undrained tomatoes, tomato paste, Italian seasoning, and garlic. Pour over chicken.

3 Cover and cook on low-heat setting for 5 to 6 hours or on high-heat setting for 2½ to 3 hours. Sprinkle with Parmesan cheese.

4 Cook fettuccine according to package directions. Drain well. Serve chicken mixture over hot cooked pasta.

Per serving: 405 cal., 7 g total fat (2 g sat. fat), 75 mg chol., 728 mg sodium, 55 g carbo., 4 g fiber, 28 g pro.

Ground turkey mellows the flavor of Italian sausage without adding lots of extra fat. This recipe directs you to cook the meat mixture in two batches, allowing for optimum browning.

TURKEY-SAUSAGE SANDWICHES

1½	pounds bulk Italian sausage
1½	pounds uncooked ground turkey
1½	cups purchased meatless spaghetti sauce
1	cup chopped onion or green sweet pepper
1	6-ounce can tomato paste
¼	teaspoon crushed red pepper
12	hoagie buns, split and toasted
1	cup shredded mozzarella cheese (4 ounces)

PREP:
20 minutes

COOK:
Low 6 hours, High 3 hours

MAKES:
12 sandwiches

1 In a large skillet cook half of the Italian sausage and half of the ground turkey until meat is brown. Drain off fat. Transfer meat to a 3½- or 4-quart slow cooker. Repeat with remaining sausage and remaining turkey.

2 Stir spaghetti sauce, onion or sweet pepper, tomato paste, and crushed red pepper into meat in slow cooker.

3 Cover and cook on low-heat setting for 6 to 8 hours or on high-heat setting for 3 to 4 hours. Serve meat mixture on hoagie buns. Top with mozzarella cheese.

Per sandwich: 559 cal., 22 g total fat (8 g sat. fat), 79 mg chol., 1,154 mg sodium, 57 g carbo., 4 g fiber, 31 g pro.

This version of the classic vegetable soup includes winter squash, such as butternut or acorn squash, which adds color and sweetness to this dish. Zesty sausage provides a spicy contrast.

WINTER MINESTRONE

PREP:
30 minutes

COOK:
Low 8 hours, High 4 hours

MAKES:
8 servings

12	ounces uncooked turkey or pork Italian sausage links, cut into ¾-inch-thick slices
2½	cups cubed, peeled winter squash (such as butternut or acorn squash)
1½	cups cubed potatoes
2	medium fennel bulbs, trimmed and cut into 1-inch pieces
1	large onion, chopped
1	15-ounce can red kidney beans, rinsed and drained
2	cloves garlic, minced
½	teaspoon dried sage, crushed
2	14-ounce cans chicken broth
1	cup dry white wine
3	cups chopped fresh spinach

1 In a large skillet cook turkey sausage until brown. Drain off fat.

2 In a 5- to 6-quart slow cooker combine squash, potatoes, fennel, onion, beans, garlic, and sage. Top with turkey sausage. Pour chicken broth and wine over all.

3 Cover and cook on low-heat setting for 8 to 10 hours or on high-heat setting for 4 to 5 hours. Stir in spinach just before serving.

Per serving: 200 cal., 5 g total fat (1 g sat. fat), 27 mg chol., 649 mg sodium, 24 g carbo., 6 g fiber, 14 g pro.

Thanks to frozen cheese ravioli, this recipe is a snap to prepare. Two types of meat—Italian sausage and ground beef—make this indulgent meal extra satisfying.

RAVIOLI CASSEROLE

Nonstick cooking spray

1	pound bulk Italian sausage
1	pound lean ground beef
1	large onion, chopped
2	cloves garlic, minced
2	26- to 28-ounce jars sun-dried tomato pasta sauce
1	15-ounce can tomato sauce
1	teaspoon dried Italian seasoning, crushed
2	25-ounce packages frozen cheese-filled ravioli
2½	cups shredded Italian blend cheese (10 ounces)

1 Lightly coat a 5½- or 6-quart slow cooker with nonstick cooking spray; set aside.

2 For sauce, in a 12-inch skillet cook sausage, ground beef, onion, and garlic until meat is brown and onion is tender. Drain off fat. Stir pasta sauce, tomato sauce, and Italian seasoning into meat mixture in skillet.

3 Spoon 1 cup of the meat mixture into prepared cooker. Add one package of the frozen ravioli and sprinkle with 1 cup of the cheese. Top with half of the remaining meat mixture. Add remaining package of the ravioli and 1 cup of the remaining cheese. Top with remaining meat mixture. (Wrap and chill remaining cheese until needed.)

4 Cover and cook on low-heat setting for 4 to 5 hours or on high-heat setting for 2½ to 3 hours. Turn off slow cooker. Sprinkle with remaining ½ cup cheese. Cover and let stand for 15 minutes before serving.

Per serving: 716 cal., 35 g total fat (13 g sat. fat), 125 mg chol., 1,597 mg sodium, 63 g carbo., 4 g fiber, 36 g pro.

PREP:
20 minutes

COOK:
Low 4 hours, High 2½ hours

STAND:
15 minutes

MAKES:
10 servings

Great Northern beans, red beans, and Italian-style green beans pack this healthful meal-in-a-bowl full of protein, vitamins, and fiber.

THREE-BEAN SOUP

PREP:
30 minutes

STAND:
1 hour

COOK:
Low 10 hours, High 5 hours; plus 30 minutes on High

MAKES:
6 servings

1	cup dry Great Northern beans
1	cup dry red beans or pinto beans
5	cups cold water
3	14-ounce cans vegetable broth
1	medium onion, chopped
2	cloves garlic, minced
2	teaspoons dried Italian seasoning, crushed
1/4	teaspoon black pepper
1	14½-ounce can diced tomatoes with basil, oregano, and garlic, undrained
1	9-ounce package frozen Italian green beans or cut green beans
2	tablespoons balsamic vinegar
2	tablespoons butter, softened
1/4	teaspoon garlic powder
1/4	teaspoon dried Italian seasoning, crushed
12	½-inch-thick slices baguette-style French bread

1 Rinse dry beans. In a Dutch oven combine beans and the cold water. Bring to boiling; reduce heat. Simmer, uncovered, for 10 minutes. Remove from heat. Cover and let stand for 1 hour. Drain and rinse beans.

2 In a 4- to 5-quart slow cooker combine beans, vegetable broth, onion, garlic, the 2 teaspoons Italian seasoning, and the pepper.

3 Cover and cook on low-heat setting for 10 to 12 hours or on high-heat setting for 5 to 6 hours or until beans are almost tender.

4 If using low-heat setting, turn to high-heat setting. Stir undrained tomatoes and frozen green beans into bean mixture. Cover and cook about 30 minutes or until beans are tender. Stir in balsamic vinegar.

5 Meanwhile, in a small bowl stir together butter, garlic powder, and the 1/4 teaspoon Italian seasoning. Spread butter mixture on one side of each bread slice. Place bread on the unheated rack of a broiler pan or on a baking sheet. Broil 4 to 5 inches from the heat for 1 to 2 minutes or until crisp and light brown. To serve, ladle soup into bowls. Add two pieces of the toasted bread to each bowl of soup. Serve immediately.

Per serving: 384 cal., 6 g total fat (3 g sat. fat), 11 mg chol., 1,384 mg sodium, 66 g carbo., 14 g fiber, 20 g pro.

A dollop of purchased pesto is a fresh, lively topper for each serving of this hearty barley soup.

PESTO-TOPPED VEGETABLE SOUP

1	9-ounce package frozen cut green beans
½	of a 16-ounce package frozen cauliflower
1	14½-ounce can diced tomatoes with basil, garlic, and oregano, undrained
1	medium onion, chopped
1	stalk celery, chopped
¼	cup regular barley
1	clove garlic, minced
¼	teaspoon black pepper
3	cups chicken broth
1½	cups vegetable juice
¼	cup purchased pesto

PREP:
20 minutes

COOK:
Low 6 hours, High 3 hours

MAKES:
6 to 8 side-dish servings

1 In a 3½- or 4-quart slow cooker combine green beans, cauliflower, undrained tomatoes, onion, celery, barley, garlic, and pepper. In a medium bowl combine chicken broth and vegetable juice. Pour over vegetable mixture in slow cooker.

2 Cover and cook on low-heat setting for 6 to 8 hours or on high-heat setting for 3 to 4 hours. Top individual servings with pesto.

Per serving: 177 cal., 7 g total fat (0 g sat. fat), 3 mg chol., 1,091 mg sodium, 23 g carbo., 4 g fiber, 6 g pro.

Seasoned tomato paste, basil, and zucchini give this hearty vegetable medley an Italian twist.

HERBED VEGETABLE SOUP

PREP:
20 minutes

COOK:
Low 7 hours, High 3½ hours;
plus 45 minutes on High

MAKES:
6 to 8 side-dish servings

1	10-ounce package frozen whole kernel corn
1	large onion, chopped
2	medium carrots, chopped
1	cup coarsely chopped zucchini
2	cloves garlic, minced
6	cups vegetable broth or chicken broth
1	6-ounce can Italian-style tomato paste
½	teaspoon dried basil, crushed
1	9-ounce package frozen Italian-style green beans
1	cup dried tiny shell macaroni
2	tablespoons snipped fresh parsley

1 In a 3½- to 5-quart slow cooker combine frozen corn, onion, carrots, zucchini, and garlic. Stir in broth, tomato paste, and basil.

2 Cover and cook on low-heat setting for 7 to 8 hours or on high-heat setting for 3½ to 4 hours.

3 If using low-heat setting, turn to high-heat setting. Stir in frozen green beans and uncooked macaroni. Cover and cook for 45 minutes more. Stir in parsley before serving.

Per serving: 198 cal., 2 g total fat (0 g sat. fat), 0 mg chol., 1,269 mg sodium, 41 g carbo., 5 g fiber, 8 g pro.

DESSERTS

11

Make this decadent torte one day in advance. While it chills, the chocolate and coffee flavors become more intense and delicious.

WALNUT-CAPPUCCINO TORTE

PREP:
25 minutes

BAKE:
40 minutes

CHILL:
4 to 24 hours

STAND:
30 minutes

OVEN:
325°F

MAKES:
12 to 16 servings

1	8-ounce package semisweet chocolate, cut up
1⅓	cups milk chocolate pieces
1	cup whipping cream
2	tablespoons instant coffee crystals
5	eggs
¼	cup coffee liqueur or brewed coffee
1	teaspoon vanilla
½	cup all-purpose flour
¼	cup sugar
1	cup chopped walnuts or pecans, toasted
1	recipe Mocha Cream
	Fresh raspberries (optional)

1 In a heavy medium saucepan combine semisweet chocolate, milk chocolate, whipping cream, and coffee crystals; cook and stir over low heat until melted. Cool to room temperature.

2 Preheat oven to 325°F. Grease and flour the bottom and side of a 9-inch springform pan; set aside.

3 In a large mixing bowl combine eggs, coffee liqueur or coffee, and vanilla; beat with an electric mixer on low speed until combined. Add flour and sugar. Beat on medium to high speed for 8 minutes. (The batter should be light and slightly thickened.) Stir about one-fourth of the egg mixture into the chocolate mixture. Stir egg-chocolate mixture into the remaining egg mixture. Stir in nuts.

4 Spread batter in prepared pan. Bake for 40 to 45 minutes or until slightly puffed around the outer edge (center will be slightly soft). Cool in springform pan on a wire rack for 20 minutes. Loosen and remove side of springform pan. Cool completely. Cover and chill for 4 to 24 hours.

5 To serve, let stand at room temperature for 30 minutes. Top with Mocha Cream. If desired, garnish dessert plates with raspberries.

MOCHA CREAM: In a chilled small bowl beat ½ cup whipping cream and 2 tablespoons coffee liqueur with a rotary beater just until soft peaks form (tips curl over).

Per serving: 462 cal., 32 g total fat (12 g sat. fat), 134 mg chol., 56 mg sodium, 35 g carbo., 3 g fiber, 8 g pro.

This cake gets better as it ages, so make it a few days before you intend to serve it.

PECAN WINE CAKE

1⅓   cups granulated sugar

1⅔   cups packed brown sugar

1   cup butter, softened (2 sticks)

4   eggs

3⅔   cups all-purpose flour

¼   teaspoon ground mace

⅛   teaspoon salt

1⅓   cups fruity white wine
(such as Viansa Frescolina Tocai or Imbianco Barbera Blanc)

1   cup pecans, coarsely chopped

Sifted powdered sugar (optional)

Fresh mint leaves (optional)

Sugared fruit (optional)

1 Preheat oven to 300°F. Grease and lightly flour a 9-inch (12-cup) fluted tube pan; set aside.

2 In a medium bowl mix the sugars together; set aside. In a large mixing bowl beat butter with an electric mixer on low speed until soft and fluffy. Add half of the sugar mixture to the creamed butter. Increase the mixer speed to high and beat until smooth. Set aside.

3 In a large bowl beat eggs with a whisk until light and fluffy (about 5 minutes). Gradually whisk the remaining sugar mixture into the eggs. Continue whisking until you have a smooth, creamy consistency. Add this mixture to the butter mixture; whisk until smooth.

4 In another large bowl combine flour, mace, and salt. Alternately add the flour mixture and the white wine to the butter-and-egg mixture, mixing well with a wooden spoon after each addition. Stir pecans into batter.

5 Pour batter into prepared pan; place on a baking sheet. Bake for 1¾ to 2 hours or until cake is golden brown and a toothpick inserted in center of cake comes out clean. Cool in pan for 30 minutes; turn out onto a wire rack. Cool cake completely. If desired, sprinkle powdered sugar over top of cake and garnish with mint leaves and sugared fruit.

Per serving: 425 cal., 18 g total fat (8 g sat. fat), 83 mg chol., 128 mg sodium, 60 g carbo., 1 g fiber, 5 g pro.

NOTE: For best flavor, age the cake by wrapping it in foil or plastic wrap and refrigerating for at least 1 day. The cake can be refrigerated for up to 10 days. Do not freeze.

PREP:
30 minutes

BAKE:
1¾ hours

OVEN:
300°F

MAKES:
16 to 20 servings

This moist, apple-filled cake is simple enough for any meal yet special enough for a dinner party.

CORNMEAL-APPLE CAKE

PREP:
30 minutes

BAKE:
40 minutes

COOL:
20 minutes + 20 minutes

OVEN:
350°F

MAKES:
12 servings

¼	cup butter
3	cups peeled, cored, and sliced baking apples (such as Granny Smith or Rome Beauty) (about 3 medium)
⅓	cup golden raisins
2	tablespoons granulated sugar
1	teaspoon ground cinnamon
¾	cup yellow cornmeal
¾	cup all-purpose flour
2	teaspoons baking powder
¾	cup butter, softened
1	cup granulated sugar
1	teaspoon vanilla
4	eggs
⅓	cup dairy sour cream
1	tablespoon milk
	Sifted powdered sugar

1 Preheat oven to 350°F. Grease the bottom and side of a 9-inch springform pan; set aside. In a large skillet melt the ¼ cup butter over medium heat. Add sliced apples and raisins. Cook about 8 minutes or just until apples are tender, stirring occasionally. Remove from heat. In a small bowl stir together the 2 tablespoons sugar and the cinnamon. Stir sugar mixture into apple mixture. If desired, reserve a few apple slices for garnish; set aside. Set remaining apple mixture aside.

2 In a medium bowl stir together cornmeal, flour, baking powder, and ½ teaspoon salt; set aside. In a large bowl beat ¾ cup butter with an electric mixer on medium to high speed for 30 seconds. Add the 1 cup granulated sugar and the vanilla; beat until combined. Add eggs, one at a time, beating well after each addition. Add sour cream and milk; beat until combined. Fold in cornmeal mixture. Pour two-thirds of the batter into the prepared pan. Add the apple mixture, arranging evenly on top of the batter. Pour the remaining batter over the apples and spread evenly.

3 Bake about 40 minutes or until a toothpick inserted near the center comes out clean. Cool in pan on a wire rack for 20 minutes. Remove side of pan; cool 20 minutes more.

4 To serve, use a serrated knife to cut warm cake into wedges. Sprinkle each wedge with powdered sugar. If desired, top with reserved apples.

Per serving: 345 cal., 19 g total fat (11 g sat. fat), 117 mg chol., 354 mg sodium, 40 g carbo., 2 g fiber, 4 g pro.

Ricotta cheese is the main ingredient in this orange-scented cake, making it extra moist. Any remaining cake can be chilled and eaten cold.

TORTA DI RICOTTA

8	eggs
½	cup granulated sugar
2	15-ounce cartons ricotta cheese
½	cup all-purpose flour
½	cup semisweet chocolate pieces
1	tablespoon finely shredded orange peel
	Sifted powdered sugar (optional)

1 Preheat oven to 350°F. Grease a deep 12-inch oven-going skillet; set aside. Separate egg whites from yolks. Place whites in a large mixing bowl; cover and let stand for 30 minutes.

2 Meanwhile, in a very large bowl beat egg yolks with an electric mixer on medium to high speed for 4 to 5 minutes or until thick and lemon-colored. Add ¼ cup of the granulated sugar. Beat until combined. Add ricotta cheese and flour, beating on low speed just until combined; set aside.

3 Wash beaters thoroughly. Beat egg whites with the electric mixer on medium speed until soft peaks form (tips curl over). Gradually add remaining ¼ cup granulated sugar, 1 tablespoon at a time, beating on high speed until stiff peaks form (tips stand straight).

4 Fold half of the beaten egg whites, the chocolate pieces, and orange peel into the egg yolk mixture. Fold in remaining egg whites. Turn mixture into prepared skillet. Bake about 40 minutes or until set, top is lightly browned, and a knife inserted near the center comes out clean.

5 Cool in skillet on a wire rack for 30 minutes. Serve warm. If desired, sprinkle with powdered sugar before serving.

Per serving: 574 cal., 25 g total fat (15 g sat. fat), 129 mg chol., 1,091 mg sodium, 63 g carbo., 3 g fiber, 24 g pro.

PREP:
25 minutes

STAND:
30 minutes

BAKE:
40 minutes

COOL:
30 minutes

OVEN:
350°F

MAKES:
12 servings

A cassata, which means "in a case" in Italian, is a traditional dessert served at Italian weddings. This version encases a filling of brandy- or rum-soaked dried fruit and whipped cream between layers of sweetened corn bread.

CORN BREAD CASSATA

PREP:
30 minutes

BAKE:
20 minutes

OVEN:
350°F

MAKES:
8 to 12 servings

*TEST KITCHEN TIP:
You'll have enough batter to make 8 individual cakes. If you don't have 8 popover or giant muffin cups, refrigerate any leftover batter while first cakes bake. Cool cups; wash and prepare cups as directed to bake remainder.

2	8½-ounce packages corn muffin mix
1	8-ounce can crushed pineapple (juice pack), undrained
2	tablespoons brandy or rum
1½	cups chopped dried cherries and/or golden raisins
1½	cups whipping cream
1	tablespoon packed brown sugar
½	cup chopped white chocolate chunks
	Dried cherries (optional)
	White chocolate chunks (optional)

1 Grease and flour eight nonstick popover or giant muffin cups* or two 9×1½- or 8×1½-inch round cake pans. Line the cake pans with waxed paper or parchment paper; set aside. Preheat oven to 350°F.

2 Prepare each muffin mix according to package directions, except stir half of the undrained pineapple into the batter of each mix along with the milk and egg. Spoon a scant ½ cup of the batter into each popover or muffin cup or spread batter into prepared 8- or 9-inch pans (use one pan for each mix). Bake about 20 minutes for popover, giant muffin, or 9-inch pans (20 to 22 minutes for 8-inch pans) or until a toothpick inserted near the centers comes out clean. Let cool in pans on a wire rack for 5 minutes for smaller pans or 10 minutes for larger pans. Remove cakes from pans; remove paper. Cool completely.

3 Meanwhile, in a small saucepan heat brandy over low heat until warm. Stir in the 1½ cups dried cherries. Let stand for 20 minutes; drain off any excess liquid. In a chilled large bowl combine whipping cream and brown sugar; beat with chilled beaters of an electric mixer on medium speed until soft peaks form (tips curl over). Fold in cherry mixture and the ½ cup white chocolate chunks. Cover and chill until ready to use (up to 2 hours).

4 For individual cakes: If necessary, trim rounded tops so inverted cakes will lay flat. Split cakes horizontally at a slight diagonal. Place each bottom layer on a dessert plate. Top with some of the whipped cream mixture, the cake top, and more of the whipped cream mixture. If desired, top with additional dried cherries and white chocolate chunks.

5 For large cakes: Place one cake layer on a serving plate; spread top with half of the whipped cream mixture. Top with remaining cake layer and remaining whipped cream mixture. Serve within 30 minutes. (Or cover and chill for up to 8 hours.) If desired, top with additional dried cherries and white chocolate.

Per serving: 604 cal., 30 g total fat (13 g sat. fat), 104 mg chol., 510 mg sodium, 76 g carbo., 1 g fiber, 9 g pro.

This luscious filled dessert uses purchased cake mix, making it extra easy to prepare. Raspberry jam provides an enjoyable flavor contrast to the chocolate and hazelnut spread.

HAZELNUT CREAM CASSATA

1	package 2-layer-size white cake mix or lemon-flavored cake mix
1	tablespoon finely shredded lemon peel (only if using white cake mix)
⅓	cup chocolate-hazelnut spread
⅓	cup ricotta cheese
⅓	cup seedless red raspberry jam
1½	cups whipping cream
2	tablespoons sifted powdered sugar
	Halved hazelnuts, toasted

PREP:
30 minutes

BAKE:
15 minutes

OVEN:
350°F

MAKES:
12 servings

1 Preheat oven to 350°F. Grease and flour three 9×1½-inch round cake pans; set aside. Prepare cake mix according to package directions using the water, oil, and eggs called for on the package. (If using white cake mix, stir in the lemon peel.) Divide batter among prepared pans.*

2 Bake about 15 minutes or until a toothpick inserted near the centers comes out clean. Let cool in pans on a wire rack for 10 minutes. Remove cakes from pans. Cool completely.

3 For filling, in a small bowl stir together chocolate-hazelnut spread and ricotta cheese. Place one cake layer on a serving platter; spread top with half of the jam. Spread half of the chocolate mixture over jam. Top with another layer of cake. Spread with remaining jam and remaining chocolate mixture. Top with remaining cake layer.

4 In a chilled mixing bowl combine whipping cream and powdered sugar; beat with chilled beaters of an electric mixer on medium speed until stiff peaks form (tips stand straight). Spread whipped cream mixture over top and side of cake. Top with hazelnuts. Cover and chill until serving time (up to 24 hours).

Per serving: 413 cal., 23 g total fat (10 g sat. fat), 45 mg chol., 310 mg sodium, 47 g carbo., 1 g fiber, 5 g pro.

*NOTE: If you have only two 9×1½-inch round cake pans, cover and chill one-third of the batter and bake it after the other layers are out of the pans.

Zwieback, which is used in the crust for this cheesecake, is a slightly sweet yeast bread that has been baked, sliced, and baked again until dry and crisp. It makes a great alternative to graham crackers for dessert crusts.

ITALIAN EASTER CHEESECAKE

PREP:
25 minutes

BAKE:
50 minutes

CHILL:
4 to 24 hours

OVEN:
350°F

MAKES:
12 to 16 servings

¾ cup crushed zwieback (9 slices)

¼ cup sugar

2 tablespoons all-purpose flour

¼ cup butter, melted

1 15-ounce carton ricotta cheese

1 8-ounce package cream cheese, softened

¾ cup sugar

½ cup dairy sour cream

2 tablespoons all-purpose flour

4 slightly beaten eggs

2 teaspoons vanilla

1½ teaspoons finely shredded orange peel

⅓ cup golden raisins

½ cup semisweet chocolate pieces

½ cup pistachios, chopped

1 Preheat oven to 350°F. Lightly grease a 9-inch springform pan. Wrap the outside of the pan with heavy foil. Place the pan in a large roasting pan; set aside.

2 In a medium bowl combine crushed zwieback, the ¼ cup sugar, and 2 tablespoons flour; stir in the melted butter. Press onto the bottom of the prepared pan.

3 In a large mixing bowl combine ricotta cheese and cream cheese. Beat with an electric mixer on medium speed until smooth. Add the ¾ cup sugar, the sour cream, and 2 tablespoons flour; beat on low speed until combined. Stir in eggs, vanilla, and orange peel. Stir in raisins. Spoon over crust in springform pan. Place the roasting pan on the oven rack. Add boiling water to roasting pan to a depth of 1 inch.

4 Bake for 50 to 55 minutes or until center appears nearly set when gently shaken. Remove roasting pan from oven. Remove springform pan and place on a wire rack. Remove foil. Cool cheesecake for 15 minutes. Using a sharp knife, loosen from side of pan; cool for 30 minutes more. Remove side of the springform pan; cool completely. Cover and chill 4 to 24 hours before serving.

5 To serve, 1 hour before serving, in a small saucepan heat chocolate pieces over low heat, stirring until melted and smooth. Sprinkle pistachios over top of cheesecake; drizzle with melted chocolate. Return to refrigerator.

Per serving: 374 cal., 23 g total fat (13 g sat. fat), 125 mg chol., 165 mg sodium, 37 g carbo., 2 g fiber, 10 g pro.

This layered dessert is a major showstopper. A pistachio-graham cracker crust is filled with a luscious cream cheese mixture and crowned with whipped cream, grated chocolate, pistachio nuts, and strawberries.

SPUMONI CHEESECAKE

1	cup finely ground pistachios
¾	cup finely crushed graham crackers
⅓	cup butter, melted
3	8-ounce packages cream cheese, softened
1	cup sugar
2	tablespoons all-purpose flour
1	teaspoon vanilla
2	eggs
1	egg yolk
2	tablespoons milk
2	tablespoons amaretto
1	cup whipping cream
¼	cup grated semisweet chocolate
	Chopped pistachios
	Sliced strawberries

PREP:
40 minutes

BAKE:
35 minutes

CHILL:
4 to 24 hours

OVEN:
375°F

MAKES:
12 to 16 servings

1 Preheat oven to 375°F. Grease the bottom and 1¼ inches up the side of a 9-inch springform pan; set aside.

2 For crust, in a medium bowl combine the 1 cup ground pistachios and the finely crushed graham crackers. Stir in melted butter. Press crumb mixture onto the bottom and about 1¼ inches up the side of the prepared pan. Cover and chill.

3 For filling, in a large mixing bowl combine cream cheese, sugar, flour, and vanilla; beat with an electric mixer on medium speed until combined. Add whole eggs and egg yolk all at once, beating on low speed just until combined. Stir in milk and amaretto.

4 Pour filling into crust-lined pan. Place in a shallow baking pan in oven. Bake for 35 to 40 minutes or until center appears nearly set when shaken.

5 Cool in pan on a wire rack for 15 minutes. Loosen crust from side of springform pan; cool for 30 minutes more. Remove side of springform pan; cool completely. Cover and chill for 4 to 24 hours.

6 Just before serving, in a medium bowl beat whipping cream with an electric mixer on medium speed until stiff peaks form. Sprinkle cheesecake with 3 tablespoons of the grated chocolate. Pipe whipping cream on top of cheesecake. Sprinkle with remaining 1 tablespoon grated chocolate and chopped pistachios. Arrange sliced strawberries on top.

Per serving: 501 cal., 40 g total fat (21 g sat. fat), 157 mg chol., 271 mg sodium, 29 g carbo., 1 g fiber, 9 g pro.

Marzipan is a sweet pliable mixture that consists mainly of ground almonds and sugar. This version also incorporates chopped pistachio nuts for an Italian twist.

RASPBERRY MARZIPAN TART

PREP:
40 minutes

BAKE:
30 minutes

CHILL:
30 minutes

OVEN:
350°F

MAKES:
12 servings

1   recipe Rich Tart Crust

⅓   cup seedless raspberry jam

1   recipe Pistachio Marzipan

2   ounces semisweet chocolate, cut up

    Chopped unsalted pistachios (optional)

1 Preheat oven to 350°F. Bake Rich Tart Crust for 10 minutes. Remove foil. Bake for 8 to 10 minutes more or until golden brown. Cool completely in pan on wire rack.

2 Preheat oven to 350°F. Spread jam onto the bottom of the Rich Tart Crust. Spread Pistachio Marzipan evenly over the jam. Bake for 30 to 35 minutes or until the filling is golden brown and firm when lightly touched. Cool in pan on a wire rack.

3 In a heavy small saucepan cook and stir chocolate over low heat until melted. Spread over marzipan. If desired, garnish with pistachio nuts. Refrigerate tart about 30 minutes or until chocolate is set.

4 Before serving, remove side of tart pan and transfer tart to a serving platter.

RICH TART CRUST: In a medium bowl stir together 1¼ cups all-purpose flour and ¼ cup sugar. Using a pastry blender, cut in ½ cup cold butter until pieces are pea-size. In a small bowl stir together 2 beaten egg yolks and 2 tablespoons water. Gradually stir egg yolk mixture into flour mixture. Using your fingers, gently knead dough just until a ball forms. If necessary, cover with plastic wrap and refrigerate for 30 to 60 minutes or until dough is easy to handle. On a lightly floured surface, slightly flatten dough. Roll from center to edge into a 13-inch circle. Wrap pastry around a rolling pin and unroll into an 11-inch tart pan with a removable bottom or a 10-inch pie plate or quiche dish. Ease pastry into pan, being careful not to stretch it. Press pastry into the fluted side of tart pan or quiche dish; trim edge. (Flute edge for pie plate.) Line pastry shell with a double thickness of foil.

PISTACHIO MARZIPAN: In a food processor or blender combine ⅔ cup sugar, ½ cup slivered almonds, and 3 tablespoons all-purpose flour. Cover and process or blend about 1 minute or until almonds are finely ground. Add ⅓ cup butter and 1 egg. Cover and process or blend until smooth. Add 1 egg, 1 teaspoon vanilla, and ½ teaspoon almond extract. Cover and process or blend until smooth. Add ⅓ cup unsalted pistachio nuts, chopped. Cover and process or blend with several on-off turns until combined.

Per serving: 344 cal., 21 g total fat (10 g sat. fat), 105 mg chol., 143 mg sodium, 37 g carbo., 2 g fiber, 5 g pro.

The dough for the lattice topper is chilled to make it easier to handle.

COUNTRY PEAR & BLACKBERRY JAM CROSTATA

2   cups all-purpose flour

⅓   cup granulated sugar

1½   teaspoons baking powder

⅔   cup butter

1   slightly beaten egg

¼   cup milk

2   teaspoons finely shredded lemon peel

1   teaspoon vanilla

¾   cup blackberry preserves or jam

4   cups thinly sliced, peeled ripe pears (about 4 medium)

¼   cup granulated sugar

2   tablespoons butter, melted

   Coarse sugar

   Lemon peel twists (optional)

PREP:
45 minutes

BAKE:
45 minutes

COOL:
30 minutes

OVEN:
375°F

MAKES:
10 servings

1 Preheat oven to 375°F. In a medium bowl stir together flour, the ⅓ cup granulated sugar, and the baking powder. Using a pastry blender, cut in the ⅔ cup butter until mixture resembles coarse crumbs. Make a well in the center of the flour mixture.

2 Stir together egg, the ¼ cup milk, 1 teaspoon of the lemon peel, and the vanilla. Pour milk mixture into flour mixture, stirring until moistened. Turn out dough onto a lightly floured surface. Knead gently for 10 to 12 strokes or until smooth. Wrap one-third of dough in plastic wrap; chill.

3 Pat the remaining dough into the bottom and up the side of a 10-inch tart pan with a removable bottom. Spread preserves evenly over pastry.

4 In a large bowl toss together pears, the ¼ cup granulated sugar, and the remaining 1 teaspoon lemon peel. Arrange pear slices over preserves in tart pan. Drizzle with melted butter.

5 On a lightly floured surface, roll chilled pastry into a 10-inch circle. Cut into ½-inch-wide strips. Arrange strips over pears in a lattice pattern. Trim strips to edge of pan. Brush lattice with additional milk. Sprinkle with coarse sugar.

6 Bake for 45 to 50 minutes or until pears are tender. If necessary to prevent overbrowning, cover loosely with foil for the last 10 minutes of baking. Cool in tart pan for 30 minutes. Remove tart from pan. Cut into wedges. Serve warm. If desired, garnish with lemon peel twists.

Per serving: 392 cal., 17 g total fat (10 g sat. fat), 63 mg chol., 235 mg sodium, 58 g carbo., 3 g fiber, 4 g pro.

Take advantage of frozen puff pastry; it provides an easy way to make elegant desserts. Here, it's topped with rich mascarpone cheese and succulent grapes.

MASCARPONE TART WITH GRAPES

PREP:
25 minutes

BAKE:
12 minutes

OVEN:
375°F.

MAKES:
10 to 12 servings

½   of a 17.3-ounce package frozen puff pastry (1 sheet), thawed

1   egg white

1   tablespoon water

1   recipe Mascarpone Filling

1   cup halved seedless red and green grapes

1 Preheat oven to 375°F. Unfold pastry; place on a lightly floured surface and use a rolling pin to roll pastry into a 12-inch square. Cut the square in half to make two 12×6-inch rectangles. From each short side of the rectangles, cut a ¾-inch-wide strip (four strips total). From each long side of the rectangles, cut a ¾-inch-wide strip (four strips total). Set the eight pastry strips aside.

2 Place the two large pastry rectangles on an ungreased baking sheet. In a small bowl whisk together egg white and the water. Brush rectangles with egg white mixture. Position four of the pastry strips on top of the edges on each rectangle to make a rim on edges, trimming to fit. Brush rims with egg white mixture. Prick bottom of pastry generously with a fork. Bake for 12 to 15 minutes or until golden brown (centers will puff slightly during baking). Cool on a wire rack.

3 Divide the Mascarpone Filling between baked pastry rectangles, spreading filling to edges. Arrange grapes on top of filling. Cover and chill until serving time (up to 2 hours).

MASCARPONE FILLING: In a small bowl stir together one 8-ounce carton mascarpone cheese or one 8-ounce package cream cheese, softened; 2 tablespoons sugar; 2 tablespoons orange juice; and ⅛ teaspoon ground nutmeg.

Per serving: 230 cal., 18 g total fat (6 g sat. fat), 29 mg chol., 110 mg sodium, 16 g carbo., 0 g fiber, 6 g pro.

MAKE-AHEAD DIRECTIONS: Prepare as directed through step 2. Cover pastry rectangles; store at room temperature for up to 24 hours. Continue as directed in step 3.

To remove these gelatin-base desserts from their molds, run a clean, small kitchen knife around the edge of the ramekin, custard cup, or mold before inverting.

ALMOND PANNA COTTA WITH MOCHA SAUCE

1   cup blanched whole almonds, toasted

⅔   cup sugar

1   envelope unflavored gelatin

2   cups whipping cream

½   cup milk

⅛   teaspoon salt

1   recipe Mocha Sauce

     Sliced almonds (optional)

PREP:
25 minutes

CHILL:
6 to 24 hours

COOL:
15 minutes (sauce)

MAKES:
6 servings

1 To make almond butter, place the whole almonds in a food processor; process until a smooth butter forms. Set aside.

2 In a medium saucepan stir together sugar and gelatin. Add whipping cream. Heat and stir until gelatin is dissolved. Remove from heat. Stir in milk, salt, and the almond butter. Pour into six individual molds, 6-ounce ramekins, or 6-ounce custard cups. Cover and chill for 6 to 24 hours or until set.

3 To serve, pool or drizzle some of the Mocha Sauce onto 6 dessert plates. Invert molded desserts onto dessert plates. If desired, garnish with sliced almonds. Serve with additional Mocha Sauce.

MOCHA SAUCE: Chop 4 ounces bittersweet or semisweet chocolate. In a heavy small saucepan heat and stir chopped chocolate over low heat until melted. Stir in ⅔ cup whipping cream, ¼ cup sugar, and 1 teaspoon instant espresso powder or instant coffee crystals. Cook and stir over medium-low heat about 3 minutes or until mixture just boils around edges. Remove from heat. Cool for 15 minutes before serving. Cover and chill any leftover sauce in the refrigerator for up to 3 days. Makes about 1 cup.

Per serving: 730 cal., 59 g total fat (30 g sat. fat), 148 mg chol., 110 mg sodium, 49 g carbo., 4 g fiber, 10 g pro.

The Italian plums used in this dish are dark bluish-purple on the outside and golden on the inside. They have a rich, sweet flavor that makes this adaptation of clafouti (a country French dessert) irresistible. It makes a terrific brunch dish.

ITALIAN DESSERT OVEN PANCAKE

PREP:
30 minutes

BAKE:
50 minutes

COOL:
15 minutes

OVEN:
375°F

MAKES:
8 servings

Butter

⅔ cup whipping cream

⅓ cup milk

3 eggs

⅓ cup all-purpose flour

¼ cup sugar

2 tablespoons butter, melted

2 teaspoons vanilla

2 teaspoons finely shredded lemon peel

⅛ teaspoon salt

2½ cups thinly sliced Italian plums
(or other plums) or pears

2 tablespoons sugar

Sweetened whipped cream (optional)

1 Preheat oven to 375°F. Generously butter the bottom and side of a 9-inch pie plate. Set aside.

2 In a medium bowl combine whipping cream, milk, eggs, flour, the ¼ cup sugar, the melted butter, vanilla, 1 teaspoon of the lemon peel, and the salt. Beat with an electric mixer on low speed until smooth.

3 Pour about half of the batter into prepared pan. Arrange plums or pears on top. Sprinkle with the remaining lemon peel. Carefully pour remaining batter over fruit. Sprinkle with the 2 tablespoons sugar.

4 Bake for 50 to 55 minutes or until puffed and lightly browned. Cool in pan on a wire rack for 15 minutes. (The pancake will fall as it cools.) Serve warm. If desired, serve with sweetened whipped cream.

Per serving: 206 cal., 13 g total fat (7 g sat. fat), 115 mg chol., 95 mg sodium, 20 g carbo., 1 g fiber, 4 g pro.

For convenience, you can substitute 1 tablespoon vanilla for the vanilla bean, adding it to the rice mixture just after cooking.

RICE PUDDING SOUFFLÉ WITH RASPBERRY SAUCE

3   cups half-and-half, light cream, or whole milk

½   cup Arborio rice or other short-grain rice

¼   cup sugar

4   teaspoons butter

1   vanilla bean, split lengthwise

½   teaspoon salt

3   eggs, separated

⅓   cup sugar

1   recipe Raspberry Sauce (optional)

     Fresh lemon balm or mint leaves (optional)

PREP:
45 minutes

COOL:
45 minutes + 10 minutes

BAKE:
45 minutes

OVEN:
350°F

MAKES:
6 to 8 servings

1 In a large saucepan bring half-and-half almost to a boil. Add uncooked rice, the ¼ cup sugar, the butter, vanilla bean, and salt; reduce heat. Cover and simmer for 20 to 25 minutes or just until rice is tender, stirring often. Remove from heat. Cool for 45 minutes. Remove vanilla bean and scrape inside of bean into rice mixture; discard bean. (If skin forms on top while rice cools, stir occasionally.) Set aside.

2 Preheat oven to 350°F. Butter a 2-quart soufflé dish; set aside. In a large bowl beat the egg yolks with an electric mixer on medium to high speed about 5 minutes or until thick and lemon-colored. Gradually add the ⅓ cup sugar, beating about 5 minutes or until thickened and sugar is almost dissolved. Set egg yolk mixture aside. Wash beaters thoroughly. In another large bowl beat the egg whites with an electric mixer on medium to high speed until stiff peaks form (tips stand straight).

3 Gently fold the cooled rice mixture into the egg yolk mixture. Fold 1 cup of the egg whites into the yolk mixture. Fold egg yolk mixture into remaining egg whites. Pour into the prepared dish. Place soufflé dish in a 2-quart square baking dish. Place baking dish on the oven rack. Pour boiling water into the baking dish to a depth of 1 inch. Bake for 45 to 50 minutes or until set. Cool 10 minutes on a wire rack. Serve warm with Raspberry Sauce. If desired, garnish with lemon balm leaves.

Per serving: 325 cal., 19 g total fat (11 g sat. fat), 154 mg chol., 293 mg sodium, 33 g carbo., 0 g fiber, 7 g pro.

RASPBERRY SAUCE: Place 3 cups fresh or thawed frozen raspberries in a food processor or blender. Process until berries are pureed. Press mixture through a fine-mesh sieve; discard seeds. In a small saucepan stir together ⅓ cup sugar and 1 teaspoon cornstarch. Add sieved berries. Cook and stir over medium heat until thickened and bubbly. Cook and stir for 2 minutes more. Remove from heat. Cool to room temperature. If desired, stir in 2 to 3 teaspoons raspberry liqueur.

This version of the traditional Italian frozen dessert is made with ingredients that are easy to keep on hand. Put it together for a tasty summertime treat.

TORTONI

PREP:
30 minutes

FREEZE:
2 to 24 hours

STAND:
5 minutes

MAKES:
6 servings

2   tablespoons finely snipped dried tart cherries

1   tablespoon dry sherry or apple juice

½   cup chocolate wafer crumbs

3   tablespoons flaked coconut, toasted

2   tablespoons butter or margarine, melted

1   pint vanilla ice cream

1   1.45-ounce bar milk chocolate with almonds, chopped

2   tablespoons slivered almonds, toasted and chopped

Chocolate-flavored syrup

1 In a small bowl combine dried cherries and sherry or apple juice; set aside.

2 In another small bowl combine chocolate wafer crumbs, 2 tablespoons of the coconut, and the melted butter. Line six muffin cups with paper bake cups; divide crumb mixture among cups. Gently press crumbs onto bottom of muffin cups.

3 In a large bowl stir ice cream to soften; fold in chopped chocolate and the cherry mixture. Divide ice cream mixture among the muffin cups. In a small bowl combine remaining 1 tablespoon coconut and the almonds; sprinkle over ice cream mixture. Cover and freeze for 2 to 24 hours.

4 Before serving, let tortoni stand at room temperature for 5 minutes. To serve, remove paper bake cups from tortoni. Drizzle chocolate-flavor syrup on six dessert plates; place a tortoni atop chocolate on each plate.

Per serving: 270 cal., 14 g total fat (8 g sat. fat), 32 mg chol., 153 mg sodium, 32 g carbo., 1 g fiber, 4 g pro.

Traditional zabaglione is made from egg yolks, sugar, and wine and is prepared just before serving. This chilled version, served on top of fresh berries, incorporates sour cream.

BERRIES WITH SHORTCUT ZABAGLIONE

2 tablespoons sugar

2 teaspoons cornstarch

¾ cup milk

1 beaten egg

¼ cup dairy sour cream

2 tablespoons sweet or dry Marsala

2 cups fresh berries
(such as raspberries, blackberries, blueberries, and/or halved strawberries) and/or fresh figs, quartered

PREP:
20 minutes

CHILL:
2 to 24 hours

MAKES:
4 servings

1 In a heavy small saucepan combine sugar and cornstarch. Stir in milk. Cook and stir over medium heat until mixture is thickened and bubbly. Cook and stir for 2 minutes more. Remove from heat. In a medium bowl gradually stir hot mixture into egg. Return mixture to the saucepan. Cook until nearly bubbly but do not boil. Immediately pour custard into a bowl; stir in sour cream and Marsala. Cover the surface with plastic wrap. Chill for 2 to 24 hours.

2 To serve, divide fruit among four dessert dishes. Spoon sour cream mixture over berries. Serve immediately.

Per serving: 119 cal., 5 g total fat (3 g sat. fat), 62 mg chol., 44 mg sodium, 14 g carbo., 4 g fiber, 4 g pro.

An elegant choice for a dinner party, this refreshing dessert will delight guests. Make sure to use ripe pears that are slightly soft to the touch.

CHOCOLATE & RICOTTA-FILLED PEARS

PREP:
25 minutes

COOK:
10 minutes

STAND:
20 minutes

MAKES:
6 servings

3	cups water
1	teaspoon finely shredded orange peel (set aside)
2	tablespoons orange juice
3	large ripe Bosc, Anjou, or Bartlett pears
1	cup ricotta cheese
⅓	cup powdered sugar
1	tablespoon unsweetened cocoa powder
¼	teaspoon vanilla
2	tablespoons miniature semisweet chocolate pieces
2	tablespoons sliced almonds, toasted

1 In a large saucepan combine the water and orange juice. Bring to boiling over medium heat. Add pears. Bring just to boiling. Reduce heat to low. Cover and cook about 10 minutes or just until pears are tender. Pears should retain shape. Using a slotted spoon, remove pears from pan; let stand for 20 to 25 minutes or until cooled. Discard cooking liquid.

2 In a medium bowl stir together ricotta cheese, powdered sugar, cocoa powder, and vanilla. Stir in chocolate pieces and shredded orange peel. Set aside.

3 Peel cooled pears and cut in half lengthwise. Remove and discard seeds and core, leaving stem intact if desired. Spoon ricotta mixture into centers of pears. Arrange filled pear halves on dessert plates. Sprinkle with almonds.

Per serving: 189 cal., 9 g total fat (4 g sat. fat), 21 mg chol., 36 mg sodium, 23 g carbo., 2 g fiber, 6 g pro.

Juicy peaches, tart cherries, and sweet figs make up the fruit compote in this impressive dessert. Fresh figs are very perishable, so use them within a day or two of purchasing.

FRUIT COMPOTE WITH LEMON CREAM

4½	cups thinly sliced white and/or yellow peaches (about 5 medium)
1	cup fresh tart red cherries, pitted, or fresh blueberries
½	cup fresh figs or quartered dried Calimyrna (light) figs
⅔	cup extra fine sugar or granulated sugar
1	teaspoon finely shredded lemon peel (set aside)
⅓	cup lemon juice
1	teaspoon ground cinnamon
½	of an 8-ounce carton mascarpone cheese
10	amaretti cookies, crushed (½ cup) (optional)
	Finely shredded lemon peel (optional)

1 In a large bowl combine peaches, cherries or blueberries, and figs. Add sugar, lemon juice, and cinnamon; gently toss to combine. Cover and chill for 2 to 4 hours, stirring occasionally.

2 Meanwhile, in a small bowl stir together mascarpone cheese and the 1 teaspoon lemon peel. Cover and chill until needed.

3 To serve, using a slotted spoon, divide fruit mixture among six dessert dishes. If desired, sprinkle with crushed amaretti cookies. Pipe or spoon some of the mascarpone cheese mixture on top of each. If desired, sprinkle with additional lemon peel.

Per serving: 260 cal., 9 g total fat (5 g sat. fat), 24 mg chol., 14 mg sodium, 47 g carbo., 4 g fiber, 5 g pro.

PREP:
20 minutes

CHILL:
2 to 4 hours

MAKES:
6 servings

While the nectarines marinate in the spiced wine syrup, they become pleasantly softened and acquire a more complex flavor that pairs perfectly with the creamy, chocolatey topping.

NECTARINES WITH CHOCOLATE-HAZELNUT CREAM

PREP:
45 minutes

COOL:
30 minutes

CHILL:
4 to 6 hours

MAKES:
6 servings

2¼	cups water
1	cup granulated sugar
¾	cup dry white wine
3	whole cloves
3	inches stick cinnamon
6	medium nectarines, pitted and sliced
⅓	cup mascarpone cheese
⅓	cup chocolate-hazelnut spread*
2	tablespoons butter, softened
¼	cup sifted powdered sugar
⅓	cup chopped toasted hazelnuts (filberts)

1 In a medium saucepan combine the water, granulated sugar, wine, cloves, and cinnamon. Bring mixture to boiling, stirring to dissolve sugar; reduce heat. Simmer, uncovered, for 10 minutes. Remove from heat. Cool for 30 minutes. Place nectarine slices in a large bowl. Pour wine mixture over nectarines. Cover and chill for 4 to 6 hours.

2 Meanwhile, for chocolate-hazelnut cream, in a small mixing bowl combine mascarpone cheese, chocolate-hazelnut spread, and butter; beat with an electric mixer on low to medium speed until well mixed. Beat in powdered sugar. Cover and chill until mixture is firm.

3 Using a slotted spoon, remove nectarine slices from syrup, reserving the syrup. Divide nectarine slices among six large shallow glasses or individual dessert dishes. Place a small spoonful of chocolate-hazelnut cream in each glass or dish. Spoon 1 to 2 tablespoons reserved syrup over nectarines in each glass or dish. Sprinkle with hazelnuts.

Per serving: 441 cal., 20 g total fat (6 g sat. fat), 27 mg chol., 127 mg sodium, 63 g carbo., 3 g fiber, 6 g pro.

*NOTE: Look for chocolate-hazelnut spread in the baking aisle or peanut butter section of large supermarkets.

Rich and tangy balsamic vinegar provides the perfect complement to sweet summer berries and creamy mascarpone cheese.

BERRIES VINAIGRETTE WITH MASCARPONE

4   cups assorted fresh berries
    (sliced strawberries, red or
    golden raspberries, blackberries,
    and/or blueberries)

2   tablespoons balsamic vinegar

1   8-ounce carton mascarpone cheese

2   tablespoons milk

2   tablespoons honey

1 Divide berries among six individual dessert bowls or dishes. Sprinkle each serving with 1 teaspoon of the balsamic vinegar.

2 In a small bowl stir together mascarpone cheese and milk. Spoon mascarpone mixture over berries. Drizzle 1 teaspoon honey over each serving.

Per serving: 234 cal., 18 g total fat (10 g sat. fat), 48 mg chol., 27 mg sodium, 9 g carbo., 3 g fiber, 9 g pro.

START TO FINISH:
10 minutes

MAKES:
6 servings

Earthy pistachios and tangy lemonade contribute an unforgettable flavor to this dense, custard-like ice cream.

PISTACHIO-LEMON GELATO

PREP:
30 minutes

CHILL:
2 to 24 hours

FREEZE:
according to manufacturer's directions

MAKES:
7 cups

4 cups whole milk

1⅓ cups sugar

12 beaten egg yolks

1 lemon

½ cup frozen lemonade concentrate, thawed

⅓ cup chopped toasted pistachios or almonds

1 In a large saucepan combine milk, sugar, and egg yolks. Use a vegetable peeler to cut long strips of peel from the lemon. Add lemon peel to saucepan. Cook and stir over medium heat just until the mixture coats a metal spoon. Remove from heat. Discard peel.

2 Transfer cooked mixture to a large bowl. Cover surface of mixture with plastic wrap. Refrigerate 2 to 24 hours to chill completely.*

3 Stir lemonade concentrate and pistachios into milk mixture. Freeze mixture in a 4- or 5-quart ice cream freezer according to manufacturer's directions.

Per ½-cup serving: 204 cal., 8 g total fat (3 g sat. fat), 192 mg chol., 41 mg sodium, 27 g carbo., 0 g fiber, 5 g pro.

***NOTE:** If you prefer, place the saucepan in a sink of ice water to chill quickly.

A wonderful summer refresher, icy strawberries get a zesty citrus twist with the addition of orange, lemon, and lime peels and juices.

STRAWBERRY ITALIAN ICE

1	cup sugar
¾	cup water
1	tablespoon finely shredded orange peel
2	teaspoons finely shredded lemon peel
1½	teaspoons finely shredded lime peel
⅓	cup orange juice
3	tablespoons lemon juice
2	tablespoons lime juice
4	cups sliced fresh strawberries

PREP:
25 minutes

FREEZE:
6 to 24 hours

MAKES:
8 servings

1 In a medium saucepan combine sugar, the water, and peels. Bring to boiling; reduce heat. Simmer, uncovered, for 5 minutes. Cool slightly. Strain and discard peels. Stir in orange, lemon, and lime juices.

2 In a blender or food processor combine half of the juice mixture and half of the strawberries. Cover and blend or process with several on/off turns until nearly smooth (leave some small chunks of strawberries). Transfer to a 2-quart freezer container. Repeat with remaining juice mixture and strawberries. Cover and freeze for 6 to 24 hours, stirring once after freezing for 3 hours.

3 To serve, scrape across frozen mixture with a large spoon and place into individual serving dishes. (If mixture is too firm, let stand at room temperature for 20 to 30 minutes before scraping.)

Per serving: 123 cal., 0 g total fat (0 g sat. fat), 0 mg chol., 2 mg sodium, 31 g carbo., 2 g fiber, 1 g pro.

To peel the oranges, use a serrated knife to cut off strips of peel, cutting from the top of the orange to the bottom. When finished, use the knife to remove any of the bitter white pith left on the orange.

FROZEN ORANGE SORBET TOWERS

PREP:
25 minutes

FREEZE:
4 to 24 hours

MAKES:
4 servings

2   pints orange or mango sorbet

2   tablespoons Grand Marnier or other orange liqueur

3   medium oranges and/or blood oranges, peeled

Fresh lavender sprigs (optional)

1 Line a 13×9×2-inch baking pan with plastic wrap, extending the plastic wrap over the sides. Place sorbet in a large bowl. Using a wooden spoon, stir sorbet to soften. Stir in liqueur. Transfer the sorbet to the prepared pan, spreading evenly. Freeze for 4 to 24 hours or until firm.

2 Using a sharp knife, slice each orange crosswise into four rounds. Wrap and place oranges in the freezer until needed.

3 Holding the edges of the plastic wrap, carefully lift the sorbet from the pan. Using a 2- to 2½-inch scalloped round cookie cutter (it should be the same diameter as an orange), cut sorbet into rounds (you should have at least 12 rounds). To serve, stack three rounds of sorbet alternately with three slices of orange. Place on individual dessert plates. If desired, garnish with lavender sprigs. Serve immediately.

Per serving: 80 cal., 0 g total fat, 0 mg chol., 0 mg sodium, 80 g carbo., 4 g fiber, 1 g pro.

Draining the ricotta cheese in a cheesecloth-lined sieve removes excess liquid so the Chocolate Filling has a rich, creamy consistency.

CANNOLI COOKIE STACKS

1	recipe Chocolate Filling
1¼	cups all-purpose flour
½	cup ground pistachio nuts
¼	cup granulated sugar
¼	cup packed brown sugar
½	cup butter
5	ounces semisweet chocolate, chopped
1	tablespoon shortening
	Finely chopped pistachio nuts (optional)
	Powdered sugar (optional)

PREP:
1¼ hours

CHILL:
overnight (filling)

BAKE:
8 minutes per batch

OVEN:
375°F

MAKES:
about 18 cookie stacks

❶ Prepare Chocolate Filling. Preheat oven to 375°F. In a medium bowl combine flour, ground nuts, granulated sugar, and brown sugar. Using a pastry blender, cut in butter until mixture resembles fine crumbs. Using your hands, work dough until it forms a ball. On a lightly floured surface, roll dough to ⅛-inch thickness. Using a 2½-inch round cookie cutter, cut dough into circles, rerolling scraps as necessary (you should have 36 to 40 circles). Place circles 1 inch apart on ungreased cookie sheets. Bake about 8 minutes or until lightly browned. Transfer cookies to a wire rack and let cool.

❷ In a heavy small saucepan combine semisweet chocolate and the shortening. Heat over low heat until melted, stirring occasionally. Remove from heat. Spread or drizzle melted chocolate on cookies. If desired, sprinkle half of the cookies with finely chopped nuts. Place cookies, chocolate sides up, on wire racks to let chocolate set. If desired, drizzle any leftover chocolate on dessert plates. Set aside to let chocolate set.

❸ To assemble each cookie stack, place a cookie round (without nuts, if using), chocolate side up, on a dessert plate. Spoon 2 tablespoons Chocolate Filling on top. Top with another cookie round (with nuts, if using), chocolate side up. If desired, sprinkle with powdered sugar.

CHOCOLATE FILLING: Line a large fine-mesh sieve with a double thickness of 100%-cotton cheesecloth. Set sieve over a bowl; spoon one 15-ounce carton ricotta cheese into sieve. Cover; refrigerate overnight. Remove cheese from refrigerator. Discard liquid in bowl. In a medium bowl combine cheese, ¾ cup sifted powdered sugar, and 1 teaspoon vanilla. Beat with electric mixer on medium speed until well mixed. Stir in 2 ounces semisweet chocolate, chopped; 3 tablespoons finely chopped pistachio nuts; and 1 tablespoon finely chopped candied orange peel.

Per serving: 248 cal., 15 g total fat (8 g sat. fat), 27 mg chol., 77 mg sodium, 25 g carbo., 2 g fiber, 5 g pro.

TEST KITCHEN TIP: Cookies may be prepared ahead and covered with chocolate for quick assembly of the stacks later. Store in an airtight container at room temperature for up to 24 hours or freeze for up to 3 months.

In these cookies, fragrant ingredients—cocoa, cinnamon, cloves, and coffee—come together for a sensational flavor experience. Finely shredded orange peel adds a bit of citrus flair.

CHOCOLATE SPICE COOKIES

PREP:
40 minutes

BAKE:
8 minutes per batch

OVEN:
375°F

MAKES:
about 3 dozen cookies

3	cups all-purpose flour
1	cup granulated sugar
¼	cup unsweetened cocoa powder
2	teaspoons baking powder
1	teaspoon ground cinnamon
1	teaspoon ground cloves
1	cup butter
2	eggs
½	cup strong coffee, cooled
1	teaspoon vanilla
½	teaspoon finely shredded orange peel
½	cup chopped walnuts or pine nuts
1	recipe Powdered Sugar Icing

1 Preheat oven to 375°F. If desired, line cookie sheets with parchment paper; set aside. In a large bowl stir together flour, sugar, cocoa powder, baking powder, cinnamon, and cloves. Using a pastry blender, cut in butter until mixture resembles coarse crumbs. Make a well in the center of the flour mixture.

2 In a medium bowl whisk together eggs, coffee, vanilla, and orange peel. Pour egg mixture into flour mixture and stir to combine. Stir in nuts. If necessary, cover and chill dough until easy to handle (1 to 2 hours).

3 Shape dough into walnut-size balls (each about 1¼ inches in diameter); place balls about 2 inches apart on ungreased or parchment-lined cookie sheets.

4 Bake for 8 to 10 minutes or until edges are firm. (Cookies may still appear soft. Do not overbake.) Transfer cookies to a wire rack and let cool. Drizzle with Powdered Sugar Icing. Let icing dry.

POWDERED SUGAR ICING: In a small bowl stir together 1 cup sifted powdered sugar and enough milk (1 to 2 tablespoons) to make a drizzling consistency.

Per cookie: 132 cal., 7 g total fat (3 g sat. fat), 25 mg chol., 54 mg sodium, 17 g carbo., 0 g fiber, 2 g pro.

NOTE: If you want to make a large batch of cookies for gift-giving, double the recipe.

Traditional Italian cheesecakes are often made with ricotta cheese and dried or candied fruits and nuts. Here, we've packaged the flavors of this classic dessert into cookie-size bars.

FESTIVE CHEESE BARS

½	cup butter
1¼	cups finely crushed graham crackers (about 18)
1	15-ounce carton ricotta cheese
1	egg
¼	cup sugar
2	tablespoons all-purpose flour
2	teaspoons finely shredded orange peel
1	teaspoon almond extract
½	cup sliced almonds or chopped hazelnuts (filberts)
⅓	cup chopped candied cherries
⅓	cup golden raisins

PREP:
20 minutes

BAKE:
25 minutes

COOL:
1 hour

CHILL:
2 hours

OVEN:
350°F

MAKES:
20 bars

1 Preheat oven to 350°F. Place butter in a 9×9×2-inch baking pan. Place the pan in the oven about 6 minutes or until butter is melted. Remove from oven. Stir crushed graham crackers into melted butter. Using a wooden spoon, press the crumb mixture firmly and evenly onto the bottom of the pan. Set aside.

2 In a blender or food processor combine ricotta cheese, egg, sugar, flour, orange peel, and almond extract. Cover and blend or process until smooth. Carefully spread cheese mixture over crumb mixture. In a small bowl combine nuts, cherries, and raisins; sprinkle over cheese layer.

3 Bake in the 350°F oven for 25 to 30 minutes or until edges are puffed and golden. Cool in pan on a wire rack for 1 hour; cover and chill for 2 hours. Cut into bars.

Per bar: 157 cal., 10 g total fat (5 g sat. fat), 34 mg chol., 83 mg sodium, 14 g carbo., 1 g fiber, 4 g pro.

This spectacular sauce is absolutely delicious served over your favorite ice cream.

ESPRESSO-ORANGE SAUCE

START TO FINISH:
15 minutes

MAKES:
1½ cups

⅓ cup packed brown sugar

4 teaspoons cornstarch

1 cup water

1 tablespoon espresso powder or 2 tablespoons instant coffee powder

2 inches stick cinnamon

2 medium oranges, peeled, halved lengthwise, and sliced

1 tablespoon coffee liqueur (optional)

1 In a medium saucepan combine brown sugar and cornstarch. Stir in the water, espresso powder, and stick cinnamon. Cook and stir over medium heat until thickened and bubbly. Cook and stir for 2 minutes more. Remove from heat. Discard stick cinnamon. Stir in orange slices and, if desired, liqueur.

2 Serve sauce warm or cooled over ice cream.

Per 3-tablespoon serving: 60 cal., 0 g total fat (0 g sat. fat), 0 mg chol., 5 mg sodium, 15 g carbo., 1 g fiber, 0 g pro.

Great on a cold winter's day, this scrumptious sipper, made from a mix of espresso, milk, and chocolate syrup, will warm you up in no time. When the weather turns warm, try the iced version.

CAFFÈ MOCHA

1¼ cups cold water

½ cup espresso roast or French roast coffee, ground as directed for your coffeemaker

2 cups milk

4 teaspoons chocolate-flavored syrup or presweetened cocoa powder

Whipped cream (optional)

START TO FINISH:
20 minutes

MAKES:
4 (6-ounce) servings

1 Using a drip coffeemaker, brew the water and coffee according to manufacturer's directions. (If using an espresso machine, use manufacturer's suggested amounts of coffee and water.)

2 Meanwhile, in a medium saucepan heat and stir milk until hot but not boiling. Divide espresso among four cups. Stir 1 tablespoon of the chocolate-flavored syrup or presweetened cocoa powder into each cup. Top each with some of the milk. If desired, add a spoonful of whipped cream to each cup.

Per serving: 79 cal., 2 g total fat (2 g sat. fat), 10 mg chol., 56 mg sodium, 10 g carbo., 0 g fiber, 4 g pro.

ICED CAFFÈ MOCHA: If desired, for chocolate swizzle sticks, drizzle melted semisweet chocolate on waxed-paper-lined baking sheets in desired lengths. Chill until set. Prepare Caffè Mocha as directed, except add the brewed espresso and the chocolate-flavored syrup or presweetened cocoa powder to the saucepan with the milk. Cool mixture. Fill four 10- to 12-ounce glasses with ice cubes or crushed ice. Pour espresso mixture over ice. If desired, top with the whipped cream. Serve with chocolate swizzle sticks, if using.

Per serving: 79 cal., 2 g total fat (2 g sat. fat), 10 mg chol., 56 mg sodium, 10 g carbo., 0 g fiber, 4 g pro.

INDEX

METRIC MEASUREMENTS

The charts on this page provide a guide for converting measurements from the U.S. customary system, which is used throughout this book, to the metric system.

Product Differences

Most of the ingredients called for in the recipes in this book are available in most countries. However, some are known by different names. Here are some common American ingredients and their possible counterparts:

■ **All-purpose flour** is enriched, bleached or unbleached white household flour. When self-rising flour is used in place of all-purpose flour in a recipe that calls for leavening, omit the leavening agent (baking soda or baking powder) and salt.

■ **Baking soda** is bicarbonate of soda.

■ **Cornstarch** is cornflour.

■ **Golden raisins** are sultanas.

■ **Green, red, or yellow sweet peppers** are capsicums or bell peppers.

■ **Light-colored corn syrup** is golden syrup.

■ **Powdered sugar** is icing sugar.

■ **Sugar** (white) is granulated, fine granulated, or castor sugar.

■ **Vanilla** or vanilla extract is vanilla essence.

Volume and Weight

The United States traditionally uses cup measures for liquid and solid ingredients. The chart below shows the approximate imperial and metric equivalents. If you are accustomed to weighing solid ingredients, the following approximate equivalents will be helpful.

■ 1 cup butter, castor sugar, or rice = 8 ounces = 1/2 pound = 250 grams

■ 1 cup flour = 4 ounces = 1/4 pound = 125 grams

■ 1 cup icing sugar = 5 ounces = 150 grams

Canadian and U.S. volume for a cup measure is 8 fluid ounces (237 ml), but the standard metric equivalent is 250 ml.

1 British imperial cup is 10 fluid ounces.

In Australia, 1 tablespoon equals 20 ml, and there are 4 teaspoons in the Australian tablespoon.

Spoon measures are used for smaller amounts of ingredients. Although the size of the tablespoon varies slightly in different countries, for practical purposes and for recipes in this book, a straight substitution is all that's necessary. Measurements made using cups or spoons always should be level unless stated otherwise.

Common Weight Range Replacements

Imperial / U.S.	Metric
1/2 ounce	15 g
1 ounce	25 g or 30 g
4 ounces (1/4 pound)	115 g or 125 g
8 ounces (1/2 pound)	225 g or 250 g
16 ounces (1 pound)	450 g or 500 g
1 1/4 pounds	625 g
1 1/2 pounds	750 g
2 pounds or 2 1/4 pounds	1,000 g or 1 Kg

Oven Temperature Equivalents

Fahrenheit Setting	Celsius Setting*	Gas Setting
300°F	150°C	Gas Mark 2 (very low)
325°F	160°C	Gas Mark 3 (low)
350°F	180°C	Gas Mark 4 (moderate)
375°F	190°C	Gas Mark 5 (moderate)
400°F	200°C	Gas Mark 6 (hot)
425°F	220°C	Gas Mark 7 (hot)
450°F	230°C	Gas Mark 8 (very hot)
475°F	240°C	Gas Mark 9 (very hot)
500°F	260°C	Gas Mark 10 (extremely hot)
Broil	Broil	Grill

*Electric and gas ovens may be calibrated using Celsius. However, for an electric oven, increase Celsius setting 10 to 20 degrees when cooking above 160°C. For convection or forced air ovens (gas or electric), lower the temperature setting 25°F/10°C when cooking at all heat levels.

Baking Pan Sizes

Imperial / U.S.	Metric
9×1 1/2-inch round cake pan	22- or 23×4-cm (1.5 L)
9×1 1/2 inch pie plate	22- or 23×4-cm (1 L)
8×8×2-inch square cake pan	20×5-cm (2 L)
9×9×2-inch square cake pan	22- or 23×4.5-cm (2.5 L)
11×7×1 1/2-inch baking pan	28×17×4-cm (2 L)
2-quart rectangular baking pan	30×19×4.5-cm (3 L)
13×9×2-inch baking pan	34×22×4.5-cm (3.5 L)
15×10×1-inch jelly roll pan	40×25×2-cm
9×5×3-inch loaf pan	23×13×8-cm (2 L)
2-quart casserole	2 L

U.S. / Standard Metric Equivalents

1/8 teaspoon = 0.5 ml	
1/4 teaspoon = 1 ml	
1/2 teaspoon = 2 ml	
1 teaspoon = 5 ml	
1 tablespoon = 15 ml	
2 tablespoons = 25 ml	
1/4 cup = 2 fluid ounces = 50 ml	
1/3 cup = 3 fluid ounces = 75 ml	
1/2 cup = 4 fluid ounces = 125 ml	
2/3 cup = 5 fluid ounces = 150 ml	
3/4 cup = 6 fluid ounces = 175 ml	
1 cup = 8 fluid ounces = 250 ml	
2 cups = 1 pint = 500 ml	
1 quart = 1 litre	

HEALTHY, FAST & FLAVORFUL RECIPES

FOR NO-HASSLE MEALS!

THE BIGGEST BOOK SERIES INCLUDES:

30-Minute Meals
Bread Machine Recipes
Casseroles
Cookies
Diabetic Recipes
Easy Canned Soup Recipes
Grilling
Italian Recipes
Low-Carb Recipes
Slow Cooker Recipes
Slow Cooker Recipes Volume 2
Soups & Stews

Available where quality books are sold.

FAMILY-FRIENDLY RECIPES
TO SATISFY EVERY APPETITE.

Meredith® BOOKS

ADT0143_0406